Private Pensions Series

Protecting Pensions

POLICY ANALYSIS AND EXAMPLES
FROM OECD COUNTRIES

No. 8

OECD

ORGANISATION FOR ECONOMIC CO-OPERATION AND DEVELOPMENT

The OECD is a unique forum where the governments of 30 democracies work together to address the economic, social and environmental challenges of globalisation. The OECD is also at the forefront of efforts to understand and to help governments respond to new developments and concerns, such as corporate governance, the information economy and the challenges of an ageing population. The Organisation provides a setting where governments can compare policy experiences, seek answers to common problems, identify good practice and work to co-ordinate domestic and international policies.

The OECD member countries are: Australia, Austria, Belgium, Canada, the Czech Republic, Denmark, Finland, France, Germany, Greece, Hungary, Iceland, Ireland, Italy, Japan, Korea, Luxembourg, Mexico, the Netherlands, New Zealand, Norway, Poland, Portugal, the Slovak Republic, Spain, Sweden, Switzerland, Turkey, the United Kingdom and the United States. The Commission of the European Communities takes part in the work of the OECD.

OECD Publishing disseminates widely the results of the Organisation's statistics gathering and research on economic, social and environmental issues, as well as the conventions, guidelines and standards agreed by its members.

> *This work is published on the responsibility of the Secretary-General of the OECD. The opinions expressed and arguments employed herein do not necessarily reflect the official views of the Organisation or of the governments of its member countries.*

Corrigenda to OECD publications may be found on line at: *www.oecd.org/publishing/corrigenda*.
© OECD 2007

No reproduction, copy, transmission or translation of this publication may be made without written permission. Applications should be sent to OECD Publishing *rights@oecd.org* or by fax 33 1 45 24 99 30. Permission to photocopy a portion of this work should be addressed to the Centre français d'exploitation du droit de copie (CFC), 20, rue des Grands-Augustins, 75006 Paris, France, fax 33 1 46 34 67 19, *contact@cfcopies.com* or (for US only) to Copyright Clearance Center (CCC), 222 Rosewood Drive, Danvers, MA 01923, USA, fax 1 978 646 8600, *info@copyright.com*.

Foreword

The protection of pension beneficiaries is one of the key topics for the work of the OECD Working Party on Private Pensions (WPPP). The work goes back to the publication of the Guidelines for the Protection of Rights of Members and Beneficiaries in Occupational Pension Plans *in 2002, and the* Guidelines on Funding and Benefit Security *which were approved as a Recommendation of the OECD Council in May 2007. Given the problems related to pension benefit losses in several OECD countries in recent years, the WPPP has returned to the topic of pension benefit security on many occasions, through discussions at its meetings and conferences. Different countries have responded to these challenges in different ways, with the WPPP providing a unique forum for policy-makers to share their experiences and seek new ways of dealing with common challenges.*

This volume n°8 of the Private Pensions Series presents a series of papers on the topic of pension benefit protection commissioned by the WPPP and prepared by pension policy analysts and practitioners. It includes an analysis of various methods of protecting pension benefits - including the advantages and disadvantages of these approaches and suggestions for best practice and practical application. In addition, in depth material is provided on how these different methods are applied in a range of OECD countries. The publication was prepared by Juan Yermo and Fiona Stewart from the OECD's Private Pensions Unit, Directorate for Financial and Enterprise Affairs, with editorial assistance from Edward Smiley.

The views expressed are the sole responsibility of the authors and do not necessarily reflect those of the WPPP, the Insurance and Private Pensions Committee, member and non-member countries.

Table of Contents

Chapter 1. **Introduction**
by David Lindeman and Juan Yermo 9

   I.   How plan design affects risk sharing.................................... 12
   II. Changes in plan design 19
   III. Regulating plan design 24
   IV. Regulating financial security 26
   V. Structure of the book 27
   VI. Lessons for policymaking 30
   Notes 32
   References 33

Chapter 2. **Reforming the Valuation and Funding of Pension Promises: Are Occupational Pensions Safer?**
by Juan Yermo 35

   Introduction 35
   I.   Measuring pension fund assets and liabilities for funding and accounting purposes 38
   II. Revisiting funding gaps and the public policy reaction 54
   III. Implications for occupational pension provision and pension funds' investment behaviour 58
   IV. Conclusion.. 65
   Notes 67
   References 72

Chapter 3. **Funding Rules and Actuarial Methods**
by Colin Pugh 75

   I.   Introduction 75
   II. Historical Development of Funding Regulations 77
   III. General Actuarial Considerations... 78
   IV. Minimum Funding Standards 82
   V. Maximum Funding Constraints 85
   VI. Challenges Facing Regulatory Authorities........................... 89
   VII. Recent Trends and Developments 94

Annex 3.A1 Actuarial Funding Methods 98
Annex 3.A2 Pension Plan Funding Regulations 104
    Austria 105
    Belgium 109
    Brazil 112
    Canada 115
    Ireland 122
    Japan 126
    Netherlands 129
    Norway 134
    Portugal 138
    Spain 142
    Switzerland 145
    United Kingdom 149
    United States 156

Chapter 4. **Pension Fund Regulation and Risk Management: Results from an ALM Optimisation Exercise**
by Sandra Blome, Kai Fachinger, Dorothee Franzen, Gerhard Scheuenstuhl and Juan Yermo 161

  I.   Introduction 161
  II.   Developments in pension fund risk management 163
  III. The impact of regulation and accounting on ALM
       for a synthetic pension fund 167
  IV. Conclusions 190
  Notes 194
    Annex 4.A1   Pension fund design and regulations in five
                         OECD countries 198
  References 211

Chapter 5. **Pension Fund Guarantee Schemes**
              by Fiona Stewart 213

  I.   Introduction 213
  II.   Arguments for Benefit Guarantee Schemes. 214
  III. Challenges for benefit guarantee schemes. 216
  IV. Practical Issues 219
  V.   Conclusion 222
  VI. Country Studies 224
        USA 225
        Canada 231
        UK 233
        Germany 239
        Sweden 242

Others 245
Notes 254
References 263

Chapter 6. **Benefit Security: Priority Creditor Rights for Pension Funds**
            by Fiona Stewart 265

I.   Introduction 265
II. Arguments for Priority Rights 266
III. Actual situation 267
IV. Arguments against priority status 269
V.   Conclusion 272
VI. Country Profiles 274
        Australia 274
        Canada 274
        Germany 278
        Italy 279
        Ireland 280
        Japan 282
        Korea 284
        Netherlands 285
        Portugal 286
        Sweden 287
        Switzerland 288
        UK 288
        USA 292
Notes 296
References 300

Annex 1.   **OECD Council Recommendation on Guidelines on Funding
             and Benefit Security in Occupational Pension Plans** 303

Guidelines on Funding and Benefit Security in Occupational Pension Plans

    I.   Funding of occupational pension plans 305
    II. Measurement of occupational pension plan liabilities 305
    III. Funding rules for occupational pension plans/funds 307
    IV. Winding-up 308

Annotations to Guidelines on Funding and Benefit Security
in Occupational Pension Plans 309

ISBN 978-92-64-02810-4
Protecting Pensions: Policy Analysis
and Examples from OECD Countries
© OECD 2007

Chapter 1

INTRODUCTION

by

David Lindeman and Juan Yermo*

Occupational pension plans – employment-based arrangements – have historically played a key role in the retirement income systems of many OECD countries. Even today, these plans cover most workers in Denmark, Finland, Iceland, the Netherlands, Norway, Sweden, and Switzerland. As shown in Figure 1, the coverage rates of occupational plans in these countries are above 90 percent of the workforce, which can be explained by their mandatory (by law or statute) or quasi-mandatory nature (as a result of bargaining at the national or industry-wide level). Occupational pension plans are mandatory in Finland[1], Iceland, Switzerland and, since 2006, in Norway. In these four countries, employers must establish pension plans and employees are obliged to join them.

Other OECD countries have also made private pension plans mandatory, but rely instead on personal pension products which are contracted directly between individuals and financial institutions acting as plan providers. Countries with mandatory personal pension plans include Hungary, Mexico,

---

* David Lindeman is an independent consultant. Juan Yermo is principal administrator, Private Pensions Unit, at the OECD. The authors would like to thank the Delegates to the OECD Working Party on Private Pensions, André Laboul, Pablo Antolín (OECD), and Colin Pugh (independent consultant) for their comments on previous versions of this paper. The views expressed are the sole responsibility of the authors and do not necessarily reflect those of the OECD or its member countries.

Poland and the Slovak republic. Australia has also made private pension plans (superannuation) mandatory but workers can choose between occupational and personal pension arrangements. Approximately half of the workforce participates in occupational plans (corporate, industry-wide or public-sector superannuation funds), while another 40 percent participates in personal pension plans.

The coverage of occupational pensions is also relatively high in other OECD countries, with rates hovering around 40-60 percent of the workforce in Belgium, Canada, Germany, Ireland, the United Kingdom, and the United States. In some of these countries, workers covered by occupational arrangements can expect to obtain a major part of their retirement income from these plans. For example, currently the average pensioner in the United Kingdom and the United States draws over one quarter of retirement income from occupational plans. Finally, there is a group of countries such as France, Greece, Hungary, Italy[2], Poland, Portugal, Spain, and Turkey with coverage rates below 10 percent. With the exception of France, these are also the OECD countries with the most generous mandatory pension benefits (including social security), which may explain the limited development of the (voluntary) occupational pension system.

Figure 1. Workforce coverage of occupational pension plans in OECD countries (2006)

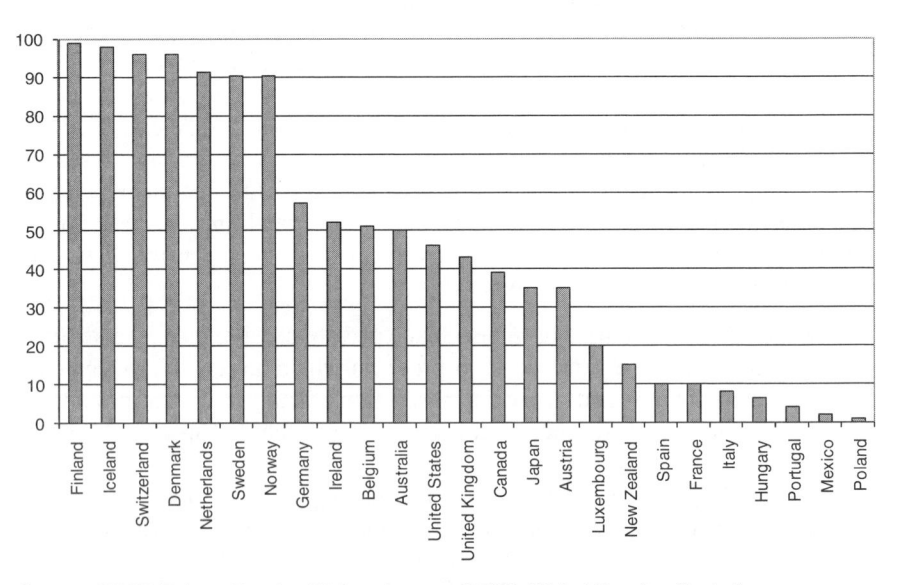

Source: OECD Private Pension Unit estimates, OECD Global Pension Statistics.
Note: The coverage of occupational pension plans in other OECD countries (Czech Republic, Greece, Korea, Slovak Republic, and Turkey) is negligible. The data for Australia include only corporate, industry and public sector superannuation funds.

The future evolution of occupational pension plans is an open question in many countries. In some countries, the growth of occupational plans has stalled or they have been overtaken by personal pension plans. An issue of particular concern is the gradual disappearance of occupational defined benefit pension arrangements in countries like the United Kingdom and the United States – at least for private sector workers - and their negligible presence or total absence in countries that have set up brand new occupational pension systems relatively recently, such as Italy, Hungary, Poland and Spain.

A priori, occupational defined benefit plans would seem to provide an attractive complement to social security, as benefits are linked to a worker's salary history, hence maintaining the standard of living into old age. Occupational defined benefit plans can also provide pensions at low administrative costs[3] and with risk-sharing features (especially between generations) that are not readily available in personal pensions or defined contribution plans. For sponsoring employers, however, one important drawback of traditional defined benefit plans that pay benefits in the form of annuities is that the cost of benefit provision increases steadily over time with improvements in life expectancy.

From the perspective of plan members, defined benefit plans are also exposed to two main risks that are specific to this type of plan: the risk of insolvency of the plan sponsor (or, more generally, plan termination) and the risk of rupture of the employment contract. Sponsor insolvency normally means the freezing of accruals and contributions. If the plan has been insufficiently funded, it may also find itself unable to pay all the accrued benefits or purchase annuities that cover all accrued rights. Employees are also exposed to potential benefit losses if they change jobs from one sponsoring company to another one. In many OECD countries, benefit portability does not guarantee a full recognition of accrued rights. In some countries, departing workers are not allowed to transfer their accrued benefits and instead maintain a right to a deferred benefit with their previous employer. The value of deferred benefits can be eroded over time as a result of inflation, except if there are indexation mechanisms in place. In the United Kingdom, for example, deferred benefits must be indexed to the rate of inflation up to 5 percent.

This book is concerned with the public policy reaction to the first of these risks. Pension regulatory and supervisory authorities intervene in occupational pension systems primarily in order to make sure that employers and pension funds make good on any promises or objectives set in the pension plan contract, that is, in order to promote a high level of "benefit security". From this follows that the regulation in occupational pension systems should be adapted to the plan's design and the nature of the contract or covenant between the different stakeholders. As explained below, there exist options other than the "final pay annuity" defined benefit plan that is under increasing economic and financing pressure and the full "investment risk" defined contribution plan that is increasingly prevalent.

Regulators' role in promoting benefit security requires a good understanding of pension plan design and how risks and responsibilities are distributed. In turn, plan design can be affected by regulations, making certain plan features more or less attractive or even requiring the implementation of specific plan designs. This two-faceted regulatory role of government, as overseer of pension plan promises and as regulator of pension plan design has the potential to strengthen the occupational pension system but it can also make it so costly as to render it unattractive for employers to sponsor pension plans. Finding the right balance between different regulatory actions is therefore one of the most difficult challenges facing governments today, as they struggle with the consequences of demographic ageing and the reform of retirement income systems.

I. How plan design affects risk sharing

Debates on pension issues are muddled by terminology. The terms defined benefit and defined contribution do not necessarily have the same content in different forums. In the world of occupational pensions, a distinction is made between arrangements in which the sponsor (an employer or group of employers) makes a unilateral or (bargained) bilateral deferred compensation promise that goes beyond just a commitment to contribute money to some kind of retirement arrangement. In such occupational, defined benefit plans the benefits are ultimately guaranteed by the employer acting as plan sponsor. Occupational pension obligations in OECD countries usually rank at the same level as other unsecured creditors such as bondholders, a status called *pari passu*[4]. A commitment only to contribute money to a retirement arrangement where the plan sponsor does not provide any investment return guarantee during either the accumulation or payment stage, or any annuity rate or other guarantees is labeled a defined contribution plan.

This definition is the one contained in the OECD classification (OECD (2005)) and is consistent with the one proposed by the International Accounting Standards Board (IASB). The classification of pension plans into defined benefit and defined contribution, however, is not sufficient to understand the risks borne by members, as some risks may be shifted to external providers, for example, buying deferred annuities from life insurance companies. For this reason, an additional sub-classification of defined contribution plans was developed by the OECD, between protected and unprotected plans. Protected defined contribution plans are those in which the pension fund itself or an external provider offers some type of benefit or return guarantee or promise.

Traditionally, the defined benefit promise has taken the form of a promised annuity – for example, 1.75% of the final five year average of salary for each year of credited employment under the pension plan. But this prototypical "final pay" annuity promise is only one of several forms that a sponsoring employer can underwrite a promised benefit. The annuity might be based on average wages or salaries throughout the employee's career (probably adjusted by some measure of average wage growth) vs. some measure of final pay.

Plan sponsors bear most risk in final salary plans, as they underwrite both investment and longevity risk before and after retirement. Moreover, these plans offer implicitly a guaranteed rate of return over the worker's career (the rate of growth of the worker's salary) that is not known until retirement. Career-average salary plans expose employers to less risk, because the value of the benefit pertaining to past service is already determined. On the other hand, employers are as exposed to longevity risk as in final-salary plans.

A less risky form of benefit promise for sponsors are defined lump-sum benefits, which are based on some measure of final or career average pay – 10 percent * years under the plan * pay measure. These defined lump-sum plans[5] can be classified as hybrid (defined benefit) arrangements; they are defined benefit in the accumulation stage as the lump sum is tied to wages and service period. But at withdrawal, each individual faces the "risk" of prevailing annuity purchase prices. From an accounting perspective and following the OECD classification, these and other hybrid plans are treated as defined benefit.

A second type of hybrid defined benefit arrangements are those that pay benefits calculated on the basis of the higher of a minimum and the actual rate of return. In Belgium, for example, all occupational pension plans must offer minimum return guarantees, and effectively pay the better of a defined contribution and a defined benefit formula. Such plans place a burden on employers that is comparable to that of traditional defined benefit plans, although sponsors of these hybrid plans do not bear longevity risk until retirement. In traditional defined plans, however, plan sponsors may have direct or indirect (via lower contributions) access to the plan's funding "surplus". In plans with minimum return guarantees, on the other hand, the whole "surplus" is effectively assigned to participants.

Another increasingly common type of hybrid arrangement (especially in Japan and the United States) is the so-called cash balance plan. These plans keep hypothetical account balances for each participant, which are credited with contributions and a specified "interest credit", which is either a fixed rate or a variable rate set with reference to a market return index, such as the return on government bonds or other market indices. Some plans offer a top-up return (one or two percentage points) on the reference instrument.[6] As plan sponsors are ultimately responsible for delivering the rate of return, cash balance plans are classified as defined benefit. However, participants also bear investment risk if the interest credit varies because it is tied to a market index. Such cash balance plans are therefore very close in risk distribution to defined contribution arrangements. This is an instance where the legal or accounting classification does not really match how risks are shared between the sponsor and participants.

Defined contribution plans also come in different forms. In the "unprotected" kind, investment and longevity risk are borne directly by each individual member at least until retirement. If the participant chooses to convert its accumulated balance into an annuity at retirement it transfers these risks to the annuity provider. Defined contribution plans of the "protected" kind also offer some form of risk pooling throughout the contribution period. These plans include occupational pension insurance products and some schemes that operate on a mutual insurance basis. The purchase by employers of annuity or life insurance products to finance retirement accumulations for salaried workers has a long history that goes back at least to the beginning of the 20th century. It continues today in a significant way in many continental European countries and is used in other countries (United Kingdom and United States) to a lesser extent to finance deferred compensation for high end employees in excess of what tax laws generally allow (so-called "top hat" or "excess" plans).

Less widespread are pooled-risk or "collective" defined contribution plans that operate within a defined contribution financing envelope but make annuity promises to participants. In the two countries in which such plans are widespread, Denmark and Iceland, the legal and accounting presumption is that these plans are defined contribution – that is, there is no legally enforceable axiomatic call back to contributing employers (or workers) to make up financing short falls between accrued rights and assets on hand. From the perspective of participants, there is reliance on the pension fund to deliver the promised benefit, just as with insurance product type arrangements where participants expect the insurance company to deliver an annuity or lump sum promise. The main difference with defined benefit plans is that the latter can have an imbalance between its liabilities and assets – even between its termination liability and assets (insolvency for a stand-alone entity) – because the funding shortfall is effectively a book reserve liability for the sponsoring firm or firms. In the case of a stand-alone entity making defined benefit promises, it has to manage investment volatility within the confines of its asset base.

These different plan designs and their implications for risk bearing can be seen in a simple quadrant – see Figure 2. Most defined benefit pension and lump sum accumulations would fall in the upper right hand quadrant where there are both a) a definite sponsor who bears legally enforceable contingent liability to make up financing deficiencies when assets are insufficient (or full book reserve responsibility) and b) the participants perceive themselves as entitled to a promise that is independent of the performance of underlying assets or the sponsor's other commitments. In contrast, most defined contribution retirement savings and pensions would fall into the bottom left hand quadrant where a) sponsors have no other obligation other than to make periodic contributions as a function of pay or similar function – that is, no contingent liability, and b) participants expect outcomes to be a function of underlying assets, whether under their investment control or otherwise.

Figure 2. Classification of occupational pension plans

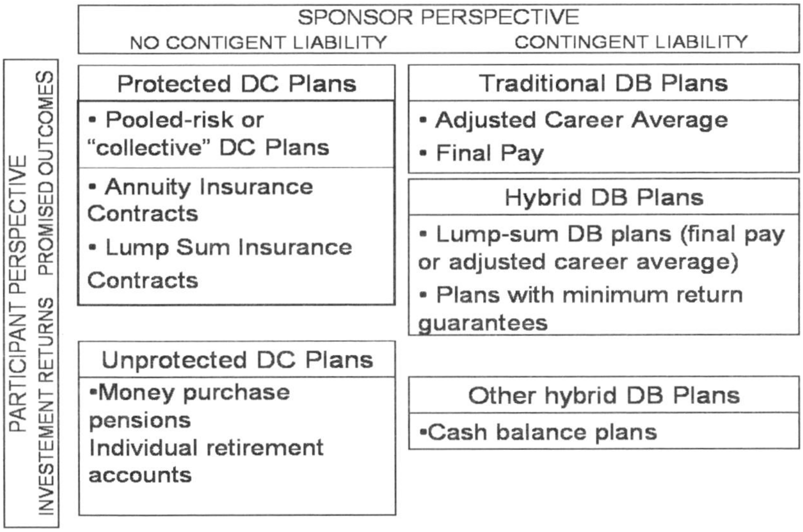

	SPONSOR PERSPECTIVE	
	NO CONTINGENT LIABILITY	CONTINGENT LIABILITY
PARTICIPANT PERSPECTIVE — PROMISED OUTCOMES	**Protected DC Plans** • Pooled-risk or "collective" DC Plans • Annuity Insurance Contracts • Lump Sum Insurance Contracts	**Traditional DB Plans** • Adjusted Career Average • Final Pay
		Hybrid DB Plans • Lump-sum DB plans (final pay or adjusted career average) • Plans with minimum return guarantees
PARTICIPANT PERSPECTIVE — INVESTEMENT RETURNS	**Unprotected DC Plans** •Money purchase pensions Individual retirement accounts	**Other hybrid DB Plans** •Cash balance plans

The bottom right hand quadrant is used to classify the increasingly popular cash balance plans in which participants bear investment risk. What makes these schemes defined benefit is that sponsor (employer, government) is promising to pay an accrued liability equal to contributions compounded by a particular rate of return, regardless of whether any segregated underlying assets are less than, or even greater than, the accrued liability. In some cash balance plans, workers have a risk/reward choice among several investment indexes, including one or more equity investment options. From their perspective, outcomes are the same as if they were investing in a standard worker-choice defined contribution plan, where members choose investment vehicles from among different options.

In the case of cash balance plans offering a fixed rate of return, the "investment risk" is that the return is a function of an "administered" return that may not reflect market conditions. While the administered return changes prospectively, the accrued liability is similar to a bond in which principal and past accrued interest are protected in nominal terms. Like a bond, however, absent inflation indexing, such cash balance "bond" can have a negative real return.

The upper left hand quadrant contains the insurance product arrangements and the pooled-risk or "collective" defined contribution plans discussed earlier. These plans are defined contribution from the employers' financing perspective (and hence from accounting perspective) but participants perceive a promised benefit. Though these arrangements contain no automatic contingent liability, it is possible that contribution rates might be raised prospectively through bargaining or otherwise such that the result is de facto, if not de jure, defined benefit.

Conversely, when defined benefit sponsors find themselves facing unacceptably high accruing liability costs (relative to defined benefit's usefulness), they can try to limit those costs through changes in plan terms, closing the plan to new entrants, freezing new accruals or even terminating a plan. Sponsor discretion, however, can be limited by collective bargaining or broader solidarity compacts, and countries have different laws and regulations about plan participants' accrued rights – are they just past accruals, based on nominal earnings or earnings adjusted for inflation (or some other factor), or the right to continue in the plan? But despite these limitations, the defined benefit bargain is economically much more contingent than often described.

It is also important to note that in some OECD countries, some aspects of the benefit formula in a defined benefit plan are not actually guaranteed and are adjusted depending on the investment performance of the pension fund. In the Netherlands, for example, the extent of benefit indexation is typically determined by the pension fund's board on the basis of the fund's solvency, rather than by the plan sponsor when the plan is set up. Benefit indexation, therefore, has a defined contribution nature from the employers' perspective. The investment risk pertaining to indexation is borne by the plan members.

As shown in Table 1, the countries with the highest coverage rates of occupational pension also tend to be ones with significant protection and risk-sharing features in their plans' design. In all seven countries with coverage rates in occupational plans above 90%, the main plan design is either of the traditional or hybrid defined benefit type (Finland, Netherlands, Norway, Sweden and Switzerland) or the protected (mainly pooled-risk or "collective") defined contribution type (Denmark and Iceland). Unprotected, defined contribution plans have only increased in importance recently in some of these countries. For example, the two main occupational pension plans in Sweden for private sector workers – SAF-LO for wage-earners and ITP for salaried employees – were reformed in recent years (1998 and 2007, respectively) and now have an unprotected, defined contribution component for new employees (see Figure 1).

Table 1. Occupational plan design in selected OECD countries

Australia	Primarily unprotected defined contribution (more than 90% of members).
Austria	Primarily unprotected defined contribution (more than 90% of members).
Belgium	Primarily hybrid defined benefit (minimum return guarantees).
Canada	Primarily defined benefit (more than 80% of members).
Denmark	Protected defined contribution (pooled-risk or "collective" DC).
Finland	Only defined benefit.
Germany	Primarily defined benefit (more than 90% of members), but new hybrid defined benefit being established (minimum return guarantees).
Hungary	The voluntary pension funds introduced by the 1993 law and the mandatory ones created by the 1998 reform can only manage unprotected defined contribution pension plans.
Iceland	Protected defined contribution (pooled-risk or "collective" DC).
Ireland	Mainly traditional defined benefit (more than 70% of members). The rest is unprotected, defined contribution.

Italy	Since 1993 pension fund law, only unprotected defined contribution allowed. Some defined benefit plans remain among employers in the financial sector.
Japan	Primarily defined benefit (more than 90% of membership). Many DB plans have switched from final pay to cash balance (hybrid).
Netherlands	Primarily "career-average" defined benefit (more than 95% of membership), but some plans are being reclassified as pooled-risk, "collective" defined contribution.
New Zealand	Mainly defined contribution (more than 60% of membership). Among private sector workers, defined contribution is more extensive (up to 80% of membership).
Norway	Mainly (more than 60% of membership) traditional defined benefit plans (final pay in the public sector and career-average in the private sector). The rest are primarily protected, defined contribution plans (deferred annuity policies).
Portugal	Primarily defined benefit (more than 90% of members)
Spain	Primarily unprotected defined contribution (more than 90% of members)
Sweden	Occupational plans in the public sector are final pay defined benefit. The defined benefit ITP plan is closed to new entrants since January 2007. New employees have a defined contribution plan. Half of the employer's contributions under the new plan must be in deferred annuity policies. Since 1998, the SAF-LO plan ("blue-collar") is an unprotected, defined contribution plan with worker choice.
Switzerland	Defined benefit and hybrid defined benefit (minimum return guarantees)
United Kingdom	Primarily defined benefit (more than 80% of members), but most plans are closed to new members and have been replaced mainly with unprotected defined contribution plans.
United States	Of private sector workers covered by occupational plans, about 60 percent rely exclusively on defined contribution plans, 10 percent rely exclusively on defined benefit plans and 30 percent have dual coverage. Among those covered by defined benefit plans, about half belong to cash balance (hybrid) plans. Public sector plans are predominantly defined benefit.

Source: OECD
Note: membership figures refer to active members. For some countries, membership figures have been adjusted to eliminate double-counting.

II. Changes in plan design

The shift from defined benefit to defined contribution arrangements concerns mainly countries with medium levels of occupational pension coverage (between 40 and 60 percent of the workforce). In terms of membership, defined benefit (traditional or hybrid) plans are still prevalent in Belgium, Canada, Germany, Ireland, and Japan, but defined contribution plans are growing in relative terms in Canada, Ireland, and Japan. Legislation on defined contribution plans was introduced in Japan in 2001, but already 10 percent of covered workers belong to them. In Canada, the coverage of occupational defined benefit plans has fallen a few percentage points over the last decade, but there are still three times as many workers in these plans than in defined contribution ones (see Figure 3). In Belgium and Germany, tax-advantaged defined contribution plans can be set up (in Germany, only since the 2001 Riester reform) but, because sponsoring employers must guarantee a minimum rate of return on contributions (see next section), these plans are classified as hybrid arrangements.

Figure 3. Shift from DB to DC in occupational plans in Canada (1991-2000)

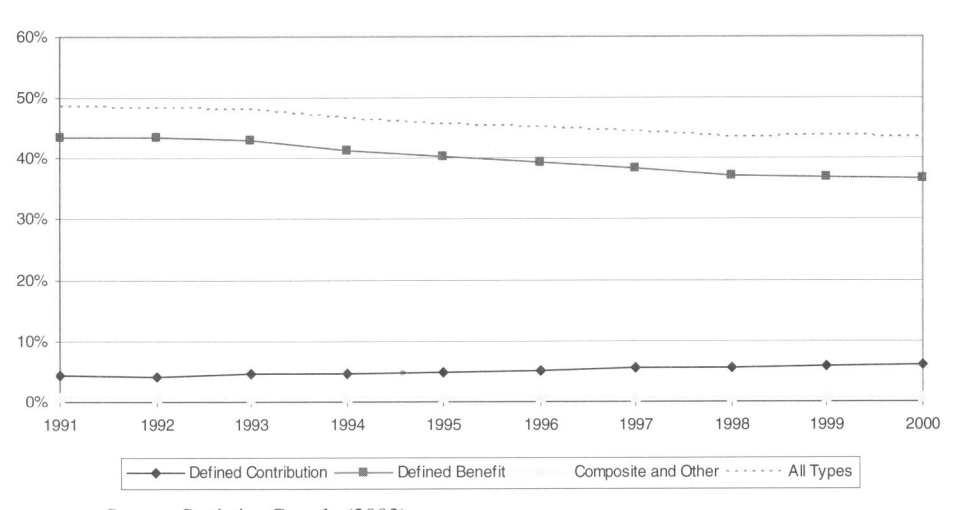

Figure 3. Percentage of Paid Workers Covered by an RPP, by Type of Plan

Source: Statistics Canada (2003)

1. INTRODUCTION

In the United Kingdom and the United States, there has been a much more marked shift towards defined contribution plans and, more recently, towards cash balance and other hybrid plans among private sector workers. This trend has intensified over the last two decades. Defined benefit plans, often paying benefits based on final salaries, were the norm until the early 1970s. Since then, these plans have been losing ground rapidly in terms of both assets and membership to defined contribution plans. As shown in Figure 4, the membership share of defined benefit plans among private sector workers in the United States fell steadily from 39 percent of the workforce in 1980 to 19 percent in 2003.[7] In the United Kingdom, the shift to defined contribution only dates back a few years, but it is proceeding at a much faster pace as most defined benefit plans have been closed to new entrants, while some have also frozen accruals.

Figure 4. Shift from DB to DC among private sector occupational plans in the United States

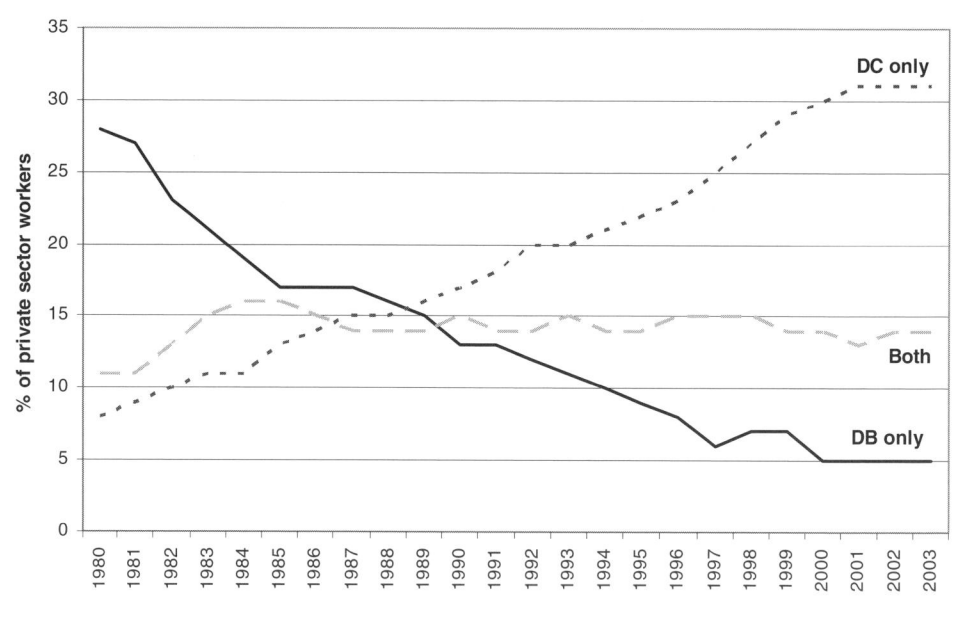

Source: Buessing and Soto (2006)

Many reasons underlie this shift. In the United States, in its initial stages this shift was documented to coincide with large employment moves from those sectors of the economy (notably manufacturing) that had traditionally sponsored defined benefit plans toward the service sector, where defined contribution plans, or no coverage, were the norm. Similar economic restructurings in other OECD countries may also be a factor in less defined benefit coverage. On the other hand, there is little evidence to support the claim that increased job mobility explains the growth of defined contribution plans. At least in the United States, causality appears to run in the opposite direction (Munnell et al. (2006)). Regulatory and taxation factors seem to have been an important factor also, and may explain why despite their similar economic structure, DB pension plans have remained much more widespread in Canada than in the United States. Among other factors, Brown and Liu (2001) argue that a lighter administrative burden on DB plans, greater freedom on coverage, the equivalent tax treatment between DB and DC plans (including tax-deductible employee contributions), and stronger unions may be factors upholding DB plans in Canada. Regulatory changes and accounting rules also appear to be partly responsible for the shift to DC in Japan and the United Kingdom. In the United Kingdom, over the space of a few years, employers have faced increased costs from mandatory revaluation of deferred DB pensions and indexation of pensions in payment, a move to market-based accounting standards, and the introduction of a guarantee arrangement (administered by the Pension Protection Fund), financed with a largely risk-based levy.

While OECD countries have experienced the move from defined benefit to defined contribution plans with different degree of intensity, the demise of final pay defined benefit plans among private sector workers is a practically universal phenomenon. In final-pay plans, older workers reap most of a plan's benefits and generate most of the costs, especially if they have had many years of coverage under the plan, which is typically the case. Generally, older workers are not hired into firms with final pay plans unless they come from firms also covered by the same plan – as can be the case in the Netherlands, for example. In contrast, workers who do not stay the course under a final pay defined benefit plan receive relatively small value. This is because their deferred annuity is based on the salary or wage at the time of separation. This "portability loss" can be mitigated if law or plan rules require the deferred pension entitlement to be adjusted between separation and when the annuity is first payable (pre-payment indexing), as is the case in the United Kingdom. In the United States, on the other hand, sponsors do not usually provide a pre-payment adjustment, precisely because it eviscerates the lock-in effect.

In some settings –manufacturing, military and, generally, the public sector – the final pay plan lock-in effect helped bind workers to the employer. This allowed the firm to invest in training and to create institutional memory in exchange for faithful service. The bargain, however, is sensitive to inflation, and as inflation has declined, the lock-in effect is less. In addition, for some caught in currents of downsizing (especially in manufacturing and even in high-tech), the final pay trade-off has become a "job mobility risk" rather than a stable bargain. Final-pay plans also reward workers with steep earnings profiles over time, leading to a more unequal distribution of benefits than career-average or cash balance plans.

Accounting standards, funding regulations and other regulatory constraints may have also contributed to sponsors reconsidering the defined benefit bargain. Long periods of high equity returns, even if punctuated with occasional but short downturns, may have led sponsors to have expectations about the costs of defined benefit commitments that are not sustainable. The negative investment returns of the early years of the millennium and continuing low discount rates (used to measure pension liabilities) have led to the emergence of funding gaps that have become more transparent on sponsors' balance sheets with the implementation of new accounting standards.

The "accounting" factor certainly appears to have played a key role in the stampede away from defined benefit plans in the United Kingdom (Klumpes and Whittington (2003)). The new fair-value based pension disclosures (FRS17) introduced in 2001 came at a particularly bad time for employers as funding levels had declined dramatically as a result of the stock market downturn and declining long term interest rates. Moreover, mandatory indexation of preserved benefits had already raised the cost of defined benefit pension provision substantially while reducing the lock-in effect provided by these plans.[8]

In the United States, accounting does not seem to have played a major role up to now. On the other hand, pension regulations can explain to some extent why some US employers have transformed final-pay plans into cash balance rather than fully replacing them with defined contribution arrangements. The 50% excise tax (15% until 1990) that employers must pay on surplus assets in the case of plan termination (and replacement with a defined contribution plan) can be avoided if the final-pay plan is instead converted into a cash balance one. Moreover, if the plan is terminated, employers must purchase annuities to cover the plan's accrued benefits in the insurance market. This is usually an expensive transaction for employers, as insurance companies' valuations of terminated pension liabilities are normally higher than plan sponsors' estimates of ongoing plan liabilities.

For the future, a further factor that will reduce further the popularity of traditional defined benefit plans is uncertainty over future increases in life expectancy. At both the national level and the firm level, the consequences of increasing longevity are better understood, particularly if retirement ages are difficult to change which is often the case in private firms. Partly this difficulty can lie in collectively bargained agreements, but often firms want to encourage workers to leave in the late 50s and early 60s for what the firms consider, rightly or wrongly, sound economic reasons. Constant fiddling with pension accrual factors to keep plan costs constant is difficult to explain to a workforce and there is only so much play with money wages and other compensation components to offset rising pension costs.

While traditional defined benefit plans suffer from serious weaknesses, the move to defined contribution plans where all risks are laid on workers may be no real panacea. Unprotected defined contribution plans expose participants fully to risks that they may be ill-prepared to handle. As the perils of these plans become clearer, the value of hybrid plans and other risk-sharing arrangements will be better appreciated. These plans, when transparently administered, can relieve participants of some of the uncertainties and difficult investment choices during the accumulation phase. However, it is unclear how much workers value this risk-transfer (vs. the more complete traditional defined benefit bargain) and whether employers believe it serves to attract a more loyal labor force.

In the OECD countries with the highest coverage levels, risk-sharing arrangements have been well established for some time. Some changes in plan design have also taken place, such as the shift among Dutch occupational plans from final pay to career-average benefits, with pre- and post-retirement indexation made conditional on funding status. Employer contribution rates are also being fixed (for 5 years or longer) which allows the plans to be qualified as defined contribution from an accounting perspective.[9]

Unlike defined benefit plans in other OECD countries, these countries' occupational pension arrangements have been generally very resilient to recent adverse market conditions. Probably the least affected occupational plans have been those in Denmark and Iceland. These countries' pooled-risk defined contribution plans generally aim at replicating defined benefit arrangements by sharing risks among participants. Unfortunately, it is not obvious that these countries' occupational pension plans designs could be easily implemented in other countries. These plans have emerged in small, homogenous countries with wide-spread collective bargaining at the industry level and are organised around occupational groups where demographic characteristics (longevity) are relatively common.

Though the conventional defined benefit plan, relative to the pooled risk defined contribution plan, has the additional layer of protection of the equity of the sponsor or sponsors, even this sine qua non of a defined benefit plan is less secure than often thought. Countries are still struggling in defining what the sponsor owes in the event of close-out – that is, to avoid the situation where plan termination by a solvent sponsor leads to benefits that are less generous than if the plan was closed to new entrants or benefit accruals were frozen. Coupled with this issue is the question of whether there should be insolvency insurance to cushion participants when both assets are insufficient and sponsors are bankrupt. While perhaps desirable in theory, no one has yet designed insolvency insurance in practice that cannot be manipulated (moral hazard) and, in the extreme, become a form of industrial subsidy.

III. Regulating plan design

Governments intervene in the design of occupational pension plans to protect what are considered basic rights of members and other beneficiaries and to promote benefit security in a direct way. There are multiple forms of regulations which affect three main areas of plan design, (i) vesting of accrued rights, (ii) benefit indexation, and (iii) investment returns.

The requirement for vesting of accrued rights is common in nearly all OECD countries. Vesting protects accrued benefits legally after a certain period of membership of the plan is completed. Two OECD countries, Japan and Portugal, do not have vesting rules, which means that employers' pension liabilities are not protected by law and can be adjusted. In Japan, the reduction of benefits accrued from past services was legalised in 1997, provided that certain conditions were met, including the explicit agreement between labour and management and the existence of business difficulties. Accrued benefits were cut during the late 1990s as investment returns deteriorated. In Portugal employers can curtail or altogether withdraw benefits from employees who leave before retirement.

Such flexibility in accrued benefits is similar to that in the "pooled-risk" or collective defined contribution schemes of Denmark and Iceland. In Denmark, the law permits pension funds to cut accrued benefits if the solvency position of the fund deteriorates substantially. The curtailment in benefits takes place by reducing the return guarantee used to calculate benefits. The mandatory occupational plans in Iceland also offer benefit promises where the risks are borne collectively by the plan members rather than the plan sponsor. Benefits accrue according to a units system in which the number of points or units earned in a year is the wage in a year in relation to the reference wage. If the performance of the pension fund over a certain number of years is insufficient to meet the targeted benefit level, benefits are scaled back or member contributions increased (or both). The only exceptions are those plans sponsored by the state and banks, where the sponsor directly guarantees the benefits.

Benefit indexation is also the subject to regulation. In the United Kingdom, pension funds are required by law to index both early leaver and retiree benefits built up on or after 6 April 1997 at the rate of the consumer price index with a 5 percent cap. Benefits accrued after the 2004 Pensions Act came into force are subject to a lower cap on statutory indexation (2.5 percent). Such requirements are rare in the OECD. Ireland has a statutory requirement to revalue deferred pensions with the consumer price index (capped at 4%), while Germany requires the indexation of pensions in payment. The specificity of the United Kingdom case arises from the fact that occupational (and personal) pension plans can be a substitute to the state second pension (the so-called S2P), which offers indexed pension benefits.

The strictness of this regulation in the United Kingdom contrasts with the situation in the Netherlands, where the indexation of both benefits accrued and benefits in payment can be left to the discretion of the pension fund's board. Most pension funds nowadays have a policy of conditional indexation that depends on the funding level. Pension funds are required to disclose the indexation policy to their members and beneficiaries in a transparent manner. The information must include whether indexation is unconditional or conditional and in the latter case, how indexation will vary.

The third main form of regulatory action concerns the rate of return that occupational pension plans must achieve on their investments and the annuity conversion rate used to transform a lump-sum or accumulated balance into a regular income stream (annuity). Such regulations turn these arrangements into hybrid defined benefit plans, as by law the guarantee is underwritten by plan sponsors. In Switzerland, the minimum return can be (and usually is) the actual return credited to members' accounts. As the annuity conversion rate is also fixed, benefits resemble those from an indexed career-average earnings DB plan. In Belgium and Germany, on the other hand, members get the higher of the guaranteed and the actual (market) rate of return on investments. The specific requirements of the guarantees are as follows:

- In Switzerland, mandatory occupational pension plans (which operate under law BVG/LPP) must guarantee a minimum nominal rate of return of 2.25 percent on investments since January 2004. The guaranteed return was 4 percent until January 2003, when it was lowered to 3.25 percent in order to better reflect market conditions. The minimum return is only applied when calculating a workers' accumulated fund when they switch plans and at retirement. The annuity rate is also fixed by law. For over twenty years, the annuity rate was set at 7.2 percent. It was recently reduced to reflect both declining interest rates and increased longevity. Employers are by law responsible for both guarantees.

- Defined contribution occupational pension plans in Belgium must since January 2004 (as a result of the Vandenbroucke Law) provide an annual minimum return of 3.75 percent on employees' contributions and 3.25 percent on their own contributions. As in Switzerland, this minimum return must be used when calculating the entitlements of workers that change plans. Unlike Switzerland, however, the actual market return must be applied if this is higher than the minimum guaranteed return. The employers that sponsor the plan are by law responsible for this engagement.

- The new German defined contribution pension plans introduced under the Riester reform must guarantee a minimum rate of return of 0 per cent in nominal terms, hence ensuring the protection of the nominal capital invested. In Germany also, the minimum return must be met only when switching plans and at retirement. Employers are by law responsible for meeting this guarantee.

Regulatory requirements on plan design such as those presented here promote benefit security but inevitably do so at the expense of flexibility in pension plan management and at potentially high cost to plan sponsors. At times of financial stress, such as the experienced by pension funds in recent years, these two objectives can come into conflict.

IV. Regulating financial security

Throughout the OECD, the basic tenet of financial security in occupational defined benefit plans is funding, that is, the provisioning for future benefits through accumulated assets.[10] Funding is also a basic requirement of the OECD Recommendation on Guidelines of Funding and Benefit Security in Occupational Pension Plans, approved by the OECD Council in May 2007[11].

Sponsoring employers can put in place various funding arrangements to collateralise their pension commitments. In most jurisdictions, in order to meet these obligations the employer creates a pension fund, a dedicated, legally separated pool of assets funded by contributions from the employer, the employee, or both. These assets are invested in order to enable the scheme to meet its pension obligations. Alternatively, the employer may contract a policy with an insurance undertaking to provide the benefits or guarantees stipulated in the pension arrangement. In a few countries (*e.g.* Germany, Luxembourg and Sweden) defined benefit pension plans need not be funded through segregated entities, but can instead be financed through so-called "book reserves", that is, pension claims on the sponsoring company's balance sheet.

Governments regulate funding in order to promote benefit security. Pension funds are subject to funding requirements, while some countries have also established guarantee funds to insure benefits against bankruptcy of the plan sponsor. All these regulations inevitably come at a cost. A key consideration for policymakers is to determine whether the goal of benefit security may be paradoxically leading to a less secure situation for some workers, especially younger ones. As defined benefit plans are increasingly regulated and protected, their burden for sponsors may have become intolerable. To the extent that these plans are unwound, and replaced by riskier and less generous defined contribution plans, younger workers may be unwittingly exposed to less benefit security.

New accounting standards are reflecting the increasing cost of defined benefit plans. In order to determine how financially secure defined benefit pension funds are, it is necessary to measure their assets and liabilities in a consistent manner. Traditionally, employers and pension regulators alike have relied on an actuarial approach to measuring funding ratios (the ratio of pension plan assets to liabilities) which involved the use of fixed or smoothed market discount rates (or, more controversially, the expected return on the fund's assets). On the other hand, assets were normally valued at current market prices, with some short term smoothing in some countries (*e.g.* the United States). The primary goal of this actuarial approach was to achieve a low and stable contribution rate.

As concern over sponsor insolvency intensified in recent years, some countries have reconsidered the appropriateness of this valuation methodology for regulatory purposes and have introduced a "fair value" approach to the measurement of funding ratios (*e.g.* Denmark, Netherlands, Sweden and the United States), which includes using a market-based interest rate for discounting future pension payments. Such approach would also be consistent with the trend in international accounting standards, and in particular the pension accounting standard of the International Accounting Standards Board (IASB) no. 19 (referred to as IAS19).

V. Structure of the book

This book addresses the question of how governments may promote the financial security of occupational, defined benefit plans and in particular in those financed via pension funds. The next chapter in this volume, by Juan Yermo, assesses current regulatory and accounting developments in the OECD area against their purported goals. It specifically considers the different approaches to valuing pension liabilities and questions the possibility of convergence between funding and business accountants' valuation standards for pension liabilities. He argues that the trend towards market-based valuation methods in business accounting is not entirely consistent with the parallel exercise undertaken by many pension regulators. Pension regulators tend to focus on a different measure of pension liabilities (that does not make salary projections when estimating pension benefits) as they are mainly concerned with the funding level for plans that risk termination as a result of insolvency of the plan sponsor.

Yermo argues that valuation methods for funding and business accounting purposes are likely to continue moving towards a market-based model. Given this trend, policymakers should be all the more cautious in setting funding regulations so as to provide sufficient flexibility to pension funds in covering funding deficits while providing incentives to establish funding buffers in good economic times. Yermo also argues that accounting rules and regulatory changes are driving reforms in plan design in some OECD countries such as Japan, the United Kingdom and the United States which may not always be in best interest of beneficiaries and can lead to procyclical investment behaviour by pension funds.

The next four chapters of this volume focus on the three basic regulatory measures to promote financial security in defined benefit plans: funding rules, insolvency insurance arrangements, and the granting of priority creditor rights of pension plan members and beneficiaries.

The chapter by Colin Pugh provides a comprehensive assessment of funding rules in selected OECD countries, the main form of regulatory action to address financial security. Such rules require a minimum contribution on the basis of a specific measure of the plan's liability or, more commonly, a minimum funding ratio and a maximum recovery period to return the fund to the minimum funding ratio in case of underfunding. In addition to minimum funding rules, the tax authorities also impose limits on contributions or on their tax deductibility when a certain funding level is attained. Regulations can also affect funding levels through the determination of the right of ownership to excess funding (where assets exceed liabilities) and, in particular, through the ability of the plan sponsor to draw part of this excess.

Pugh's review shows that the United Kingdom is the only OECD country that does not directly apply a single, uniform minimum funding requirement to all defined benefit pension plans. Instead, pension plan trustees must develop a funding policy specific to the plan and the plan sponsor, and any funding shortfalls should be eliminated as quickly as the plan sponsor can reasonably afford. There is a more specific requirement for sponsors to cover any funding deficit if a plan is terminated and there are insufficient assets to buy annuities from life insurance companies.

Pugh also argues that there is a danger in excessive regulatory zeal. Given the long-term nature of pension liabilities and the sponsor guarantee, there is a danger in regulations that focus on "full-funding at all times", especially when such regulations are based on fair value methodologies that heighten volatility in funding ratios. If smoothing methodologies are abandoned, Pugh recommends extending amortisation or recovery periods in order to ensure the attractiveness of pension provision to employers. Pugh also calls for reform of tax rules in some countries, allowing the build-up of larger buffers in good times and of a more consistent treatment of responsibility for pension surpluses and deficits.

In the next chapter, Blome, Fachinger, Franzen, Scheuenstuhl, and Yermo assess the impact of regulations and accounting standards on funding costs and investment strategies via the use of a stochastic asset liability model (ALM). They find that the impact depends critically on how regulators measure liabilities. Regulations affect funding costs primarily through the choice of investment strategy. Funding regulations that require full funding at all times and rely on fixed discount rates to calculate liabilities generally lead to higher investment in lower yield, lower risk instruments, raising the net funding cost.

Their paper also shows that the different valuation methodologies used for accounting and funding purposes leads to a dilemma in an ALM context, as the optimisation target becomes ambiguous. Low volatility in cover ratios (the accounting measure) that satisfy sponsors may mean high volatility in funding levels that violate regulatory requirements, especially in countries where discount rates are fixed by regulators. Hence, they claim, greater coherence in valuation methodologies under accounting and regulatory standards would go a long way towards facilitating the implementation of optimal ALM strategies by pension funds.

The chapter by Fiona Stewart looks at the operation of insolvency insurance arrangements, which she finds exist only in a few OECD countries. They are most prevalent in cases where pension funds or private insurance contracts are not used (*i.e.* the case of book reserves in Germany and Sweden)[12]. In Germany and Sweden, such schemes are run by a single mutual insurance company. Insolvency insurance arrangements also exist in the Canadian province of Ontario, Japan, the United Kingdom and the United States to protect defined benefit pension funds.

Stewart recommends careful consideration before introducing such arrangements. Governments need to address the complexity of ensuring efficient pricing of the guaranty in order to avoid unwarranted incentives for risk taking and undesirable cross-subsidisation from well managed to badly managed plans. It is also critical to endow the guarantee fund with sufficient powers. In Sweden the guaranty arrangement is further strengthened by priority rights for the insolvency insurer over the employer's assets in case of insolvency. The insurer can also demand that companies with a weak credit rating purchase insurance with the SPP insurance company and can thus gradually limit its exposure.

Governments may also consider using existing market mechanisms, such as the derivative default market and existing life insurance companies to provide the necessary protection. For example, in Luxembourg, employers must contract a policy with a life insurance company to cover the risk of insolvency.

The final chapter of the publication, by Fiona Stewart, addresses the issue of the rights of pension creditors within bankruptcy proceedings of the plan sponsor. Stewart finds that such rights are often not readily recognised, either because the obligations of the plan sponsor are not clearly laid out in the plan document or because plan beneficiaries lack proper representation in proceedings. She points at the German bankruptcy system as a reference as all unsecured creditors are treated equally, including the guarantee fund, the PSVaG. Stewart also echoes the OECD Recommendation of Guidelines on Funding and Benefit Security, which call for priority creditor rights for due and unpaid contributions, equal to the position of due and unpaid taxes.

The final section of this volume contains the OECD Recommendation mentioned above. This set of non-binding guidelines was approved by the OECD Working Party on Private Pensions in September 2006 and later endorsed by the OECD Council. They set out basic guidance for regulators in the three policy areas considered in the previous chapters.

VI. Lessons for policymaking

Defined benefit occupational pension plans are under increasing stress throughout the OECD area. Sponsors' reaction to the recent funding gaps has not been symmetric across OECD countries. Underfunded occupational pension commitments have created most strain for plan sponsors when they are the sole or main contributors to the plan and when accrued benefits are protected by law, as is the case in Canada, Ireland, the United Kingdom and the United States. The consequences of unfunded pension obligations are less drastic for companies in countries where accrued benefit rights can be cut back in situations of financial stress (as in Denmark, Iceland, Japan, and Portugal), or where future obligations can be readily adjusted by changing benefit formulas, revaluation or indexation parameters (as in the Netherlands) or by changing minimum rates of return on investment and annuity rates (as in Switzerland).

In occupational plans in the United Kingdom and, to a lesser extent, the United States, employers are responding by shifting risks to workers, closing down defined benefit plans to new entrants and replacing them with "pure" (unprotected) defined contribution plans. This trend, however, is not inevitable. It need not be the onset of a new era where workers are helplessly exposed to investment and longevity risks. Some employers in these countries have transformed traditional defined benefit plans into hybrid arrangements, where investment risks are shared during the accumulation phase and longevity risks are shared or shifted to insurance companies at retirement. Other countries such as Denmark, Iceland, and the Netherlands also show that it is possible to devise occupational pension systems where pension obligations fall on pension funds, hence allowing the plans to be classified as defined contribution from an accounting perspective. Workers in these countries bear pension-related risks collectively through the pension funds.

Policymakers' action can also help strengthen defined benefit plans by addressing employers' concerns over the costs of benefit security. The mistakes of the past, such as excessively long contribution holidays, low maximum funding ratios, and opaqueness in accounts are being replaced by a focus on fair values and short recovery periods for correcting underfunding. While the move to greater transparency in pension plan accounts is welcome, the existing fair value approach as exemplified by the FRS17 accounting standard in the United Kingdom seems to misrepresent the cashflow challenges and opportunities faced by pension funds. Even more, the introduction of volatility in measures of funding ratios would justify a more lenient approach to recovery periods as the funding situation one day may be suddenly overturned.

At the end of the day, the risk that policymakers need to be most concerned about in occupational defined benefit plans is that of bankruptcy of the plan sponsor. From a policy perspective, there are two main solutions to this problem: ensuring high funding ratios on an ongoing basis and establishing insolvency insurance protection. Some OECD countries, like Canada (excluding Ontario), Ireland and the Netherlands, have focused exclusively on the former route. One OECD country, the United Kingdom, is following mainly the latter route. In between are countries that have both minimum funding rules and insolvency guarantee schemes, like Japan and the United States.

There is no inherent superiority to any combination of these two policy actions as long as they are designed efficiently. However, history has shown that it is difficult to operate insurance insolvency arrangements in a way that accounts appropriately for risks. At the same time, strict funding rules can make defined benefit plans very expensive to manage, especially if sponsors are called to make up any funding gaps at times of economic weakness. Time will tell which approach is best at encouraging benefit security while maintaining the attractiveness of defined benefit plans for employers.

Notes

1. The OECD definition of occupational pension plans includes also those that operate under social security law, as is the case in Finland (e.g. the TEL scheme).

2. The coverage rate increased in Italy in 2007 as a result of the introduction of an automatic default transfer of severance funds (TFR) to pension funds.

3. For example, the operational costs of occupational defined benefit plans in the Netherlands have been estimated at 0.14 percent of assets under management (Bikker and de Dreu (2006)).

4. In some OECD countries, certain occupational pension obligations have a preferred status, and must be met by a company before debt. This is the case, for example, of severance schemes in Italy (the so-called TFR).

5. Defined lump-sum plans are known as pension equity plans in the United States.

6. In the United Kingdom, cash balance plans have also started to emerge, sometimes as a result of discontent with the results of defined contribution arrangements. However, UK cash balance plans tend to be less generous than their Japanese or US counterpart as the interest credit is usually limited to revaluation of the account balance with the retail price index, that is, a 0% return in real terms. Some plans offer additional returns on a discretionary basis (Department of Work and Pensions (2005)).

7. These figures are derived from 5500 forms. They tend to overestimate the number of participants because they include non-vested and non-participating employees, as well as involving double-counting.

8. Wesbroom and Reay (2005) estimate that the cost of early leavers' benefits went up by a factor of four in the late 90s as a result of revaluation and indexation requirements.

9. See Ponds and van Riel (2007) for an analysis of the shift to collective DC plans in the Netherlands.

10. See Lindeman (2004).

11. The Guidelines are contained in the Annex of this publication.

12. Severance schemes, which in many ways resemble defined benefit pension plans, are often protected solely by priority credit rights.

References

Bikker, J. and de Dreu, J. (2006), Pension fund efficiency: the impact of scale, governance and plan design, *DNB Working Paper*, No. 109, August 2006.

Blome, S., Fachinger, K., Franzen, D., Scheuenstuhl, G. and Yermo, J. (2007), "Pension Fund Regulation and Risk Management: Results from an ALM Optimisation Exercise", this volume.

Brown, R. L. and Liu, J. (2001), The Shift to Defined Contribution Pension Plans: Why Did It Not Happen in Canada?, *North American Actuarial Journal Vol. 5 No.3*, July 2001

Buessing, M. and Soto, M. (2006), "The State of Private Pensions: Current 5500 Data", Issues in Brief No. 42, Center for Retirement Research at Boston College, February 2006.

Department of Work and Pensions (2005), "Risk Sharing and Hybrid Pensions Plans", Research Report 270.

Klumpes, P., Li, Y. and Whittington, M. (2003), "The Impact of UK Accounting Rule Changes on Pension Terminations", *Warwick Business School Working Paper*, August.

Lindeman, D. (2004), "A Note on Benefit Security", *Financial Market Trends*, No. 86, March 2004, pp. 121-131, Paris: OECD.

Munnell, A., Haverstick, K. Sanzenbacher, G. (2006), "Job Tenure and the Spread of 401(k)s", *Issues in Brief No. 55*, Center for Retirement Research at Boston College, October 2006.

OECD (2005), "Private Pensions: OECD Classification and Glossary", Paris: OECD.

Ponds, E. H. M. and van Riel, B. (2007), "The Recent Evolution of Pension Funds in the Netherlands: the Trend to Hybrid DB-DC Plans and Beyond", *Center for Retirement Research at Boston College Working Paper 2007-9*, April 2007.

Pugh, C. (2007), "Funding Rules and Actuarial Methods", this volume.

Statistics Canada (2003), Canada's Retirement Income Programs: A Statistical Overview, No. 74-507.

Stewart, F. (2007a), "Pension Fund Guarantee Schemes", this volume.

Stewart, F. (2007b), "Priority Creditor Rights for Pension Funds", this volume.

Wesbroom, K. and Reay, T. (2005), "Hybrid Pension Plans: UK and International Experience", Department of Work and Pensions Research Report 271.

Yermo, J. (2007), "Reforming the Valuation and Funding of Pension Promises: Are Occupational Pensions Safer?", this volume.

ISBN 978-92-64-02810-4
Protecting Pensions: Policy Analysis
and Examples from OECD Countries
© OECD 2007

Chapter 2

REFORMING THE VALUATION AND FUNDING OF PENSION PROMISES: ARE OCCUPATIONAL PENSIONS SAFER?

by
Juan Yermo*

Introduction

Since 2001, occupational[1] defined benefit (DB) pension plans in OECD countries have experienced an adverse funding situation, that is, a low ratio of assets to liabilities. The decline in funding ratios can be traced to the low interest rate environment and poor equity market returns, together with longer term pressures such as revisions in life expectancy assumptions.[2] Various regulatory initiatives have been undertaken to address these funding gaps, some providing forbearance to plan sponsors, others aiming at improving benefit protection outright.[3] At the same time, new accounting standards have been introduced which aim at shining a bright light on what

---

* The author is principal administrator of the private pensions unit at the OECD. He would like to thank the Delegates to the OECD Working Party on Private Pensions, André Laboul (OECD), Chinu Patel (Watson Wyatt) and Colin Pugh (independent consultant) for their comments on previous versions of this paper. The views expressed are the sole responsibility of the author and do not necessarily reflect those of the OECD or its member countries.

has been historically a rather obscure but major component of the balance sheet of pension plan sponsors.

Policymakers face a difficult dilemma. If funding rules are tightened too much, employers may altogether abandon DB plans. On the other hand, lax funding rules may expose workers to benefit losses if underfunded plans are terminated by insolvent employers. A key question for policymakers (and the actuarial and accounting professions) is to determine whether certain valuation methods used by regulators and accountants may portray a misleading picture of the health of DB plans. In addition, it may be asked why funding ratios were not higher in the good years, like the 1990s, given the possibility of adverse developments in asset values and interest rates. Policymakers need to consider how regulations should be reformed in order to best protect pension promises. Such deliberations should also take into consideration the reform in accounting standards, as shareholders can be a powerful agent of change.

This chapter extends the discussion on funding by assessing current regulatory and accounting developments in the OECD area against their purported goals. It specifically considers the different approaches to valuing pension liabilities and questions the possibility of convergence between funding and business accountants' valuation standards for pension liabilities. The main conclusions are as follows:

Valuation methods for funding and business accounting purposes are likely to continue moving towards a market-based model. Given this trend, policymakers should be all the more cautious in setting funding regulations so as to provide sufficient flexibility to pension funds in covering funding deficits while providing incentives to establish funding buffers in good economic times.

While market-based valuation methods are becoming more prevalent, the measure of the pension liability used for funding rules is likely to differ from that used in business accounting, because of their different objectives. In particular, pension regulators are most concerned with the value of accrued benefits (the accumulated benefit obligation or ABO), ignoring the impact of salary increases. Accounting standards, on the other hand, take salary increases into account in order to develop a measure of liabilities (the projected benefit obligation, or PBO) consistent with the view of the enterprise as an ongoing concern.

The current application of fair value principles[4] to pension accounting standards is the subject of much controversy. There is an ongoing debate about the right measure of liabilities (ABO or PBO), the extent to which pension benefits are a debt of employers or can be adjusted, the appropriate discount rate to be used, and the way to recognise actuarial gains and losses.

Given the uncertainty surrounding valuations based on "mark-to-model" principles, accounting disclosures by sponsoring companies should be at least accompanied with information about the assumptions made and a sensitivity analysis. Policymakers should also consider the impact of the volatility created by market-based valuations on companies' balance sheets and income statement. In particular, the removal of the smoothing options currently permitted by international accounting standards could have an adverse impact on DB pension provision, the application of efficient risk management strategies, and could potentially lead to procyclical investment behaviour by pension funds.

This chapter is structured as follows. Section I provides a comparison of valuation methods for pension assets and liabilities for both funding and business accounting purposes. There is special focus on selected OECD countries (Denmark, Japan, Netherlands, Sweden, United Kingdom and the United States) that have already or are in the process of moving towards a market-based approach to measuring pension fund liabilities for regulatory funding purposes (insurance purposes in the UK case). Asset valuation methodologies, which have been traditionally market-based but allowed some degree of smoothing, are also moving towards a fair-value model. Market-based valuations have made even greater in-roads in the domain of business accounting, as most OECD countries have implemented some variation of the International Accounting Standards Board's pension standard (IAS 19).

Section II describes the recent trends in funding levels and recent regulatory initiatives in this sample of OECD countries. There are substantial differences in many aspects of the regulation, namely what the funding target should be, how quickly funding gaps should be eliminated (the recovery period), and what the maximum funding level may be. These differences can be explained by a variety of factors. In particular, it is argued that the regime of funding rules cannot be discussed in isolation from other policy initiatives that affect benefit security, such as insolvency guarantee funds and priority rights in bankruptcy. Funding rules should also take into consideration the extent to which pension funds have an automatic claim on sponsor contributions from the plan sponsor, the extent to which benefit promises can be cut back (in particular, revaluation and indexation factors), and whether employees may also be asked to make additional contributions to the fund.

Section III reviews the aftermath of the funding gaps and these regulatory and accounting initiatives. Changes in valuation standards (for both funding and accounting purposes) and the reform of funding rules are likely to bring about higher funding levels, greater protection of pension rights and greater use of asset-liability modeling techniques. At the same time, it is quite possible that these initiatives will push some plan sponsors to terminate their defined benefit plans. The demise of defined benefit plans may not be a problem in itself if new arrangements appear that maintain some of the attractive features of those plans (such as the targeting of salary related benefits via "protected" defined contribution plans). However, in some countries the emerging plan model is of the "unprotected" defined contribution type, which offers members investment choice and correspondingly lays all investment risks on individual members.

I. Measuring pension fund assets and liabilities for funding and accounting purposes

A transparent, consistent measurement of DB pension fund assets and liabilities is essential to ensure good governance and effective supervision. While pricing pension fund assets is normally straight forward (as long as they are traded in liquid markets), there are different views as to what is the relevant measure of pension fund liabilities as (i) they are not traded in markets, (ii) they have special design characteristics stemming from wage-benefit bargaining which can cause discretionary changes in future (and, in some cases, even accrued) benefits, and (iii) there are no hedging assets that closely match the cashflows of pension funds, which could be used to price their liabilities.

Various observers (*e.g.* Bader and Gold (2003), Exley (2006)) argue that such characteristics are not obstacles to calculating "market-equivalent" values of DB pension funds, applying what is referred to as the fair value principle. Others (*e.g.* Day (2003), Plantin et al. (2005)) have argued that attempts at "marking to market" pension fund liabilities can lead to a narrow focus on the short-term impact of financial decisions, inducing sub-optimal long-term results. While the academic debate on the application of fair valuation principles to pension funds (or indeed banks and insurance companies) is far from closed, there is a general shift towards some form of fair value among pension fund regulators and accounting standard-setters.

In most countries, there are at least two statutory measures of liabilities, one designated by the pension regulator for funding purposes[5] and another one used by plan sponsors for business accounting purposes. In addition, some countries like the United Kingdom and the United States require other measures to be calculated for purposes of determining premiums to a guarantee fund (the Pension Protection Fund – PPF – in the United Kingdom and the Pension Benefit Guaranty Corporation – PBGC - in the United States). A market measure of the liabilities may also exist in the quoted premia that life insurance companies charge for taking over pension liabilities. This so-called buy-out market has gained importance in the

United Kingdom in recent years and has established a fourth measure of pension liabilities.

The difference between these measures can be significant. One rating agency, using the PBO measure estimated a shortfall in the United States for the S&P 500 companies of US$140billion (a funding ratio of 90.4 percent) in 2005, as against a surplus of some $250billion five years earlier.[6] On the other hand, the PBGC – which uses a measure similar to the ABO to calculate funding ratios – estimated a shortfall for all insured single-employer DB plans of a record US$339billion as of December 2005, for an average funding ratio of 72 percent[7]. The funding deficit in multi-employer plans was over US$170bn, meaning a total funding gap (for single and multi-employer plans) in the country of over US$500bn.

The main differences between regulatory and accounting measures of liabilities relate to:

- the actuarial cost method to be used;
- the benefits to be considered, including benefit revaluation (for early leavers) and indexation (for retirees) factors, and assumptions over the rate of withdrawal from the plan;
- the choice of discount rate to calculate the present value of accrued benefits; and
- the mortality tables and the adjustments to be made for future mortality trends, including those specific to the plan.

With respect to the actuarial cost method, benefit allocation methods are becoming increasingly popular over cost allocation methods, but different approaches exist with respect to other aspects of the cost method. Regulators usually calculate benefits on the basis of current salaries (as in the current unit credit method used to calculate the ABO)[8] while business accountants do so on the basis of future, projected salaries (as in the projected unit credit method used to calculate the PBO). Actuarial cost methods also differ in the extent to which extent actuarial gains and losses[9] and other supplemental liabilities (like plan amendments and initial plan liabilities) may be amortised (spread) over time.[10]

Regulators and accountants also differ on the type of benefits that they include in their liability measures. Regulators normally exclude revaluation and indexation factors from their measure of liabilities unless they are required by law (as in Ireland – revaluation only - and the United Kingdom). Business accountants, on the other hand, tend to account for these factors if they are considered a "constructive" obligation on the plan sponsor, where "constructive" is defined as a reasonable expectation on the basis of past behaviour or informal agreements. Regulators and accountants also make different assumptions with respect to employees that leave the plan early. Regulators usually require that measures of liabilities exclude withdrawal from service, while accountants use withdrawal rate assumptions.

The choice of discount rate also varies between regulators and business accountants. Many regulators still apply a maximum discount rate, while accounting standards are based on market yields of fixed income securities, typically those of corporate bonds. As shown in Table 1, the differences in discount rates are substantial in most countries, the accountants' discount rate being normally higher than that used by regulators. The recent trend towards market-based discount rates among regulators is likely to bring about some convergence in this key parameter. In particular, at the beginning of 2007, the Netherlands joined Japan and the United States in linking the regulatory discount rate to the market yield of fixed income securities.

Table 1. Discount rates used in regulatory and accounting measures of pension liabilities in selected OECD countries (2005)

	Regulator	Accountant
Belgium	6	4.87
Canada	4.5	5.98
Germany	2.75-4	4.91
Ireland	4.6-7.25	4.82
Japan	1.0-1.6	2.07
Netherlands	4	4.94
Portugal	4.5	5.12
Spain	4.0	4.87
United Kingdom	4.0	5.41
United States	4.7	5.83

Source: each country's respective regulatory authority, Watson Wyatt (2005)
Note: regulators' discount rates are maxima, except in Canada, Japan, and the United States where they are market-based. Accountants' rates are averages of a sample of companies in each country.

The mortality tables and projections used by regulators and accountants also differ, although in principle they should be the same. Few regulators require pension plans to take into account the expected future evolution of mortality or to use the latest mortality data available. However, the main differences in mortality assumptions occur not between regulatory and accounting measures in the same country but across countries. A study by Cass Business School (2005) shows that only in some countries do pension plans incorporate an allowance for expected future improvements in mortality. Most use tables that relate to mortality observed over a period in the past. As shown in Figure 1, countries like Denmark and Switzerland use mortality assumptions based on the national population mortality tables, without allowing for expected future increases in life expectancy. The implications of these different assumptions for liability measures are substantial. Antolin (2007) shows that an unexpected improvement in life expectancy at birth of 1 year per decade would increase the liabilities of a typical pension fund by 10 percent, and up to 20 percent for a fund with mainly young workers.

Figure 1. Difference between assumed life expectancy of DB plan male members aged 65 and the observed general population life expectancy in selected OECD countries (2005)

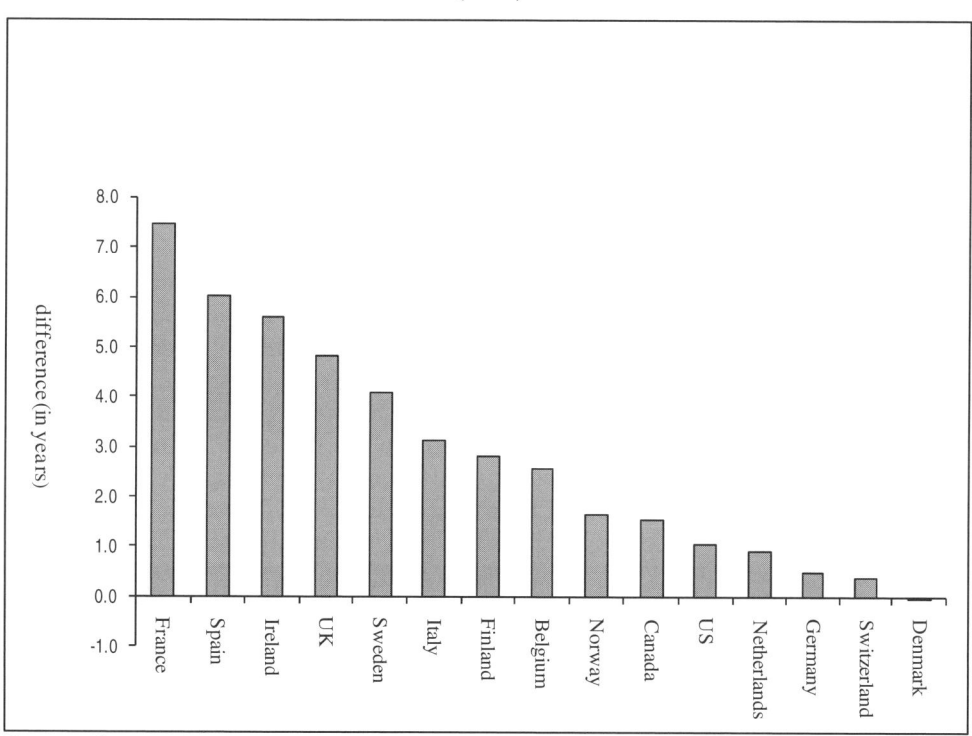

Source: Cass Business School (2005)

Valuation methods for funding purposes

While wide differences still exist across countries in valuation methods of pension fund[11] assets and liabilities for funding purposes (see Pugh (2007)), there has been some degree of convergence in recent years. In particular, regulators are increasingly requiring the use of discount rates that reflect market yields of government bonds. This move towards market-based valuation is consistent with the regulator's goal of promoting funding levels high enough to cover benefit promises in the case of plan termination. However, the situation in some countries is still one where regulatory measures of pension liabilities are below the plan termination liability. Like the termination liability and the ABO, the regulatory measure of pension liabilities is based on accrued benefits, where no allowance is made for future salary increases.[12] However, at termination, some countries like the United Kingdom and the United States require the pension fund's assets to be used to buy deferred annuities (from a guarantee fund or from a private insurance company[13], depending on whether the termination was caused by the insolvency of the plan sponsor). As annuities are priced above the regulator's liability measure, funding rules can give a false sense of security. The elimination of the minimum funding requirement in the United Kingdom in 2005, and its replacement by a scheme-specific funding standard is in part an answer to this concern.

Benefit allocation methods that projects benefits by taking into account future salary growth (PUC method used to calculate the PBO) are more likely to value the actuarial liability above the plan termination liability (all else, such as amortisation periods, actuarial assumptions and discount rates, being equal). Yet even this method is the subject of some controversy. This method still creates a climbing ratio of contributions to salary (contribution rate) over the service period of the worker. Before accounting standards were adopted based on this method, employers in some countries used cost allocation methods that aimed at a roughly constant contribution rate over the service period. In the United States, for example, the percentage of large final pay plans using cost allocation methods declined from 90 percent in 1983 to 31 percent by 2002, while the percentage using a PUC-based benefit allocation method increased from 10 percent to 69 percent (McGill et al (2005)).

A key aspect of the valuation of pension liabilities is the choice of discount rate. Regulatory authorities often specify the discount rate to be used for calculating the present value of such accrued benefits (*i.e.* the accrued liabilities). The prescribed discount rate usually takes the form of (i) a specific or maximum rate, (ii) the current market yield on an identifiable group of securities or (iii) the rates implicit in the purchase from insurance companies of immediate and deferred annuities. The choice of discount rate can make a large difference to the measured value of accrued liabilities. An increase of one percent in the discount rate can lead to as much as a 30 percent increase in the liability. Market valuation methods usually rely on bond yields as discount rates, instead of fixed rates set on a discretionary basis by the authorities. Market discount rates can also be chosen to reflect the nature of the plan's liabilities such as the maturity of the fund or the extent of benefit indexation. The new funding rules introduced in the United States under the 2006 Pension protection Act, for example, require that discount rates are based on the high-quality corporate bond yield curve, choosing maturities consistent with the duration of the plan's liabilities.

The main OECD countries that have introduced market-based liability valuations of DB pension funds are Japan, the Netherlands, and the United States, while the United Kingdom has introduced such valuations for purposes of calculating the insurance premia (levy) to be paid to the PPF. Discount rates in all these countries are based on spot or a historic average of bond yields or equivalent swap rates.

In Japan, funding rules were reformed in 1997. Prior to this date, the discount rate used for calculating liabilities was prescribed. Since then, the fund can decide its discount rate, which must within 80% to 120% of the average yield of 10-year government bonds issued during the previous five years. The measure of accrued benefits also excludes future salary increases and early withdrawals from the plan by departing employees.

In the Netherlands, the new regulatory framework, effective from 1 January 2007 requires a market-based valuation of pension liabilities for funding purposes, without any amortisation or smoothing options. As in other countries, estimated future salary growth is not to be considered in the measure of accrued liabilities. Future benefits are discounted using the current yield curve on default-free capital market instruments, rather than the fixed rate of 4 percent as has been historically the case.[14] The market yield is corrected for expected inflation if indexation of accrued pensions is "unconditional", that is, if it does not depend on the performance of the pension fund. Liability measures are also expected to take into account further increases in longevity. Sponsor companies are also required to separate the liabilities that are "conditional" on the investment performance of the pension fund from those that are "unconditional". Funding requirements are applied only to unconditional liabilities.

In the United States, one measure of pension liabilities is used for minimum funding requirements while a different one is calculated by the PBGC. The PBGC's measure assumes plan termination and is therefore market-based. The measure for funding purposes, on the other hand, has historically allowed long amortisation periods[15] and the smoothing of both asset returns and discount rates over many years.[16] It also relies on the current unit credit method (current salaries). The Pension Protection Act of 2006 has overhauled funding requirements, including changes to pension liability measures. Transition measures have been introduced for 2006 and 2007, but starting January 1st 2008, pension benefits will be discounted using a corporate bond yield curve, where the timing of future benefit payments would determine the yield to be used (based on the actual curve or three main rates for different maturity segments). The actual discount rate used must be between 90% and 100% of the average over the last two years. Plan assets under the new rules are also based on market value with permitted smoothing over 24 months. Smoothed assets must be within 10% of market value. The Act has also introduced a true termination measure for plans with funding ratios below 80%. Such plans are required to measure their at-risk liability which takes into account additional costs incurred when a plan terminates. These costs are calculated by assuming that workers eligible to retire within the next ten years will do so as early as possible and assuming that beneficiaries choose the benefit option that creates the highest liability. Also, if a plan were at risk for at least two of the preceding four years, its funding target would be increased by the administrative costs of group annuity contracts.[17]

Meanwhile, in the United Kingdom, the new guarantee fund, the PPF, relies on market values of pension fund assets and liabilities when calculating premiums to insure pension plans against the bankruptcy of the plan sponsor. On the other hand, the new funding framework from the Pensions Regulator (released in 2005) does not make any specific requirements with respect to valuation methods of assets or liabilities, other than requiring trustees, under the advice of actuaries, to decide on the funding objective appropriate for their plan and choose the actuarial assumptions prudently.[18] The flexibility of the UK approach stems from their elimination of statutory funding rules. However, disclosure requirements have been strengthened, and trustees are now required to instruct their scheme actuary to draw up at least two actuarial valuations: one reflecting the liabilities as an ongoing concern and another one reflecting the cost of securing benefits by the purchase of insurance policies.

In several other OECD countries that have not yet moved to market-based valuations of DB pension fund liabilities, policymakers have at least required a change in the fixed or maximum discount rates used in line with market developments. In Switzerland, for example, it is regulated that for the calculation of accrued benefits the discount rate must be set at 3.5 to 4.5%. In practice, a specially authorised second pillar expert sets this parameter according to the long-term return rate of a low-risk instrument (*e.g.* the Swiss Confederation bond with a maturity of 10 years) or according to the average return of the pension fund minus a safety margin. In Germany, the discount rate for calculating *Pensionskassen* liabilities was lowered from 3.25 percent in 2003 to 2.75 percent in 2004 (same as for other pension insurance contracts). A further lowering to 2.25 percent is envisaged from 2007 onwards. In Austria, the discount rate was lowered to 3.5 percent in 2003. In Finland, the statutory discount rate is being reduced gradually from 4 percent in 2003 to 3.5 by 2013. Countries where discount rates have not been changed in recent years include Spain (4 percent) and Portugal (4.5 percent).

The move towards market-based valuations has also taken place in countries such as Denmark where occupational pensions are DC from an accounting (sponsor) perspective, but the pension funds offer minimum return and benefit guarantees. Industry-wide pension funds (and other pension companies[19]) have been able to present their account on the basis of fair values since 1 January 2002. Starting on 1 January 2003, this has been made compulsory. The main features of the Danish market-based approach are the use of an adjusted yield curve of euro swap rates to set discount rates[20], the immediate recognition of actuarial gains and losses and the use of current salaries to calculate benefits (CUC method).

Similarly, in Sweden, the move to market valuation came into force on January 1, 2006 for life insurance companies and other insurance undertakings qualifying as institutions for occupational pension provision as defined under the EU Directive. The reform to valuations took place together with the adoption of the prudent person rule for regulating investments. Starting 1 January 2007, market discount rates are set based on an average of government bond yields and swap rates, replacing the current fixed 3 percent rate (3.5 percent until April 2003).

Valuation methods for accounting purposes

In the past, business accounting standards in some OECD countries (*e.g.* the Netherlands, Switzerland) did not require companies that sponsor DB pension plans[21] to show on their balance sheet the net balance of the pension fund's assets and liabilities. Sometimes, disclosure was only required in the notes to the accounts, as was the case in the United States until the reform by the Financial Accounting Standards Board (FASB) in September 2006. Even where disclosure was required, local accounting standards permitted a significant degree of flexibility in the recognition of certain liabilities, with long amortisation periods for initial plan liabilities, plan amendments, and actuarial gains and losses. Assets were sometimes measured at book values, or market values smoothed over some years. In addition to the opaqueness of reporting, the lack of an international valuation standard for pension expensing hampered cross-country comparison of company accounts by investors.

This situation has been changing rapidly in recent years with the advent of international accounting standards for post-employment benefits, including pensions. There is currently a high degree of convergence in business accounting standards towards market-based valuation, driven by the efforts of the International Accounting Standard Board (IASB) and FASB. IASB's standard for net pension liabilities, the so-called IAS19 standard, was approved in May 1999 and has been gradually adopted by many OECD countries. A new standard based on IAS19 was introduced in Japan in April 2000, while in the United Kingdom the new standard FRS17 was introduced in November 2001. The European Council adopted a resolution in June 2002 which required all listed companies based in the European Union to comply with this IASB accounting standard (and other International Financial Reporting Standards) in the preparation of their consolidated group accounts for years commencing on or after 1 January 2005.[22]

IAS19 is based on market valuation principles, using the PBO measure of pension liabilities (projecting benefits including the effect of future salary growth). Benefits are discounted at a suitable corporate bond rate and actuarial gains and losses may be either amortised over the remaining service period of plan members (above a 10 percent corridor) or immediately recognised in the profit and loss account (see Box 1). A revision in December 2004 introduced a third option, immediate recognition in a separate income statement (see Box 1). The latter is actually the only method permitted under the United Kingdom's own accounting standard, the so-called FRS17. Under FRS 17, actuarial gains and losses are fully and immediately recognised in a Statement of Recognised Gains and Losses (STRGL), which can be viewed as a supplementary profit and loss account.

The IAS 19 standard has been integrated into other EU countries' national accounting standard for listed companies. However, some countries permit a rather different accounting for non-listed companies. This is the case in Germany, which may be explained by the book reserving method which is still popular among mid-sized employers[23]. Although local German accounting rules (HGB) permit pension obligations incurred prior to 1987 to be ignored entirely for balance sheet accrual purposes (they must be disclosed in the notes to the accounts), almost all companies fully recognise pension plan liabilities on the balance sheet. The actuarial valuation method and the assumptions (*e.g.* a discount rate of 6 percent) are usually transposed unaltered from the tax accounts to the financial statements primarily on the grounds of simplification and the desire not to have diverging tax and financial statements. Under German accounting rules, the valuation of liabilities is made on the basis of current salaries and there is a requirement for immediate recognition of past services costs as well as actuarial gains and losses. This contrasts with the valuation method under IAS 19 (projected salaries and option to defer recognition of actuarial gains and losses). Hence, the actual liability reported on the balance sheet under German accounting standards may be higher or lower than that recognised under IAS 19. The German accounting standards board recently rejected a draft accounting standard (E-DRS 19) that followed similar principles to those of IAS 19, but required immediate recognition of actuarial gains and losses in annual expense.

The implementation of IAS19 was smoother in the Netherlands, although there has been some debate over the classification of some Dutch pension plans. Dutch accounting guideline RJ 271, while based on IAS 19, leaves some discretion when determining whether a plan is defined benefit or defined contribution. In 2003, the Dutch accounting standards board, RJ, ruled that the sponsoring company only bears the defined benefit liability if that fact is specifically stipulated in its financial agreement with the pension foundation. This contrasts with IAS 19 which requires plans to be classified as defined benefit (and liabilities to be recognised on the sponsor's balance sheet) if there is a "constructive" obligation on the part of the plan sponsor to meet pension promises. Following this debate, the government has proposed that plan documents specify whether benefit promises are conditional (on pension fund performance) or not and whether the plan sponsor is responsible for meeting any funding shortfalls. This should help clarify the accounting treatment of pension fund liabilities.

Accounting reform has also taken place outside the EU. The Japanese accounting standard (ASRB) was introduced in 1998 and became operative for financial years starting April 1, 2000. As is the case under IAS 19, Japanese employers must recognise their pension liabilities on the balance sheet. The main difference with IAS 19 is that the Japanese standard does not use the corridor method for actuarial gains and losses. Also, the discount rate used to calculate the pension liabilities can be based on yield fluctuations during the previous five years of long-term government or high quality corporate bonds. In practice, the 5-year average of the 30-year government bond yield is often used as the reference rate, as annuity conversion rates used by the Pension Fund Association for members who leave their employer or at plan termination are based on this rate.

> **Box 1. International pension accounting standard IAS19**
>
> IAS 19 prescribes the accounting and disclosure rules with respect to employers' benefits, in particular "post-employment benefits such as pensions, other retirement benefits, post-employment life insurance and post-employment medical care". Post employment benefits plans are classified as either defined contribution plans or defined benefit plans. Under IAS 19 recommendations, unfunded pension benefits are to be recorded, as a general rule, as liabilities in the balance sheet of the sponsoring employer. The International Accounting Standards Board (IASB) clearly distinguishes two categories: defined contribution plans and defined benefits plans. In defined contribution plans, the employer's annual contribution under the terms of the occupational plan should be recognised as an expense. For defined benefit plans, the rule's most noteworthy aspects are the following:
>
> - In general, unfunded pension benefits in defined benefit plans should be recorded as a pension liability in the employer's balance sheet (see amortisation rules below). Actuarial gains and losses (including investment) can be either (i) immediately recognised in the earnings statement, (ii) not reflected on the balance sheet if within a range of 10% of plan assets or obligations (actuarial gains and losses above/below this level can be amortised over the working life of employees.), or (iii) immediately recognised in a special, below-the-line statement.
>
> - The projected unit credit method should be used for valuing pension liabilities, as in the PBO measure. Under IAS19, these pension liabilities are referred to as the defined benefit obligation (DBO). The valuation method involves the projection of salaries to the estimated time of realisation of the insured event (retirement, disability, death, departure from company, etc). The discount rate to value liabilities should be based on high quality corporate bond yields at the balance sheet date. Indexation and other benefit increases should be taken into account to the extent that they are part of the formal or constructive terms of the plan.
>
> - Pension plan assets should be valued at fair value (smoothing is not permitted). Discount cash flows should not be used if market values exist. A pension plan surplus may be deemed as an asset of the sponsoring employer to the extent the surplus might be refunded to the company or used to reduce future contributions.

A new pension accounting standard was also introduced in Australia in January 2006, while in March 2007, the Korean Financial Supervisory Commission and the Korea Accounting Institute made a similar announcement. Both standards are largely consistent with IAS 19, requiring the recognition of the net value of DB pension plans on the company's balance sheet and changes therein in the profit and loss statement. The implications for the Australian pension system, however, are quite limited, as DB pension funds represent only a small part of the overall market.

The other main pension accounting standard, the United States' FAS 87, was reformed in September 2006 as a result of FASB's approval of the Statement of Financial Accounting Standards No. 158 (SFAS 158). The reformed standard is very close to the United Kingdom's FRS17, as immediate recognition of actuarial gains and losses is now required (see Table 2). The other main features of the US standard, such as the use of the PBO as the measure of pension liabilities and the use fair values for the investment portfolio are also in line with FRS 17 and IAS 19. A new pension accounting standard is also expected to be introduced in Canada by the end of 2007 which would bring it into line with the new US standard. Among the main changes, the new standard would bring the difference between the pension assets and liabilities onto the balance sheet.

Table 2. Comparison of FAS87 before and after SFAS 158

	Before	After
Disclosure	In the footnotes to the annual report	In the balance sheet
Actuarial gains and losses	Amortised over the remaining service period of plan members (above/below a +/-10 percent corridor), although faster amortisation is permitted	Immediate recognition
Asset values	Smoothing of actual asset values permitted over a period no longer than five years (and only for first time adoption)	Fair value (with limited exceptions)
Valuation date	Early measurement date permitted	As of the date of the employer's fiscal year-end

The pros and cons of market-based valuations for accounting and funding purposes

The move towards market-based valuation of pension liabilities by accounting standard-setters is driven, in the words of the IASB, by a desire to increase the understandability, relevance, reliability and comparability of company accounts. International efforts to create convergence in national pension standards and to improve the transparency of pension disclosures are to be commended and further encouraged. However, it is essential that the standards also promote the reliability and relevance of accounts for investors and company managers.

The new pension accounting standards are expected to portray more accurately the exposure that shareholders have to unfunded pension liabilities by calculating their "fair value". Yet, DB pension funds exist precisely because there is no security in the market with a similar pay-off schedule as the cashflows generated by a DB pension fund.[24] Pension liabilities have very long durations and are related to economic variables (such as prices, salaries, and labour turnover rates) and demographic factors (such as mortality rates), that, with the exception of inflation, are not incorporated into existing securities. Hence, attempts at "marking-to-market" pension liabilities represent modelled predictions of value, rather than observed market prices.[25]

The application of market valuation to pension liabilities can nevertheless be facilitated if pension liabilities can be sold to third parties. The development in the United Kingdom of the bulk annuity market for pension buyouts could therefore lend further support to the application of market-based valuations.[26] However, accounting standards must first solve the internal inconsistency of attempting to derive a market value for pension liabilities while at the same time aiming at estimating the value of liabilities as an ongoing concern. In particular, the PBO, which is the required measure of pension liabilities by IAS 19 and other accounting bodies, does not correspond to the liability that would be sold by an employer to a third party. The liability at termination should not take into account the effect of future salary increases (like the ABO), but should normally be based on insurance company valuations. In most cases, such valuations would be higher than the accounting measure.

The choice of discount rate under IAS 19 is also the subject of controversy. In principle, the discount rate should reflect the duration of pension liabilities and take into the account their stochastic nature. If assets are measured at fair values, benefits should be discounted using stochastic, not fixed discount rates. For the purpose of pricing pension liabilities, the level of the discount rate should be determined by factors such as the covariance between wage inflation (the driver of defined benefit pension liabilities) and financial asset prices. Yet, under international accounting standards the market value of corporate bond yields are used to discount liabilities, without any allowance for the riskiness of pension liabilities and their covariance with equity returns. While it may be argued that the use of corporate, rather than government, bond yields already provide an allowance for risk (as corporate yields are normally above government ones), the adjustment may not be appropriate for pension liabilities.[27] Moreover, if fair valuation was strictly applied, each pension fund's liabilities should require a specific discount rate adjustment to reflect the risk of default of the specific sponsor.

A final area of contention is that in some countries the net pension liability of the plan sponsor may be lowered via additional employee contributions or reductions in benefits. In a few countries pension liabilities take the form of promises, rather than contractual obligations.[28] These promises may be adjusted in adverse states of the world, creating embedded options that are open to subjective valuation. It is only through the initiative of pension regulators that some of these promises have become a true debt on the plan sponsor. For example, regulators in many OECD countries prohibit reductions in accrued benefits in nominal terms, and some (*e.g.* in Ireland and the United Kingdom) even require the protection of benefits in real terms for employees that depart before retirement (up to a specific revaluation factor).

Given all these considerations, it may be questioned whether the move towards market-based valuations has been correctly undertaken by accounting bodies. Moreover, it is not clear that the volatility created on the sponsoring company's balance sheet and income statement (especially with immediate recognition of actuarial gains and losses, as under FRS 17 and the reformed US standard, SFAS87) is conducive to better decision-making by company managers or better asset allocation decisions by pension funds.[29] In mature industries, with large pension funds, even small changes in the pension fund's funding status can cause wide swings in the reported earnings of the firm. There is actually little evidence that fair value accounting of pension plans better meets the information needs of investors.[30] Even if it did, the impact of fair valuation on companies' willingness to sponsor DB pension funds should be carefully considered by policymakers, as pension funds offer retirement income products that are not available in the market.[31] There are also important ramifications for financial stability and the possible procyclical behaviour induced by fair value accounting standards that should also be carefully considered.[32]

Given the uncertainty surrounding market-based valuation of pension liabilities for accounting purposes, it seems as a minimum necessary to carry out a thorough assessment of the risks underlying pension funds, to provide a detailed description of the assumptions behind any valuation model, and to subject any estimates to sensitivity analysis.[33] Such sensitivity analysis, based on stochastic modelling of the cashflow streams, can provide more relevant information about the funding status of a pension fund than the static deficit measure required by international accounting standards.[34] Such information, which may be incorporated in the notes to the company's annual report, may improve investors', company managers', and pension fund members' understanding of the relevance and reliability of the accountants' estimates.

Accounting standard-setters also need to resolve the various approaches currently permitted for recognising actuarial gains and losses (see Box 1). The spreading of actuarial gains and losses over time and the use of 10% "corridor" may be justified by the limited reliability of the "mark-to-model" valuation approach. However, the possibility of smoothing values also gives an incentive to companies to make unrealistic assumptions about rates of return on invested assets. Under international accounting standards, the assumed rate of return on assets should reflect historic investment performance of the pension fund. However, accounting rules often do not provide detailed instructions for picking each year's rate. In the United States, the use of high assumed rates of return helped companies smooth out the impact of investment risk on the company's financial performance. Throughout the 1990s, investment rate assumptions of over 8 percent were common. Since the bursting of the stock market bubble, however, most companies have continued to use such assumptions despite the fact that returns have been substantially lower for the past five years. According to Coronado and Sharpe (2003), return smoothing contributed to an overvaluation of equity prices of 5% on average after the bubble burst in 2000. Gold (2001) argues that the "opaque" pension accounting system has encouraged an overexposure to equities that would be corrected if it was based on a fair value methodology.

A priori, market-based valuation of pension liabilities seems more relevant for regulatory purposes. The regulator's focus is on the value of accrued benefits if the plan is terminated (or "frozen" -accruals are discontinued) as well as the transfer value of accrued benefits for workers that switch to a different pension fund. Market-based valuations can provide a more realistic picture of the pension fund's solvency and can be used to calculate transfer values in a fair, independent manner. However, some of the concerns raised over the potential for short-termist and procyclical investment behaviour also arise in a regulatory context, especially if regulations require pension funds to restore full funding - measured on a market-basis - or the build-up of buffers (or solvency margins) over relatively short periods.

The regulators' concern solvency contrasts with the accountant's goal of assessing as accurately as possible the present value of these long-term commitments as an ongoing concern. In particular, regulators are increasingly concerned about the termination value of liabilities and are often taking this measure of liabilities into account when designing funding rules. For regulators, therefore, the ABO, rather than the accountants' PBO, is the relevant measure of pension liabilities.

There are other important differences between accounting and funding perspectives on pension fund liabilities. First, from a funding perspective, the valuation of liabilities is also an issue for defined contribution plans that carry some return or benefit collectively guaranteed by the plan members or the pension fund, without any risk on the plan sponsor.[35] Regulators of these so-called pooled-risk or collective defined contribution plans, which exist in countries like Denmark and Iceland and are becoming popular in the Netherlands, require measures of their liabilities, but they have no impact on the balance sheet of the plan sponsor. The accounting treatment of the sponsoring employer is that of a defined contribution plan under both the OECD and IASB definitions. Hence, the difference between the pension fund's liabilities and assets should not be shown on the sponsor's balance sheet.

Second, pension regulators do not allow pension funds to make an allowance for sponsor default risk when calculating pension liabilities for funding purposes, as it would defeat the purpose of funding requirements.[36] Regulators also tend to prefer a conservative estimate of pension liabilities, rather than one purely reflecting market conditions in an unbiased manner. For these reasons, regulators' discount rates tend to be below those stipulated by accounting standards. Regulators also tend to make more conservative assumptions about vesting and withdrawal rates.

For these reasons, and despite the potential advantages in terms of lower administrative burdens and higher transparency, single-track reporting for accounting and funding purposes seems rather far-fetched. On the other hand, establishing coherence between funding and accounting requirements should be on the agenda as one of the key objectives of any future reform to international accounting standards and regulators' valuation rules. In particular, the economic and demographic assumptions used for funding and accounting purposes should be consistent, and where relevant (*e.g.* wage or inflation forecast or mortality risk estimates over a common period for the same group of individuals) they should be identical. Such objectives call for closer cooperation between accounting standard setters, the actuarial profession, and pension regulators.

II. Revisiting funding gaps and the public policy reaction

The funding status of DB pension funds deteriorated throughout the OECD after 2000.[37] Figure 2 below shows the two main accounting measures of pension liabilities, the ABO and PBO, for a sample of pension funds in selected OECD countries. On a PBO basis, the highest funding ratios in 2005 were observed in Australia and Norway, while the lowest ones were those of pension funds in Japan. As expected, also, ABO funding ratios are substantially higher than PBO ones. On the basis of ABO measures, pension fund solvency is mainly a concern in Japan, though funding ratios were also low in Canada, Switzerland and the United Kingdom (around 0.90).

Figure 2. Accounting measures of funding ratios (ABO and PBO) in selected OECD countries in 2005

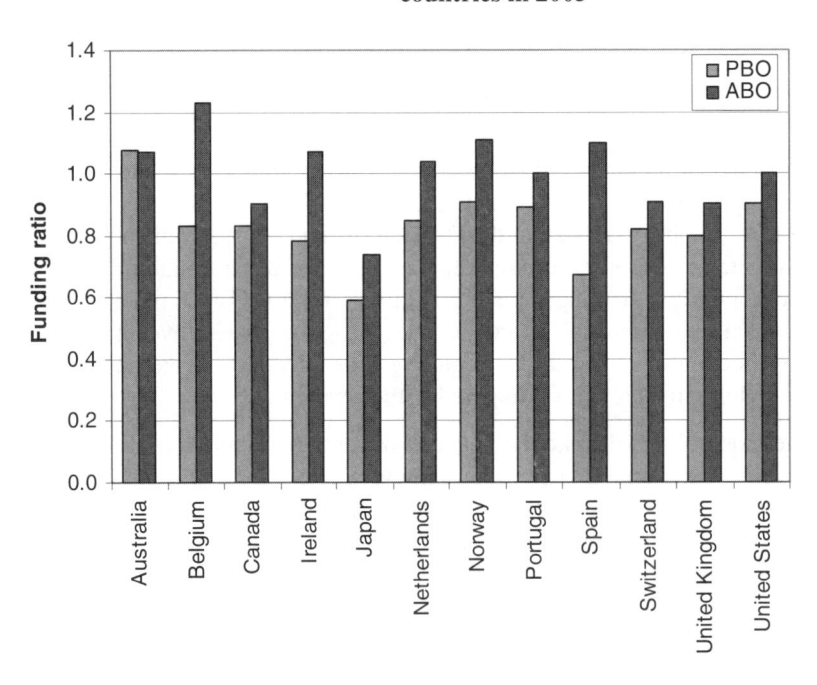

Source: Watson Wyatt (2005)

While the "perfect storm" of negative investment returns and low discount rates accounts for these historically low funding ratios, policymakers are also reconsidering some aspects of regulations which may have constrained the build-up of buffers during the benign 1990s. Part of the blame for today's troubles lies in opaque valuation methods, weak funding regulations, and rules on overfunding that discouraged the high funding levels necessary to withstand adverse market conditions such as the ones experienced over the last six years. At the same time, regulators should act with moderation at times of market distress and unusual, transitory valuations, such as those observed on long-term bonds in recent years.

As accountants and regulators adopt market-based valuation standards, the volatility in security prices means that funding levels can fluctuate drastically in relatively short periods. It is therefore even more important to reform maximum funding rules so that they take into account this inherent volatility of security prices and in particular the infrequent, but big risks, the so-called "fat tails" of frequency distributions. Maximum funding rules may need to be relaxed while minimum funding requirements may need to be tightened. One particularly astonishing statistic is that approximately one quarter of UK companies with defined benefit schemes were still enjoying contribution holidays at the beginning of 2003, despite the growing funding hole.

Policymakers also need to consider the impact of other regulations that are intended to protect the rights of beneficiaries but may make DB pension provision excessively costly for employers, especially under the new regulatory and accounting environment. Employers in most OECD countries have an additional disincentive to overfund their pension liabilities stemming from the plan members' ownership of any plan surplus in case of plan termination. The main exceptions are Portugal, the United Kingdom and the United States, where employers can seek a refund, but there are hefty taxes involved (especially in the United States). To the extent that employers bear the downside risk but do not ultimately benefit from the upward potential it is unlikely that they will aim at high funding levels, irrespective of the presence of maximum funding rules. Other regulations that increase the cost of pension provision for employers include those requiring the revaluation and indexation of benefits. Such rules reduce employers' incentives to fund benefits above what is required by minimum funding rules, as they reduce the value of DB plans to employers in managing labour turnover.

Even worse, such regulations may be diminishing companies' willingness to sponsor defined benefit plans altogether if they feel that they are faced with an asymmetric risk: funding shortfalls are the employer's problem while funding excesses belong to the members. Key plan design decisions such as the division of contributions between employers and employees, responsibility for underfunding and the reaction to overfunding should ideally be left to market participants, as the parties to each pension plan may find solutions best suited to their particular circumstances. Pension regulations should not impair employers' and employees' ability to adapt the pension plan's design and operation to their specific needs and objectives, especially where such plans are established on a voluntary basis. Instead, what pension regulations should do is to require clarity in the plan documents over rights and responsibilities in cases of overfunding and underfunding. Regulations should also limit benefit enhancements, contribution holidays, and asset reversions to the plan sponsor in a way that encourages high funding levels and the build-up of substantial buffers during favourable periods.

Reforming funding regulations

Minimum funding standards aim at ensuring that the pension plan's assets at least match and, preferably, exceed by some margin the plan's accrued liabilities. Countries differ on the extent to which they aim at this goal at every measurement date rather than over time. Indeed, in countries where bankruptcy is a rare event, policymakers may be more willing to permit underfunding over long periods of time. On the other hand, increasing competition in world markets makes market positions and profitability increasingly unstable. A company sponsoring a defined benefit plan runs the risk of assuming liabilities that can grow dramatically relative to its revenues. By running a pension plan in an underfunded manner, a healthy, profitable company can expose itself to a heavy double blow to its earnings if its market position deteriorates at the same time as its workforce ages and the drawdown of benefits intensifies. This is precisely what happened to the steel and airline companies that went bankrupt over the last decade in the United States.

The presence of insolvency guarantee funds also affects the design of funding requirements. If premiums to the guarantee fund are risk-based, taking into account the market value of liabilities if the plan was to be terminated, funding rules could theoretically be superfluous. This seems to be the rationale behind the elimination of the minimum funding requirement in the United Kingdom and its replacement by risk-based premiums to the PPF. The level of protection afforded by the PPF could, if the premiums were truly risk-based, be as high as it would be under a strict funding requirement. In practice, however, it is very difficult to set fully risk-based premiums as they typically imply higher costs for sponsoring employers with lower credit ratings (often smaller companies). Any departure from risk-based premiums creates incentives for underfunding (moral hazard) that are best corrected with funding rules.

The level of minimum funding required by regulators also depends on how accrued benefits are defined and how assets and liabilities are measured. In general, regulators use an ABO-type measure, the main exception being Spain where a PBO-type measure is used. Most countries also assume that all workers in the plan will qualify for full vesting of their accrued rights and exclude withdrawals from the plan. This produces a more conservative (higher) measure of liabilities than on a plan termination liability, all else being equal.

The valuation method must also be considered when determining the funding requirement. A fully-funded pension plan may reveal itself underfunded on a plan termination basis and therefore insolvent if a "slow" actuarial cost method is used to allocate liabilities or discount rates are above market values. In such cases, a higher funding target may be established, although a better solution may be to reform the valuation method. In general, the valuation method used for funding purposes should not lead to a measure of liabilities lower than that calculated on a plan termination basis. Otherwise, the funding ratio will give a false impression of the solvency of the plan.

The move towards market-based measures of liabilities, and in particular the use of discount rates based on bond yields, also calls for gradualism in correcting underfunding. Otherwise, an unnecessary and counterproductive degree of contribution volatility will be introduced. Regulatory forbearance may be specially required at times of market distress. Good examples of this are the province of Quebec in Canada and Ireland, where recovery periods were extended after the 2000 market downturn.

In general, countries where DB funding shortfalls are solely or largely the responsibility of the sponsoring employer tend to allow longer recovery periods (*e.g.* 5 years in Canada, 7 years in Japan and the United States, between 3 and 10 years in Ireland, depending on the pension fund). As pension benefits are effectively backed by the sponsoring employer's capital, funding rules can be more lenient than in countries where pension funds effectively operate independently of the sponsors, receiving contributions from both employers and workers.

Industry-wide pension funds in countries such as Denmark and Iceland cannot fall back on the sponsoring employer to cover funding shortfalls. Employers' liabilities are limited to specified contributions (contribution rates are fixed), which means that pension fund members collectively bear investment and longevity risks. As a result of pension funds' arms-length relationship with their sponsors, regulators in these countries require relatively rapid recovery of funding shortfalls and also require a "buffer" or solvency margin above the full funding level, as is the case for insurance undertakings. In Denmark, for example, the market value of the euro swap curve is used to value pension fund liabilities every six months. Pension funds must at all times have sufficient assets to cover their technical provisions (the pension fund's liabilities) and a solvency margin which can be no less than 4 percent of technical provisions plus 0.3 percent of a measure of the investment risk exposure. If funding levels decline below the stipulated solvency margin, the institution must draw up a plan to restore its financial position. The supervisor decides the maximum recovery period, depending on the size of the shortfall. When the pension fund's capital is less than one third of the solvency margin (or less than the minimum capital requirement), the recovery period is usually stated in months and does not normally exceed one year. The recovery plan may include raising employee contributions, cutting bonus reserves and, ultimately, reductions in minimum benefit or return guarantees (as happened in 1994 and 1999).

In the Netherlands, pension funds are in intermediate situation with respect to their independence from the sponsors. The revaluation and indexation of benefits is the responsibility of the pension fund, which can alter it in line with the funding level. Hence, this risk is borne collectively by plan members. On the other hand, nominal benefits are a shared responsibility of plan sponsors and workers. This situation is reflected in the regulatory approach. Under the new regulatory framework, effective from 1 January 2007, as long as indexation is conditional (on the funding ratio, normally), nominal pension commitments are measured once a year using the market value of the Euro swap curve for discounting. The funding ratio must be at least 105% at any time and the DNB must be informed immediately of any shortfall. A strategy must be developed within three months, and actions must be taken within three years to enable the asset value to be brought back up to the 105% level. Pension funds are also required to meet a solvency test; the probability of underfunding within one year cannot be higher than 2.5 percent. Pension funds have 15 years to correct funding levels if the test is not met. Finally, pension funds must provide evidence to the supervisor that their funding and investment strategy is consistent with their indexation ambition, under a so-called continuity test.

III. Implications for occupational pension provision and pension funds' investment behaviour

The most immediate effect of the emergence of funding gaps in various OECD countries since 2000 has been the need to increase contributions to occupational pension plans. In countries like the United Kingdom or the United States where employers had been taking contribution holidays throughout most of the 90s, the sudden jump in pension contributions has dealt a severe blow to company cash flows and in some cases may have contributed to debt downgrades. Yet, some corporations have been able to dampen the impact of funding requirements by borrowing in capital markets and transferring the proceeds to the pension fund or allocating physical assets owned by the company to it. For example, in the United States an airline can plug a funding gap by transferring a plane to the pension fund and leasing it back from the fund.

The largest increases in contribution rate have actually taken place in Canada the Netherlands. As shown in Figure 1, pension fund contributions in Canada went up from 0.5 percent of GDP in 2001 to 2.2 percent in 2005. In the Netherlands, contributions went up from 2.8 percent of GDP in to 4.5 percent over the same period.

Figure 1. Contributions to Pension Funds as a % of GDP, 2001-2005

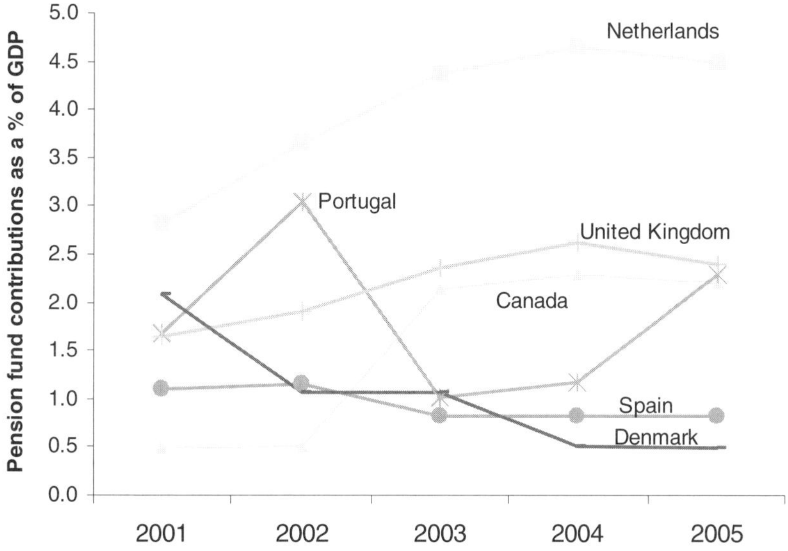

Source: OECD Global Pension Statistics

In addition to this short term effect, the funding gaps and the regulatory and accounting initiatives of the last few years are bringing about deeper, structural changes in the design and operation of occupational pension plans in OECD countries. Three in particular are noteworthy. First, the move to funding in what have been traditionally occupational pension systems dominated by book reserve systems. Second, the increased popularity of asset-liability risk management techniques by pension funds. Third, the closure of defined benefit plans and their substitution by a whole spectrum of new plans with different degrees of risk sharing features.

New funding initiatives in book reserve systems

In countries like Germany that have traditionally financed significant parts of their occupational pension liabilities through book reserves, the move towards market-based accounting standards has driven some sponsors to separate pension assets into special purpose entities called contractual trust agreements (CTAs).[38] These entities are not subject to any of the regulations that apply to the two main types of German pension funds (*Pensionskassen* and *Pensionsfonds*) and other financing vehicles (*e.g.* direct insurance with a life insurance undertaking). For local German accounting purposes they are treated on-balance sheet as occupational pension plan assets. Under international accounting standards, CTAs are treated as plan assets if it can be shown that they enable protection against the insolvency of the sponsor. Among other factors, sponsors' preference of CTAs over *Pensionskassen* or *Pensionsfonds* has been influenced by the higher discount rates applied under the CTA-book reserve system, typically 6 percent. The other two financing vehicles, on the other hand, are required to use a 2.75 percent discount rate.

The growth in ALM, changes in pension fund investment, and financial stability considerations

A largely positive upshot of the move to market valuations for both funding and accounting purposes is that pension funds will need to take a closer look at their liabilities when deciding on their investment strategy. This is leading to a significant departure from standard practice in countries like the United Kingdom or the United States, where the investment focus was on benchmarking performance relative to a market index, with little regard to variations in the funding ratio. While asset-liability management (ALM) has been used for some time, it had not played such a central role in the assessment of pension fund investments.

In the United Kingdom, investment policies are being revised paying due regard to market valuations of the pension fund's liabilities. Of all OECD countries, the United Kingdom used to have the highest pension fund allocation to equities, up to 70 per cent on average. This allocation has been coming down in recent years (to less than 60 percent by December 2005[39]), largely as a result of the reform of accounting standards and the introduction of the PPF. However, it is unlikely that pension funds will go as far as one large pension fund (Boots), which in 2000 shifted to a fully fixed income-based portfolio, as it was felt that it was the closest match to the fund's liabilities and maximised tax benefits for the sponsoring employer.[40] Most pension fund trustees, employers and consultants consider that there is no perfect match for DB pension liabilities (especially for active workers) and that some exposure to equities and alternative asset classes is worth the risk involved.

A similar shift towards bonds (especially inflation-indexed) has also taken place in Canada in recent years. In Denmark, after the new fair valuation system and risk-based supervision were introduced in 2001, pension funds increased their exposure to bonds by up to 40 percent (and increased their duration) and decreased their allocation to equities by approximately 70 percent. In Switzerland, where fixed discount rates are still being used, there is also evidence of a significant effect of the nature of liabilities on pension fund portfolios (Gerber (2005)).

Even in other countries like the Netherlands, where ALM techniques have been in use for some years, the arrival of new funding rules and accounting standards has also caused some changes in pension fund portfolios. While the percentage allocation to bonds by pension funds has hardly increased, there has been a rise in the duration of the bond portfolio. (Kakes and Broeders (2006)). This has improved the matching with the pension funds' liabilities, though the current duration gap is still about ten years, according to the central bank (DnB).

An investment strategy consistent with the pension fund's liabilities (including those aiming at cashflow matching, so-called liability-driven investment or LDI) is in principle a desirable outcome of market-based funding and accounting valuations. However, the potential implications for the long-term efficiency of the asset allocation and financial stability need to be carefully considered. When accompanied with strict funding rules, the result may be suboptimal long-term asset allocation, higher funding costs[41], and a decrease in financial stability. The potential disruptive effect of rapid changes in pension fund asset allocation is exemplified by the sharp decline of yields on UK inflation-indexed bonds (gilts) between 2004 and 2006, substantially below those in the euro area. UK pension funds were partly responsible for this phenomenon, together with the "scarcity" of these bonds.[42] This evidence highlights the potential for procyclical behaviour among pension funds. New regulations, such as the Dutch FTK, remain to be tested in this regard. Up to now, Dutch pension funds have tended to steer changes in their asset allocation by altering the ratio of net purchases of different asset classes, rather than through net sales.[43]

The increasing popularity of ALM and LDI strategies also calls increasingly into question regulatory frameworks based on portfolio limits as certain asset classes may be a best match for pension funds trying to immunise their liabilities. While diversification within asset classes is still a relevant investment principle, diversification applied to assets classes needs to be considered in the context of the liabilities of long term investors like pension funds. Asset allocations should be based on liabilities, and in some cases, a high investment in certain assets classes may be in order.

Further policy focus is also needed in the implications of ALM and LDI strategies for public debt management. The government is the only entity capable of issuing riskless (*i.e.* inflation-linked) long-term paper that employers can use to match long-term interest rate guarantees. Bonds indexed to wages or economic growth would be even more attractive for DB pension funds, given the link of their liabilities to real variables. In addition, policymakers need to pay more attention to the measurement and management of mortality risk by pension funds. ALM-based investment strategies need as much a focus on demographic risks as on investments.

The decline in DB plans

Ironically, while funding concerns in occupational DB systems are in the vanguard of the public policy debate, their constituency is slowly (or rapidly in some cases) shrinking. Only a few countries like Germany, the Netherlands and Japan have experienced some resistance to the decline in the number and coverage of defined benefit plans that has affected other countries like Australia, Canada, the United Kingdom, and the United States. Even in these countries, it is not clear how long their popularity will last. Changes have taken place already in the Netherlands, with the shift over the last few years from final salary to career average plans with conditional indexation, and a further shift to pooled-risk or collective defined contribution arrangements expected. In Japan, most defined benefit plans have been transformed into cash balance arrangements (still treated as defined benefit under both the IASB and the OECD classifications, as the sponsoring employer bears investment risk until up to retirement).

Underlying changes in the economy, such as the shift in jobs to the service sector appear to explain much of the decline in DB plan coverage in some countries like the United Kingdom or the United States. The service sector in these countries has been traditionally less unionised and there was therefore weaker pressure for DB type pension provision. However, the more recent decline in coverage over the last decade in the United Kingdom appears to be linked to the impact of market-based accounting standards and the increasing cost of regulations (such as the revaluation and indexation requirements).[44] In particular, the introduction of FRS 17 seems to have been an important factor in some firm's decision to terminate DB plans, especially highly leveraged ones (Klumpes and Whittington (2003)).

The introduction of the PPF may also affect DB provision. The portfolios shift to bonds by pension funds in the UK since 2003 appears to be at least partly related to the decision by corporate treasurers acting as scheme trustees to avoid hikes in the PPF levy by locking in as far as possible the funding status of the plan through better matching of the FRS17 value of their assets and liabilities (pension funds with funding ratios above 130 percent do not pay the levy[45]). The PPF introduced risk-based premiums in 2006/7[46] and raised the total value of the levy in 2007/8. Some employers, especially smaller ones, may find the additional cost of sponsoring DB plans exacting. However, if premiums are unrelated to risks, the danger would be potentially undesirable subsidies and inefficient allocation of capital.

In the United States, tax regulations setting low ceilings on overfunding and rules over the ownership of any funding excess (such as the tax on reversion to the sponsoring employer) may have reduced the attractiveness of prudent funding. In addition, the presence of a guarantee fund (the PBGC) may have also facilitated employers' withdrawal from DB pension provision. This moral hazard risk is being addressed with changes to the premium charged and new regulations that limit benefit increases by underfunded plans.

The impact of minimum funding requirements on DB pension provision is more complex. Employers have an interest in stable contribution rates, so a funding requirement based on an economically meaningful funding target is likely to be consistent with their own funding objectives, while at the same time enhancing the retirement benefit security for workers. However, complex funding rules and short recovery periods can raise the cost of DB pension provision dramatically, especially as additional contributions may be required during bad economic times.

The new pension landscape

As DB plans decline in importance, the question needs to be raised whether workers are better served by the new DC arrangements being put in place. Certainly, for employees in the growing service sector and in dynamic industries such as information technology DB arrangements may not be attractive if they expose them to benefit losses because of the lack of portability of accrued benefits and the absence of revaluation regulations (as is the case in the United States, for example). However, portable DB plans such as those in place in the Netherlands (at least for workers who move within the same industry), would seem to be superior in a welfare sense to "pure" (unprotected) defined contribution plans where all risks and costs are borne individually by workers.[47]

Ultimately, employers and policymakers need to focus on solutions that provide for efficient risk sharing of the two main risks in retirement provision: investment and longevity. Solutions that are in between traditional DB plan and "pure" DC plans (where members bear investment and longevity risks on an individual basis) have been around for some time. In the US, for example, employers can sponsor cash balance plans that can offer protection against investment risk (through an interest rate guarantee) but lay all longevity risk on the individual (since benefits are usually paid as a lump-sum). Employers in the UK and other countries are exploring similar arrangements to replace their traditional DB arrangements.

It is also possible to design a defined benefit plan where only nominal benefits are guaranteed, while revaluation and indexation are adjusted on the basis of the performance of the fund, as is the case in the Netherlands. The risks of a defined benefit plan can also be shifted to the members on a collective basis by transforming the pension fund into a mutual insurance entity that provides guarantees similar to those of a defined benefit plan. Such entities are wide-spread in countries like Denmark and Iceland and are also common for public sector workers in Spain. Such plans are treated as defined contribution under accounting standards but provide some degree of protection against market volatility and longevity risk. In the Netherlands, some listed companies that have adopted international financial reporting standards have also had their plans classified as defined contribution by fixing their contribution rate over long periods.

These "protected" DC plans (including the mutual insurance model of Denmark and Iceland and the "collective" DC plans of the Netherlands) may be superior – in a welfare sense - not just to "unprotected" DC arrangements but also to traditional and hybrid DB plans, as they offer a higher level of protection against sponsor insolvency and greater flexibility to address investment and longevity risks. Pension funds in these countries offer an efficient form of intergenerational risk sharing between different generations of workers tied to the same fund through their employment contract. Such risk sharing cannot be replicated via "unprotected" DC plans, because of the general requirement to grant members choice of investment.

The shift to "pure" or unprotected DC plans also raises additional challenges for policymakers. In countries that have had a marked shift from DB to such DC plans, employer contributions to the latter tend to be much lower. This has been widely reported in the United Kingdom, a country where private pension plans are expected to account for a large portion of retirement income. In the United States DB plans tend to be offered as part of the employment contract and have automatic enrolment, while employees must specifically request membership of DC plans. DC plans also involve investment decisions that may not be easily understood by plan members. In addition to difficult risk-return analysis, plan members must be able to compare different fee structures. Financial education is clearly necessary to overcome some of these deficiencies. Policymakers also need to play a role to ensure that the latest academic wisdom on retirement saving quickly filters through to the financial industry. Employers, too, can play a key role in educating their employees, in facilitating investment choice among a few suitable investment options, and providing low cost default alternatives that meet as best as possible the retirement benefit security goal of workers.

The risk transfer to individual households is all the more worrying given the decreased appetite among insurers for bearing long term risks such as those underlying pension products like annuities. In the United Kingdom, for example, despite the requirement to buy annuities before 75, there are only two main annuity providers. The possible move towards fair valuation of life insurance companies could lead to a further retrenchment from these markets. The controversy over accounting of life insurance companies[48], which mirrors that of DB pension plans, calls at least for a closer scrutiny by policymakers of its potential consequences for private pension provision and a reassessment of the importance of social security systems.

IV. Conclusion

The trend towards market-based valuation of pension plan liabilities is in general a welcome development as it may offer a more realistic picture of the solvency position of DB pension funds and improve the transparency and international comparability of company accounts. For financially weak plan sponsors, market-based measures of the plan termination liability can help supervisors decide on appropriate remedial action. Market valuations should also help improve the coherence between valuations for funding and accounting purposes, particularly with respect to the choice of economic and demographic assumptions. Differences in actuarial cost methods are likely to remain, however, as pension regulators and accountants often take different perspectives when valuing pension liabilities. In particular, pension regulators are increasingly concerned about the termination value of benefits (ABO), tend to make more conservative assumptions about vesting and withdrawal rates and use lower discount rates.

Both accountants and regulators should also require that economic and demographic assumptions are based on best estimate points, with the necessary sensitivity analysis and risk (prudent) margins built into the valuation framework. The assumptions used for calculating pension benefits and comparing assets and liabilities should also be tailored for each fund in order to take into account the specific economic and demographic experience of the covered population. These best estimate assumptions should be updated in each reporting period to reflect new information on the actual experience of the pension plan over that period that is expected to continue into the future.

The review of valuation methods has also shown some inconsistencies in the accounting standard for pension liabilities (IAS19), which has been implemented in most OECD countries. Business accountants value pension liabilities for the firm as an ongoing concern, using the PBO measure which includes salary increases up to retirement. Yet, market prices for such long-term, non-traded liabilities cannot be found. If employers were to sell their liabilities, as has been occurring in the United Kingdom recently, they would pay a price based on the ABO measure, which is based on accrued benefits. A move to fair value accounting, where smoothing or amortisation of actuarial liabilities over time is no longer possible, therefore risks misrepresenting the long-term economic cost of pensions as an ongoing concern. It can also lead to sub-optimal asset allocation decisions and have negative implications for financial stability as employers and pension funds overreact to short term changes in asset values and engage in procyclical investment behaviour.

The introduction of market-based valuation also calls for a different approach to funding regulations. A certain moderation in rectifying underfunding problems is in order. When setting maximum recovery periods, regulators should take into account the potential disruption to long-term investment. At the same time, regulators need to provide the necessary incentives for the build-up of buffers in good economic times. The goal of high funding specifically calls for higher overfunding ceilings than is currently the case in some countries.

Ultimately, however, many sponsors may prefer to move away from defined benefit plans that expose them to significant risks without any upside potential, as "surpluses" cannot normally be recovered by the sponsoring employer, and when they can they are often subject to heavy taxes. New pension arrangements, like cash balance and other hybrid pension plans, can encourage more meaningful risk sharing, where, in particular, the cost of anticipated increases in life expectancy are borne by each generation of workers. The transformation of pension funds into mutual-type entities that underwrite retirement risks may also be attractive in some countries, as long as it can mean the reclassification of the pension plan as a defined contribution one for business accounting purposes. In some OECD countries, however, the main type of plan replacing defined benefit ones are "pure" defined contribution ones, where members bear the full weight of investment and longevity risk, at least until retirement. Further analysis of these plans and their policy implications is needed to avoid their pitfalls.

Notes

1. According to the OECD pensions taxonomy, an occupational pension plan is linked to an employment relationship between the plan member and the entity that establishes the plan (the plan sponsor). Occupational plans may be established by employers or groups of employers (e.g. industry associations), professional and labour associations (e.g. trade unions). Generally, the plan sponsor is responsible for making contributions under the terms of occupational pension plans, but employees may be also required to contribute. Sponsors may also have administrative or oversight responsibilities for these plans.

2. See, for example, Schich (2005). Funding ratios recovered in 2006 as a result of rising long-term interest rates.

3. See Pugh (2007) in this volume for a description of recent reforms to funding regulations. The OECD Recommendation on Guidelines on Funding and Benefit Security in Occupational Pension Plans is the international standard on these regulatory issues (OECD (2007)).

4. Fair value is usually defined as the amount for which an asset could be exchanged, or a liability settled, between knowledgeable, willing parties in an arm's length transaction.

5. Some jurisdictions, such as most Canadian provinces, require a minimum funding valuation and an ongoing funding valuation. This paper discusses only the minimum funding valuation, which is the main concern for regulators. For a description and discussion of ongoing funding valuations and methods, see Pugh (2007).

6. Standard & Poor's (2006).

7. PBGC (2006).

8. The main exception is Spain, where regulators require DB plans to use a PBO measure of pension liabilities.

9. Actuarial gains (losses) are assets (liabilities) created by a positive (negative) departure of the experience of the plan from the assumptions that underlie the actuarial cost estimates. They include both changes in

actuarial assumptions and experience gains and losses, the latter being deviations of actual from expected experience.

10. For further information on actuarial methods, see the chapter by Pugh (2007) in this volume, Groupe Consultatif Actuariel Europeen (2001), and Groupe Consultatif Actuariel Europeen (2006).

11. Throughout this paper we refer to pension fund assets and liabilities, even though in some countries the liabilities are assigned to the pension plan, rather the pension fund itself (which is only a vehicle to hold the plan assets). The term pension plan is not used because a plan can be funded through vehicles other than pension funds, such as pension insurance contracts. These funding vehicles are not the subject of this paper.

12. Like the PBO, the ABO accounting measure is based on assumptions about employee turnover and death for a continuing plan. Pension regulators, on the other hand, require the use of assumptions that reflect to a greater extent the conditions of plan termination.

13. In the United Kingdom, it is also possible to use the newer "buy-out" firms, most of which have been set up as single-line insurers but can also be authorised as pension companies.

14. There would be a three year transition period during which an institution may use a single discount rate aligned as closely as possible with the duration of the institution's liabilities.

15. The initial unfunded liability and plan amendments could be amortised over 30 years. Experience gains and losses could be amortised over 5 years in the case of single-employer plans and 15 years in the case of multi-employer plans. Changes in actuarial assumptions could be amortised over 15 years in the case of single-employer plans and 15 years in the case of multi-employer plans. Neither statutes nor regulations defined the amortisation period applicable to changes in unfunded liabilities resulting from changes in actuarial cost methods and asset valuation methods.

16. Since 2004, the discount rate can be chosen from a range between 90 and 105 percent of the weighted average yield of 30-year Treasury securities during the four-year period preceding the plan year. Between 2001-5, when issuance of this bond stopped, the Treasury used a proxy monthly interest rate that attempted to mimic what this rate would have been.

17. See Warshawsky (2007).

18. When choosing discount rates, trustees should take into account either or both the yield on assets held by the fund to pay for future benefits and the anticipated future returns on those assets and the market redemption yields on government or other high-quality bonds.

19. Other pension companies include life-insurance companies and labour-market related life-insurance companies. All these pension companies are subject to the Act on Insurance Companies. Other pension providers, e.g. the Danish Labour Market Supplementary Pension Scheme (ATP) and LD Pensions, and company pension funds are subject to separate acts.

20. The spread allows for the difference between euro rates and swap rates in Danish krone. Until the beginning of 2009, pension funds will be able to use instead a flat discount rate based on the average yield on three government bonds with an average duration of 10 years.

21. The accounting definition of defined benefit plans is similar to that of the OECD and includes all plans in which the sponsor has a legal or constructive obligation to pay further contributions to an ongoing plan in the event of unfavourable plan experience. Following this definition, so-called hybrid plans (such as cash balance plans), where the sponsor is responsible for meeting a minimum of fixed rate of return on investment investments, are classified as defined benefit. On the other hand, if such guarantees are underwritten by the pension fund itself and there is no potential claim on the sponsor, the plan is classified as defined contribution.

22. The International Accounting Standards Board has revised IAS 19 in three occasions, in 2000, in 2002 and in December 2004. Another, broader revision of IAS19 is expected to start soon.

23. Currently, 55 percent of occupational pension plans are financed through book reserves, compared to 65 percent ten years ago.

24. As argued by Whittington (2006), laying off a salary-linked DB liability to a third party would raise a moral hazard problem because the sponsoring employer retains control over salaries and hence over the debt.

25. This type of valuation method is also referred to as "marking-to-model".

26. There are limits to bulk buy-outs stemming in the first instance from price considerations, because insurers are subject to stricter prudential standards in their valuations than pension funds (and must return a competitive return to their shareholders' capital). Buy-out valuations of pension liabilities are even higher than those under FRS17 (by 20-30 percent, according to market sources). Furthermore, there are practical problems with buy-outs of the larger funds. The market pricing of these termination liabilities may therefore not be ascertainable.

27. Khorasanee (2004) has estimated the equilibrium risk premium for discounting UK defined benefit liabilities at about 0.4% per annum. This small risk premium is caused by the low standard deviation of real salary growth and the relatively high long-term correlation between equity returns and salary growth.

28. This is the case of nominal benefits in Japan and Portugal and of revaluation and indexation factors in the Netherlands.

29. Borio and Tsatsaronis (2005) argue that "accounting standards might distort valuations and induce "artificial" volatility in a firm's financial statement, thereby also influencing its behaviour, not least its risk management decisions, in ways that are contrary to economic logic." Groome et al (2006) argue that "it is not clear that the volatility associated with fair value accounting measures properly focuses insurance companies or pension funds on effective risk management objectives".

30. See Hann et al. (2004).

31. This argument applies even if fair value valuation methods can be reliably applied (see Kortleve and Ponds (2006).

32. Burkhardt and Strausz (2004) and Plantin et al. (2005) show how fair value accounting may heighten incentives for procyclical investment behaviour among banks and insurance companies. A similar argument can be made about pension funds.

33. Borio and Tsatsaronis (2005) also suggest disclosing information on "measurement error, be this as a result of model error or of intentional misreporting".

34. A report by the Association of British Insurers (2007) models a pension fund's cash flows and compares them against the FRS 17 pension deficit measure. It finds that "there is no clear correlation between the size of the FRS 17 deficit and the financial health of the plan. A decrease in staff turnover, for example, had the largest impact on the FRS 17 deficit even though the scheme remained financially solvent".

35. The EU Directive on Institutions for Occupational Pension Provision actually requires that pension entities that underwrite any investment or biometric risk are subject to the solvency regulations contained in the Third Life Insurance Directive. The OECD Recommendation on Guidelines on Funding and Benefit Security in Occupational Pension Plans (OECD (2007)) also refers to the need for additional buffers or a solvency margin in such cases.

36. If a higher discount rate is used to value pension liabilities linked to weak plan sponsors, the resulting required funding level will be lower. An adjustment for default risk would be made in a true market-based system. Accounting standards require the use of a common discount rate, based on AA corporate discount rates, while regulators tend to prefer government bond discount rates.

37. The funding ratios disclosed by regulators are not comparable across countries because of the differences in valuation methodologies mentioned earlier. For international comparisons, it is better to refer to the pension disclosures by companies that present their accounts according to international accounting standards.

38. The first major German company to set up a CTA in Germany was Hewlett Packard in the 1980s. By December 2006, all the 30 companies that make up the DAX stock market index all used off-balance-sheet funding for their pension liabilities, with the CTA being the most popular vehicle. A recent survey by Towers Perrin (2007) has estimated that nearly two-thirds (65%) of the pension liabilities at these firms were externally funded in 2006.

39. See OECD (2006) for data on pension fund asset allocation in OECD countries.

40. Recently, the Boots' pension fund decided to shift back up to 15% of its portfolio to other assets.

41. See Blome et al. (2007) in this volume.

42. See the report by the Committee on the Global Financial (2007) of the Bank for International Settlements. On bond "scarcity" see Ervin and Schich (2007).

43. See Kakes and Broeders (2006).

44. By April 2005, almost half of all UK DB plans active members were in a plan closed to new entrants (Government Actuary's Department (2006)).

45. Since 2006, any plan that is more than 125% funded on a Pension Protection Fund basis will not be liable to pay the risk based element of the pension protection levy.

46. See Stewart (2007). The risk-based part of the levy makes up 80% of the total. It is based on a plan's underfunding risk and the sponsoring company's insolvency risk. The main risk that is not considered in the levy is investment risk.

47. Forcing portability of DB plans in countries like the United States by introducing statutory revaluation of accrued benefits by departing employees does not appear the right solution. Such policies simply shift portability costs to a single company, rather than sharing them among different companies, as in the Dutch industry-wide arrangements.

48. See e.g. Fore (2003).

References

Antolín, P. (2007), Longevity risk and private pensions, *OECD Working Paper on Insurance and Private Pensions No. 3*, January 2007.

Association of British Insurers (2007), Understanding Companies' Pension Deficits: Occupational Defined-Benefit Schemes, *ABI Research Paper 3*, March 2007.

Bader, L. and Gold, J. (2003), "Reinventing Pension Actuarial Science", in *The Pension Forum, Volume 14, No. 2*, Society of Actuaries, January 2003.

Blome, S., Franzen, D., Scheuenstuhl, G. and Yermo, J. (2007), "Pension Fund Regulation and Risk Management: Results from an ALM Optimisation Exercise", this volume.

Borio, C., and Tsatsaronis, K., (2005) *"Risk in financial reporting: status, challenges and suggested directions."*, BIS workshop on "Accounting, risk management and prudential regulation", Basel, 11-12 November 2005.

Burkhardt, K. and Strausz, R. (2004), *"The Effect of Fair vs. Book Value Accounting on the Behavior of Banks"*, mimeo, Berlin: Free University of Berlin.

Cass Business School (2005), Mortality Assumptions Used in the Calculation of Company Pension Liabilities in the EU, Cass Business School.

Committee on the Global Financial System (2007), Institutional Investors, Global Savings and Asset Allocation, *CGFS Papers No. 27*, February 2007, Basel: Bank for International Settlements.

Coronado, J. L. and Sharpe, S. A. (2003), Did Pension Plan Accounting Contribute to a Stock Market Bubble?", *Brookings Papers on Economic Activity*, 1: 323-371.

Day, A., (2003) *Financial Economics and Actuarial Practice* In "The Great Controversy: Current Pension Actuarial Practice in Light of Financial Economics Symposium", Society of Actuaries, June 2003.

Ervin, C. and Schich, S. (2007), *Institutional Intermediation of Retirement Saving: Challenges for Defined Benefit Pension Funds*, in "Challenges to the Financial System – Ageing and Low Growth", Third Conference of the Monetary Stability Foundation.

Exley, J. (2006), *The Fair Value Principle*, in Niels Kortleve, Theo Nijman and Eduard Ponds (eds.) "Fair Value and Pension Fund Management", Elsevier: Amsterdam.

Fore, D. (2003), "The Impact of Fair Value Accounting Standards on the Portfolio Composition of Life Insurance Companies", *TIAA-CREF Institute Working Paper*, 13-050103, May.

Gerber, D. S. (2005), "How Demography Impacts Asset Allocation and Costs: Evidence for the Pension Fund Industry in Switzerland", mimeo, April 2005.

Gold, J. (2001), "Accounting/Actuarial Bias Enables Equity Investment by Defined Benefit Pension Plans.", Pension Research Council Working Paper 2001-5, The Wharton School.

Government Actuary's Department (2006), Occupational Pension Schemes 2005: The thirteenth survey by the Government Actuary, London: The Government Actuary's Department, June 2006.

Groome, T. Blancher, N., Haas, F., Kiff, J., Lee, W., Mills, P., Nakagawa, S., Ramlogan, P., Khadarina, O. and Kim, Y. (2006), "The Limits of Market-based Risk Transfer and Implications for Managing Systemic Risks", *IMF Working Paper No. 217*, September 2006.

Groupe Consultatif Actuariel Europeen (2001), Actuarial Methods and Assumptions used in the Valuation of Retirement Benefits in the EU and other European countries, edited by David Collinson, December 2001.

Groupe Consultatif Actuariel Europeen (2006), Minimum Technical Provisions for Defined benefit Occupational Pensions in the EU: A Summary of Minimum Funding Requirements, edited by Chinu Patel, December 2006.

Hann, R., Heflin, F., and Subramanyam, K. R. (2004), *Fair-value based pension accounting*, mimeo, December 2004.

Kakes, J. and Broeders, D. (2006), "The Sustainability of the Dutch Pension System", *Occasional Studies Vol. 4/No. 6*.

Khorasanee, Z (2004), "What Discount Rate Should be Used to Value Defined Benefit Liabilities", *Pensions Institute Discussion Paper* PI-0402, January 2004.

Klumpes, P., Li, Y. and Whittington, M. (2003), "The Impact of UK Accounting Rule Changes on Pension Terminations", *Warwick Business School Working Paper*, August.

Kortleve, N. and Ponds, E. (2006), *Pension Deals and Value-Based ALM*, in Niels Kortleve, Theo Nijman and Eduard Ponds (eds.) "Fair Value and Pension Fund Management", Elsevier: Amsterdam.

McGill, D., Brown, K. N., Haley, J. J., and Schieber, S. J. (2005), Fundamental of Private Pensions, eighth edition, Oxford: Oxford University Press.

OECD (2006), Pension Markets in Focus, Issue 3, October 2006, Paris: OECD.

OECD (2007), Recommendation on Guidelines on Funding and Benefit Security in Occupational Pension Plans, this volume.

PBGC (2006), Annual Management Report, Fiscal Year 2006, November 15, 2006.

Plantin, G., Sapra, H., and Shin, H. S. (2005), *"Marking to market: Panacea or Pandora's Box?"*, London: London School of Economics, September 2005.

Pugh, C. (2007), "Funding Rules and Actuarial Methods", this volume.

Schich, S. (2005), "Corporate Pension Liabilities and Funding Gaps", *Financial Market Trends*, Volume 2005/1, No. 88.

Standard and Poor's (2006), Pensions & Other Post Employment Benefits Report, June 6, 2006.

Towers Perrin (2007), *Pensionsverpflichtungen DAX 2006*, Rauser-Towers Perrin, May 2007.

Warshawsky, M. (2007), The New Pension Law and Defined Benefit Plans: A Surprisingly Good Match, *Pension Research Council Working Paper WP2007-6*, February 2007.

Watson Wyatt (2005), 2005 Global Survey of Accounting Assumptions for Defined Benefit Plans, Watson Wyatt Worldwide.

Whittington, G. (2006), 'Accounting Standards for Pension Costs', in 'The Oxford Handbook of Pensions and Retirement Income' edited by Gordon L. Clark, Alicia H. Munnell, and J. Michael Orszag, Oxford University Press, 2006; Oxford.

ISBN 978-92-64-02810-4
Protecting Pensions: Policy Analysis
and Examples from OECD Countries
© OECD 2007

Chapter 3

FUNDING RULES AND ACTUARIAL METHODS

by
Colin Pugh[*]

I. Introduction

Basic Objectives of this Report

This report outlines the regulatory framework within which defined benefit (DB) pension plans are financed and addresses the challenges facing the funding of such plans. The Appendices include a summary and discussion of the funding regulations in selected OECD countries, most of which have a long history of externally funded DB pension plans. This report attempts to draw on the positive and negative experiences in these countries and then ***develop ideas and recommendations for the regulation of pension plan financing in OECD countries and elsewhere***. This paper will address such central issues as:

- What funding and actuarial costing methods may be considered as best practice? In particular, should the projected unit credit method be the universal norm? How desirable is consistency with accounting principles?

---

[*] Independent consultant. The author would like to thank the OECD for financial support, for the information provided by the Delegates to the Working Party on Private Pensions, as well as for comments from André Laboul, Fiona Stewart, and Juan Yermo (OECD Financial Affairs Division). The views expressed are the sole responsibility of the author and do not necessarily reflect those of the OECD or its member countries.

- What are the pros and cons of imposing minimum and maximum funding requirements? How much flexibility should companies have to adjust their funding levels to meet these requirements?

- Should regulators establish a precise set of actuarial assumptions (economic and demographic) to be used in actuarial valuations? Alternatively, how much flexibility should actuaries have in setting assumptions?

We live in difficult times.

The first version of this report was written in 2003, following a three-year period during which the funded positions of defined benefit pension plans deteriorated rapidly. Some governmental authorities reacted by creating yet another layer of regulations to protect the current funding position of DB plans. Other countries concluded that these were not normal times and that a temporary relaxation of funding rules would better serve the overall economy and the longer term interests of the various stakeholders. Although pension fund assets have performed relatively well since 2002, a large percentage of defined benefit pension plans continue to be underfunded. The situation has been aggravated particularly by abnormal increases in plan liabilities resulting from declining interest rates and increased pensioner longevity. The challenges to the regulatory authorities thus continue. There are no easy solutions. There is still no clear best practice that (i) reassures the pension plan beneficiaries and conservative regulatory authorities in sustained periods of severe economic downturn, but (ii) does not aggravate the country's wider economic problems and (iii) still encourages the sustainable development of occupational pension plans in the years ahead. It will be counter-productive to become excessively distracted by the current economic issues, so each issues addressed in this report first will be analysed in the environment of more normal times. The effectiveness of each conclusion in a sustained economic downturn then will be tested, but without the automatic expectation that it will always satisfy the concerns of all stakeholders.

Pension plans that are the focus of this report.

Although various aspects of this paper have wider application, the focus is on <u>occupational</u> <u>defined benefit</u> pension plans financed through <u>autonomous pension funds</u>. Clarification of these terms will be provided throughout this report, and reference also should be made to the OECD's "Taxonomy for pension plans, pension funds and pension entities".

Lump sum pension benefits.

For the purposes of this paper, it does not matter whether the retirement benefit is paid in periodic installments (generally for the lifetime of the retired employee and spouse) or whether it is paid in a single lump sum at retirement. The advance funding considerations are virtually identical.

Long service or termination indemnities.

Long service indemnities or termination indemnities of the defined benefit type also would fall within the scope of this paper - if they are paid automatically on retirement to anyone fulfilling the eligibility requirements, and if such obligations are or were to be externally funded.

II. Historical Development of Funding Regulations

This report will focus almost exclusively on the roles of the regulatory authorities as they relate to the **external funding** of DB pension plans. Pension plan regulators clearly have broader responsibilities, but the OECD is addressing these issues in other research papers and other conference sessions. "Funding" is already a large subject, and a very topical subject, so it will be productive to focus the mind on this single issue.

Development of Regulatory Environment.

There are primarily two governmental bodies concerned with the regulation of occupational pension plans and pension funds – the labour, social affairs and social security ministries on the one hand and the economic and financial authorities on the other. Among the latter, the **tax authorities** have played historically the more dominant role. They set the conditions under which employees and employers could make contributions – often tax deductible contributions – to a plan, and they still control this aspect. Their regulations affect both plan design and plan funding. The tax authorities were, and still are, concerned about (a) the payment of excessive benefits to some or all plan members and (b) the deposit of unnecessarily high, tax favoured contributions into the pension fund. These are, of course, legitimate concerns. In the 1990s, they perceived their greater challenge to be the accumulation of large funding excesses (surpluses) within pension funds – not because of deliberately excessive employer contributions, but simply because investment performance far outstripped the actuary's expectations for a sustained period of time. The knee jerk reaction was additional, and often very counterproductive legislation, although it is unfair to place all the blame on the tax authorities. This point will be covered in more detail in other sections of this report.

It was only later (the mid-1960s in Canada, 1974 in USA, etc…) that the **labour and other ministries** became more actively involved in pension plans, and their focus was substantially different. The thrust of legislation from this quarter is the establishment and protection of plan members' rights. This involves many aspects of plan design, as well as prudent investment of fund assets and sound funding of the pension plan obligations. The last item is of direct relevance to this report. Minimum funding standards were an integral part of the original legislation, but (in retrospect) the initial requirements were not particularly onerous. In simple terms, the general requirements were for payment of:

- the current year's normal costs (as defined by the actuarial funding method);
- a slow amortisation of any initial unfunded liability existing at the time the legislation was introduced or a new pension plan was established;
- slow amortisations of subsequent increases in past service liabilities resulting from retroactive plan improvements;
- sensible amortisations of "experience deficiencies", *i.e.* unfavourable deviations from the actuary's forecasts (high salary increases, low investment returns, etc…).

The legislation in some countries did not break down the payments in this manner, but the overall intent was similar. Later, for a variety of both positive and misguided reasons, the legislation in many countries became far stricter. There was, and continues to be, considerable emphasis on "minimum funding standards", but the rules of the game have changed. These requirements will be discussed in Section 4 of this report and analysed in detail in the country appendices.

III. General Actuarial Considerations

This section will address actuarial funding methods and actuarial assumptions from the perspective of the regulator. The fundamental question is the extent to which pension law or the pension regulator should mandate the use of a single actuarial funding method or prescribe the actuarial assumptions? These and other questions will be addressed in general terms in this section and then analysed in more specific detail in the subsequent sections on minimum funding requirements (Section 4) and maximum funding constraints (Section 5). Annex 3.A1 summarises the most important actuarial funding methods and identifies their key characteristics and objectives. Anyone unfamiliar with actuarial methodology should first read the Annex and then return to this section. Country-specific legislation on actuarial methods and assumptions is provided in Annex 3.A2.

Should regulators mandate a single actuarial funding method?

It is difficult to justify mandating a single actuarial funding method. Employers in different industries or at different stages of their development (from start-up to mature) will have correspondingly different funding objectives. All the actuarial funding methods described in Annex 3.A1 are sound and systematic, and the use of any of these methods should not cause concern to a regulator.

Is "Projected Unit Credit" becoming the norm?

In the absence of any particular legislative constraints or other outside influences, there has been a trend in many countries towards Projected Unit Credit. An easy example is the UK, where the Aggregate method was dominant for a very long time and Projected Unit Credit (PUC) was hardly to be seen. However, long before UK accounting standards pushed PUC for pension expensing purposes, the method took hold. In Canada, PUC has been dominant for decades, again before outside influences. One must then ask whether the popularity of PUC is justified, and the answer is almost certainly "yes". It is more transparent than most other methods, and it produces a form of *balance sheet* that most people can understand. Its definition of accrued liabilities is clear and readily comparable with the accumulating fund assets. Favourable and unfavourable experience is easy to identify and understand. Finally, and more recently, there is one major defensive reason for using PUC. It is the method selected by the major accounting bodies for the pension expensing requirements that are being imposed on plan sponsors. Perhaps, accountants were also convinced of the transparency and other advantages just described. There is certainly no *necessity* to use the same actuarial method for funding and expensing, but there are obvious advantages.

Should regulators prescribe the actuarial assumptions?

In answering this question, there are a number of separate issues to be addressed. If we start by focusing on the regular funding of the plan, and we temporarily set aside any concerns of minimum funding standards and maximum funding constraints, then the regulators should mandate nothing more than the use of reasonable and appropriate assumptions. In this context, the major assumptions should be independently realistic, with perhaps a margin of conservatism (prudent assumptions). The reasonableness of the minor assumptions can be evaluated in aggregate. This is already the legislative environment in many countries, although a combination of cultural, psychological and legislative factors restricted the use of this approach in the Netherlands and Switzerland until quite recently (see appendices). As regards minimum and maximum funding constraints, the question is more difficult to answer, simply because assumptions can be used to manipulate the results. For example, a high discount rate and a weak mortality table can make a plan appear to be better funded than is really the case … and vice versa.

Should regulators prescribe the valuation of assets?

This question should not be answered in isolation. Assuming a realistic and somewhat market-related valuation of the liabilities, most players now agree that fund assets should be brought into the equation on the basis of either their straight market value or some smoothed market value. The disagreement is over the validity of smoothed values. The accounting profession clearly does not like them, and others claim that smoothed values are a distortion of reality and tend to shield the plan sponsor from facing up to such realities. However, the objective of a pension fund is to accumulate assets on a sound and systematic basis. From a long-term funding perspective, is a market valuation on a single date (that is already some months in the past) really so important?

Forcing or encouraging plan sponsors to take dramatic corrective actions based on this single market value can be very counterproductive, and it is an issue that is developed in greater detail in Sections 4 and 5. Numerous proposals are provided in these sections, so only one additional point will be made at this time. Even if smoothed market values are rejected, and fair market values must be used at all times, large and unnecessarily volatile swings in contribution rates can still be avoided. This is where the question of asset values cannot be answered in isolation. If the effects of experience gains and deficiencies revealed in an actuarial valuation are allowed to be spread over a reasonable period of time (*e.g.* at least five years), then there is still implicit smoothing. If the market value of the assets was only a temporary aberration, the amortisation can be stopped before it aggravates the real funded position of the plan. Some smoothing is highly desirable – in one form or another – but which form?

Correction of overfunding and underfunding.

With the sole exception of the Aggregate method, the actuarial funding methods described in Annex 3.A1 do not prescribe the amortisation of any experience gains or deficiencies. [At this point, we are concerned with the overall effect of positive and negative deviations from the actuarial assumptions, not just the investment gains and losses.] These actuarial methods, including the Projected Unit Credit, simply indicate that the plan is overfunded or underfunded. There are then subjective decisions to be made regarding whether to ignore the excess or the shortfall or, alternatively, how to correct it. Unless the funded status of the plan is close to the minimum funding requirement or the maximum funding constraint, the plan sponsor should be allowed a fair degree of flexibility.

Frequency of Mandated Valuations?

The choice is usually between one and three years. It is rather strange that nobody has thought of two years, although it is clear that one year is too short in most circumstances and three years is too long. The accountant's pension expensing standards may push plans towards annual valuations. Furthermore, annual valuations make sense when the plan is seriously underfunded or the experience is volatile. From a regulatory standpoint, a *maximum* interval of three years is probably still appropriate, with more frequent valuations of poorly funded plans.

Pension expensing considerations.

Many of the accounting-related issues and influences on funding have already been addressed. One remaining question is then whether a plan sponsor should try to match the pension plan funding with the pension expense, primarily in order to eliminate any pension asset or liability on the company's balance sheet. The answer to this question is "no". Some American employers attempted this in the late-1980s. In practice, it does not work. Now, given the proposed changes in accounting standards, it would generate highly volatile and thus highly undesirable funding requirements.

IV. Minimum Funding Standards

Background.

Minimum funding requirements usually are to be found in legislation focused on protecting the plan members' benefits and, in particular, on ensuring the security of the payment of such benefits. The source is normally labour and social affairs legislation, but financial and tax authorities also regulate funding requirements. As already indicated in Section 2, traditional minimum funding requirements focused on payment by the plan sponsor of the normal or current service cost plus maximum amortisation periods for various categories of unfunded liabilities and experience deficiencies. These requirements still exist in many jurisdictions, but they have been overtaken in importance by straight asset/liability measures.

Asset/liability measures.

In many countries, the minimum funding standards focus on the pension fund assets exceeding the pension plan's accrued liabilities on every measurement date. Almost every country with such a standard has its own way of defining "accrued liabilities", and often there are various requirements for valuing the fund assets (see below). However, the basic philosophy is the same. The authorities are focused on "benefit security" (a laudable objective), and the standards equate such benefit security with the crude size of the pension fund assets. In truth, benefit security depends on many other factors, such as the financial strength of the sponsoring employer, its future intentions regarding the pension plan and the funding thereof, the quality of the fund assets relative to the liabilities, verifying whether the assumed rate of return is reasonable, etc... It is easy to accept the weaknesses of the simple asset/liability solvency measures. It is far more difficult to develop a viable and effective alternative.

Calculation of Accrued Liabilities.

For the purposes of minimum funding standards, most regulatory authorities define the "accrued benefits" and then specify the discount rate to be used for the calculating the present value of such accrued benefits (*i.e.* the accrued liabilities). For these purposes, common definitions of accrued benefits include vested benefits payable on termination of employment and benefits payable to the members in the event the plan were immediately terminated. The prescribed discount rate usually takes the form of (i) a specific rate, (ii) the current market yield on an identifiable group of securities or (iii) the rates implicit in the purchase from insurance companies of immediate and deferred annuities. In some countries, it is simply a maximum rate (*e.g.* 6% pa in Belgium).

Basic criticism of annuity purchase assumption.

As already indicated, many solvency tests implicitly or explicitly assume (i) immediate termination of the pension plan, followed by (ii) immediate liquidation of the fund assets and (iii) immediate purchase of insured annuities. If a pension plan cannot successfully discharge all three of these assumed steps, it is deemed to have serious funding problems that requires drastic actions. However, in all except the rarest circumstances, none of these assumptions is logical. Even if the plan were terminated, the solvency test makes an unwarranted assumption as to the future strategy of the pension entity administering the plan. An immediate sale of all assets and transfer of the proceeds to an insurance company is most unlikely, especially for a large fund or if market conditions are unfavourable. These concerns become even more worrying if the solvency test explicitly assumes annuity purchases, and the current annuity market is (for one reason or another) simply uncompetitive. Ireland is one country where this issue is already being discussed.

Over-regulation.

Over-regulation of DB pension plans is an unfortunate and growing phenomenon; see Section 5. The Myners' report in the UK, when reviewing the UK's minimum funding requirement and other UK regulations, argued that increased protection under DB plans will deprive employees of having any DB plan at all. Instead, such plans will be replaced by DC plans, and *all* the risks will then be thrown at the employees. In the area of minimum funding, as with other areas of legislation, there is a fine line between (over)protecting the interests of DB plan members and destroying the incentives for employers to sponsor such plans.

Minimum funding vs. fraud.

The UK's minimum funding standard (the MFR) was a reaction to the Maxwell scandal, where pension fund assets were fraudulently removed from the Mirror Group pension fund. Minimum funding standards of the asset/liability type described above do not prevent fraud. Indeed, most pension legislation cannot stop a determined criminal. However, minimum standards that pay more attention to the quality of the fund assets and the good intentions of the employer can be an important step in the right direction.

Conclusions.

The assumptions used for calculating and comparing assets and liabilities should not necessarily be the same for all pension funds. A single set of assumptions fails to recognise fund-specific factors such as the maturity of the fund, the strength and future intentions of the plan sponsor, and the investment strategy of the pension entity.

The whole situation becomes even further detached from reality under the plan discontinuance and annuity purchase type of solvency test.

Solvency tests should not protect against all possible economic scenarios (such as the fourth or fifth consecutive year of an economic downturn). The costs would be too high. Pension funding should not take priority over the very survival of the plan sponsor, and the wider economic impacts could be disastrous. See "Netherlands" in Annex 3.A2.

Solvency tests would be better focused if they encouraged optimal investment of the fund assets and protected plan members against inappropriate investment strategies. Such assessments should be fund-specific. Asset liability modelling (ALM) studies can play an important role in this regard.

Of course, the final question is whether minimum funding tests serve any useful purpose. If not, they should be abandoned in favour of other requirements on the sound management of the plan and fund (governance and other issues). If they are still deemed to be necessary, they should be more plan-specific and they should avoid the imposition of volatile funding or other detriments to the smooth functioning of the plan. In moving away from the MFR, the UK authorities are indeed trying to move towards a more plan-specific approach.

Recommendations.

Monitor the discussions taking place among regulators and within the actuarial profession in both Canada and the USA, and in the UK and elsewhere in Europe. Many experts are searching for better alternatives to today's crude asset/liability measures for measuring funding adequacy and protecting the members' security. Their efforts should be encouraged.

If an asset/liability type of minimum funding measure is to be introduced or retained, then legislation should not require the immediate and complete correction of any underfunding that the test purports to reveal. Actuarial calculations are an inexact science. Asset values fluctuate, and funding shortfalls may disappear as quickly as they had appeared. It is counterproductive for a plan sponsor to make high additional contributions and then find, one or two years later, that the markets have recovered and the plan now has an embarrassing funding excess (see next section).

Continue to refine approaches that avoid excessive knee jerk reactions to underfunding, include ignoring small funding shortfalls (say, 10% of liabilities), smoothing asset values and amortising shortfalls over five years. Whilst acknowledging the inherent weaknesses of any asset/liability solvency measures, and recognising the slight differences between the various supervisory authorities in Canada, there is much to recommend the general Canadian approach to minimum funding. The objective is clear and logical. The five-year period for corrective action avoids dramatic knee jerk reactions to deficits in times of temporarily distorted market conditions. The combined smoothing of asset values and discount rates, as allowed by some of the Canadian regulators, also can work well.

The regulator should allow additional flexibility in a sustained economic downturn.

V. Maximum Funding Constraints

Background.

Maximum funding constraints are imposed by tax authorities to prevent either the deliberate or accidental build-up of excessive assets within the pension fund. Deliberate build-ups were the result of a plan sponsor consciously contributing far more to the pension fund than was needed to finance the promised benefits. Only pension people with long memories can remember those days! Accidental build-ups of excess funds result primarily from favourable experience under the plan. With the benefit of hindsight, the actuary's assumptions were too conservative. High investment returns or other favourable plan experience caused the assets to grow at a faster pace than the accruing liabilities. This was the focus of attention of the tax authorities during the late-1980s and the 1990s.

Sanctions and Corrective Actions.

In most countries, tax legislation does not impose direct *sanctions* on plan sponsors or pension funds in the event of overfunding. There are examples of special excise taxes (USA) or additional taxes on withdrawals of excess assets (UK), but most jurisdictions focus on requiring the plan sponsor to take *corrective actions*. The most common, and most obvious, corrective action is the reduction of future contributions. Even in the absence of government legislation, these downward corrections of contribution rates are an automatic part of ongoing discussions between the actuary and the plan sponsor. Then, in the 1990s, plan sponsors were happy to go even further than the actuary would normally recommend. They happily agreed to complete contribution holidays, and they explained their actions as being a consequence of government legislation.

Another important approach to reducing overfunding is for the plan sponsor voluntarily to spend the money, through improvements in the accrued benefits of non-retired members, increases to pensions-in-payment and guarantees of future pension indexing. This approach only becomes contentious when the regulator mandates such actions. The third main approach to reducing overfunding is the refund of excess assets to the plan sponsor. Such withdrawals are explicitly forbidden in some countries, *e.g.* Belgium and Switzerland. For all practical purposes, Canada can also be categorised as a country where withdrawals of excess assets have become impractical.

Of course, one has to ask whether any of these corrective actions were really necessary or desirable. We are now facing a pensions funding dilemma, for which blame can be widely apportioned. Without excusing plan sponsors and their advisors, it is clear that government legislation is counterproductive when it encourages or requires rapid and vigorous corrections of either the perceived overfunding of the 1990s or the subsequent (and somewhat consequential) underfunding of the early 2000s.

Ownership of Funding Excesses.

In the very large majority of countries and situations, it is the plan sponsor (the employer) that is fully responsible for correcting any underfunding situations. It should therefore not be a great leap of faith to conclude that the employer should be the beneficiary of any temporary overfunding. Indeed, some of the actuarial costing methods involve the conscious creation of such advance funding, to underpin the basic objective of a smooth employer contribution rate. However, overfunding or advance funding is frequently re-categorised into the far more emotive word "surplus". Anyone familiar with the pension environment during the 1990s will remember the highly emotional, and even confrontational, discussions on the ownership and application of such *surpluses*. The equation has become unbalanced in several countries where, in practical terms, funding shortfalls are the employer's problem and funding excesses belong to the members. In such an environment, no employer is going to move beyond minimum funding. This is very unfortunate. Unless plan sponsors can be convinced of their right to the upside gains as part of their responsibility to accept the downside risks, solid funding of pension obligations will become history. Future generations of plan members and plan sponsors will curse our short-sightedness. It should be noted that there are some countries where the responsibility for covering any funding deficiency is shared, or can be shared, partly with the plan members; in these circumstances, the treatment of any funding excess would need to follow a consistent approach.

Accelerated funding under some actuarial funding methods.

As discussed in Section 3 and Annex 3.A1, some actuarial funding methods require heavier contributions in the early years in order to stabilise future contribution rates. A practical side effect of these accelerated contributions is an additional hedge against unanticipated and unfavourable future experience. If government legislation then requires the funded position of all pension plans to be assessed on an accrued benefit basis, these particular plans will appear to be overfunded even when plan experience has conformed largely to actuarial expectations. If this factor is not taken into account in any governing legislation, then the practical effect is to restrict the choice of actuarial funding methods and reduce funding levels.

Investment reserves and smoothing techniques.

Notwithstanding some of the above concerns, the tax authorities still have a right to be concerned about any plan sponsor that attempts to abuse the generally tax-favoured status of occupational pension plans. However, their concerns should not be aimed at penalising prudent plan sponsors that simply want to fund their pension obligations on a sound and conservative basis. The other main challenge for the regulator is to avoid demanding drastic corrective actions when overfunding is simply the result of recent, and perhaps temporary, market conditions. As events have shown, overfunding can disappear as quickly in the years immediately following an actuarial valuation as it had been generated in the years immediately preceding such a valuation. From a regulator's standpoint, there are three solutions to these challenges that parallel a sensible treatment of underfunding, namely:

- **Smoothed asset values.** For the purposes of determining whether a plan is genuinely overfunded, and the extent to which it is overfunded, the plan sponsor should be allowed to use a smoothed market value for the assets. Alternatively, fair market values can be specified, but a pension fund would be allowed to maintain an additional investment reserve when asset values are high. The end result is the same, but there are important differences in the presentation.

- **Margins**. In the same manner as most authorities do not require any action to be taken for underfunding of less than 10%, a similar (but preferably higher) margin could be allowed for overfunding.

- **Amortisations.** Any "correction" of overfunding should be allowed to take place over a sensible period of time.

However, there is one additional consideration that differentiates overfunding from underfunding. While it is clearly undesirable to continuously ignore a funding shortfall, is there any reason to prevent a pension fund continuing to retain a modest funding excess? If pension funds had been allowed to retain contingency reserves, and if the "ownership" issues surrounding such reserves could be more favourable to the plan sponsor, pension funds would have been in a better position to weather the current underfunding problems.

Conclusions and solutions.

Using the term "pension plan regulator" in the narrower sense, namely the administrators of legislation protecting members' rights, these regulators would have no problems in allowing or even encouraging overfunding. The legislation surrounding the ownership of excess funds is usually found elsewhere, and often in the Courts. The legislation establishing maximum funding constraints usually emanates from the tax authorities. This is a classic example of the need for effective cooperation between the somewhat competing priorities of various parts of government. Desirable solutions include:

- Resolution of the current no-win situation for plan sponsors in many countries regarding the correction of experience shortfalls (deficits) and the utilisation of funding excesses (surpluses);

- Tolerance of a reasonably large amount of overfunding by the tax authorities. There should continue to be measures to prevent abuse, which is normally confined to small plans. Ireland is one country where the focus of the regulators is the correction of genuine abuse without the penalisation of plan sponsors seeking conservative funding.

- To the extent that overfunding is so high as to demand corrective action, the plan sponsor should be permitted to amortise the corrective actions over a reasonable period of time. In Canada, for example, there are no requirements for dramatic action even when the surplus exceeds the established threshold. The plan sponsor can simply take a contribution holiday until the excess funding is used up. If the funding excess was just the result of temporarily distorted market conditions, then the contribution holiday will be short and regular funding can resume.

It will not be easy to persuade some legislators to make these changes. However, there will never be a better time than now. People are coming to understand that aggressive and counter-productive treatment of overfunding in the 1990s is one of the primary reasons for the current underfunding.

VI. Challenges Facing Regulatory Authorities

Introduction.

The challenges identified in this section are particularly relevant to the regulation of pension plan funding, although some are equally applicable to plan design or the investment of fund assets. There can also be complicated areas of overlap, for example when an apparently sound funding regulation has the potential to create adverse consequences on plan design or the investment of fund assets.

The primary objective of this section is to set out the difficulties facing any legislator and to learn from the positive and negative experiences in other countries. The challenge for the government and the regulator is to move towards pension funding regulation that:

- has clear and agreed objectives;
- is transparent, avoiding convoluted methodology or artificial assumptions;
- is capable of being understood by non-experts;
- is effective in practice, avoiding unnecessary cost burdens such as administrative overload or inefficient investment practices; and most importantly
- encourages the establishment and continued maintenance of occupational pension plans.

In most of those countries with a long history of pension plans, there is a widespread fear in the business community that pension plan and pension fund laws and regulations can become excessive and even counterproductive. Regulators have a very important role to fulfill. It is a great challenge for them to satisfy the legitimate concerns of all stakeholders (pension plan sponsors, their shareholders, pension plan members and other beneficiaries, etc…) whilst avoiding unforeseen or undesirable consequences for the plan sponsor or the general economy. From the perspectives of both the regulator and the regulated, some of these challenges now will be identified. For those countries in the development stage of pension plan regulation, there are many useful lessons to be learned.

Challenges

A stable legislative environment. An environment of constantly changing legislation and regulations is not conducive to the smooth and efficient operation of pension plans and funds. Countries such as the United Kingdom might be a consultant's dream, but they can be an employer's nightmare. The competing effects of the UK's minimum funding requirement (MFR) and maximum funding constraints caused considerable confusion. More recently, the frequent changes to Dutch funding legislation have become a cause for concern. The Dutch regulator prides itself on "continuously updating it supervisory regime", but this can be a two-edged sword. It was not so long ago that Dutch past service liabilities could be book reserved on a tax effective basis and other unfunded liabilities and experience shortfalls could be amortised through to retirement (the so-called 65-x method). In 2000, the 65-x method was abandoned in favour of full and immediate funding; a 10-year transition was allowed. In 2003, additional reserves were then required in connection with equity investments and for the unamortised portion of the 10-year transition. Although some of the early changes had little practical effect at the time, because of inflated asset values, an environment of constantly shifting sands was discouraging. Further, very significant changes in funding regulations were then promised for 2006 (since deferred until 2007); see Annex 3.A2.

Although plan sponsors may not like some parts of any country's pension legislation, they eventually learn to adapt and comply. Obviously, this is easier when the legislation is not undergoing constant change and where there is a consistency of approach. Switzerland provides a good example of a more stable environment. Swiss pension legislation is scheduled for a thorough review only every ten years, and there is comprehensive input from all quarters. There is only fine-tuning of the legislation in the intervening years, and usually as a consequence of well-reasoned requests from plan sponsors and others. One example has been the acceptance of asset liability modelling studies to support efficient pension fund investment strategies that otherwise contravened the quantitative investment restrictions.

A stable funding environment. Plan sponsors should be allowed to fund their pension obligations in a controlled manner, without the knee-jerk volatility imposed by funding legislation in some countries and without the pressures imposed by other outside influences. Plan sponsors are very concerned about the extreme volatility of pension *expense* that can be imposed by evolving accounting requirements. Translating that level of volatility into pension *funding* could be catastrophic. The next two points expand on this issue.

Smooth correction of underfunding. This issue has already been developed in detail in Section 4. Even if smoothing is allowed in the calculation of accrued liabilities or the valuation of assets, actuarial calculations are an inexact science and asset values are volatile. Amortisation of any funding shortfall should be allowed over a reasonable period of time. If no smoothing is allowed in the underlying calculations, then such amortisations (and the use of "corridors") become even more important. The minimum funding approach developed by the Canadian Institute of Actuaries achieves a fine balance in this regard (the problems in Canada lie elsewhere, in that customary funding could default to this minimum funding standard). The challenge for the regulator is to allow some smoothing, either in the calculations or through amortisations, without completely destroying the credibility or transparency of the results.

Constructive approach to overfunding. Some of the same considerations apply to overfunding. However, there is an important fundamental difference. Underfunding is a problem, whereas overfunding is an opportunity – an opportunity to set aside reserves to protect against future adverse experience and to introduce further stability into the funding of the plan's obligations. In many countries, the various arms of government need to work in a more coordinated manner to ensure a constructive approach to overfunding.

Additional flexibility in difficult times. More than 70 years have passed without a sustained economic downturn of the type recently experienced. As a result, many governments and regulators explicitly relaxed their funding requirements on a temporary basis (*e.g.* Ireland, UK and USA). In a number of other countries, the regulators have taken a more flexible attitude to short term funding (*e.g.* Portugal). In contrast, in the Netherlands, the regulator called for a speedy recovery in funding levels, and found it necessary to engage in a close dialogue with the pension funds, for whom the requirements were too restrictive given the difficult economic environment they faced.

A Pension Fund is not an Insurance Company. A pension fund of the closed type, which is the primary focus of this report, does not sell products. Indeed, it is the opposite, as it is a buyer of services and products. It does not deal with the general public. Only in rare circumstances does a pension fund make guarantees. It is the plan, and thus the plan sponsor, that normally makes promises (or even guarantees) to the plan members; it is not the fund. Yet, many countries persist in regulating pension funds as if they were insurance companies or insurance products. Funding standards, and especially minimum funding standards are erroneously geared to insurance company products, guarantees, reserving and overall philosophy. Pension fund legislation that talks about "premiums" rather than contributions, and "mathematical reserves" rather than accrued liabilities, often reflects this approach. The debate about the requirements for a "level playing field" between pension funds and insurance companies may have complicated these issues.

The insurance supervisory authority is, in several countries, responsible also for pension fund supervision - this is not always a problem, and it is sometimes necessary in smaller pension markets with limited actuarial expertise, but the regulator (and the legislation itself) must recognise the unique characteristics of pension funds. Portugal is a good example of an insurance supervisory authority that has been charged with pension fund supervision and is able to make the clear distinction. In contrast, the Dutch Central Bank published a so-called White Paper on the Solvency Test, "by means of which the capital adequacy of a pension fund or an insurer is assessed" – and which appears to assume that a pension fund and an insurance company are identical twins and should be regulated as such.

Problems (real and perceived)

Unrealistic expectations. Some plan members, their representatives and other parties have developed unrealistic expectations about the roles of regulators in curing all the world's pension problems. One obvious example was the UK's minimum funding standard (MFR). It was not only supposed to prevent fraud of the Maxwell type, but it gave most people the impression of providing iron-clad guarantees of the funding of their accrued benefits. Iron-clad guarantees are too expensive, and fundamentally inefficient, but that is a separate and even more complex issue. The MFR was nothing more than its name indicates – a minimum funding requirement. However, it created unrealistic expectations, and regulators need to be aware of this type of potential problem.

Over-regulation. There is strong evidence that this is the second most important reason for employers switching from defined benefit (DB) pension plans to defined contribution (DC) pension plans, with the first reason being the potentially volatile costs of DB plans. Over-regulation is indeed a serious problem, and it should not be underestimated by government authorities in developing pension plan markets. DB pension plans are inherently superior to DC plans in a number of important areas, but they are being legislated to death in some countries. This point is covered below in more detail.

Counter-productive legislation. There is a lot of discussion on this point at the present time. In the same way as a doctor treats a sick patient, the regulator must be careful to cure a problem without creating numerous and more serious side-effects elsewhere. One example will serve to illustrate the point (see next paragraph).

Distortion of investment decisions. Much very valuable work has been done in recent years to improve the effectiveness of pension fund investments. Asset liability modelling (ALM) studies have played a major role in this regard. For various degrees of risk tolerance and with the specific demographic and other characteristics of an individual plan, it is now relatively simple to develop a range of efficient portfolios for the fund. The results have been revealing, sometimes surprising and always useful. As already indicated, Switzerland has agreed to relax its complicated asset mix restrictions, if it can be shown that they are "inefficient" for a particular fund. The EU pension fund directive almost completely abandons quantitative investment restrictions, in exchange for a prudent person rule and the encouragement to use ALM. However, the progress achieved through the front door is in danger of being lost through the back door. For example, minimum funding standards in many countries are designed around insurance company annuity rates or current market yields on long-term bonds. In order to avoid problems, especially in jurisdictions that require immediate correction of the (perceived) underfunding, a plan sponsor is tempted to over-invest in such long-term bonds. Some legislation on the indexation of pension benefits can have the same effect. Although outside the realm of the pension regulator, proposed amendments to international, UK and perhaps US pension expensing standards may again push plan sponsors away from equities and into more bonds. However, pension plans in the long term, especially those providing benefits based on final-average salaries, need substantial investments in equities. Otherwise, the investments may be inefficient, and the cost of the pension plan to the plan sponsor will therefore increase.

Undesirable Consequences.

A funding strategy based on avoidance of overfunding. This issue has already been mentioned, but it bears repeating. Unless issues surrounding ownership and control of funding excesses can be resolved, plan sponsors will simply aim for minimum funding, perhaps with the smallest of contingency margins. This type of approach is in nobody's long term interests. The negative impacts were painfully illustrated during the recent economic downturn.

Increases in costs. One point is the direct administrative and consulting costs incurred in complying with a growing body of pension legislation. Plan sponsors repeatedly complain about these costs, especially in regard to defined benefit plans. Filling out government forms, and hiring advisors to provide numerous certifications, is a reality of life - an easy source of frustration, but a necessary part of doing business. As regards pension plans, the real concerns are elsewhere. As already described, the most serious *indirect* cost impacts stem from the legislative requirement or encouragement to invest the fund assets in an inefficient manner. There are other examples.

Switching to DC plans for the wrong reasons. For a while, many employers believed they were switching from defined benefit to defined contribution plans because they thought it was a good idea for everyone concerned. However, DC plans are not inherently superior. They are different, and they have many weaknesses that are only starting to be understood by the majority of the population. Employers now readily acknowledge that the switch to DC was really because of their concerns about the uncertainty and potential volatility of DB plan costs. Their concerns are only partly justified, because a well-designed DB plan that is funded in a systematic manner can be quite stable. Much of the fuel for their concerns was supplied by legislation that removed the basic flexibility to fund "in a systematic manner", and probably also by accounting standards.

Abandoning pension plans altogether. This is simply an extreme extension of the concerns expressed in the previous paragraph.

In Summary.

In an era of reducing (first pillar) social security benefits, there must be proactive encouragement to employers to establish and maintain occupational pension programs. Tax legislation can provide important incentives. In a minority of countries (*e.g.* Ireland), the pension regulator also is charged with encouraging the growth of occupational pension plans. In all countries, pension regulators have the challenge of discharging their supervisory responsibilities without discouraging the continuation of the very plans they are attempting to protect. Not an easy task.

VII. Recent Trends and Developments

As already indicated, the first version of this report was written in 2003. Much has happened on the regulatory front during the intervening period. Indeed, several jurisdictions have started directly to address many of the concerns identified in this report. This Section 7 will highlight and comment on several of these changes. Technical descriptions are to be found in the updated individual country profiles in Annex 3.A2.

Plan-specific funding requirements. As part of its Pensions Act 2004, the UK is moving towards plan-specific funding requirements. These will replace the misunderstood and much maligned Minimum Funding Requirement (MFR). Each occupational pension plan now is required to adopt a Statutory Funding Objective. The actuarial costing method is not prescribed, although it must be one of the family of accrued benefit costing methods. Similarly, the economic and demographic assumptions and the discount rate for calculating the liabilities are not prescribed, but they must be prudent. In preparing a recovery plan to address any funding shortfall, the trustees (in consultation with the plan sponsor) must take into account the asset and liability structure of the plan, its risk profile, its liquidity requirements and the age profile of the members. It is anticipated that amortisation periods will be relatively short, although this will require some level of consultation and even negotiation between the trustees and the plan sponsor.

Relaxation of minimum funding requirements. Several jurisdictions have relaxed their minimum funding requirements, most specifically in the area of longer amortisation periods for addressing funding shortfalls. Some of these concessions are announced as being temporary, and conditions often are attached. Bill 102 in the Province of Quebec, proposals under discussion in other Canadian jurisdictions, Ireland and Switzerland all provide examples of these changes.

Tightening of minimum funding requirements. The Dutch minimum funding requirements were replaced by new rules laid down in the Pension Act and the regulations based upon this act, which came into force on 1 January 2007, with the exclusion of some transitional arrangements. The primary supervisory body is the Dutch Central Bank (DNB). As the new rules require the calculation of assets and liabilities on a market basis, periods of low interest rates result in higher funding requirements than under the old rules. The new Dutch regulations would be classified as conservative in relation to almost all other jurisdictions.

Letters of Credit. There are several variations of this theme. A typical example would be the plan sponsor purchasing a letter of credit from a bank, as part of the plan sponsor's general credit facility. The letter of credit could, for example, cover the pension plan's solvency deficit or the foregone solvency amortisation payments. The letter of credit would be held by the trustee of the plan and fund, and it would be called upon in the event the plan sponsor defaults. The letter of credit would be counted as a plan asset, but normally only for minimum solvency valuation purposes. This concept has been introduced in Quebec Bill 102, and it is being widely discussed in other North American jurisdictions.

No benefit improvements by severely underfunded plans. Relaxed funding requirements in some jurisdictions have been accompanied by tighter constraints on making plan improvements. The basic thrust is to avoid further aggravation of the funded position of an already seriously underfunded plan. For example, Quebec Bill 102 forbids all plan improvements unless any resultant increase in accrued liabilities is fully and immediately funded. The new pension funding reform in the USA would, with few exceptions, forbid plan improvements being made by severely underfunded plans. Indeed, if the funding ratio falls below 60%, future regular benefit accruals also would be in jeopardy.

More constructive approaches to overfunding. Many jurisdictions are becoming increasingly cognisant of the problem, but no simple and effective solutions have yet been found. Indeed, it is the tax authorities and the courts that are the sources of many of these unfortunate constraints on conservative funding, so the pension legislator often is unable unilaterally to address the issues. Some progress has been made in regard to relaxing the tax regulations on maximum funding, *e.g.* in the USA, where current pension reform envisages a return to the higher limits of prior years. The tight UK 105% maximum funding limit also is being changed. From the perspective of both jurisprudence and pension law, the 2005 Canadian federal government consultation paper on funding reform requests input on "whether there are any disincentives or obstacles preventing plan sponsors from adequately funding their plans and building up a funding cushion". The document acknowledges that: "Many plan sponsors and experts have argued that there may be an apparent asymmetry in surplus ownership under (government regulations). They argue that (government regulations) have the effect of requiring plan sponsors to share any surplus while remaining fully responsible for pension plan deficits." The problems have already been discussed in Section 5 of this report. They are important, and solutions need urgently to be found. Otherwise, plan sponsors will just aim for minimum funding at all times, and this is in nobody's best interests. This is not to pretend that the solutions are easy. Some countries do not even see it as a problem; they legislate that funding excesses belong entirely to the plan members … in full, and under all circumstances. For most plan sponsors operating in these countries, conservative funding and overfunding are unsound philosophies.

DC funds retaining the annuity and Hybrid Plans. A hybrid plan is generically defined as a pension plan that shows features of both defined benefit and defined contribution plans, and there have been at least four main developments in this area. First, cash balance and other hybrid pension plans have simply become more widespread. Second, there are a growing number of plans that seem to be defined contribution, but that include a minimum guaranteed rate of return. The cause either may be government legislation (*e.g.* Belgium and Germany), plan sponsor choice or collective bargaining. These plans are, in effect, "better of" plans, where the plan member receives the higher of a pure DC accumulation and a defined benefit. Third, there are defined contribution plans in some countries (*e.g.* Brazil) where the pension fund converts the retiring employee's DC accumulation into an annuity *and retains* the annuity obligation in the fund – rather than purchasing an annuity from an insurance company. The fourth development is an inevitable consequence of the first three; governments and accountants, actuaries and other specialists acknowledge that all of these types of arrangements need to be treated as defined benefit plans for the purposes of expensing and actuarial funding. In particular, governments and pension regulators now are explicitly requiring in their legislation and regulation that conventional DB actuarial funding valuations must be performed for these plans. Spain recently has identified the problem of DC plans with minimum guarantees ... most of which were created when plan sponsors tried to move away from the complex Spanish regulation of conventional DB plans. Ireland recently has recognised the problem of DC plans retaining the annuity risk. While admitting that there are few such plans in Ireland, it is an explicit recognition of the general issue. The new UK pension reform explicitly addresses the definitions, and the USA has long regulated cash balance plans as defined benefit. The list goes on.

EU Pension Fund Directive 2003/43/EC. The two year period for implementation of the directive at the national level in all 25 EU member states has expired, and indeed governments have already taken implementing actions. However, there are still unanswered questions as to the practical meaning in each member state of the requirement in article 16.3 of the directive for cross-border pension plans to be fully funded at all times. The provisions in article 16.2 of the directive setting the basic conditions whereby domestic plans can be underfunded "for a limited period of time" also are still being interpreted. In conjunction with the pension reform concurrently being undertaken in the UK and other EU member states, this has led to some (hopefully temporary) confusion.

Annex 3.A1

ACTUARIAL FUNDING METHODS

In the widest possible description of actuarial funding methods, there are up to six very broad categories of financing approaches. However, we can quickly dismiss the two approaches at each extreme. At the minimalist end, there is "pay-as-you-go" and "terminal funding". Pay-as-you-go is a financing method, but not a funding method, as no assets are set aside. Benefits are paid simply when they become due. Under terminal funding, the liability is discharged in full when the employee retires, and usually by the purchase of an annuity from an insurance company. No assets are set aside while the employee is working. At the other extreme, there are two classes of financing that involve heavy pre-funding of future benefits. These approaches also can be ignored. We will now focus on the two important categories of actuarial funding methods, namely:

- **Accrued benefit funding methods.** These methods focus on maintaining a certain level of funding. They are security driven, in that they attempt to establish and maintain a sound relationship between the fund assets and the accruing liabilities. The funding requirement is then the contributions required to achieve the funding objective. The two most important methods within this category are Current Unit Credit and Projected Unit Credit. Variations included Partially Projected Unit Credit (used in Canada and UK for various purposes) and methods that focus on the assumed termination of the plan.

- **Prospective benefit funding methods.** In contrast, these methods define a certain level of contributions. They are contribution driven, and the primary objective is stability of such contributions. These contributions then define the targeted level of the fund at any point in time. The three most important methods within this category are Entry Age, Attained Age and Aggregate.

The funding method does not affect the true overall cost.

It is important to remember that the ultimate cost of any pension plan to the plan sponsor is:

- Total benefits paid to plan beneficiaries; less
- Member contributions to the plan; less
- Investment income earned by the pension fund; plus
- Expenses incurred in the operation of the plan and the fund.

It can readily be seen that there are no actuarial calculations or actuarial estimates in this formula. Nevertheless, because certain actuarial funding methods require higher employer contributions in the early years, which will hopefully result in greater investment income, the eventual employer cost is indirectly affected by the funding method. This is a timing issue, and indeed actuarial funding valuations are all about "timing" – setting aside assets in an organised fashion to discharge the eventual benefit obligations. Brief descriptions of each of the main actuarial funding methods will be described, after two brief, but important definitions.

Accrued and Prospective Benefits.

"Accrued benefits" are generally understood to mean pensions-in-payment, deferred pensions of ex-members, and benefits earned by active plan members in respect of accrued pensionable service (service already performed, or years of contribution already made, up to the date of the actuarial valuation). By extension, "prospective benefits" for the third group (the active members) include the effect of projected future service. The treatment of these active members differentiates various funding methods.

Current Unit Credit.

The objective is to maintain a fund equal to the "accrued liabilities", defined as the present value of accrued benefits. Under the Current Unit Credit method, the accrued liabilities for active employees exclude any allowance for the effect of future salary increases. For example, the accrued benefits under a final-average earnings plan generally would be calculated by reference to each employee's current salary. In many cases, the accrued liabilities would approximate the value of the benefits the employee would receive on immediate termination of service or on plan termination. This is a simplistic comparison, but it helps focus the mind on the approximate level of assets the Current Unit Credit method is trying to achieve. The basic contribution for the next year is then (a) the present value of the increase in accrued benefits, primarily the effect of one year's salary increase, plus (b) the present value of the benefits to be earned by the active members because of an additional year of service. The rules of the plan would govern the allocation of this contribution between the employees and the employer.

Projected Unit Credit.

This method is similar to the Current Unit Credit, except that the calculation of the accrued liabilities includes an allowance for the effect of future salary increases on accrued pensionable service and accrued benefits. The normal cost, the so-called "current service cost" or simply "service cost", is then the present value of benefits to be earned by active members because of an additional year of service – as with the accrued liabilities, this service cost includes the predicted effect of future salary increases. There is no second element in the current service cost under the *Projected* Unit Credit method (cf. the "updating" of accrued liabilities under the *Current* Unit Credit method), as this is already incorporated into the calculation of the accrued liabilities.

This is arguably the most important actuarial funding method, so it is important to understand its fundamental objectives. The goal is to maintain the pension fund assets at such a level that, with future investment income but without any future contributions, the fund will be able to pay all accrued benefits until the last plan beneficiary dies. In this regard, we can think of the plan being *suspended*, rather than *terminated* - there are no further contributions and no further accruals of pensionable service, but the plan continues, future salary increases are recognised, and benefits become payable in the normal manner on retirement or prior death, disability or termination of service.

The contribution to the fund is then the current service cost plus an adjustment to correct (over an agreed period of time) any imbalance between the accumulated assets and the accrued liabilities. In the event of overfunding, this adjustment is negative. In the event of heavy overfunding, the adjustment matches the current service cost, and a contribution holiday is initiated.

It is important to understand that this type of actuarial funding method does not prescribe the amortisation of any underfunding or overfunding. It just calculates the accrued liabilities, compares the result with the assets (however valued) and identifies the difference. Any action to correct underfunding or take credit for overfunding is then to be discussed. The final decision normally rests with the plan sponsor, after consultation with the trustees, board of foundation or equivalent pension entity. It is at this point that the regulator frequently places constraints on the choices available (see Sections 5 and 6).

Attained Age.

For most plans that provide salary related pension benefits, the future normal funding rate under the Attained Age method is calculated by dividing (a) the present value of all benefits accruing after the valuation date by (b) the present value of future salaries. The normal cost is then obtained by applying this *funding rate* to the current payroll of the plan members. As these calculations ignore accrued benefits, another calculation is required to compare the accrued liabilities with the accumulated fund assets. The accrued liabilities are calculated in *exactly* the same manner as under Unit Credit methods, and adjustments to correct any overfunding or underfunding are handled in the same manner. Although the Attained Age method shares some similarities with accrued benefit funding methods, its focus on stability of future normal costs places it in the family of prospective benefit funding methods.

Entry Age.

The normal cost under Entry Age method is the level amount (or the level percentage of pay) that would exactly fund each member's prospective benefits if contributed from the member's date of eligibility until normal retirement date. Unfunded accrued liabilities can exist on the plan's inception date, if the member's pensionable service date precedes the plan's effective date. Otherwise, accrued liabilities at any point in time are simply the present value of prospective benefits over the present value of future normal costs. "Prospective benefits" recognise both accrued pensionable service and projected future service. Note that this definition of accrued liabilities does not correspond in any manner to the present value of accrued benefits described under the accrued benefit funding methods. Future funding contributions are then the Entry Age normal cost plus an adjustment for the difference between accumulated assets and these accrued liabilities.

Aggregate.

For most plans that provide salary related pension benefits, the normal funding rate under the Aggregate Funding method is obtained by subtracting the accumulated fund assets from the present value of all prospective benefits and then dividing the result by the present value of future salaries. The resulting *funding rate* is then applied to the current payroll of the plan members. "Prospective benefits" recognise both accrued pensionable service and projected future service. There is no unfunded liability under this approach, as all experience gains and losses are absorbed into the single calculation. In effect, they are amortised through to retirement age. There is a common misconception that the Aggregate method generates conservative funding. This is generally true if the plan experience conforms to the actuary's assumptions. It is certainly true if the plan experience is favourable, because the process of taking credit for the funding excesses is extremely slow (right through to retirement age). However, if a plan is underfunded in a conventional sense, then it will stay underfunded for a long time – again, because of the slow amortisation implicit in the method.

Sample Calculations

Simple illustrations of the fundamental differences between the calculations of the funding rates under four of the above actuarial funding methods will now be provided. The same asset value is used in all cases. This common starting point helps to highlight the effects of moving forward with each of the different funding methods. In reality, if each funding method had been followed in the past, the contributions to the pension fund - and the resultant accumulation of the assets - would have been different.

(PV = present value)	Value	CUC	PUC	AttAge	AGG
Assets in the pension fund	120	Yes	Yes	Yes	Yes
PV of accrued benefits (current salaries)	80	Yes			
PV of benefits accrued one year from now	88	Yes			
PV of one year's benefits (projected salaries), *i.e.* (current) service cost under PUC method	11		Yes		
PV of accrued benefits (projected salaries)	150		Yes	Yes	Yes
PV of future benefits (projected salaries)	130			Yes	Yes
PV of total projected benefits (150 + 130)	280				Yes
PV of future salaries	1,000			Yes	Yes
Current payroll	110		Yes	Yes	Yes

Abbreviations:
- CUC: Current Unit Credit actuarial funding method.
- PUC: Projected Unit Credit actuarial funding method.
- AttAge: Attained Age actuarial funding method.
- AGG: Aggregate actuarial funding method.

Current Unit Credit:
- Basic contribution = 88 – 80 = **8**.
- But, there is a funding excess of 40 (120 assets – 80 liabilities) that can be applied to reduce contributions.

Projected Unit Credit:
- Basic contribution = Service Cost = 11 = **10.0%** of payroll.
- But, there also is a funding shortfall of 30 (150 liabilities – 120 assets) that will need to be addressed. For example, by being amortised over the next five years.

Attained Age:
- Future funding rate = 130 divided by 1,000 = **13.0%** of payroll, so contribution = 14.3.
- But, there also is a funding shortfall of 30 (150 liabilities – 120 assets) that will need to be addressed. For example, by being amortised over the next five years.

Aggregate:
- Funding rate = (280 total liabilities – 120 assets) ÷ 1,000 = **16.0%** of payroll = 17.6.

Annex 3.A2

PENSION PLAN FUNDING REGULATIONS

Occupational defined benefit pension plans financed through autonomous pension funds are to be found in all of the countries analysed in this Annex. In summary:

1. Employers or group of employers can establish occupational plans where they bear the risk for a certain benefit formula or lump-sum benefit (generally based on salary and service), or the higher of a defined benefit and a defined contribution pension;

2. Plan sponsors are permitted or required to establish autonomous pension funds as a means of financing the obligations created under such a pension plan; and

3. Plan sponsors are permitted or required to establish pension entities (*e.g.* trust, foundation, corporate entities) that own and may control the autonomous pension fund on behalf of plan members.

Although these countries also permit other financing arrangements, such as insurance contracts, the individual country summaries in this Annex focus on the different regulatory approaches taken by the tax and supervisory authorities to the funding of defined benefit pension plans using autonomous pension funds.

AUSTRIA

Supervisory Control.

The 1990 Company Pensions Act (BPG) authorises four different financing arrangements for company pension plans and also establishes minimum vesting, portability and other requirements. Three of the financing arrangements (book reserves, support funds and direct insurance) are not relevant to this report. The fourth is a Pensionskasse (Pensionskassen, in the plural), which is a special form of pension fund. Around half of company pension plans in Austria are financed by book reserves, over one third by pension funds and the rest by insurance contracts. The 1990 Pension Fund Act (PKG) regulates the establishment, operation and supervision of single and multi-employer pension funds, as well as laying down rules concerning asset management, minimum funding and accounting. The Financial Market Authority (FMA) supervises pension funds, insurance companies and other financial service providers. The funding rules for pension funds (pensionskassen) will be discussed below.

Minimum Funding Requirements

The basic objective of the minimum funding requirements is for the fund assets to exceed the sum of the accrued liabilities and a contingency fund.

For these purposes:

- Assets are taken at fair market value.

- The only permitted actuarial costing methods are those that recognise the liabilities over the active service life of each plan member (current unit credit, individual entry age, attained age).

- The liabilities to be funded include the full value of pensions in payment and deferred pensions.

- The maximum discount rate for calculating the liabilities is between 3.0% and 6.5%, depending on the date of creation of the fund and the form of benefit indexation.

The maximum period for correcting any underfunding resulting from plan experience differing from the actuarial assumptions is ten years. All other underfunding must be corrected immediately.

In order to compensate for potential investment losses, every Austrian pension fund must establish a contingency or volatility reserve ("Schwankungsrueckstellung"), designed to equalise profits and losses from the investment of the assets and from the technical account balance. The mechanism for calculating the "contingency reserve" is described in detail in the Austrian Pension Companies Act (PKG); it can range from a maximum of 20 % to a minimum of –5 % of assets, and operates according to boundaries. The targeted value for the "volatility reserve" is between 10-15% of pension liabilities, and it must be financed from employer contributions. If the volatility reserve exceeds this target value, 10% of the excess shall be immediately released (with the management board allowed to determine exceptions). The upper boundary is 20%. If the volatility reserve exceeds 20% of the allocated assets, these are released to the extent of the difference. In terms of the lower boundary, if the application of the reserve rules results in a negative volatility reserve, the reserve for future beneficiaries is immediately released in full. For plan members who have already retired or are receiving benefits, only the part of the negative reserve exceeding 5% of allocated assets is immediately released.

Customary funding practices

Customary funding practice is prescribed in the pension fund contract and in accordance with the collective agreement or equivalent document. As multi-employer Austrian pension funds can cover a wide variety of plans, there also can be a variety of actuarial methods involved in calculating liabilities and contributions. The most commonly used include the following:

- Most pension companies use the attained age method to calculate liabilities and contributions. The underlying assets are recognised at their market value smoothed by the contingency reserve.

- The individual entry age method is not commonly used to calculate annual contributions, but it is often used to calculate initial transfer amounts when changing an unfunded, book-reserved plan into a plan financed by a pensionskasse. In some cases, the calculated transfer amounts are increased by an initial contingency reserve.

- The projected unit credit method is used primarily by pension funds established by large companies that are members of a multinational group.

- The discount rate used to calculate liabilities depends mainly on the benefit-increases (indexation) prescribed in the plan rules; the rate varies from 3.5-6.5%. Explicit allowances for salary increases are only made when they are not implicitly recognised in the discount rate; they range from 2%-5% and in some cases depend on age and/or years of service. Similarly, explicit allowances for benefit indexation are only made when they are not implicitly recognised in the net discount rate; they range from 1%-4%, depending on the plan. Turnover assumptions are not included.

- Demographic assumptions can be chosen by the actuary. In 1999, a new set of generational mortality tables was published by the Austrian Association of Actuaries (AVÖ). There are different tables for 'white-collar employees' only and 'mixed white-collar and blue-collar employees'. These new tables are generally used when calculating book reserves and have been used for almost all pension fund calculations since 2001. In some cases, the tables published in 1989 (which are for 'mixed white-collar and blue-collar employees' and do not include any generational allowance for improving mortality) are still used.

Maximum funding limits

From a pension law perspective, there are no maximum funding limitations. However, tax law specifies several maximum limits for both defined benefit and defined contribution plans.

Frequency of actuarial valuations

A report by an independent external actuary must be prepared annually and submitted to the Financial Market Authority (FMA).

Bankruptcy of plan sponsor

In the case of the bankruptcy of the plan sponsor, the fund assets belong to the plan members. There is no possibility of a refund of surplus assets to the bankrupt plan sponsor. Correspondingly, further creditors rights do not exist. There is no mandatory insolvency insurance program, and the plan sponsor is not required to insure the pension rights of the members.

Termination of an overfunded plan

In general, the surplus assets belong to the risk sharing group and go into technical account balance. Depending on the individual claims, the surplus is distributed to the members of the risk sharing group.

Who appoints the actuary?

The pension fund appoints the actuary. The appointment of a member of the pension fund board as an actuarial expert must be approved by the supervisory board. In addition, the pension fund must appoint an independent external actuary to conduct the annual actuarial audit; this appointment also must be approved by the supervisory board. Actuaries must have proven proficiency in the field of actuarial analysis, and external actuaries must be independent (defined as not receiving more than 30% of yearly income from, and not carrying out any other function for, the pension fund). The appointment of both employed actuaries and external actuaries must be notified to the FMA, which may disapprove of the appointment within one month.

Role of the actuary

The independent external actuary must monitor compliance with the pension fund's "business plan": examining whether the business plan is being correctly implemented; whether any changes to the current contribution rates or benefit structure are necessary; whether any funding shortfall exists; and whether and to what extent and by what deadline the employer has to address any such underfunding. The actuary has to exercise his activity with due regard to the statutory provisions relevant to his activity as well as all technical standards in accordance with recognised actuarial principles.

A pension fund must prepare the aforementioned business plan outlining its actuarial and technical provisions. The business plan must be reviewed by an independent external actuary and approved by the FMA. The business plan contains any and all details and parameters required for the operation of the pension fund, in particular:

- the types of benefits offered;
- the presentation of the circumstances which are significant for the safeguarding of the interests of the beneficiaries and for assessment of continued compliance with the pension fund's obligations;
- the bases of calculation (mortality tables, economic assumptions, assumed discount rate, expense loadings, targeted technical surplus);
- the type and management of the volatility reserve;
- the investment policy, as well as the method for apportioning the assets of a multi-employer fund between the various plans and the various groups of beneficiaries;
- the principles of, and the formulas for, calculating the plan sponsor contributions.

BELGIUM

Supervisory Control

There are specific minimum funding requirements in Belgium. These requirements are established by government regulation, in particular a Royal Decree of 7 May 2000, and administered by the insurance supervisory authorities (*l'Office de Contrôle des Assurances* in French, and *Controledienst voor Verzekeringen* in Dutch). Customary funding practices are established by the actuarial profession. There are no direct maximum funding requirements.

Minimum Funding Requirements

Under the minimum funding requirements, fund assets must equal or exceed the sum of the following:

- accrued liabilities; plus
- if the plan provides disability and death-in-service benefits, an additional solvency margin.

For these purposes:

- Accrued benefits equal the highest of (i) the vested rights as defined in the plan rules, (ii) the past service benefits based on current salaries, and (iii) the employee's own contributions accumulated with interest.
- The accrued liabilities are valued using the current unit credit method.
- The maximum discount rate is 6%pa.
- The mortality tables are specified by the authorities, namely the MR 88-90 table for males and the FR 88-90 table for females.
- No assumptions are permitted regarding employee turnover.
- Pensions are assumed to commence at normal retirement age, although an adjustment must be made for plans that provide subsidised early retirement benefits.
- Special rules apply to a pension funds that supplement group insurance contracts (a common arrangement in Belgium, generally with employee contributions going to the insurance contract).

- The additional solvency margin for death and disability benefits is a complicated function of total sums at risk, the five largest sums at risk, etc… If all or a portion of the death and disability benefits are reinsured, the solvency margin may be reduced proportionately, but not to below 50% of the full solvency margin.
- Assets are taken at fair market value.

In the event of a shortfall (assets less than accrued liabilities):

- A plan to liquidate the shortfall must be submitted to, and approved by, the regulator.
- The effect of an increase in liabilities caused by the Royal Decree of 7 May 2000 or by any subsequent modifications of the minimum standard can be amortised over as long as 20 years.
- There are severe penalties for plan sponsors that fail to comply with the agreed financing plan.

Customary funding practices

There are no government constraints in this area.

However, the following observations can be made:

- The most common actuarial valuation methods are Projected Unit Credit and Aggregate.
- It would be normal to use the same MR and FR mortality tables as are specified for the minimum funding test.
- Otherwise, the economic and demographic assumptions are established by the actuary in accordance with standard actuarial practices.
- Disability and death-in-service benefits may be insured, in which case the annual insurance premium will be added to the current service cost for the retirement benefits. Even if these benefits are not (re)insured, the actuary may still cost them on an annual "risk premium" basis.
- The minimum funding requirement is a funding constraint, rather than a funding objective.
- Fund assets are usually taken at market value.
- These valuations serve as the basis for claiming employer tax deductions.

Maximum funding limits

There are no direct limits on the maximum amount of assets that can be held in a pension fund.

However, there are two indirect constraints:

- The maximum pension that can be provided under a tax-effective Belgian pension plan is 80% of final salary - after a full career, and inclusive of social security benefits.
- The "financing plan" prepared by the actuary and submitted to the insurance control authorities must take account of the 80% limit.

The financing plan must take into account any overfunding when developing its future funding costs. There are no requirements to suspend contributions until the funding excess is exhausted, but the financing plan must address the overfunding in a systematic manner; the regulator takes a dim view of dramatic changes in financing plans. The plan sponsor is not allowed to withdraw excess assets from the fund, so that is not an option.

Frequency of actuarial valuations

Valuations are required to be performed annually.

Bankruptcy of plan sponsor

Whether the plan is overfunded or underfunded, the entire assets of the fund are allocated between the plan members. There is no government insurance program to cover shortfalls.

Termination of an overfunded plan

The entire assets are allocated between the plan members. In other words, each plan member receives an appropriate share of the funding excess. As already indicated, there are no circumstances under which excess assets can revert to the plan sponsor.

Who appoints the actuary?

The actuary is appointed by the pension fund. He or she must hold a European degree in actuarial sciences and must have relevant experience over a period exceeding five years.

Role of the actuary

The appointed actuary has to advise on the financing of the plan, the reinsurance arrangements and the calculation of the technical provisions.

BRAZIL

Supervisory Control

Funding requirements are described in detail in Complementary Law 109/01 of 30 May 2001 and associated regulations. Complementary Law 108/01 describes additional requirements for pension plans sponsored by public companies. Different supervisory regimes apply to closed funds (covering a single employer or group of companies, an association or a union) and open funds (insurance company and similar products available to both individuals and employers). The legislation covering closed funds is of more direct relevance to this report. Closed pension funds are supervised by the *Secretaria de Previdencia Complementar* (SPC), reporting to the Ministry of Social Security and Assistance. Regulations are issued by the *Conselho de Gestão de Previdência Complementar* (CGPC), a special board comprised of heads of the SPC and the social security administration, together with representatives from other ministries and from pension fund associations. Open pension funds are supervised by the *Superintendencia de Seguros Privados* (SUSEP), reporting to the Ministry of Finance.

Minimum Funding Requirements

Article 18.3 of the aforementioned Pension Law 109/01 states that "accumulated assets of each benefit plan must at all times fully cover existing obligations under the plan". This statement has caused considerable confusion within the industry, and a clear interpretation of its meaning is still being sought. In the meantime, CGPC/MPAS Resolution n°11 of 21 August 2002 provides the basic guidance on actuarial funding issues. The rules regarding minimum funding can be summarised as:

- Liabilities shall be calculated using the current unit credit actuarial costing method applied to the closed group of existing plan members and beneficiaries.

- Accrued benefits are to be calculated using historical salaries, *i.e.* without future projections.

- The *real* discount rate cannot exceed 6% pa.

- The AT 49 mortality table must be used. There are already active discussions on replacing this mortality table with a table more up-to-date and appropriate to the Brazilian working population.

- The employee turnover assumption cannot exceed 5% per year, unless a higher rate can be justified by the plan sponsor.

- Disability and survivor *pensions* can be financed on a terminal funding basis, whereby the entire liability is funded at the time of the death or commencement of disability benefits. Death and disability *lump sums* can be financed on a pay-as-you-go basis.

- Alternatively, such death and disability benefits can be reinsured (CGPC/MPS Resolution n°11 of 27 May 2004).

The maximum period for correcting any underfunding of the liabilities for active members is the weighted average future working lifetime. The maximum period for correcting any underfunding of pensioner liabilities is the weighted average life expectancy. These provisions closely follow the methodology in North American and international accounting standards.

Customary funding practices

Any actuarial funding method is permitted, as long as it generates contribution requirements that equal or exceed the minimum funding requirements. Current Unit Credit is widely used, although Projected Unit Credit and Aggregate also are to be found. Under Resolution CGPC/MPAS n°3 of 19 December 2001, an independent actuarial audit must be completed at least every five years and the conclusions submitted to the SPC. The requirements of such an audit are extremely rigorous.

Maximum funding limits

Article 20 of Pension Law 109/01 directly addresses the issue of maximum funding. Basically, plan sponsors are allowed to establish a *contingency reserve* of up to 25% of the accrued liabilities. For these purposes, the accrued liabilities are calculated under the funding method used for customary funding. The implication is that plan sponsors desiring faster or conservative funding of their obligations should use the projected unit credit or aggregate funding method. However, there must be a consistency of approach from one year to the next. Any fund assets beyond the 25% limit then constitute a *special reserve*. This special reserve can be maintained for three years, or it *can* be used in the interim for benefit improvements or contribution reductions. If there is a positive balance in the special reserve for three consecutive years, then it *must* be spent on benefit improvements or used to reduce both employee and employer contributions.

Frequency of actuarial valuations

Valuations are required to be performed annually.

Bankruptcy of plan sponsor

Whether the plan is overfunded or underfunded, the entire assets of the fund are allocated between the plan members. There is no government insurance program to cover shortfalls.

Termination of an overfunded plan

The entire assets are allocated between the plan members. In other words, each plan member receives an appropriate share of the funding excess.

Who appoints the actuary?

The pension fund appoints the actuary.

Role of the actuary

The actuary provides advice on the sound funding of the plan, including the minimum funding requirements, and provides most of the input for the actuarial report that must be submitted each year by the pension fund to the regulator (the SPC).

CANADA

Supervisory Control

The division of responsibilities between the federal government and the various provincial governments complicates the pension supervisory structure in Canada. Except for a relatively small percentage of workers who are governed by federal employment legislation, it is the role of the provinces to regulate pension plans and set standards in all the traditional areas such as minimum vesting, disclosure, minimum funding, etc… Federal and provincial pension law in Canada is harmonised through the Canadian Association of Pension Supervisory Authorities (CAPSA). In general, CAPSA may propose changes to existing pension legislation and regulations, though it must receive Ministerial approval. Of necessity, this paper will make generalisations concerning the various minimum funding standards, but this should not distract from the basic conclusions. Through CAPSA and through its close liaison with the Canadian Institute of Actuaries (CIA), there is considerable consistency of approach.

The federal government controls the maximum amount of funding in defined benefit pension plans through limits, set out in the federal income tax rules, on the type and level of benefits that such plans may provide, and on the amount of surplus that a pension plan may hold.

Customary funding practices are established by the actuarial profession.

Legislation and consultation in 2005

In 2005, there were several important initiatives by legislators and the actuarial profession regarding further improvements to the funding (and the regulation of the funding) of defined benefit pension plans.

These initiatives included:

- Quebec Bill 102 concerning (i) a temporary relaxation of the minimum funding requirements, (ii) authorising the use of letters-of-credit and (iii) severely restricting plan improvements by underfunded plans (5 May). Details are provided below.

- Quebec working paper on "towards better funding of defined benefit plans" (24 May). Builds on the temporary measures in Bill 102.

- Federal consultation paper on "strengthening the legislative and regulatory framework for defined benefit pension plans registered under the Pension Benefits Standards Act" (May). In a similar vein to the Quebec legislation and working paper. Of particular interest is the request for input on the controversial subjects of disincentives and obstacles to adequate funding or overfunding of pension plan liabilities, the ownership of surplus assets and related matters.

- CAPSA discussion paper on "proposed funding principles for a model pension law" (20 June). A more technical paper that primarily transforms current common provincial and federal funding regulations into a single model. Of particular interest is its stated objective that "A funding requirement should provide appropriate assurance that sufficient plan assets are maintained to deliver the promised benefits in defined benefit plans, *particularly in the situation of employer bankruptcy*". In other words, full funding at all times is neither required nor realistic.

- Canadian Institute of Actuaries "statement on revised actuarial standards of practice for reporting on pension plan funding" (March). For going concern valuations, the paper discusses "unbiased measurement" of assets (market value) and liabilities (best estimate assumptions) and then describes explicit "provisions for adverse deviations" (contingency reserves) and "adjustments to unbiased measurements" (positive or negative adjustments, such as asset value smoothing).

All except the CAPSA paper talk about (a) a possible relaxation of solvency funding requirements, (b) alternative financial instruments such as letters-of-credit, (c) severe restrictions on making benefit improvements to underfunded plans and (d) reform of the current 'asymmetrical' surplus ownership rules.

Minimum Funding Requirements (solvency basis)

Each supervisor requires minimum funding sufficient to provide the accrued vested benefits to which the members would be entitled in the event of plan termination. For these purposes:

- Solvency valuation, as defined, means a valuation of the assets and liabilities of a plan using actuarial assumptions and methods that are in accordance with accepted actuarial practice for the valuation of a plan, determined on the basis that the plan is terminated at the valuation date.

- Assets are taken at market value, although some supervisors will allow a smoothing method over up to five years, if a smoothing method over the same time period also is used for the initial interest assumption in the valuation of the liabilities. Alternatively, this smoothing alternative generally is allowed when the plan is experiencing problems because of poor investment performance or when there has been a rapid drop in interest rates.

- The accrued liabilities are valued using the accrued liability (current unit credit) method.

- Most supervisors require the actuary to make assumptions concerning the proportion of members who would elect a commuted value (and transfer from the plan) and the remainder who would leave their deferred or immediate pension benefits in the plan. In turn, the commuted value normally must assume the most advantageous early retirement date provided by the plan for terminated members. For older or long service employees (age + service = 55 years), some supervisors require the commuted value to be determined assuming the active member will remain active and will retire at the most advantageous early retirement date for active members. Note – early retirement is an important issue under most union and many other Canadian pension plans.

- When calculating commuted values, the actuary must follow a Standard of Practice prescribed by the CIA. This standard currently prescribes the UP-94 mortality table projected forward to the year 2015 using mortality projection scale AA, no pre-retirement mortality or other decrement, and an interest rate of x% per annum for 10 years and y% per annum thereafter. The rate "x" is equal to the market yield on 7-year Government of Canada benchmark bonds plus 0.5%. The rate "y" is a more complicated blend of market yields on such 7-year bonds and on long term Government of Canada benchmark bonds, again plus 0.5%. Lower interest rates apply when the plan provides indexation of pensions; the formulas are specified in the CIA Standard of Practice.

- Proxy assumptions for annuity purchases from an insurance company would be used for the members who are assumed to retain their benefits within the plan.

- Some regulators require unisex mortality; others require sex-distinct mortality.

Any shortfall (assets less than accrued liabilities) revealed in an actuarial valuation must be eliminated within five years. Each shortfall has its own five-year amortisation schedule, so new shortfalls discovered in subsequent valuations involve new five-year amortisations, whilst the earlier amortisation schedules are continued until they expire.

Under Quebec Bill 102 of 5 May 2005, the minimum funding requirements have been relaxed (temporarily) for Quebec-registered plans. As a first step, all existing solvency deficits can be aggregated and re-amortised over five years. Subject to certain conditions, the payments in the first five years can be calculated as if a ten-year amortisation period had been adopted; the balance at the end of the five years is then re-amortised in the conventional manner. This second approach is available only if: (a) the plan sponsor is a municipality, a university or an education institution at the university level; or (b) both the active and inactive members give their consent (which is deemed to be given unless 30% of one group or the other explicitly objects); or (c) the plan sponsor provides a guarantee (*e.g.* a letter-of-credit). The idea of employing letters-of-credit is discussed in further and more general detail in Section 7 of this report. Plan amendments that create immediate unfunded liabilities will not be allowed during the application of the second approach, unless such additional liabilities are fully and immediately funded.

Customary funding practices (and minimum funding on a going concern basis)

Regulations typically require actuarial valuations to follow the professional requirements of the Canadian Institute of Actuaries. The regulations also include minimum funding requirements calling for funding of unfunded liabilities and solvency deficiencies over specified periods.

- Going concern valuation, as is defined in the regulations, means a valuation of the assets and liabilities of a plan using actuarial assumptions and methods that are in accordance with accepted actuarial practice for the valuation of a plan, assuming that the plan will continue to operate indefinitely. The assumptions and methods are selected by the actuary and normally include margins for adverse deviations.

- The most common actuarial valuation method for final average salary plans is, and always has been, the Projected Unit Credit. The Current Unit Credit method generally is used for flat benefit and career average earnings plans.

- None of the actuarial assumptions is prescribed, although a supervisor will question the actuary about the appropriateness of high interest rates or old mortality tables (previous to GAM 1983).

- Assets can be taken at current market value or smoothed over a period not exceeding five years. The smoothing method is losing favor, perhaps because of concern about pension expensing (accounting) standards.

- Most supervisors will allow the funding of any going-concern experience deficiency or other unfunded liability (*e.g.* retroactive plan improvements) over a period not exceeding 15 years.

In accordance with the proposed minimum funding target highlighted in the January 2003 "Final Report of the CIA Task Force on Pension Plan Funding", the minimum funding target should be achieved within five years of solvency funding (item 5 above) plus a margin; guidelines are provided to help the actuary establish the appropriate margin. It is important to note that the proposed minimum funding target has not yet been approved. In effect, the Partially Projected Unit Credit method is used, in that salaries, etc… are projected for the five-year period, but not beyond.

Maximum funding limits

Under the federal income tax rules, which are administered by the Canada Customs and Revenue Agency (CCRA), "full funding" is permitted on either the customary funding basis, with methods and assumptions determined by the actuary (item 6 above), or on the solvency basis, with assumptions and methods prescribed by the supervisors (item 5 above). There are then specific limits on the amount of any "funding excess" or surplus. An actuarial surplus can be retained or otherwise ignored to the extent it does not exceed the lesser of:

- 20% of the actuarial liabilities; and
- the greater of 10% of the accrued liabilities and twice the combined employee/employer current service costs for the first year following the valuation.

Effectively, for a mature plan with many pensioners and few active employees, the surplus cannot exceed 10% of accrued liabilities. For a relatively immature plan, the limit is the lesser of 20% of liabilities and two years' current service costs. An important aspect is that the government does not prescribe the actuarial method or assumptions, so the actuary can introduce stability into the funding exercise by smoothing the asset values, etc… In effect, this establishes investment reserves when the market is temporarily bullish and smoothes the effects of downturns.

In the event of surplus in excess of the above limits, the employer must stop its contributions to the pension fund. Employee contributions are permitted to continue. In lieu of an employer contribution holiday, the plan sponsor could amend the plan to provide enhanced benefits such as ad hoc indexing for pensioners, formalised future indexing, or enhanced early retirement provisions. However, enhancing benefits based on what may be a temporary surplus would have to be assessed against the long-term funding implications. Furthermore, retroactive increases in the basic benefit or basic accrual rate can be complicated by the immediate tax impacts on plan members.

The Government of Canada has recently proposed a change for plans where funding shortfalls and excesses are shared equally between the employer and the employees (fixed cost-shared plans). In a fixed cost-shared plan, an employer contribution holiday automatically triggers a corresponding employee contribution holiday. The proposed change will allow employee and employer contributions under such plans to continue to be made when there is a funding excess of between 10 per cent and 25 per cent of accrued liabilities. The contributions would be calculated as a declining percentage of the normal annual pension costs. The change will put these plans on a more equal footing with traditional defined benefit plans for which employee contributions may continue regardless of the amount of surplus.

Under most pension regimes, it is difficult for an employer to recover surplus assets from the fund in an ongoing situation without the approval of virtually all the members – even when the plan provisions state that the employer owns the surplus!

Irrespective of the limits on funding excesses contained in the tax rules, it is important to remember that there is little incentive for overfunding of medium and large scale Canadian pension plans because of the uncertainties regarding surplus ownership. If the employer is fully responsible for deficits, and if the employees are the full or primary beneficiaries of overfunding, then the result is inevitable. Some employers will simply take all possible measures to avoid any overfunding in the first place. Nonetheless, the surplus limits are required to prevent overfunding that could arise from other considerations. In particular, for smaller defined benefit plans where the interests of the plan members and the employer may be one and the same, the limits on excess surplus are key to preventing excessive deferrals of tax that could otherwise be achieved through deliberate overfunding.

Frequency of actuarial valuations

Valuations are required to be performed every three years. However, the federal regulator (the Office of the Superintendent of Financial Institutions) and one provincial regulator (Ontario) require annual valuations if the solvency ratio (see earlier) is less than 100% and 80% respectively.

Bankruptcy of plan sponsor

Creditor rights of plan members fall behind numerous other secured lenders. Only Ontario provides a guarantee fund (the PBGF) in the event of plan sponsor insolvency, and then only for single employer plans. These single employer plans must pay an annual assessment fee to the PBGF, based on the number of plan members and any (solvency basis) unfunded liability.

Termination of an overfunded plan

Surplus funds usually are applied to provide extra plan benefits to members. Any surplus paid to members in cash usually would be allocated in proportion to each member's accrued liabilities. In some jurisdictions an employer may access surplus on plan wind-up, subject to obtaining the consent of at least two-thirds of members, former members and other persons within prescribed categories, and if the prescribed funding margins have been satisfied. If fewer than two-thirds but more than one-half of each category consent, legislation in some jurisdictions allows the employer to go to binding arbitration. All funds dispersed are treated as income to the members or to the employer in the year received, and they are taxed accordingly. No special, additional taxes apply.

Who appoints the actuary?

Each pension plan must have an "administrator" which bears ultimate responsibility for the plan. This administrator is either the plan sponsor or a board of trustees. The administrator then appoints the actuary and other professionals who are required for the smooth operation of the plan.

Role of the actuary

The current and future role of the pension actuary is a topic of ongoing discussion within the profession. Basically, the actuary acts as a pension consultant to the administrator. The actuary is expected to prepare a valuation report using assumptions and methods which provide some contribution flexibility for the employer, but which ensures that the pension fund eventually will protect the future interests of the plan members. However, the actuary is not (and does not want to be) a plan fiduciary. The actuary can recommend certain actions to the administrator but cannot compel the administrator to act. An actuary sometimes may feel compelled to resign, and the supervisor may require an explanation from the administrator concerning any change of actuary.

IRELAND

Supervisory Control

Minimum funding requirements are established under the Pensions Act. The Social Welfare and Pensions Bill 2005 introduced considerable changes to the Pensions Act, some provisions of which affected the minimum funding requirements. The supervision of pension plans and pension funds is carried out by the Irish Pensions Board. Customary funding practices are established by the actuarial profession.

Minimum Funding Requirements

The basic objective of the minimum funding requirements (the so-called Funding Standard) is for the assets to at least equal the accrued liabilities. The Pensions Act prescribes the use of a plan discontinuance basis, but it does not prescribe all the detailed assumptions to be used. In practice, the actuary must conduct such valuations in accordance with professional guidance issued by the Society of Actuaries in Ireland. The applicable guidance notes are GN3, GN3A and GN9. Highlights include:

- Fund assets are to be taken at realisable value, *i.e.* fair market value less selling costs.

- In respect of pensions in payment, the actuarial basis should be consistent with the cost of buying matching annuities in the marketplace. In respect of non-retired members, the value shall be no less than the sum of the individual transfer values to which each member would be entitled under the standard transfer value basis contained in Guidance Note 11 issued by the Society.

- Allowance must be made for the estimated expenses of winding up the plan.

In the event of the fund assets being less than the discontinuance liabilities, the shortfall normally must be liquidated within 3 years (but see next paragraph).

The Social Welfare (Miscellaneous Provisions) Act, 2003 amended the Pensions Act to give additional flexibility to the Pensions Board in its administration of the Funding Standard. These somewhat temporary provisions were consolidated and expanded in the Social Welfare and Pensions Bill 2005. As a result, the Pensions Board now has the power to extend the three year period for correcting a shortfall to as much as ten years (or even longer) if certain conditions are met. These include:

- the shortfall was due to adverse experience resulting from (a) an exceptional fall in the value of markets, (b) a sharp drop in the interest rates used to calculate liabilities, (c) unusual price inflation or salary increases or (d) payment or early retirement and similar enhanced benefits;

- the actuary's reasonable expectations as to the return on the fund assets, as well as other elements of the plan's experience, would show that the plan could reasonably be expected to fully satisfy the funding standard within the agreed period;

- the proposed funding contributions are weighted to ensure a funding level of at least 85% of the discontinuance liabilities within three years of the effective date of the funding proposal; and

- the trustees inform the plan members of the new funding proposal.

Customary funding practices

The actuary conducts regular funding valuations and produces actuarial valuation reports in compliance with a number of Guidance Notes issued by the Society of Actuaries in Ireland; these include GN3, GN3A, GN9 and GN11. The Pensions Act requires actuarial valuations to be prepared every three years. The most common actuarial funding method is the Projected Unit Credit, although Attained Age and Aggregate methods are still to be found. The actuary has wide discretion in setting the assumptions used to calculate the liabilities. Assets are usually taken at fair market value or smoothed market value.

Maximum funding limits

There are no direct quantitative limits concerning the maximum amount of assets that can be held in a pension fund. There are procedures to prevent abuse, although they rarely are applied. The tax authorities require that the matter be brought to their attention when a valuation discloses a surplus in excess of 10% the liabilities, with assets and liabilities being valued under the chosen method.

Frequency of actuarial valuations

Full actuarial valuations are required to be performed at least every 3 years. The traditional 3½ year period was reduced in 2005 to 3 years, in line with the EU pension fund directive. Actuarial *reviews* now must be carried out between full valuations in order to establish whether the plan continues to satisfy the Funding Standard. If a positive statement cannot be made in this regard, then an actuarial funding certificate must be prepared.

Bankruptcy of plan sponsor

In the event of the wind up of a defined benefit plan in any circumstances, an order of priorities for allocating the assets is prescribed in Section 48 of the Pensions Act, namely: (a) expenses associated with the wind-up; (b) benefits arising from additional voluntary contributions, including AVCs forming part of any transfer payment received; (c) pensions-in-payment, excluding future discretionary increases in such pensions; (d) benefits in respect of "reckonable service" (as defined in the law), together with revaluation of post-1991 preserved benefits and benefits generated by transfer payments received; (e) revaluation of pre-1991 preserved benefits and any uplift to provide minimum contributory benefit for members entitled to an immediate retirement benefit at the date of plan windup; and (f) any other benefits in accordance with the priorities specified in the plan rules.

Termination of an overfunded plan

The fund assets first would be allocated in accordance with the priorities prescribed in the Pension Act (see previous paragraph), and then in accordance with the priorities in the plan rules. If there are still excess assets, and if the plan rules so provide, such assets can be refunded to the plan sponsor.

Who appoints the actuary?

The Irish equivalent of the "pension entity" in OECD parlance is the board of trustees. The trustees appoint the plan actuary. In order to sign an Actuarial Funding Certificate for the purposes of the Pensions Act, the actuary must be a Fellow of the Society of Actuaries in Ireland who has been granted and holds a valid pension plan actuary practising certificate under the rules of the society.

Roles of the actuary

The appointed actuary is required to conduct regular actuarial valuations, inter-valuation reviews, prepare Actuarial Funding Certificates and assist in the development of Funding Proposals for addressing any underfunding.

Specifically:

- The actuary must certify that the funding proposal being submitted to the Pensions Board meet the requirements set out in the Pensions Act.
- The actuary must certify the reasons for the failure of the plan to meet the minimum funding standard.
- The actuary must prepare a prescribed statement (certificate) for the plan's annual report.

It should be noted that actuarial certificates also are required from *defined contribution* plans that pay pensions from fund assets, rather than buying annuities from an insurance company. This requirement was introduced in the Social Welfare and Pensions Bill 2005. Although it is expected only to affect a very small number of plans in Ireland, it serves to identify an issue that needs to be addressed, or may eventually need to be addressed, in other countries.

JAPAN

Supervisory Control

Pension plans are supervised by the Ministry of Health, Labor and Welfare (MHLW). Plans are also subject to rules and regulations set by the Tax Administration Authority.

As a result of the Pension Reform that became effective in April 2002, there are now several financing arrangements for defined benefit pension plans. In this context, defined benefit plans include those that are contracted-out of social security (historically, the common approach), contracted-in plans and cash balance plans. The most important funding vehicles are as follows:

- Employees' Pension Fund (EPF). Introduced in 1966, it is the traditional funding vehicle for large plans that "contract out" of the earnings-related portion of social security (EPI). In 1989, termination insurance was added.

- Tax-qualified pension plan (TQPP). Introduced in 1962, it is for "contracted-in" plans, and its use generally has been confined to small plans. This funding arrangement is being phased out, and existing plans must convert to one of the other arrangements by 31 March 2012. (TQPPs will be ignored for the balance of this analysis.)

- Contract-type corporate pension fund with a trust company, life insurer, etc…

- Fund-type corporate pension fund. A separate legal entity with the same structure as an EPF.

The first two are the traditional arrangements, and the last two financing vehicles were introduced under the Pension Reform Law. The new arrangements have the same funding requirements as the traditional EPFs (to be described below). However, they only can be used for contracted-in plans, and there is no insolvency insurance. Also, the tax treatment of employee contributions, investment income and benefit payments is different.

Minimum Funding Requirements

Traditional minimum funding requirements were undemanding. Past service liabilities and actuarial losses could be amortised over a minimum of 7 years and a maximum of 20 years.

- In 1997, the 7-year minimum amortisation period was reduced to three years.

- Also in 1997, a solvency test was introduced. If the value of accumulated assets is less than 105% of the termination liabilities of the contracted-out portion or 90% of the termination liabilities of total plan benefits, the shortfall must be eliminated within a maximum period of 7 years.

- However, if the plan is severely underfunded and the employer is in financial distress, it is possible to reduce benefits. Conditions for reducing benefits include approval by two-thirds of the plan participants and agreement of the labour union.

- Following further downturns in the stock market, the government introduced temporary relaxations of the minimum funding requirements, including a possible two-year suspension of deficit amortisations and an extension of the 7-year maximum amortisation period to 10 years.

- Prior to 1997, the discount rate for calculating liabilities was prescribed. Now, the fund can decide its discount rate. The government only implies a rate within the range of 80% to 120% of the average yield of 10-year government bonds issued during the previous five years.

Customary funding practices

Actuarial valuations are performed on both an ongoing plan basis and a plan discontinuance basis. Various actuarial costing methods are allowed. However, the minimum funding tests described in the previous section are the dominant consideration.

Maximum funding limits

Although somewhat academic at the present time, there is an upper limit on the funding of pension liabilities. The prescribed amount is the greater of 150% of actuarial liabilities calculated under the customary funding valuation (see previous paragraph) and 150% of the actuarial liabilities calculated using a minimum interest rate specified by the regulator. When the fund assets exceed this limit, the plan sponsor is required to reduce or suspend contributions.

Frequency of actuarial valuations

Full actuarial valuations are required to be performed at least every five years.

Bankruptcy of plan sponsor

Whatever the circumstances, the windup of a pension plan entails the allocation among the non-retired participants of the remaining fund assets, after deduction of the amounts necessary to pay benefits to current pensioners. In the case of a continuing employer, the remaining unfunded benefits for non-retired employees usually would be paid directly by the employer at the time of each employee's retirement or termination of employment (effectively, on a pay-as-you-go basis). In the case of an insolvent employer, there is a termination insurance program covering Employees' Pension Funds (EPFs), but it covers at most only about 30% of the contracted-in portion of EPFs and it does not cover the other types of pension funds.

Termination of an overfunded plan

The entire surplus assets would be allocated among the plan participants.

Who appoints the actuary?

Pension funds (in the case of EPFs and Fund-Type plans) or plan sponsors make actuarial service contracts with third party actuarial service providers recognised by the regulator (the MHLW). Each of these recognised service providers must employ at least one licensed pension actuary within the company. Qualification of a pension actuary is decided by the MHLW, based on experience and capabilities.

Role of the actuary

The licensed pension actuary performs the roles of (a) confirming the actuarial calculations performed by the pension fund or plan sponsor and (b) certifying the validity and appropriateness of the actuarial documents submitted by the pension fund or plan sponsor to the Minister.

NETHERLANDS

Supervisory Control.

The supervisory rules regarding pensions are laid down in the Pension Act and the regulations based upon this act. This act and these regulations which came into force on 1 January 2007, with the exclusion of some transitional arrangements. The primary supervisory body is the Dutch Central bank (DNB).

Minimum Funding Requirements (historical basis)

Until 1999, the Dutch funding standards focused on the so-called "65-x" method, with 65 being the assumed normal retirement age and "x" being the plan member's current age. The objective was to ensure full funding by age 65, and the effect was to amortize the remaining costs over the period until age 65. The accrued and projected liabilities were calculated using a discount rate of 4% p.a., with no allowance for future salary increases, employee turnover, etc. The 4% discount rate was in effect for a very long time, including periods when interest rates were much higher (but adjustments were then possible).

New legislation then outlawed the 65-x method and introduced a new minimum funding standard. It required the market value of the assets to equal or exceed the accrued liabilities. A ten-year transition period was established, but "full funding" would thereafter be required at all times. On the liabilities side, this meant full and immediate funding of the effects of salary increases, pension indexing and retroactive plan improvements. On the assets side, it meant full and immediate correction of poor investment results. Notwithstanding the ten-year transition, the regulator began paying close attention to plans that were less than 100% funded on the above basis.

Minimum funding requirements (effective 1 January 2007)

Assets and liabilities have to be valued at market value.

Accrued liabilities are calculated on a unit credit base, without allowance for the effects of future salary increases on accrued benefits. The DNB stipulates the term structure of risk free interest rates used to discount the liabilities. During a short transitional period, pension funds may use a simplified method, based on the spot rate of appropriate duration.

"Conditional benefits", such as non-guaranteed increases to pensions-in-payment and to accrued benefits of present and former members, do not have to be included in the liability calculations for the required funding level.

Pension funds are required to achieve a coverage ratio sufficient to meet nominal obligations with a 97.5 percent probability. This level is determined in the so-called "solvency test". There are three alternative methods to perform a solvency test.

In the standardized method the level is a function of (a) the interest rate risk, (b) the equity and real estate risk, (c) the foreign exchange risk, (d) the commodity risk, (e) the credit risk and (f) the underwriting risk, taking into account possible correlation between interest rate and variable-yield securities risks. In practice, this implies a coverage ratio of 125–130 percent for an average pension fund.

A "simplified method" is available (a) when the plan is simple and unambiguous, (b) the funding ratio is at least 130% and (c) the strategic asset mix involves less than 25% of the fund being invested in variable-yield securities. An "internal model method" (an internal capital adequacy model) is allowed for large and sophisticated funds, but the requirements for following this route are demanding.

A pension fund must conduct the "solvency test" yearly and a "continuity analysis" at least every three years. The aim of the continuity analysis is to assess the financial position of the plan against the background of realistic long-term scenarios and related risks.

If the coverage ratio is less than the required level, the required level should be restored within a period agreed on with the supervisor not exceeding 15 years. A coverage ratio below 105 percent has to be restored within three years, subject to certain conditions. Otherwise, the coverage ratio of 105 percent has to be restored within one year. The Minister of Social Affairs and Employment can extend these periods in times of severe macroeconomic downturns or systemic risk.

Customary funding practices

Up to 2006 the majority of Dutch pension funds used to focus on the traditional 4% interest rate without taking future salary increases into account.

However, this will all change under the new supervisory regime from 1 January 2007. Some funds already perform actuarial funding valuations using independently explicit assumptions, *i.e.* a market-related discount rate and explicit allowances for future salary increases, employee turnover, early and disability retirements, etc… The Projected Unit Credit method is already widely used in this context, with the calculations also being used to support pension expensing requirements.

Maximum funding limits

There are no maximum funding levels.

Frequency of actuarial valuations

Valuations are required to be performed every year.

Bankruptcy of plan sponsor

Whether the plan is over funded or underfunded, the entire assets of the fund are allocated between the plan members. There is no government insurance program to cover shortfalls, although regulation of ongoing plans is focused on constant avoidance of any such under funding.

Termination of an over funded plan

The entire assets are allocated between the plan members. In other words, each plan member receives an appropriate share of the funding excess. Regarding the termination of an over funded plan the Pension Act stipulates:

- the performance agreement which has to be concluded between employer and the pension implementer must (among others) include the premises and procedures applicable in relation to the decision-making on capital deficits and capital surpluses or profit-sharing (article 25, paragraph 1, point g);
- the pension fund will allow the participants council to give advice on any proposed resolution of the pension fund for (among others): liquidation of the pension fund (article 111, paragraph 2, point g.

Who appoints the actuary?

The board of the pension fund appoints the actuary. This board generally is comprised of an equal number of employee and employer representatives.

Role of the actuary

The Pension Act stipulates the following provisions regarding the roles of the actuary:

Article 147

The actuary authenticates the actuarial statements, including an actuarial report accompanied by an actuary's statement, which the pension fund, as part of the periodic statements has to be submitted to the supervisor (DNB). The actuary will confirm that he/she has ascertained to his/her satisfaction that the provisions in the Pension Act are met regarding:

- the determination of technical provisions;
- the financing of old-age pension
- the amount of cost-covering premium
- the restitution or premium reduction
- the statement of premium in annual accounts and annual report
- the minimum required own funds
- the required own funds
- the coverage by assets
- the reduction of pension claims and pension rights by pension fund
- the investment-related requirements
- the loans
- the financing provisional granting of supplements
- the long-term recovery plan
- the major changes during performance of long-term recovery plan
- the short-term recovery plan

Article 148

The competent actuary authenticating the actuarial report will be independent of the pension fund and will perform no other work for the pension fund.

Article 170

The actuary performing the audit of the statements will disclose to the supervisory body as quickly as possible any circumstance of which he/she learns in the performance of the audit and which:

a. is in contravention of this act;

b. threatens the fulfilment of the obligations undertaken by the pension fund; or

c. will lead to the refusal to issue the statement concerning the reliability or to reservations being made.

The auditor or actuary will provide to the supervisory body, as quickly as possible and at no cost, all information it may reasonably require for the supervision of the compliance with this act. The supervisory body will grant the pension fund the opportunity to be present at the provision of information by the auditor or actuary.

At the request of the supervisory body, the auditor or actuary will provide the supervisory body with the records of the audit activities."

NORWAY

Supervisory Control

The majority of the occupational Norwegian pension plans are insured, and they are regulated and supervised as far as possible in line with insurance companies. A small number of the largest plans hold around 25% of overall pension fund assets in *'pensjonskasser'*, a form of independent trust regulated by the Financial Supervisory Authority. The minimum funding rules are contained in the 1988 Insurance Activity Act. The 1956 Financial Supervision Act provides for the supervision by the Financial Supervisory Authority (FSA) of financial institutions such as pension funds and insurance companies. This Act also defines the powers of the FAS and requires auditors to notify the FSA of special events (whistle-blowing). Pension funds must register with the FSA, and this registration is subject to authorisation of the plan rules.

Minimum Funding Requirements

Separate from the regular minimum funding requirement, each *pensjonkasse* must comply with a minimum capital standard defined by the Ministry of Finance. It is the same for both insurance companies and pension funds and equals 8% of the total of risk-weighted asset items and off-balance sheet items. In addition, the capital base of pension funds must exceed a certain Norwegian Krone threshold that is adjusted on a yearly basis according to changes in the Consumer Price Index. From 1998 an additional requirement was introduced that pension funds should have financial strength to be able to absorb an adverse development in the financial markets of a certain order.

All pension plans, whether defined contribution or defined benefit, and whether financed through insurance contracts or a *pensjonkasse*, must be administered on an individual allocation basis. The minimum reserves held for each plan member in a *pensjonskasse* should equal the value of that member's accrued benefits (but without allowance under final-salary plans for the effects of future salary increases on such accrued benefits). If the annual report reveals underfunding, or underfunding is revealed in some other way, the pension fund shall immediately take the necessary actions to regain full funding. Legislation does not, however, indicate the length of the time period within which full funding should be achieved. Deficits arising from wage increases are assumed to be spread equally over the remaining time to retirement.

The maximum permissible technical interest rate for calculating liabilities and contributions is 4% per annum. If the pension fund was established after 1993, the maximum technical interest rate is 3% pa. Furthermore, the maximum rate of interest is 3% for all contributions (premiums) due after 1 January 2004, even for insurance contracts and pension funds established prior to 1993, and for the technical provisions derived from these premiums. Fund assets are taken at market value.

Premium Fund and Other Reserves

In addition to the payment of regular premiums, and with the objective of smoothing the funding, the tax authorities allow tax-deductible payments into a so-called "Premium Fund". The annual payment to the Premium Fund cannot exceed 50% of the average annual premium during the last three years, and the accumulated amount in the Premium Fund should not exceed six times the regular annual premium. Any excess must be refunded to the plan sponsor. The main application of the premium fund is paying future contributions, thus helping plan sponsors through difficult economic times.

Legislation also allows for the accumulation of additional provisions, up to a maximum of 8 per cent of the regular mathematical reserves. Then, if the return on fund assets falls short of the interest rate for discounting liabilities, these additional provisions can be used to compensate for the shortfall and thus maintain the prescribed level of mathematical reserves.

Customary funding practices

All regular actuarial calculations employ one or other of the following methods.

- **Level annual premium method.** Benefits are funded by charging a level annual premium over the active service period, based on current salaries. Each subsequent increase in projected benefits (arising from salary increase etc.) is charged over the subsequent future service period by further series of level annual premiums. Historically, this was the traditional method.

- **Current unit method.** Benefits are funded as they are accrued, again without any allowance under final-salary plans for the effects of future salary increases on such accrued benefits. Premiums for the following year reflect both the cost of purchasing an additional year of pension accrual plus, if applicable, the cost of updating past accruals to current salary levels. Effective from January 1, 2001, the current unit method replaces the level annual premium method in the majority of pension plans.

There are no other prescribed actuarial assumptions, but the basis of valuation for pension funds (also including mortality, disability and expenses assumptions) must be approved by the Financial Supervisory Authority. A valuation basis which is not prudent will not be approved. Generally used actuarial assumptions are as follows:

- **Economic assumptions:** No further assumptions are made regarding future pension increases or the effects of future salary increases. The discount rate has already been discussed.

- **Demographic assumptions:** The demographic assumptions used in all calculations are usually chosen according to standard tables. The assumptions have to be approved by the supervisory authority. The standard tables currently being used are the IR73 tables (disability) and K63 tables (old age and death).

- **Allowance for expenses.** A separate allowance normally is made for the administration expenses associated with operating the pension plan and fund.

Maximum funding limits

No maximum funding rules apply.

Frequency of actuarial valuations

Pension funds must submit annually to the FSA a standard report prepared by the appointed actuary. The contents of this report must conform to the guidelines set down by the supervisory authorities. Funds must also produce a report proving compliance with the capital standard requirement and providing certain statistics on their operations. The Financial Supervisory Authority recommends that an actuarial valuation is performed more frequently, at least semi-annually.

Bankruptcy of plan sponsor

There is no requirement to insure against financial loss, and no compensation fund exists. In the case of bankruptcy of the plan sponsor when the fund has insufficient assets, the fund (and, thus, the plan members) will normally be among the creditors in the legal sense and its claims will be handled by the court as a part of the overall bankruptcy treatment. The fund itself, being a separate legal entity, is protected from creditors. It should be noted that there have not yet been any cases of a bankrupt plan sponsor with an underfunded plan, presumably due to the stringent funding requirements.

Termination of an overfunded plan

Detailed legal rules govern the conditions under which a plan may be wound up and the resultant allocation of plan assets. When a terminated plan is overfunded, the surplus assets normally are applied to enhance members' benefits.

Who appoints the actuary?

All institutions administering pension plans must appoint an auditor and an actuary. The actuary is appointed by the board of the pension fund, but he/she must be explicitly approved by the FSA.

Role of the actuary

The roles, duties and rights of actuaries are laid down in the law. The calculations performed by actuaries for self-administered pension funds include:

- calculation of the pension fund's contingency reserve;
- calculation of the premium rates (tariffs) and resultant pension plan contributions;
- calculations for accounting purposes;
- calculation of the value of the pension rights when an employer or group of employees terminates the pension contract;
- calculation of transfer values in the case of bulk transfers arising from company takeovers or mergers.

PORTUGAL

Supervisory Control

Occupational pension plans are supervised by the insurance supervisory authority, *o Instituto de Seguros de Portugal* (ISP). Pension funds assets must be held and managed by a pension fund manager, which can be either an insurance company or a pension fund management company. The primary legislation governing the operation of pension plans and funds is Decree Law n° 475/99 of 9 November 1999.

Minimum Funding Requirements

Minimum funding requirements are established by the ISP. The basic objective of the minimum funding standards is for the assets to exceed the accrued liabilities. For these purposes:

- Assets are taken at fair market value.
- Accrued liabilities are equal to the sum of (a) the present value of accrued liabilities of non-retired members, calculated using the current unit credit method without salary projection, and (b) the present value of pensions-in-payment to retirees and other beneficiaries.
- Pensions of non-retired members are assumed to commence at normal retirement age, although an adjustment must be made for plans that provide subsidised early retirement benefits.
- The TV 73/77 mortality table must be used.
- The discount rate is $4\frac{1}{2}\%$ pa.
- No assumptions are permitted regarding disability or employee turnover.
- If indexing of pensions is contractually guaranteed, then an allowance for the effect of future indexing must be included in the calculation of the accrued liabilities.

In the event the fund assets are less than the value of pensions already in payment, the pension fund manager shall instruct the plan sponsor to contribute the necessary funds. The pension fund manager must issue this notice within 15 days of verifying that there are insufficient assets, and the plan sponsor then has 180 days following the notice in which to make the necessary contributions. If the contributions are not made, the fund shall be wound up. Furthermore, the pension fund manager may only pay new pensions under the plan if the fund assets are equal to or exceed the present value of both the pensions currently in payment and the new pensions due – calculated according to assumptions set out in the minimum funding regulations. This constraint does not apply when a funding program already has been approved by the ISP.

In the event the fund assets are less than the total accrued liabilities, and the shortfall is not immediately addressed through additional contributions, the pension fund manager shall propose the correction of this situation to the plan sponsor. If no suitable funding plan has been drawn up within one year, the pension fund manager should wind up the fund in accordance with procedures laid down by the ISP.

Customary funding practices

Customary funding practices are established by legislation, the actuarial profession and the ISP. It is established practice that the interest rate used in the calculations should be chosen in a prudent way, taking into account any adverse fluctuations. Additional constraints apply to pension plans in the banking sector, where the law specifies maximum permissible spreads between the discount rate and the salary and indexing assumptions. Otherwise, the following observations can be made:

- The most common actuarial funding methods are Projected Unit Credit and Attained Age.

- It is normal to use the same mortality table for females and males.

- The appointed actuary establishes the economic and demographic assumptions, taken into account the general ISP rules.

- The minimum funding requirement is a funding constraint, rather than a funding objective.

- Fund assets are taken at market value.

- Amortisation periods for unfunded liabilities and experience deficiencies are to be agreed with the ISP. Regulations only establish a maximum amortisation period of 20 years for unfunded liabilities at plan inception, but most amortisation periods do not exceed 10-15 years. The funding requirements for the banking sector are strict and more prescriptive.

- In the event of a shortfall due to plan improvements or experience losses, the appointed actuary proposes the amortisation period. This will be analysed by the ISP on a case-by-case basis and usually varies between 3 and 10 years.

- Disability and death-in-service benefits may be insured, in which case the annual insurance premium will be added to the current service cost for the retirement benefits. Even if these benefits are not (re)insured, the actuary may still cost them on an annual "risk premium" basis.

Maximum funding limits

There are no *direct* limits on the maximum amount of assets that can be held in a pension fund, but there are limits on employer contributions for tax purposes. Employer contributions to plans that do not provide pre-retirement vesting are only tax deductible up to a limit of 15% of annual payroll (25% if the employees are not covered by social security). Employer contributions to plans that do provide pre-retirement vesting are fully tax deductible. In an overfunding situation, the plan sponsor can reduce or suspend contributions. A plan sponsor can request prior approval for a return of surplus, which will only be possible if the surplus exists for structural reasons over five consecutive years and annually exceeds a set percentage of the accrued liabilities, whilst maintaining a minimum funding percentage in accordance with ISP regulations.

Frequency of actuarial valuations

Valuations are required to be performed at least every three years, but in practice are performed annually.

Bankruptcy of plan sponsor

In the event of the bankruptcy of the plan sponsor and the subsequent termination of an underfunded plan, the fund assets are allocated among the plan members in accordance with a set of priorities defined in law. They are:

- Members' individual accounts (under contributory plans);
- Pensions-in-payment;
- Pensions for members of an age equal to or greater than normal retirement age;
- Vested rights of members existing at the time of the plan wind-up;
- Accrued pensions not covered by the previous paragraphs;
- Contractual indexing of pensions-in-payment.

Termination of an overfunded plan

Once all vested and non-vested accrued benefits have been guaranteed, the allocation of any excess assets is decided jointly between the pension fund manager and the plan sponsor and requires prior approval from the ISP. Whenever the excess assets result from a drastic reduction in the number of non-vested plan members, such assets first shall be used to guarantee accrued pensions for such ex-members. If it is decided that surplus assets are to revert to the plan sponsor, a special tax will be applied unless the plan sponsors proves that the surplus is due to a cessation of labor contracts, previously accepted by the Directorate General of Taxation.

Who appoints the actuary?

The pension fund manager shall appoint an *appointed actuary* for each defined benefit or hybrid pension plan when submitting an application to incorporate a closed pension fund or add a new group of members to an existing open pension fund. The appointed actuary shall be chosen from a list of approved actuaries who comply with the conditions laid down by the ISP.

Role of the actuary

In addition to preparing the annual actuarial report, the appointed actuary is required to verify:

- the actuarial calculations and the pension plan's funding level;
- the suitability of the technical and actuarial funding plan;
- the present value of the *total* liabilities (for the purposes of determining whether there is any funding excess); and
- the suitability of the nature of the fund assets in relation to the pension plan liabilities (an assessment required periodically by the ISP and in accordance with its regulations).

The duties of the appointed actuary are described in more detail in Regulation 06/2004-R.

SPAIN

Supervisory Control

Occupational pension plans are supervised by the General Directorate of Insurance and Pension Funds, which is part of the Ministry of Economy.

Regulatory Framework

Royal Decree 1/2002 consolidates the Pension Plan and Pension Funds Law of 1987 (*Ley de Planes y Fondos de Pensiones*) and all its modifications. It regulates the establishment of pension plans, pension funds and pension fund management entities, defines maximum contribution limits and includes measures concerning protection of rights. These issues have been further developed by the Royal Decree 304/2004 that endorses the Pension Plans and Pension Funds Regulations and repeals the prior Royal Decree 1307/1988. The 1999 Royal Decree on the implementation of employers' pension agreements with employees and beneficiaries (*Reglamento sobre la instrumentación de los compromisos por pensiones de las empresas con los trabajadores y beneficiarios*), based on the Insurance Law of 1995 (*Ley de Ordenación y Supervisión de los Seguros Privados*), requires plan sponsors to implement occupational pension agreements through group insurance contracts and/or the creation of a pension fund. The decree also restricts the establishment of book reserves to certain occupational pension agreements in the financial sector and provides for transitional arrangements for pre-existing plans.

Statutory Funding Requirements

Pension plans must follow an actuarially recognised capitalisation funding method. The funding must be on an individual, fully allocated basis. Funding requirements include the following:

- Assets must be sufficient to cover the accumulated benefit obligation.
- The valuation methods for fund assets differ by asset class. With some exceptions, assets are taken at their fair or market value.
- A minimum solvency margin requirement applies. It is 4% of actuarial liabilities in the case of defined benefit plans and 4% of accumulated contributions in the case of defined contribution plans that provide a guaranteed rate of return. There is also an additional requirement of

0.3% of death and disability lump sums. There is a minimum, overall solvency margin.

- The two actuarial costing methods approved by the 21st July 1990 regulation are the Individual Entry Age method and the Projected Unit Credit method. The latter has been the most commonly adopted, but other methods are now growing in popularity.

- The maximum discount rate for calculating liabilities is 4% per annum. Other economic assumptions affecting the benefits (*e.g.* salary inflation, price inflation) should be appropriate when considered in conjunction with the choice of discount rate.

- The mortality and morbidity tables must be based on local or foreign experience that is no more than 20 years old at the valuation date and projected using recognised actuarial techniques. For plans existing on 1 November 2000, the generation tables PERM/F -2000 C is recommended, with the possibility of a ten year transition to its full adoption. For new plans, PERM/F 2000 P tables are acceptable. It should also be possible to use GRM/F-95 tables. Another alternative is to use tables that are based on the actual experience of the pension plan population; strict conditions are imposed.

The time period over which shortfalls must be corrected is not currently specified, although new rules are expected to be issued on this matter in the near future.

Maximum funding limits

No maximum funding rules apply. In the case of an overfunded position, the plan rules specify how the excess assets will be allocated. The current practice is to reduce the plan sponsor's contributions or to increase the members´ benefits.

Frequency of actuarial valuations

Actuarial valuations are required every three years from all defined benefit plans and from defined contribution plans that provide a guaranteed rate of return. However, those plans that require a solvency margin to be set aside (basically, all non-insured plans) must perform annual valuations.

Bankruptcy of plan sponsor

In the case of the bankruptcy of the plan sponsor, the plan members have the right to their accrued vested benefits. In case of a defined benefit plan, the vested right will be adjusted and reduced depending on the existing "Technical Provision and the Solvency Margin" at the time of the bankruptcy of the plan sponsor. Insolvency insurance protection is not required, and no compensation fund exists.

Termination of an overfunded plan

If a plan is terminated with surplus funds, these will be distributed to the plan members and beneficiaries in proportion to their vested rights. The same rules apply whether the plan is terminated as a result of the sponsoring employer ceases its activities or the plan's approval is revoked. Under certain circumstances, the General Directorate of Insurance and Pension Funds may take part in the winding up of a plan and/or a fund, in order to ensure the protection of rights.

Who appoints the actuary?

The actuary is appointed by the Control Commission of the pension plan. The actuary must be independent and comply with legally established professional requirements. The regulator currently does not maintain a register of approved actuaries, so regulation is through the actuarial association.

Role of the actuary

The roles of the actuary include recommendations concerning assumptions, the resultant valuation of the pension plans´ liabilities and funded ratio, and contribution requirements.

SWITZERLAND

Supervisory Control

Each canton designates an authority that supervises the pension institutions headquartered in that canton. The federal government directly supervises pension institutions that have a national or international character, as well as certain other pension institutions such as those of the federal government and the national bank. The federal social insurance office oversees the 26 cantonal supervisory authorities.

Switzerland has extensive legislation concerning the design and operation of pension plans. The first focus of this legislation is on the mandatory benefits, whereby all employers must provide second pillar pensions for their employees. The minimum contributions are age-related and cover a specific slice of salary. The interest rate credited to such contributions is set by the government; it was 4% pa for many years, but has since fluctuated (reaching a low of 2.25% in 2004). The annuity conversion rate is also specified. It also has been changed in recent years, as a result both of declining interest rates and increased longevity. Mandatory death and disability benefits are also specified. In summary, mandatory pension plans are classified as defined benefit plans for actuarial purposes, and they do indeed require the preparation and submission of actuarial valuation reports. The legislation on mandatory pension is known as BVG in German and LPP in French. Many employers sponsor defined benefit or defined contribution pension plans providing higher benefits than those required under the mandatory pension legislation. It is then necessary to maintain BVG/LPP shadow accounts, to ensure that each member receives at least the mandatory benefit (whether on death, disability or retirement).

Minimum Funding Requirements

The main funding requirements are documented in the 1984 Ordinance BVV2/OPP2, as subsequently amended. Prior to 2005, pension funds were required to fully fund their liabilities at all times, but new regulations now allow plans to be underfunded for a limited time. Highlights of the new regulations are:

- For the purposes of determining the funded position, the liabilities must *include* the asset fluctuation reserves. The assets must *exclude* any employer contribution reserve (see below), unless the employer has renounced the use of such reserves.

- Subject to guidance from the appointed actuary, the pension fund sets the method for determining its technical reserves and its asset fluctuation reserves. The methodology cannot subsequently be changed without good reason.

- Whatever the degree of underfunding, the supervisory authority must immediately be notified of the size of the deficit and explain how the deficit arose.

- In normal situations, a funded ratio of at least 90% is deemed not to present serious problems and not to require immediate remedial action.

- In contrast, a funded ratio of less than 90% is deemed to be "important", and a program to eliminate the underfunding must be established. An amortisation period of 5-7 years would generally be deemed reasonable. An amortisation period exceeding ten years is not allowed.

- Such special "recapitalisation contributions", whether paid entirely by the employer or by both the employer and the employees, will not vest when the employee subsequently leaves the plan.

- In the case of serious underfunding, and if the plan rules allow, more drastic measures can now be contemplated. Such potential actions can include reduction or elimination of interest credits and reduction of future benefit accruals.

- In the case of serious underfunding of a plan with a large proportion of pensioners, temporary contributions from the pensioners themselves also can be required. Understandably, the conditions for taking such drastic actions are strict.

Customary funding practices

The actuary works with the plan sponsor to develop a sound funding program. The traditional approach to calculating accrued and projected liabilities involved using a discount rate of around 3.5%-4.5%, with no allowance for the effects of future salary increases, no employee turnover assumptions, etc… However, many plans now use explicit assumptions concerning interest rates, future salary growth, employee turnover, early retirement and disability decrements, etc… There are various approaches to the valuation of the fund assets.

The regulator is primarily concerned that the employer contribution rate will be sufficient, together with future employee contributions and existing fund assets, to fund all the prospective obligations. In some defined benefit plans, the employer's contribution rate is set in the plan rules or is constrained in some other fashion. Overfunding is then defined as the excess of the fund assets and the present value of future contributions over the projected liabilities. Thus, two different plans with identical fund assets and accrued liabilities can be deemed overfunded or underfunded depending solely on the prescribed (or otherwise established) levels of their future contributions. A plan deemed underfunded on this basis can still have fund assets that exceed the accrued liabilities, and vice versa.

It should also be noted that the plan sponsor cannot contribute less than the employees. This is a cumulative test. If the plan maintains an "employer contribution reserve" that is credited with employer contributions in excess of employee contributions, then any credit in the reserve can be used in subsequent years to reduce employer contributions below the level of employee contributions.

Maximum funding limits

There are no direct limits on maximum funding. However, there are now upper limits on the benefits that can be provided under pension plans and the contributions that can be made to such plans. There is also now a maximum on the annual salary that can be recognised for pension purposes, although the limit is high (SFr 744,000 in 2005). The Swiss tax authorities can withdraw tax exemption from contributions to overfunded plans, but there is a certain margin before considering a plan as overfunded for these purposes. Anyway, given that it is impossible to return any funding excess to the plan sponsor, overfunding is not a sound philosophy for most employers.

Frequency of actuarial valuations

Valuations are usually performed every three years, although larger plans may conduct annual valuations. Pension expensing requirements are also pushing plan sponsors towards annual valuations.

Bankruptcy of plan sponsor

Whether the plan is overfunded or underfunded, the entire assets of the fund are allocated between the plan members. There is a guarantee fund which covers any shortfalls in case of sponsor or pension fund bankruptcy, but with an upper limit on the insured benefits payable to an individual plan member.

Termination of an overfunded plan

The entire assets are allocated between the plan members. In other words, each plan member receives an appropriate share of the funding excess. As already indicated, there are no circumstances under which excess assets can revert to the plan sponsor.

Who appoints the actuary?

The board of foundation appoints the actuary. However, unless constrained by the plan rules, funding decisions are within the control of the plan sponsor. In this important regard, one can say that the actuary also works for the plan sponsor.

Role of the actuary

The primary roles of actuary are (a) to advise on future funding requirements and (b) to certify to the regulator that plan's funding is sufficient to meet its obligations.

UNITED KINGDOM

Supervisory Control

As a result of changes introduced by the Pensions Act 2004, a new pension regulatory authority named "The Pensions Regulator" (TPR) has been created. It has more powers than the Occupational Pensions Regulatory Authority (OPRA) which it replaced.

Important developments in 2004-2005

The Pensions Act 2004 also introduced the concept of a new funding standard to replace the Minimum Funding Requirement (MFR). Implementation of the new standard (summarised below) was twice delayed, but eventually came into force on 30 December 2005. The final "Regulatory Code of Practice" (n°3) then was issued by TPR and became effective on 15 February 2006. As there is an inevitable transition period from the MFR to the new "Statutory Funding Objective", and because the MFR provides some interesting lessons for everyone, descriptions of both approaches are provided.

Trustee/plan sponsor agreement under the new funding legislation

The trustees are responsible for the overall management of the valuation process, although the trustees normally must reach agreement with the plan sponsor on certain key funding matters. The legislation requiring the employer's agreement is modified where the plan rules give someone other than the employer the power to determine the contribution rate, as follows:

- If the trustees have the power, unrestrained by conditions, to determine the contribution rate and no other person has the power to reduce or suspend contributions – the trustees are required to consult the plan sponsor but the plan sponsor's agreement is not required.

- If the trustees have the power, subject to certain conditions, to determine the contribution rate and no other person has the power to reduce or suspend contributions – and if such conditions are satisfied – the trustees are required to consult the plan sponsor but the plan sponsor's agreement is not required.

- If the contribution rate is determined by, or on the advice of, a person other than the trustees or the plan sponsor (usually the actuary) – the trustees must obtain the plan sponsor's agreement. They must take into account the recommendations of the other person on the method and assumptions for calculating the technical provisions and on the preparation of any recovery plan.

New Funding Legislation

Part 3 of the Pensions Act 2004 requires every occupational pension plan to adopt a "Statutory Funding Objective" aimed at ensuring that the plan has "sufficient and appropriate assets to cover its technical provisions". Highlights of this legislation include:

- The trustees are required to set out the funding principles in a document to be made available to the plan members. The document should identify the statutory funding objective and a policy on how to eliminate any funding deficit, including the period over which this is to be achieved.

- Under the MFR legislation, the old regulator (OPRA) had the power to extend the period for funding a deficit. There is no comparable provision under the new legislation.

- The regulations do not prescribe the actuarial valuation assumptions to be used. Similarly, the regulations do not prescribe the actuarial cost method, although it must be an accrued benefits funding method (projected unit credit, partially projected unit credit, current unit credit or discontinuance basis). "It is for the trustees to determine which method and assumptions are to be used in calculating the scheme's technical provisions. This is another matter on which they must take advice from their actuary and reach agreement with the employer."

- The individual economic and actuarial assumptions should be chosen prudently. The trustee must consider whether, and to what extent, account should be taken of a margin for adverse deviation. However, the legislation does not require technical provisions to be set so conservatively as to match the level needed to buy out the accrued liabilities from an insurance company.

- The trustees should aim for any funding shortfall to be eliminated as quickly as the plan sponsor can reasonably afford. In preparing a recovery plan to address a funding shortfall, the trustees (in consultation with the plan sponsor) also must take into account the asset and liability structure of the plan, its risk profile, its liquidity requirements and the age profile of the members.

- If the trustees cannot obtain the agreement of the plan sponsor on one or more funding matters (most specifically, contribution increases), the trustees - with the employer's agreement - can reduce or otherwise modify the plan's future benefit accruals.

Previous Minimum Funding Requirements (MFR)

The basic objective of the existing "Minimum Funding Requirement" (MFR) is that fund assets should be sufficient to cover, in the event of plan termination:

(a) for pensioners, the purchase of insurance company annuities; and

(b) for those who have not retired, the payment of an amount which, on transfer to another pension arrangement, would give individuals a reasonable expectation of receiving their plan retirement pension.

The actuarial assumptions to be used are prescribed in considerable detail. The calculations are complex, and there have been many criticisms of the MFR in recent years. Although the government intends to abolish the MFR, it is worth reviewing the standard in order to learn lessons for the future and for other countries.

For these MFR purposes:

- Assets are taken at realisable market value.

- The accrued liabilities are valued using the current unit credit method.

- Accrued benefits for active employees are calculated on the assumption of immediate termination of employment (accrued, vested rights).

- There are complicated rules on the "MFR pension age", *i.e.* the age at which pension payments are assumed to commence.

- If partial cash commutation is permitted at retirement, then the calculations should assume the member exercises this option to the maximum allowed.

- Allowance must be made for discretionary benefits already granted (*e.g.* ad hoc pension indexing), but there must not be any allowance for future discretionary benefits.

- The discount rate for valuing pensions-in-payment is the prevailing market yield on UK government securities (gilts). However, pensioner liabilities in excess of £100 million may be valued using the assumed long term return for UK equities (plus the market value adjustment factor – see below).

- For the period up to retirement, the discount rate for valuing the pension rights of members who have not yet retired is broadly the assumed long-term return on equities. For the ten years up to MFR pension age, the discount rate gradually moves from the equity return to the gilt return. For the period after retirement, the discount rate is the assumed long-term return on gilts. A "market value adjustment" factor then is applied to the resultant liabilities, to reflect prevailing UK equity dividend yields. This market value adjustment factor in relation to equities is the ratio of 3.00% to the current dividend yield on the FTSE Actuaries All-Share Index.

- Pre-retirement and post-retirement mortality is generally to be determined in accordance with the PA(90) standard mortality table, rated down two years.

- Other assumptions are prescribed in some detail.

- There should be an allowance for termination expenses. The formula is prescribed.

In the event of a shortfall (assets less than accrued liabilities), additional contributions must be made to the fund such that:

- the fund assets reach at least 90% of the MFR level within three years (formerly, one year).

- the fund assets reach at least 100% of the MFR level within ten years (formerly, five years).

The plan actuary, as part of the regular valuation (see below), also is required to make a statement regarding the adequacy of the fund assets to meet its liabilities if the plan were to be discontinued. This should not be confused with the MFR.

Customary funding practices

There are no government constraints in this area. The actuary works in accordance with the requirements of his profession. In particular, generally accepted valuation methods for pension plan actuarial valuations are set out in "Actuarial Guidance Note GN26".

- Pension plan liabilities are generally calculated on the assumption that the plan is ongoing.

- The most common actuarial valuation method is now Projected Unit Credit, prompted in large part by the accounting standards for pension costs in company accounts. Historically, the objective has been a stable future funding rate, in the form of a level percentage of salary. Thus, Aggregate, Attained Age and Entry Age methods were more common, and they are still sometimes used. The minimum funding standard uses the Current Unit method and the maximum funding method uses the Projected Unit Credit method.

- The method of calculating the actuarial liability for pensions-in-payment and deferred pensions is common to all the funding methods.

- There must be an explicit allowance for future expenses that are a responsibility of the fund.

- The actuary establishes the economic and demographic assumptions in accordance with standard actuarial practices and unconstrained by government regulations.

- Disability and death-in-service benefits may be insured, in which case the annual insurance premium will be added to the current service cost for the retirement benefits. Even if these benefits are not insured or reinsured, the actuary may still cost them on an annual "risk premium" basis. In this regard, it is important to understand that most UK pension plans provide large lump sum death-in-service benefits that are not a function of accrued pensionable service.

- The MFR was deemed to be a funding constraint, rather than a funding objective. Clearly, the maximum funding limitation also is a funding constraint.

- Fund assets are now usually taken at market value, although other approaches are still used.

- These valuations serve as the basis for claiming employer tax deductions.

Maximum funding limits

The Inland Revenue (tax authorities) imposes strict limits on the maximum amount of assets that can be held in a pension fund without the loss of tax advantages. In simple terms, the assets should not exceed 105% of the accrued liabilities (as calculated under the projected unit credit method). The key actuarial assumptions are prescribed. In the event of assets exceeding the maximum, there are a number of choices available:

- all or part of the excess can be used to reduce or suspend employee or employer contributions during the next five years;
- all or part of the excess can be used to fund retroactive plan improvements;
- any excess still remaining must be withdrawn from the fund (special taxes apply).

The whole issue of maximum funding limits is under review.

Frequency of actuarial valuations

Valuations are generally required to be performed every three years. Under the new regulations, formal actuarial valuations still must be performed at least every three years; however, in the absence of annual valuations, the actuary will be required to produce interim annual actuarial reports.

Bankruptcy of plan sponsor

Under the Pensions Act 2004, and in the event of the bankruptcy of the plan sponsor, the pension fund has the status of an unsecured creditor. Associated parties, such as the UK or non-UK parent company, are required to help fund any deficit, whether on bankruptcy of the plan sponsor or conventional plan termination by a solvent plan sponsor. Any shortfall on plan termination by a not-insolvent plan sponsor will be treated as statutory debt, and the shortfall will be calculated based on the cost of securing indexed immediate and deferred annuities from an insurance company. A government compensation fund, the Pension Protection Fund (PPF) also was introduced as part of the 2004 pension reform.

Termination of an overfunded plan

The plan rules govern the application of excess assets arising in the event of a plan termination. If allowed by these plan rules, excess assets can be refunded to the plan sponsor; in which case, a special tax will be applied.

Who appoints the actuary?

The UK equivalent of the "pension entity" in OECD parlance is the board of trustees. The trustees appoint the plan actuary.

Role of the actuary

The roles of the actuary are (a) to assess the funding level and advise on the contributions needed to achieve and maintain the desired level, (b) to make a statement regarding the MFR, (c) to make a statement regarding the plan's ability to meet plan termination liabilities, (d) to provide a contracting out certificate, where required, (e) to make calculations required for the plan sponsor's commercial accounts, and (f) to provide a statement to the tax authorities regarding the 105% limit. Typically, the plan sponsor and the trustees agree on the employer's future funding rate, based on the advice of the actuary.

The roles of the actuary in regard to the new statutory funding objective include confirmation that the agreed contributions are sufficient to enable the statutory funding objective to be met, or to continue to be met, by the end of the recovery period.

Pursuant to the requirements of Section 230(1) of the Pensions Act 2004, the Faculty and Institute of Actuaries issued a new guidance note (GN 49) on "occupational pension schemes - scheme funding matters on which the advice of an actuary must be obtained". It also revised guidance note GN 9 on "funding defined benefits – presentation of actuarial advice". Both guidance notes became effective on 30 December 2005.

UNITED STATES

Supervisory Control

Funding requirements are enforced by the Internal Revenue Service (IRS), which is part of the U.S. Department of the Treasury. The minimum funding requirements are established under identical provisions in the Internal Revenue Code (IRC) and the Employee Retirement Income Security Act of 1974 (ERISA). Maximum deductible funding constraints are established in the IRC. Customary funding practices are established by the actuarial profession, but are constrained by the minimum and maximum funding limits.

The legislation governing pension plan funding is long and complex. At first glance, it would also appear to be very prescriptive, but there are still some important areas where the actuary has control over the all-important aspects of choosing the actuarial funding method and actuarial assumptions. Given the massive detail in the U.S. legislation, this summary will serve only to highlight the key points and issues.

2005 Pension Funding Reform

Various proposals have been introduced in Congress and by the Bush administration regarding improving the funding position of occupational defined benefit pension plans. Themes running through most of the proposals include:

- Funding deficits would have to be amortised over much shorter periods of time, *e.g.* 7 years.

- With certain exceptions, severely underfunded plans would not be allowed to make plan improvements or otherwise increase benefits. In the same vein, lump sum payments from severely underfunded active plans (and generally underfunded plans of bankrupt employers) would be strictly limited. The underlying objective of these restrictions is to avoid further aggravating the already severe underfunding of such plans.

- Future benefit accruals would be frozen under seriously underfunded plans, *e.g.* plans with a funded ratio of less than 60%.

- "Shut-Down" benefits would be prohibited. These are payments that some pension plans make to long service employees when a plant is shut down. These benefits are typically negotiated between employers and trade unions, and they are generally unfunded. Similarly, other contingent-event benefits would be prohibited.

- The maximum funding limit would be relaxed, and plan sponsors would be allowed to make additional contributions during favourable economic times; *e.g.* the deductible limit could increase to (a) 150%-180% of the *funding target*, plus (b) the target normal cost, less (c) the plan's assets. However, the problem remains that plan sponsors have unattractive choices (*e.g.* special excise taxes) when trying to access any subsequent overfunding.

- "Funding target" is the new phrase that is equivalent to the "current liability" found in existing legislation and described below. The mortality table would be specified. There is considerable ongoing discussion concerning the most appropriate discount rate(s) for calculating such liabilities.

Minimum Funding Requirements

The current minimum funding requirements need to be understood in two parts. The first requirement, which was part of the original 1974 ERISA legislation, requires the establishment of a "***Funding Standard Account***". In simple terms, ignoring the complexities of interest credits and debits, the Funding Standard Account now requires the accumulated payment of at least the following:

- the normal costs (*i.e.* the current service cost under the plan's funding method);

- amortisation over 40 years of the initial unfunded past service liability for plans in existence on 1 January 1974;

- amortisation over 30 years of the cost of plan improvements and of the initial past service liability for plans that were not in existence on 1 January 1974 (even longer amortisation periods can apply to some multi-employer plans);

- amortisation over 10 years of the effects of changes in actuarial assumptions; and

- amortisation over 5 years of experience gains and losses.

For these purposes:

- all the above costs "shall be determined under the funding method used by the actuary to calculate funding costs"; there are few constraints.

- the value of plan assets "shall be determined on the basis of any reasonable actuarial method of valuation that takes into account fair market value and which is permitted under regulations", *i.e.* fair market value or smoothed market value.

References to "**accrued liability**", as opposed to the "current liability" described below, mean the accrued liabilities calculated under the method and assumptions chosen for these calculations.

As can readily be appreciated, a pension plan comfortably could comply with the above minimum funding requirements and yet still maintain a very poor ratio of plan assets to accrued liabilities. A second, more conventional *minimum funding requirement* then was introduced, and it does indeed focus on accrued liabilities and accumulated assets. For these purposes:

- The assets are to be taken at actuarial value, which may be fair market value or smoothed market value.

- The "*current liability*" is the value of accrued benefits – calculated under prescribed mortality tables and discount rate, and with ongoing plan assumptions as to retirement rates, turnover, etc;

- The discount rate for calculating liabilities is prescribed. It was equal to the four-year weighted average yield on 30-year Treasury bonds, and the actuary then could calculate the *current liability* using a rate in the range of 90%-105% of this rate. The 105% was temporarily relaxed to 120%, as Treasury bond yields had been at historic lows relative to conservative long-term corporate bond rates, and the basis was artificially inflating the calculation of the *current liability*. The whole basis currently is being reviewed.

If the unfunded *current liability* is less than 10% (*i.e.* the ratio of assets to current liability is at least 90%), the plan sponsor is not required to make any supplemental contributions. [There is also a temporary relaxation in this area – if the funded ratio is at least 80% and two consecutive of the previous three years' ratio were at least 90%, then no action is required]. If the ratio is less than 90%, then a supplemental contribution must be made to bring the otherwise required contributions up to the "amortisation percentage" of the unfunded current liability. The "amortisation percentage" is 30% for funded ratios below 60%, and for funded ratios above 60% it is 30% less 0.40 times the excess over 60% (*e.g.* a funded ratio of 75% means an amortisation percentage of 24%) – complicated, but logical. These minimum funding requirements cut off when the plan assets reach the "*full funding limitation*"; see below.

Customary funding practices

All regularly acceptable actuarial funding methods are allowed, but the Projected Unit Credit method is dominant, especially among large plans. However, the method and assumptions need to be chosen very carefully, as they impact both the Funding Standard Account and the Maximum Funding Limit (see below). In the event that the selected actuarial funding method does not produce a value for accrued liabilities, then this value must separately be calculated under the Entry Age Normal method.

Maximum funding limits

The *"full funding limitation"* is the greater of 90% of the *current liability* and 100% of the accrued liability. Assets are taken at the lesser of the smoothed market value (if such smoothing is used for minimum funding purposes) and the fair market value. In general, a plan sponsor cannot make contributions, or at least cannot make immediately tax-deductible contributions, when the full funding limitation is reached. In addition to the loss of a tax deduction, special excise taxes are payable on some contributions in excess of the maximum tax deductible contribution.

In the years prior to 2004, the full funding limitation was equal to the higher of (a) 90% of the plan's *current liability* and (b) the lower of (i) 100% of the *accrued liability* and 150%-170% of the *current liability*. The measure of 150%-170% (depending on the year) was then dropped, but alternative forms of this measure are re-appearing in proposed 2005 pension reform.

Frequency of actuarial valuations

Valuations are required to be performed every year.

Bankruptcy of plan sponsor

In the event of the bankruptcy of the plan sponsor and an underfunding in the pension plan, the plan may continue. However, if the plan meets the conditions for termination, the Pension Benefit Guaranty Corporation (PBGC) steps in and pays benefits up to certain guarantee limits. Plan sponsors pay annual premiums to the PBGC, based on the number of plan members and the size of the unfunded liability. The PBGC has become severely underfunded in recent years, although opinions differ widely as to the extent of the problem. Various proposals for increasing PBGC premiums and taking other measures to increase the financial solvency of the PBGC are actively under discussion.

Termination of an overfunded plan

Upon termination of a plan, the plan sponsor must purchase annuity contracts in the private insurance market (or make lump sum payments if the participant and the participant's spouse agree). Surplus assets can revert to the plan sponsor. However, plan sponsors that terminate overfunded defined benefit plans are subject to an excise tax penalty of up to 50% of the excess (20% under certain limited conditions). In addition, the proceeds are taxable income to the plan sponsor, and thus subject to corporate income taxes. In effect, the plan sponsor must take all necessary steps to avoid overfunding – now and in the future. These rules strongly discourage conservative funding, as the plan sponsor has no effective way to recoup excess assets if future investment returns and other plan experience are more favorable than expectations.

Who appoints the actuary?

The plan administrator appoints the actuary.

Role of the actuary

In contrast to most other countries, the actuary may be a fiduciary – with all the associated additional responsibilities. The roles and responsibilities of the actuary are prescribed in some detail.

ISBN 978-92-64-02810-4
Protecting Pensions: Policy Analysis
and Examples from OECD Countries
© OECD 2007

Chapter 4

Pension Fund Regulation and Risk Management: Results from an ALM Optimisation Exercise[*]

by
Sandra Blome, Kai Fachinger, Dorothee Franzen,
Gerhard Scheuenstuhl and Juan Yermo

I. Introduction

This paper provides a stylised assessment of the impact of investment-relevant pension fund regulations and accounting rules on contribution and investment strategies within the context of an asset-liability model (ALM) specifically designed for this purpose.[1] The regulations and accounting rules considered represent, in a simplified way, the situation in Germany, Japan, the Netherlands, United Kingdom and United States.[2] These countries were studied for their differences in regulations, including some major regulatory initiatives in recent years, as well for the size of their defined benefit (DB)

---

[*] This article was prepared by Sandra Blome (IFA, Germany), Kai Fachinger (risklab germany), Dorothee Franzen (Oxford University, United Kingdom), Gerhard Scheuenstuhl (risklab Germany), and Juan Yermo (OECD). It is the result of a joint research project between Allianz GI, risklab Germany, and the OECD, and received useful inputs from Brigitte Miksa (Allianz GI), a group of external advisers, including Con Keating (Finance Development Centre, United Kingdom), Niels Kortleve (PGGM, Netherlands), Colin Pugh (independent consultant), Peter Vlaar (DNB, Netherlands), as well as the Delegates to the OECD Working Party on Private Pensions and Pablo Antolín, André Laboul and Fiona Stewart from the OECD Secretariat. The views expressed are the sole responsibility of the authors and do not necessarily reflect those of the OECD or its member countries.

systems. The analysis could in principle be extended to other countries or regulations.

The pension fund industry in these countries has undergone a major upheaval over the last few years. Japanese pension funds were first to be affected, as weak economic conditions have prevailed for most of the period since the prickling in 1990 of the property and stock market bubble. Occupational DB plans in the United Kingdom and the United States were dealt a severe blow by the 2000-1 stock market crash and the ensuing low interest rate environment, creating large funding gaps after almost a decade of contribution holidays. On the other hand, pension funds in Germany and the Netherlands, while also adversely affected by these market corrections, have generally maintained funding levels (the ratio of pension plan assets to liabilities) above the solvency level established by the regulation.

Short term regulatory action has taken diverse forms, some corrective (leading ultimately to increases in contributions), some lenient (allowing temporary reduction in statutory contributions). Going forward, however, there is a general consensus among OECD countries for reforming regulatory and supervisory systems so that they better meet the objective of benefit security without jeopardising plan continuity. New pension fund regulations have been approved in the Netherlands, the United Kingdom and the United States with precisely these goals in mind. The general trend is towards greater surveillance of funding levels, to avoid situations where pension plans need to be closed (normally, because of bankruptcy of the plan sponsor) but plan assets are insufficient to meet benefit promises.

Looking closer, however, two rather different models of regulation can be identified, epitomised by the new UK and Dutch regulatory systems. The UK system is characterised by a flexible approach to funding (there is no statutory minimum funding requirement) and a strict, risk-based sponsor insolvency insurance fund, the Pension Protection Fund. The Dutch system, on the other hand, offers no explicit insolvency insurance but has relatively strict funding rules, including a requirement to fund at least 105% of the pension fund liability in nominal terms (excluding both salary projection for revaluing accrued benefits and indexation of benefits in payment) and a regular assessment of the buffers built to finance the fund's revaluation and indexation ambitions.

Another important aspect of the external environment that affects pension fund investment decisions is the accounting of pension expenses by DB plan sponsors, which have changed substantially over the last two decades. Starting with the US standard SFAS87 in 1985, actuarial valuation methods have been gradually replaced throughout the OECD by a market-based valuation approach. The traditional actuarial approach focused on the long-term stability of estimated contributions necessary to fund pension payment. Pension funds' assets and liabilities were valued at fixed, smoothed or long-term expected rates. The market-based approach, on the other hand, applies market prices to pension funds' assets and liabilities thereby enhancing the transparency and comparability of the financial position of the fund.[3] According to advocates of the new approach only the consistent and consequent application of fair value principles enables pension funds to conduct an objective risk assessment. On the other hand, this approach has been criticised for introducing inappropriate volatility to the liabilities and for leading to short-termist investment strategies. Some observers[4] also argue that market-based valuations, and in particular the UK's FRS17 standard, may have contributed to the decline of DB plans.[5]

Also, the new accounting standards require pension liabilities to be calculated applying the projected unit credit method, thereby leading to a different measure of liabilities compared to regulatory standards, which typically require the recognition and funding of the accrued benefits only (without projecting salaries at retirement).[6]

Assessing the pros and cons of different regulations and accounting standards requires an evaluation of their impact on funding levels (hence, benefit security), investment performance (hence, benefit levels) and funding cost (hence, plan continuity). While a full assessment of these regulations and accounting is beyond the scope of this exercise, the present paper attempts to elucidate some basic facts through an ALM exercise. Such models are increasingly being used by pension funds to assess their investment strategies.

The paper is organised as follows. Section 2 provides an introduction to the literature on risk management models and their application to pension funds. Section 3 presents the risk management model and the main results of the assessment of five different regulatory systems which are simplifications of the existing framework in five OECD countries (Germany, Japan, the Netherlands, United Kingdom and the United States). The last Section concludes. The annex describes the typical DB plan design and regulations in each of the five countries covered in the study.

II. Developments in pension fund risk management

Risk management is becoming an increasingly sophisticated and central function within financial institutions. In DB pension funds, risk management involves the measurement and assessment of pension fund risks and the design, monitoring and revision of the fund's parameters (contributions, benefits, and investments) in order to address these risks in line with the funds' objectives.

The main risks that DB pension funds are exposed to are investment, inflation, and longevity risk.[7] In turn, plan members are exposed to the risk that pension fund assets will be insufficient to cover benefit promises if the plan is terminated (typically, because of bankruptcy of the plan sponsor). In order to meet the needs of both plan sponsors and plan members, risk management should have the following two goals:

- Minimising the pension cost to contributors.
- Minimising the risk of benefit cuts to beneficiaries.

These goals involve trade-offs between contributions, asset allocation and risk, as the objectives of the stakeholders can (and do) vary. Plan sponsors are most interested in minimising the net funding cost of a plan by optimising the risk-adjusted return on plan assets. Plan members usually follow multiple goals that change over time: In case of member contributions, they share employers' goal of minimising pension costs. As active members, they are generally concerned with maximising their plan benefits without running the risk of losing vested benefits. Retired members usually place higher emphasis on benefit security as they have less or no time left to make up any shortfalls. As the pension promise is ultimately backed by the employer, insolvency of the plan sponsor forms the most basic risk to beneficiaries. This risk can be either dealt with by pension insurance arrangements (publicly set-up protection funds or private insurance) or via high funding buffers in the pension fund itself. Risk management's task, therefore, consists in unravelling these different objectives and constraints into a consistent combination of benefit and contribution policies and funding and investment strategies that satisfy plan sponsors and plan members, both active and retired.

Asset-liability modelling (ALM) is a key method in strategic risk management.[8] ALM is a financial risk assessment and asset planning tool used by pension funds to help them choose the strategic pension policy under uncertainty in a coherent and consistent balance sheet approach.[9] ALM involves developing mathematical scenarios of the future evolution of pension fund assets and liabilities, given certain assumptions about the statistical properties of economic, financial and biometric variables that affect the evolution of assets and liabilities. There are many ways to generate economic, actuarial and financial market scenarios. The traditional method was to create a central scenario and to carry out some stress testing around it.

With time the models have become more sophisticated, moving from the 'one-period static' type to 'multi-period dynamic' models involving the consistent stochastic simulation of assets and liabilities (which run multiple 'Monte Carlo' simulations). Modern ALM studies rely on stochastic models that generate thousands of scenarios with different probabilities attached to each. While the traditional ALM studies focused on asset-optimisation with a deterministic view on liabilities, today the ALM context is increasingly used to simulate the consequences of pension policies on different stakeholders while complying with the requirements of the regulating authorities. In this sense, ALM systems are used as integrated planning systems to simultaneously determine investment, funding and – if applicable – indexation policies thereby balancing the goals of the different stakeholders[10]. Risk is usually conceptualised as adverse development of the key variables, *e.g.* funding level, which has explicitly to be decided on. This has been taken further: by discounting the results of the ALM study back to present by applying risk-adjusted discount rates, risk becomes endogenous. Under such a 'value-based ALM' contributions have a higher opportunity cost in bad economic times. As poor equity returns coincide with periods of economic weakness, a 'value-based ALM' may lead to lower optimal equity allocations.[11]

ALM studies are common in all the countries covered by this paper, however there are differences in how they are carried out, and the stringency with which the resulting strategic asset allocation is implemented. In all countries, ALM studies are carried out by outside actuaries or consultants; only the very large Dutch and US funds run ALM studies internally, often in parallel to an externally conducted study. Dutch pension funds can be regarded as most sophisticated in terms of ALM. In the Netherlands, ALM is a widely accepted risk management tool. The new regulatory framework introduced in January 2007 requires the use of ALM studies, with stochastic analysis prescribed as of 2010. Germany also requires 'Pensionskassen' to regularly perform an ALM study, although the German market still lacks the Dutch sophistication. In the United Kingdom, on the other hand, there are still reservations against ALM, as the ALM models do not take account of the sponsor's covenant, on which the pension promise in the UK is based. There are also some reservations against the mathematical approach dating back to the Myner's Review.[12]

Though dynamic models have proven a better fit for the real world scenarios encountered by pension funds they do have their drawbacks, partly due to their complexity, making it harder for fund trustees or directors to understand and interpret. Arguably, in some countries investment oversight and trustee training have not always been able to keep pace with improvements in the sophistication of mathematical modelling techniques.

Furthermore, it has been proclaimed that many ALM studies generated high-risk, high-return portfolios, rather than strictly liability- matching portfolios[13], as it is proposed by a school in financial economics that proclaims pension funds should avoid exposing sponsoring employers to risks that can be taken directly by shareholders of the sponsoring company[14]. The coherent implementation of risk-immunising portfolios lies at the heart of the new 'Liability-Driven-Investment' (LDI) strategies, the understanding of which, however, varies across countries. In its general meaning, which is mostly applied in the Netherlands, for example, LDI refers to an investment strategy that is aligned with the liabilities of an investor and explicitly considers their stochastic nature. The impact of relative differences between liabilities and assets on the goals and constraints set by the decision maker make it crucial to look at both sides simultaneously. In the UK context, LDI concepts aim to immunise the sponsor from certain risk factors. Duration and cash flow matching strategies aim at eliminating interest rate risks. Other risk dimensions like inflation or mortality risks however cannot be properly addressed for lack of adequate financial products. In general, liabilities have become much more important for determining the optimal investment policy, and therefore the valuation methodology applied to pension funds' liabilities.

The use of risk management techniques such as ALM and LDI has been felt most strongly in investment strategies. Two main developments have been observed in the countries covered by this study:

- A move towards greater duration of fixed income portfolios and greater use of derivative instruments to hedge interest rate risk.

- Greater investment in so-called alternative instruments, such as private equity, real estate and hedge funds in search of the elusive "alpha".

Professional players with superior risk management systems in place focus increasingly on the analysis of 'fat tails', that is, tails of the frequency distribution of returns that have higher density than what is predicted under the assumption of normality. At the same time, ALM studies and LDI techniques are being used to either monitor or hedge basic liability risks, such as interest rate risk.

Some pension fund regulators are also starting to use ALM techniques to assess the resilience of the pension fund sector to different shocks. For example, in Austria, the financial supervisory authority (FMA) has developed a scenario analysis model in order to simulate the consequences for members and beneficiaries, pension funds (Pensionskassen) and employers of different investment returns on asset classes. In the Netherlands, the pension fund supervisor (DnB) has developed an elaborate ALM model that allows it to evaluate different regulations and model the future evolution of the sector.[15] The Pensions Regulator in the United Kingdom has also made use of risk management tools in considering its regulation of the funding of pension funds.

III. The impact of regulation and accounting on ALM for a synthetic pension fund

Pension fund regulations aim at promoting high levels of benefit security at an acceptable cost. Accounting standards in turn aim at ensuring the transparent disclosure of information to shareholders regarding a company's pension obligations. This section investigates in which ways investment and risk management activities of pension funds are affected by the regulatory and accounting framework. The goal of the following analysis is to show:

- how the valuation of pension fund liabilities differs across regulatory regimes;

- how different regulatory regimes induce what is considered a "liability-optimal" investment strategy;

- the consequences of regulation on liquidity demands, funding cost, cover ratios (business accountants' measure of pension assets to liabilities), and funding levels (pension regulators' measure of pension assets to liabilities).

Some of the key variables analysed such as the funding cost and the volatility of contributions provide an order of magnitude for the potential cost of regulations. A full cost-benefit assessment of different regulatory regimes requires comparing these costs against the benefits, in terms of greater benefit security achieved. The funding level can be used as a rough proxy for benefit security, though in none of the countries studied does the value of the liabilities measured under this ratio correspond to the amount that would have to be paid to an insurance company in order to buy out the accrued benefits in case of plan termination.

In order to isolate the impact of regulations, the analysis is based on a common (synthetic) pension fund liability, which illustrates a typical situation in an OECD country. Similarly, the same stochastic economic scenarios are developed. As the goal of the exercise is to measure funding costs to plan sponsors and their volatility, it is further assumed that investment and contribution decisions are made by the plan sponsor.[16] The objectives of members and beneficiaries (benefit security) are subsumed under those of the pension regulators. Under such identical plan and economic conditions, the effects of different pension regulations can be consistently compared.

The plan designs and regulations modelled in this exercise are simplifications of the real life situation. The results of the modelling exercise, therefore, cannot be used to judge the overall quality and suitability of any specific regulatory regime. The complexity of the pension context in each of these countries and, in particular, the degree of flexibility in plan design, risk sharing, and regulations do not permit a conclusive comparison of pension systems.[17] A full, rigorous comparison of private pension designs is beyond the scope of this analysis. The focus is also on funding and asset regulations only. Other important regulations (such as vesting and portability rules) are considered as common across all the cases considered.

III.1 Methodology

While there have been some studies addressing similar questions to the ones in this report, they have considered only one country-specific type of regulation.[18] To our knowledge, this is the first time such a cross-country, or rather, cross-system investigation has been undertaken.

The simplified regulatory regimes considered resemble some aspects of the pension regulations in place in Germany, Japan, the Netherlands, the United Kingdom, and the United States. Our comparison includes four representative corporate DB pension plans all of which are based on the same synthetic liabilities. The valuation considered is based on traditional actuarial methods for valuing the pension liabilities.[19] We consider both final pay and career average plans both with and without indexation of benefits.

The asset and investment management is modelled under consistent and rational behaviour. To avoid systematic biases, it is assumed that the pension investor applies the same Liability Driven Investment (LDI) policy based on the same, integrated ALM study incorporating the particular regulatory framework. Thus for each regulatory regime, the LDI optimal asset portfolio will be used and provides the respective best possible results under each regulation. LDI is here applied in its general meaning, which is basically a dynamic ALM.

The effects of regulatory rules are studied over a long horizon. This is achieved by applying a simulation analysis with 10 000 capital market scenarios over an investment horizon of 30 years. To assess the various impacts of regulation we proceed as follows: First, we look at the specific characteristics of liabilities and the implied LDI portfolios. In a second step, the pension fund's funding situation under the particular regulation is investigated. This will provide an initial asset-liability reconciliation. Finally, the corporate sponsor's view under its International Financial Reporting Standards (IFRS) framework will be used to optimise asset allocation and contribution strategies. The model simulates the liquidity situation (cash contributions to the pension fund), the profit and loss statements (pension expenses), and ratio of pension assets to liabilities measured under IFRS (referred to as the cover ratio).

As is always the case in stochastic exercises, the methodology applied is dependent on the underlying assumptions about asset returns, and in particular about the correlations between different asset classes. We do not attempt to model the implications of different tax structures, except those concerning the maximum funding level that pension funds can build without losing their tax advantages. It is also important to consider the results of such modelling as part of the broader debate about financial stability and economic development.

III.2 Synthetic Pension Plans and Structure of Underlying Liabilities

Pension plans under investigation

The focus of this report is on DB plans that pay out benefits in the form of annuities only.[20] In order to provide a common and realistic basis for the analysis, a synthetic plan is constructed that reflects the main characteristics of prevailing plans in the countries covered in the study. We assume that lifelong annuities are paid annually beginning either at age 65, in case of disability[21], or in case of death if there is a surviving spouse[22]. In order to simplify the modelling, no waiting or vesting periods are considered.

The amount of benefits depends on the type of pension plan, with a common accrual rate for all types of plans of 1% of the reference salary per year of service. Two main types of pension plans are considered: final pay and career average plans. For each of these two types of plan we consider two variations regarding indexation of benefits in payment (with and without indexation to last year's inflation[23]). The plan design details are summarised in Table 1.

Table 1. Overview of the different types of pension plans under investigation.

name	type of pension plan	benefit accrual rate	indexation of benefits in payment
FP_incr	Final Pay Plan with indexation	1% of final salary per year of service	Increase based on last year's inflation.
FP_const	Final Pay Plan without indexation	1% of final salary per year of service	Benefits remain constant.
CA_incr	Career Average Plan with indexation	1% of specific salary in each year of service	Increase based on last year's inflation.
CA_const	Career Average Plan without indexation	1% of specific salary in each year of service	Benefits remain constant.

To assume a realistic and representative situation we consider a corporate plan with 10,000 persons who have an existing entitlement or already receive pensions. It is a synthetic group of plan members, which is mixed in respect of status (*i.e.* active members, old-age pensioners, disabled and widows/widowers), gender, salary and age (see Box 1).

The demographic evolution of plan members is projected using mortality and morbidity assumptions normally used for occupational DB plans in Germany.[24] It is assumed that there are no early leavers from the plan. As the valuation of the plan's liabilities under both IFRS and regulatory methodologies includes current plan members only, the liabilities modelled do not include new entrants. The question of whether the plan is open or closed to new members is therefore irrelevant for our analysis. We also assume that salaries increase annually by productivity growth (constant factor of 1.017), by advancement in one's job or position (constant factor of 1.0025), and by last year's inflation, which is stochastic.

Valuation of liabilities under IFRS accounting rules

The valuation of the pension fund from the sponsor's perspective follows IFRS, and in particular standard IAS19, which addresses pension benefits. Under IAS19, pension plan liabilities, or the defined benefit obligation (DBO), are valued according to the projected unit credit method, using market yields of high quality corporate bonds (as discount rates) and estimated term of benefit obligations. Regarding mortality and morbidity, best estimate assumptions are made.[25] Furthermore, the calculation includes future increases of salaries and pensions as best estimate assumptions. The valuation used also applies the option under IAS 19 for immediate recognition of actuarial gains and losses (which is the basis of the UK's FRS17 standard and a basic feature of fair value). The lack of spreading or amortisation options heightens the impact of the pension fund on the sponsor's balance sheet.[26]

Box 2. Characteristics of plan members at the start

At the start, the synthetic plan has the following membership composition:

- 60% active members, 25% old-age pensioners, 5% disabled and 10% widows/widowers.

- The gender composition is equally split between males and females.

- There are five main categories of active members according to annual salary: 1% earn 200,000 monetary units (board members), 4% earn 100,000 monetary units (upper management), 15% earn 80,000 monetary units (middle management), 20% earn 60,000 monetary units (lower management), and 60% earn 40,000 monetary units (blue collar workers).

- The age distribution of active members mirrors the OECD average working population (see figure below), while old age pensioners, disabled and windows/widowers are equally distributed across specific age ranges (65 and 85, 45 and 64, and 45 and 85, respectively).

Age Distribution of Active Members

The sponsor's annual service cost is also calculated as per IAS 19. Service cost is primarily an accounting figure entering into the sponsors P&L statement. Cash contributions into the pension fund are typically related to service cost but can be very different from service costs (*e.g.* contribution holidays). Contribution strategies are an integral part of the investment policy. A detailed specification of the contribution strategies used here will be given in the next section on investment policies.

Valuation of liabilities and funding rules under different regulatory systems

The previous section described the valuation of liabilities from the sponsor's point of view. We now characterise the valuation of liabilities from the pension fund's point of view under different regulatory regimes. Table 2 shows the main differences between the regulatory systems under investigation. A regulatory system with no specific rules apart from the prudent person principle is considered (Reg-1). The valuation of liabilities under this system follows IFRS (IAS19). The main differences in valuation across regulatory systems are driven by discount rate assumptions and whether future salary and benefit increases are taken into account. Other key features of the regulatory system considered are minimum funding rules (which state recovery periods in order to reach a specific funding level) and premia paid into insolvency protection funds, which guarantee a certain level of benefits in case of bankruptcy of the plan sponsor.[27]

Table 2. Main characteristics of different types of modelled regulatory systems.

Regulatory system to be modelled Resembling	Reg-1 IFRS	Reg-2 UK	Reg-3 Germany	Reg-4 Netherlands	Reg-5 US	Reg-6 Japan
Discount rate	depending on market yields of high quality corporate bonds		3.5% fixed	current AA-swap rate curve. In case of indexation guarantees, the real market yield curve.	four year average of 30-year treasury bond rate	20-year government bond rate
Future salary and pension increase	taken into account		not taken into account	implicitly taken into account if revaluation and indexation are guaranteed[28]	not taken into account	

Regulatory system to be modelled Resembling	Reg-1 IFRS	Reg-2 UK	Reg-3 Germany	Reg-4 Netherlands	Reg-5 US	Reg-6 Japan
Minimum funding level	no	no	104.5%	105%	90%	90%
Additional contributions due to minimum funding rules	no	no	FL < 100%: immediate FL <104%: 3 year plan	FL < 105: 1 year plan Prob(FL>100%) < 97.5%: 15 year plan	Additional contributions if FL < 90%	FL < 90%: 7 year plan
Legal maximum funding rule	none	105%[29]	none	none	100%[30]	150%[31]
Contributions to Protection Fund	no	yes	no	no	yes	yes

Note: FL is the funding level.

The models we apply capture only some of the main features of the respective national regulation systems and do not reflect very recent legislative reforms, such as the new funding rules introduced in the United States as a result of the entry into force of the Pension Protection Act or the increase in the FTK recovery period from one to three years.[32] Therefore, the analysis cannot be directly associated with the respective national regulation systems. We therefore refer to the modelled regulatory systems as Reg-1 to Reg-6.

In order to be able to compare contribution and investment strategies under different regulatory systems, the pension fund is endowed at the start with the same amount of assets, equal to 100% of the DBO according to Reg-1 (IAS19). Under Reg-3 to Reg-6 there is a restitution of assets to the employer at the beginning of the period so that the funding level equals a target above the minimum required by regulators. The precise target funding level chosen reflects market practice. For Reg-3, it is 110%, for Reg-4 it is 120%, and for Reg-5 and Reg-6 it is 100% of the regulatory DBO.[33] At the end of the modelling period, the funding shortfall relative to the IAS19 DBO measure of liabilities is covered via a lump-sum payment by the plan sponsor. Hence, under all regulatory regimes, the start and end period endowments are exactly the same.

DBO projections

Figure 1 to 4 show the evolution of the DBO for the four different types of plan calculated according to the valuation methods under the different regulatory systems. A range of value of liabilities is provided around a central best estimate, the variability being determined by the stochastic future development of inflation and discount rates. The range of outcomes is assigned different levels of likelihood, each indicated by a different coloured bar. For example, liability valuations within the dark grey bar have a 50% probability of occurring. In all cases, the DBO projection is shown at its current level (2006), and two future dates (2015 and 2030).

For the period considered, the DBO rises gradually as a result of salary growth. Over a longer period, however, the DBO declines as the impact of death of members and beneficiaries overrides that of salary growth. This can be observed in Figure 5, which plot the evolution of the DBO in a deterministic setting (central best estimate) for the final pay plan with indexation under Reg-1.

The differences in DBO between the different types of plan are substantial under Reg-1, Reg-2 and Reg-4. Under these regimes, the DBO of the career average plan without indexation (Figure 4) is about half of that of the final pay plan with indexation throughout the first 24 years of the simulation period, 2006-2030 (Figure 1). In the other regulatory regimes, the differences in DBO between the different types of plan are much smaller, mainly because indexation is not taken into account in the regulatory measure of the DBO.

The differences in measures of liabilities (DBOs) for a given plan type are driven by two main parameters, namely the choice of discount rate and the extent to which salary revaluation and benefit indexation factors are taken into account. For example, in the case of the final salary plan with indexation (Figure 1), the central best estimate of the current liability valued with the Reg-6 rules (576) is only about 60% of the liability applying Reg-1 rules (925). On the other hand, for the career average plan with indexation (Figure 3), the central best estimate of current liability valued under Reg-6 rules (486) is 75% of that using Reg-1 rules (642). By moving from a final salary to a career average plan, therefore, differences in valuations across regulatory regimes are diminished.

The removal of indexation causes yet greater convergence in DBO measures (see Figures 2 and 4). Moreover, the highest central estimate of liabilities in both plans without indexation (final pay and career average) is the one using Reg-3 valuation rules rather than the one using Reg-1 ones as a result of the lower discount rate used.

4. PENSION FUND REGULATION AND RISK MANAGEMENT

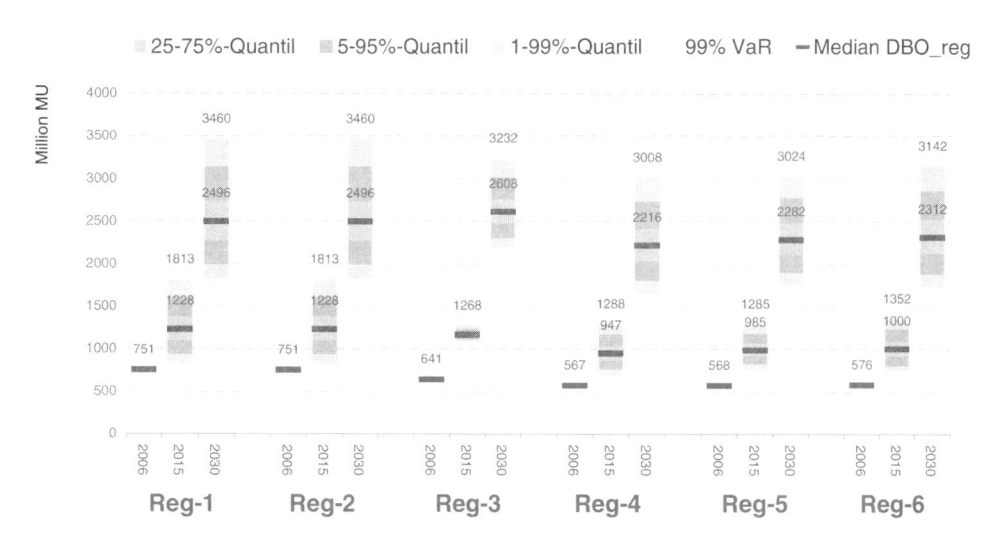

**Figure 1: Final pay plan with indexation of benefits in payment (FP_incr)
– DBO projections under different regulatory systems**

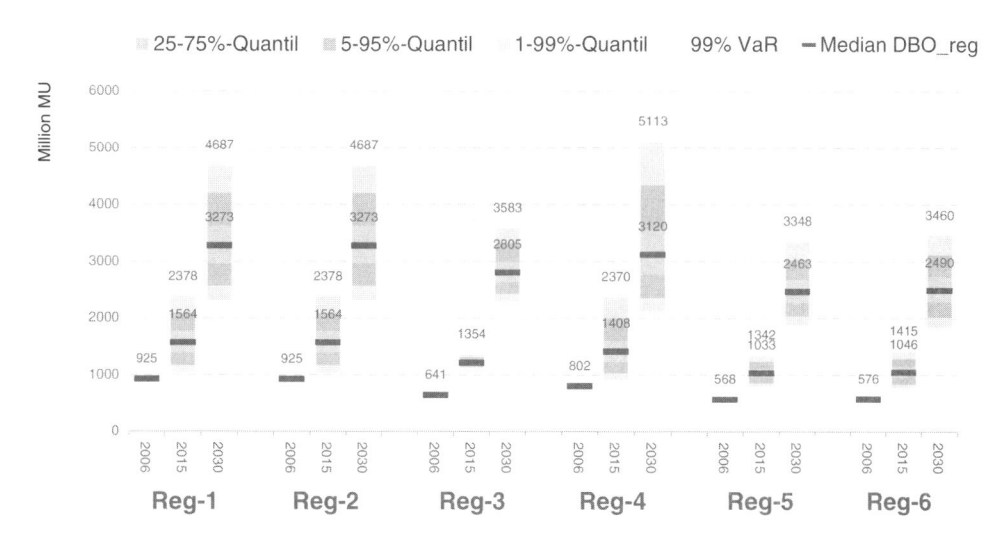

**Figure 2: Final pay plan without indexation of benefits in payment (FP_const)
– DBO projections under different regulatory systems**

4. PENSION FUND REGULATION AND RISK MANAGEMENT

Figure 3: Career average plan with indexation of benefits in payment (CA_incr) – DBO projections under different regulatory systems

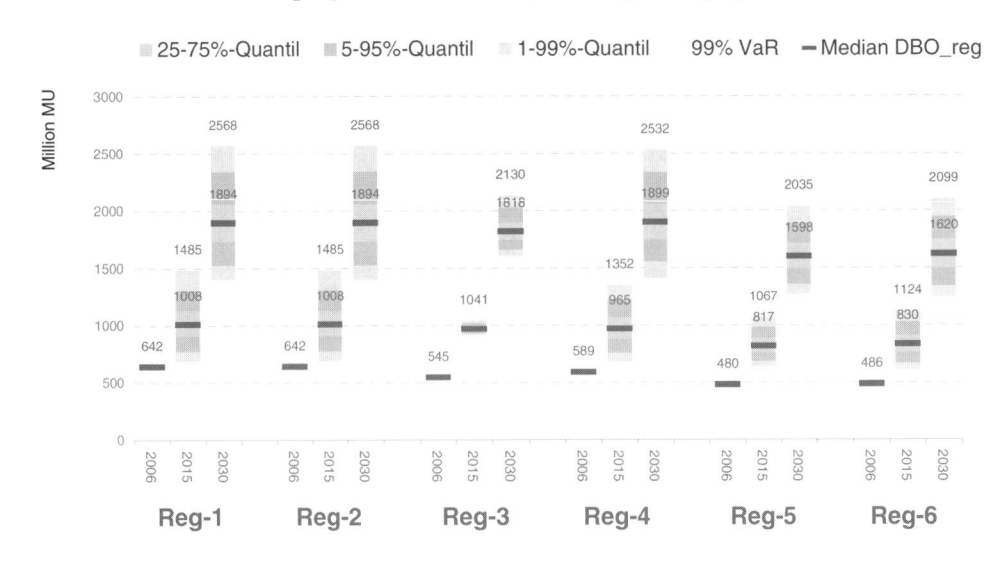

Figure 4: Career average plan without indexation of benefits in payment (CA_const) – DBO projections under different regulatory systems

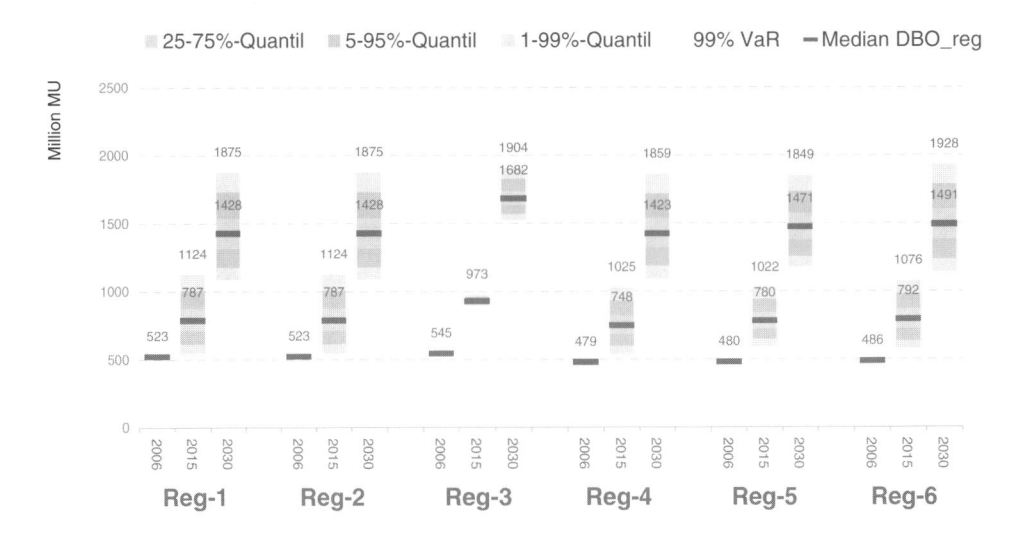

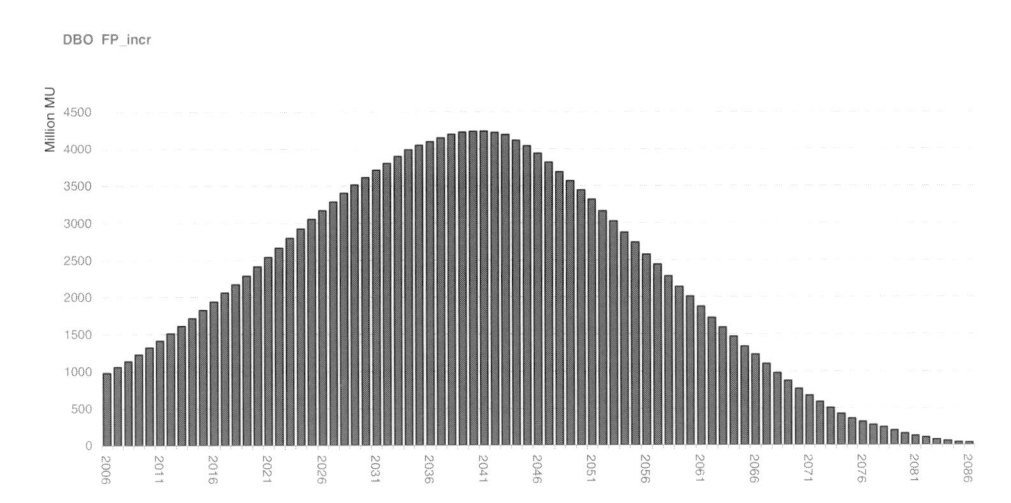

Figure 5. Deterministic projection of DBOs over 80 years for the final pay pension plan with indexation under IAS19 (Reg-1).

III.3 Liability based Investment Philosophy

The ALM Framework

The ALM framework is based on a surplus optimisation approach. The process starts with a systematic assessment of the stochastic characteristics of the underlying liabilities and their sensitivities to all relevant risk factors. These risk factors, such as inflation, the term structure of interest rate, and the growth rates of salaries, need to be modelled individually and consistently. Based on a set of different scenarios of possible future economic environments[34], a consistent stochastic description of liabilities can be given. This stochastic modelling of liability behaviour goes beyond the traditional actuarial modelling with deterministic expected cash flows. In a stochastic framework, the statistical properties of the liabilities, such as volatility and duration (sensitivity to interest rates), are key factors driving the asset allocation decision. The regulatory systems considered, as they determine the measures of the liabilities, are therefore expected to affect the investment strategy. Table 3 shows the statistical properties of the liabilities in a final pay plan with indexation under the different regulatory frameworks Reg-1 to Reg-6. The highest volatility and highest duration of liabilities are those measured under Reg-1 and Reg-2. The duration of the liabilities under Reg-3 is zero, because of the use of a fixed discount rate. The liabilities also grow faster under Reg-3 to Reg-6 than under Reg-1 or

Reg-2 because the latter incorporate salary increases from the start, whereas these adjustments are only progressively incorporated into the other measures of liabilities.

Table 3. Statistical properties of liabilities of the four types of pension plans under different regulatory regimes.

	FP_incr			FP_const			CA_incr			CA_const		
	DBO RoR	Vola DBO RoR	Interest rate sensitivity	DBO RoR	Vola DBO RoR	Interest rate sensitivity	DBO RoR	Vola DBO RoR	Interest rate sensitivity	DBO RoR	Vola DBO RoR	Interest rate sensitivity
Reg-1	5.0%	15.2%	21.0	4.9%	14.3%	20.7	5%	14.0%	20.4	4.3%	13.2%	19.8
Reg-2	5.0%	15.2%	21.9	4.9%	14.3%	20.7	4.9%	14.0%	20.4	4.3%	13.2%	19.8
Reg-3	6.7%	0.7%	-	6.0%	0.5%	-	5.4%	0.5%	-	4.5%	0.2%	-
Reg-4	6.3%	15.2%	16.1	7.0%	11.4%	14.2	5.0%	15.6%	16.6	5.2%	11.6%	14.9
Reg-5	7.3%	4.1%	4.0	6.6%	4.1%	4.0	6.0%	4.2%	4.1	4.9%	4.1%	4.6
Reg-6	7.7%	10.4%	16.6	6.9%	10.5%	17.0	6.4%	10.6%	17.1	5.3%	10.7%	18.0

Note: DBO RoR is the growth rate of DBO (Rate of Return), Vola DBO RoR is the volatility of the growth rate of DBO. The interest rate sensitivity is measured as the duration of the surplus risk minimising portfolio with respect to the regulatory DBO.

The identification of a liability benchmark serves as a first orientation of the characteristics needed on the asset side. The number of possible investment strategies is indefinite. However, rational behaviour suggests using efficient portfolios only, that is, those that are not dominated by others with respect to their risk-return characteristics. The portfolio efficiency frontier considered is one that offers the best possible trade off between the mean excess return of the pension fund's assets over the growth of the liabilities and the volatility of this excess return. Based on its specific goals (like minimising the expected net funding cost of the pension plan), risk preferences and other constraints, the corporate sponsor would choose one of those investment portfolios in the efficiency frontier as his strategic asset allocation (SAA-LDI). In case of a dynamic strategy (DSP-LDI[35]) the sponsor would additionally formalise a management rule of when to switch from one of the risk efficient portfolios to another.

When considering the choice of investment portfolio, the prudent person requirement is interpreted as using risk-efficient and well-diversified portfolios. Risk in the ALM framework measures the deviation with respect to a liability-hedging portfolio, where the liability is the DBO calculated under each regulatory regime. The surplus return, meanwhile, is the excess return obtained on the assets above the rate of growth of the liabilities. The surplus risk-return efficiency frontier can hence be calculated under each regulatory regime, as shown in Figure 6a for the final salary plan with indexation (FP_incr) and in Figure 6b for the career average plan with indexation. Each of the lowest surplus risk portfolios represents the "mismatch minimising portfolio". This portfolio tries to replicate the stochastic nature of the respective liabilities as well as possible given the universe of assets available. The mean excess return of the mismatch minimising portfolios is negative in cases Reg-2 to Reg-6 because the growth of the liabilities (the compounded effect of interest cost and salary growth) is greater than the return on low risk assets.

If the pension fund is also subject to a specific type of quantitative investment regulation (only the case in Reg-3) then regulatory requirements may override the sponsor's primary choice of investment strategy. The portfolios under the shaded area on the efficiency curve of Reg-3 are not feasible because of regulatory limits on risky strategic asset allocations. These portfolios are therefore excluded from the optimisation process.

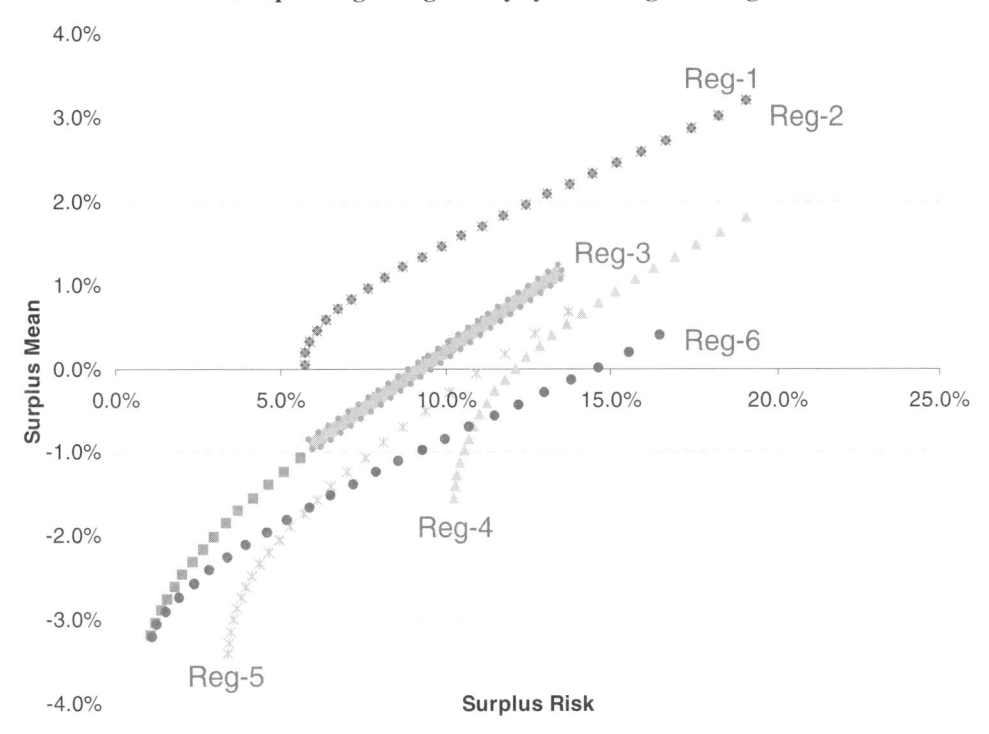

Figure 6a: Surplus efficiency frontiers for the final salary plan with indexation (FP_incr) under the liability measures corresponding to regulatory systems Reg-1 to Reg-6

Figure 6b: Surplus efficiency frontiers for the career average plan with indexation (CA_incr) under the liability measures corresponding to regulatory systems Reg-1 to Reg-6

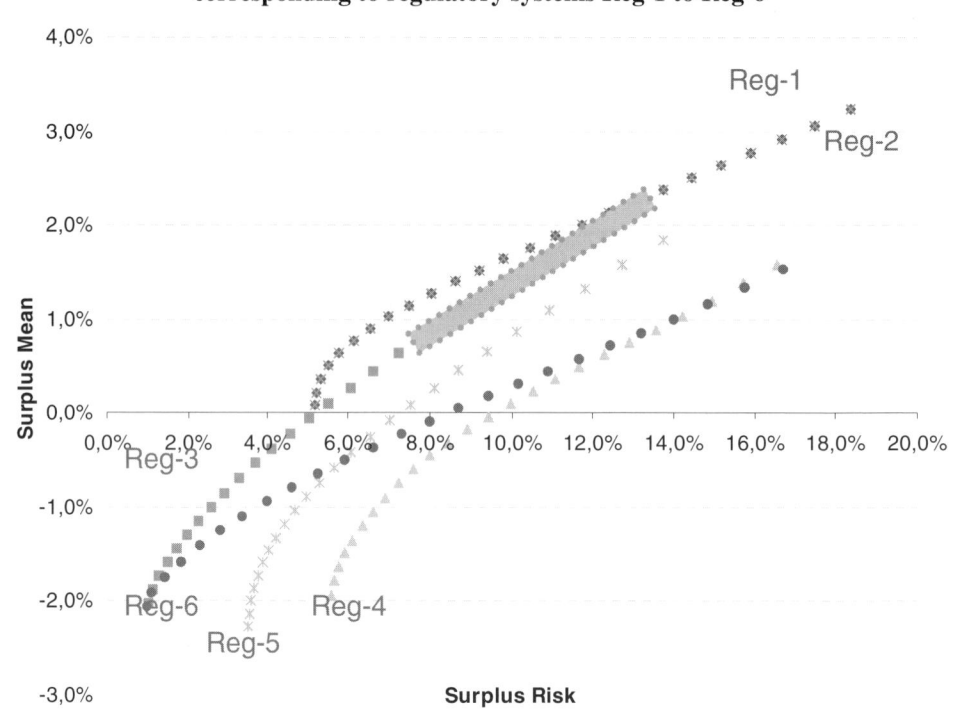

All portfolio allocations are "well-diversified" over various asset classes such as government and inflation linked bonds (with different maturities up to 30 years), corporate bonds, international stocks, real estate and absolute return funds.[36] However, due to the different characteristics of the underlying liabilities (*i.e.* their sensitivity with respect to interest rates[37] and inflation) for different regulatory regimes the portfolios on these risk-efficient frontiers can be substantially different. For example, the mismatch minimising portfolio has a zero duration under Reg-3, but 22 years under Reg-1 and Reg-2. Portfolios for Reg-3 regulation try to establish an absolute return type of investment. They hold a high proportion in alternative investments to match as well as possible biometric risks as hedging instruments are not available (6% in real estate and absolute return funds in the mismatch minimising portfolio). Bond investments consist primarily of inflation-linked instruments since this is the only remaining sensitivity to address.

The contribution strategy is the other main parameter driving the ALM. In the IFRS context, the corporate sponsor has a large degree of freedom of when to fund pension liabilities and in what amount. Unfunded liabilities need to be shown on the balance sheet and might influence the credit rating and re-financing costs of the company. Accounting standards, therefore, can provide an incentive to sponsoring companies to fully fund their pension plans. Regulators also impose funding requirements on pension funds, though these are usually based on the regulatory DBO that often exclude the impact of salary projections.

In order to make comparisons between the different regulatory regimes, we model the same contribution strategies (funding policy). All strategies consist of a lower funding level, an upper funding level, and a withdraw level, as the example in Figure 7 shows. The corporate sponsor's contribution strategy is entirely determined by the current funding level. If the funding level is below the critical threshold of "lower level" the amount of contributions is set above the regular service costs so that the "lower level" is reached within a certain recovery period of, for example, 10 years. When the funding level is between the lower and upper threshold, contributions equal the amount of regular service costs. For situations when the funding level is above the "upper level" the mechanism assumes contribution holidays and no cash contributions flow into the pension fund. In cases of substantial over-funding the policy allows restitutions to the corporate sponsor in order to bring back the funding level back to a withdraw level.

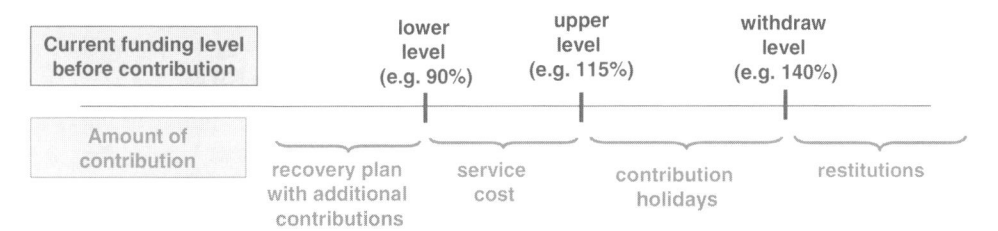

Figure 7: Basic action mechanism of a contribution strategy.

Current funding level before contribution	lower level (e.g. 90%)	upper level (e.g. 115%)	withdraw level (e.g. 140%)
Amount of contribution	recovery plan with additional contributions	service cost · contribution holidays	restitutions

Since different funding policies chosen by the sponsor induce different liquidity demands, the choice of the contribution strategy will be identified within the ALM optimisation framework. For simplicity, we consider a set of seven alternative contribution strategies, shown in Table 4. The funding levels under each strategy are defined according to the DBO measure of the regulatory system considered.

Table 4. Contribution strategies under investigation.

ContributionStrategy_Basic				
ID	lower_level	upper_level	Withdraw_level	RecPlan
1	70%	90%	140%	10
2	70%	95%	140%	10
3	80%	100%	140%	10
4	90%	105%	140%	10
5	95%	110%	140%	10
6	100%	115%	140%	10
7	100%	120%	140%	10

Funding regulations set an additional constraint on the sponsor's contribution policy. Table 2 shows the funding and contribution requirements set by different regulatory regimes. The strategically intended corporate funding rule (as described in Table 4) can therefore be overridden by regulatory requirements and additional contributions might be necessary. The amount of additional contributions depends on the type of regulatory system.

Deriving optimal strategic asset allocations and contribution strategies

The optimal ALM strategy for the corporate sponsor consists of a combination of an asset allocation and a corresponding contribution strategy. The corporate sponsor's preferred combination of asset portfolio and contribution strategy would be derived for example by solving the following (stylised) type of optimisation problem:

-- Minimise the expected Net Funding Cost (NFC) of the given pension plan subject to a set of sponsor specific risk constraints, such as

- (Liquidity) Avoid extreme cash requests in a single period, and, over the entire investment period, keep total excess contributions low.
- (Profit & Loss Statement) Avoid extremely high pension expenses.
- (Balance Sheet) Avoid extreme shocks to the cover ratio.
- (Investment) The investment portfolio has to comply with asset regulations or quantitative asset limits.
- (Solvency) The contribution strategy has to comply with funding regulations requirements.

For the goal function we use "Net Funding Costs" (NFC). This is in line with earlier studies on dynamic ALM modelling for DB pension funds.[38] More recently, some models have applied utility functions[39], but given the different governance structures and therefore different patterns of influence for the stakeholders in the analysed countries, formulating one utility function that can be applied for all countries was not regarded as feasible. The NFC function used characterises the economic value needed to ensure that at the end of the considered investment horizon (*i.e.* in 30 years) the funding level is again at 100%, assuming that we started at a 100% funding level at time t=0. Contributions into the pension fund mean cash outflows for the corporate sponsor. The (expected) net funding cost therefore comprises all cash outflows the sponsor has to put into the fund – either due to his own funding preferences or imposed by regulatory funding requirements. Contribution components comprise[40] "normal contributions", "additional contributions" and for some systems also "protection fund contributions". Negative contributions, which would mean a cash inflow would be "restitutions from the fund to the sponsor" in cases, the fund has a substantial over-funding.[41] Taking the promised, accrued benefits as given, the corporate sponsor's goal is to implement the best possible investment and contribution strategy so that the net funding cost is as small as possible.

Investment strategies with "higher surplus returns" provide lower net funding costs on average but go along with a more volatile annual funding cost and larger swings in the cover ratio. These risks need to be taken into account when choosing the contribution and investment strategy.[42] The risks are limited by the constraints imposed on cash requests, the cover ratio and pension expenses reported in the sponsor's profit & loss account. Hence, the contribution and investment strategy is driven by the IFRS accounting framework. This case study considers three different sponsors. A "High Risk Tolerance", a "Medium Risk Tolerance" and a "Low Risk Tolerance" sponsor, that tries to match his liabilities as well as possible (LDI-matching). In this study, risk is not endogenous as in the case of applying state prices[43] but conceptualised as adverse development for the key variables which have to be explicitly taken into account.

Based on an integrated and comprehensive simulation analysis[44] for all combinations of asset allocations and contribution strategies the resulting consequences on liabilities, assets, funding status, contributions, pension expenses, etc., for the pension fund are projected into the future. This is done separately for all regulatory regimes. With these simulation results, the optimisation problem can be solved directly by selecting the combination with the minimal NFC among all feasible combinations.

III.4 Comparing the Impact of Regulation

Regulations act at different levels, changing the profile of cash contributions and hence affecting the sponsor's liquidity and its investment strategy. As under each regulatory regime there is a different funding target, the funding cost will also necessarily differ. Ultimately, the impact of regulations can be assessed by comparing the net funding cost against the resulting funding levels and cover ratios. From the sponsor's perspective the key objective is minimising the net funding cost taking benefits as given. From the regulator's perspective, this cost must be traded off against the extra security afforded to the pension fund in the form of higher funding levels.

Impact on Contributions and Corporate Sponsor's Liquidity Situation

Liquidity aspects are crucial for the company's investment policy. Especially, high demands on cash contributions in a single year can cause financial distress to the sponsor and must be avoided. Figure 8a and 8b provide a detailed view on additional contributions for the final pay and career average plans with indexation.[45] Additional contributions are mainly triggered by regulatory requirements such as recovery plans.

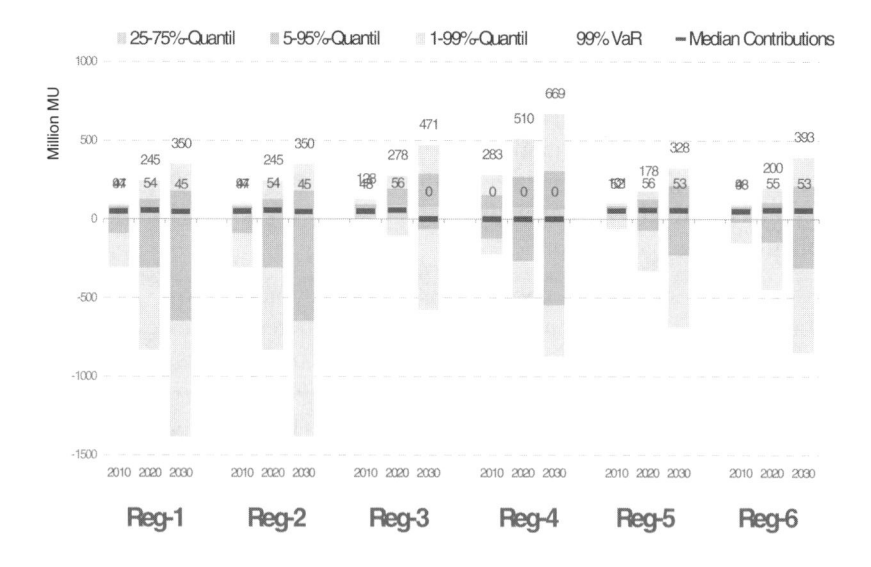

Figure 8a: Percentile plots of cash contributions in selected years for different regulations in a final pay plan with indexation (FP_incr) for the High Risk Tolerance sponsor

Figure 8b: Percentile plots of cash contributions in selected years for different regulations in a career average plan with indexation (CA_incr) for the High Risk Tolerance sponsor

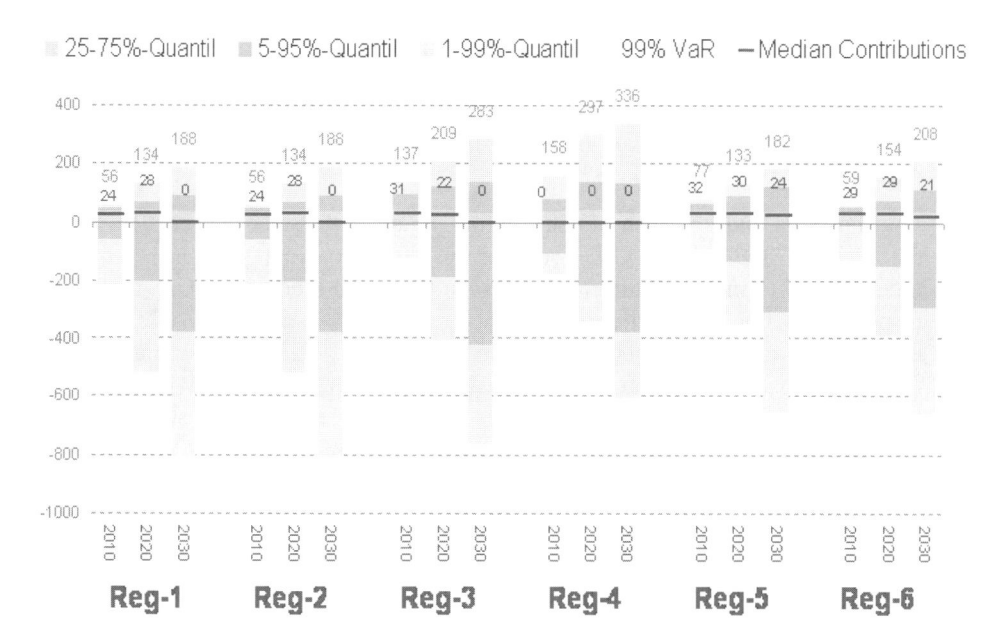

Regulations influence the optimal choice of an investment policy by affecting the liquidity constraints. Regulation systems (like Reg-3 and Reg-4) with strict solvency rules on the funding level (100 percent for Reg-3 and 105 percent for Reg-4, respectively) in combination with very short recovery plan periods (immediately for Reg-3, or 1 year for Reg-4, respectively) cause much higher demand on liquidity. Systems with longer recovery periods (like Reg-5 and Reg-6) or those without explicit recovery periods (like Reg-1, or Reg-2) provide more flexibility. Ad-hoc liquidity demand is much smaller since the additional funding can be spread over several years.

Impact on cover ratios and funding levels

Two main measures of the funding status of pension funds are considered. The funding level is defined as the ratio of assets and liabilities from the pension fund's point of view, using the methodology required by pension regulators. The cover ratio is defined as the ratio of assets and liabilities from the plan sponsor's point of view, measured under accounting standard IAS19 (IFRS, as under Reg-1).

The corporate sponsor wants to avoid disturbances in its financial statements triggered by the pension fund for its reports to investors. Both the absolute level of the cover ratio and its volatility are important in this regard. The different volumes of DBOs given by different regulation regimes (for the same pension plan) lead to substantially different funding situations (cover ratios) from the corporate balance sheet view. From the regulator's (and beneficiary's) point of view, on the other hand, the relevant measure of solvency is the funding level, measured under the specific valuation rules of the regulatory system in place.

Figure 9a and 9b illustrate the funding situation for selected years from the view of the sponsor (the cover ratio) for the final pay plan with indexation (FP_incr) and the career average plan with indexation (CA_incr), respectively. For the final pay plan, the highest cover ratios are achieved under Reg-1 and Reg-2, because sponsors face no regulatory constraints on their funding and focus on the impact of the net pension liability on their balance sheet, as well as Reg-4, a regulatory system requires the use of real interest rates to calculate the DBO measure. In the other cases, funding regulations override balance sheet considerations, so pension funds end up with a cover ratio (measured under IAS19) that is substantially below 100%. For the career average plan with indexation, Reg-3 also leads to higher cover ratios than under Reg-1 and Reg-2, as a result of the lower (fixed) discount rate used (see Figure 9b).

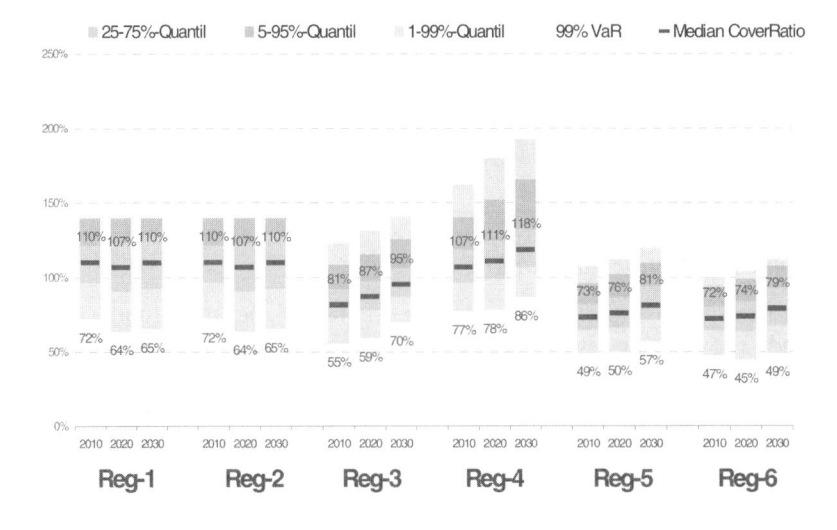

Figure 9a: Percentile plots of Cover Ratio under different regulations for the final pay plan with indexation (FP_incr) for the "High Risk Tolerance" sponsor

4. PENSION FUND REGULATION AND RISK MANAGEMENT

Figure 9b: Percentile plots of Cover Ratio under different regulations for the career average plan with indexation (CA_incr) for the "High Risk Tolerance" sponsor

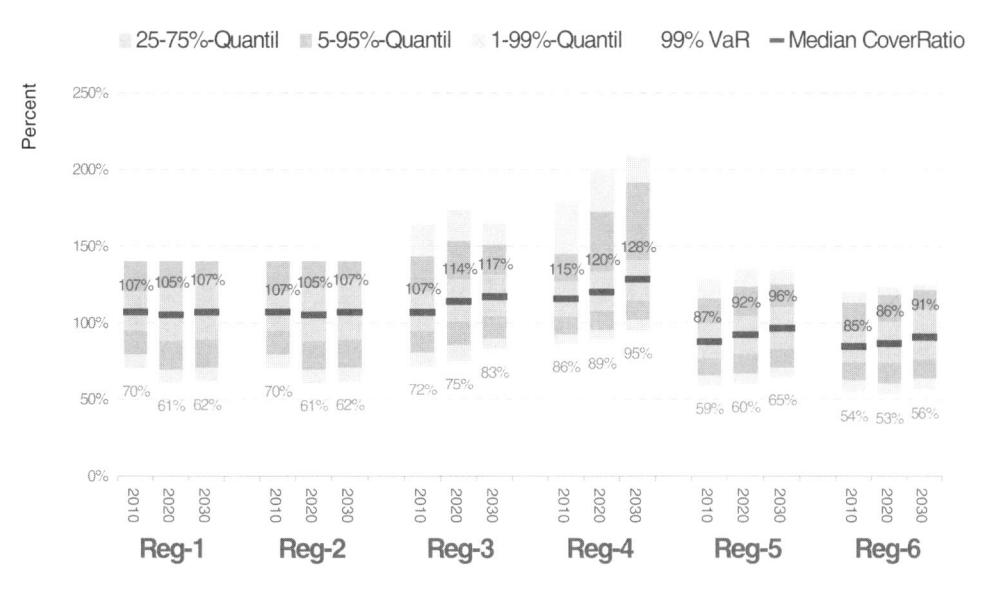

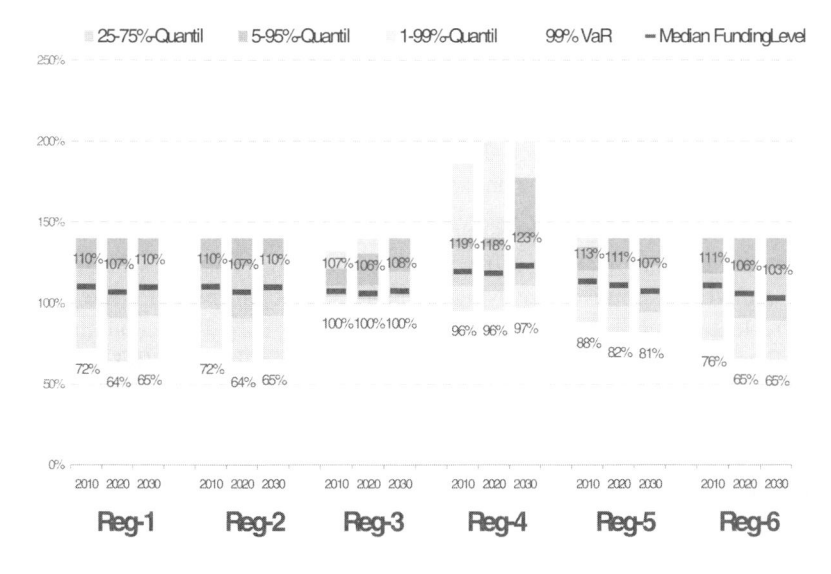

Figure 10a: Percentile plots of regulatory Funding Levels for different regulation (FP_incr) for the "High Risk Tolerance" sponsor

PROTECTING PENSIONS: POLICY ANALYSIS AND EXAMPLES FROM OECD COUNTRIES – ISBN 978-92-64-02810-4 – © OECD 2007

4. PENSION FUND REGULATION AND RISK MANAGEMENT

Figure 10b: Percentile plots of regulatory Funding Levels for different regulation (CA_incr) for the "High Risk Tolerance" sponsor

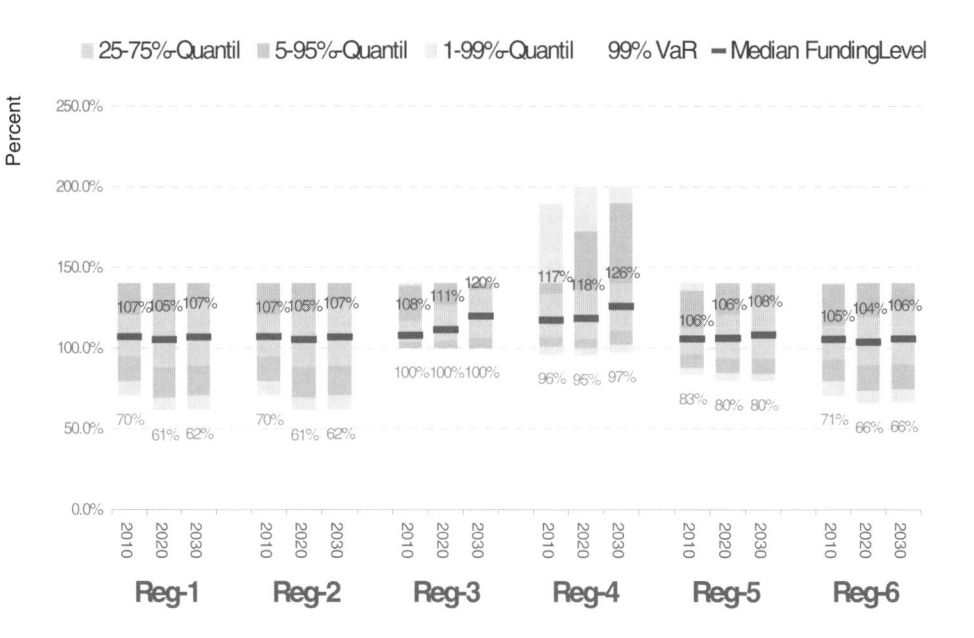

[Chart: Percentile plots showing 25-75%-Quantil, 5-95%-Quantil, 1-99%-Quantil, 99% VaR, and Median FundingLevel for Reg-1 through Reg-6 across years 2010, 2020, 2030. Key values: Reg-1: 107%/105%/107%, 70%/61%/62%; Reg-2: 107%/105%/107%, 70%/61%/62%; Reg-3: 108%/111%/120%, 100%/100%/100%; Reg-4: 117%/118%/126%, 96%/95%/97%; Reg-5: 106%/106%/108%, 83%/80%/80%; Reg-6: 105%/104%/106%, 71%/66%/66%]

In Figure 10a and 10b the corresponding regulatory funding levels are shown. As argued earlier, the regulatory funding level under Reg-1 and Reg-2 is the same as the sponsor's cover ratio, as there are no additional funding regulations.[46] As expected, the stricter the funding regulations, the lower the range of outcomes in funding levels. In particular, under Reg-3 the funding level never falls below 100%, while under Reg-4, it does not fall below 96%. The funding levels, however, are specific to each regulatory system. For example, a substantial under-funding in 2010 according to Reg-2 of some 30% would still be an over-funding according to Reg-6.

The example underscores the sometimes very different views between accounting and regulation. Such differences in measuring liabilities cause a dilemma: an ALM optimised investment policy and contribution strategy can only reflect either the characteristics of the DBO used for accounting purposes (here IAS19) or the possibly very different regulatory DBO. This results in a mismatch on either the cover ratio or the funding level. If, for example, the investment policy is tailored to the regulatory funding level, we will see additional volatility of the cover ratio. For Reg-3 we see for example a small surplus risk of the asset portfolio with respect to the DBO-Reg-3 (6.7%). However, the volatility of the cover ratio with respect to the

DBO-IAS is substantially larger (14.7%). Regulatory systems that apply a similar methodology to measuring liabilities as that used in the corporate accounting system would reduce cover ratio volatility and allow for a consistent policy framework but may lead to higher net funding costs.

Impact on Net Funding Costs

In addition to the expected level of net funding costs (median NFC) its risk needs to be considered. The risk is that in adverse economic situations the resulting funding cost could be substantially higher than expected. The "worst case" situation is here described by the 99% Value at Risk (VaR).[47] 5a summarises the resulting median net funding costs (NFC) as well as the 99-percent VaR for the three sponsors in a final pay plan with indexation, while Table 5b shows the same variables for the career average plan with indexation.

5a and 5b clearly show the impact of strategic asset allocations on the NFCs. The "High Risk Tolerance" NFC is two to three times smaller than that of the "Low Risk Tolerance". The absolute amount of NFC underscore the different effectiveness of the regulation systems given the projection model applied here. It does however not necessarily mean that one system is always more expensive compared to the others. Assumptions about opportunity costs of capital are crucial in the comparison of systems with different absolute initial funding levels. We assume the risk free market interest rate as the relevant opportunity costs. As consequence, regulations with higher contributions towards the end of the period (as under Reg-5 and Reg-6) tend to be more expensive since the pension plan does not earn the risk premium on the plan assets before. The analysis also indicates that regulatory systems with stricter solvency rules and shorter recovery periods (such as we find in Reg-3 or Reg-4) reduce the spectrum of possible outcomes and increase the average net funding cost for the "Low Risk Tolerance". The Reg-3 NFC is in fact the highest of all regulatory regimes. This result is determined by the greater exposure to low yielding assets (short term bonds and deposits) that is needed to maintain regularly a high level of funding, as liabilities are calculated using a fixed discount rate of 3.5%. But this higher cost also goes along with higher average funding levels. Interestingly, the highest NFC is that under Reg-5 for the "High Risk Tolerance" and the "Medium Risk Tolerance" sponsor.

4. PENSION FUND REGULATION AND RISK MANAGEMENT

Table 5a. Median and 99 percent Value at Risk of the NFC of a final pay plan with indexation (FP_incr) for the three different sponsors

Figure / Regulation	HRT		MRT		LRT	
	Median NFC	VAR (99%) NFC	Median NFC	VAR (99%) NFC	Median NFC	VAR (99%) NFC
Reg-1	375	2,416	427	2,348	1,076	1,948
Reg-2	387	2,442	446	2,430	1,089	1,989
Reg-3	530	2,218	668	2,100	1,342	2,358
Reg 4	577	2,301	643	2,164	1,194	2,362
Reg 5	657	2,175	720	2,099	1,310	2,257
Reg 6	514	2,330	554	2,275	1,239	2,074

Note: HRT is the high risk taker, MRT is the medium risk taker and LRT is the low risk taker.

Table 5b. Median and 99 percent Value at Risk of the NFC of a career average plan with indexation (CA_incr) for the three different sponsors

Figure / Regulation	HRT		MRT		LRT	
	Median NFC	VAR (99%) NFC	Median NFC	VAR (99%) NFC	Median NFC	VAR (99%) NFC
Reg-1	166	1,350	189	1,312	623	1,052
Reg-2	173	1,368	201	1,361	631	1,065
Reg-3	232	1,334	294	1,267	829	1,326
Reg 4	205	1,440	230	1,355	710	1,120
Reg 5	279	1,285	304	1,239	779	1,248
Reg 6	231	1,330	249	1,299	726	1,144

Note: HRT is the high risk taker, MRT is the medium risk taker and LRT is the low risk taker.

IV. Conclusions

This paper provides a stylised assessment of the impact of investment-relevant regulations on the investment and contribution policy of DB pension funds. The main findings of the ALM analysis underscore the substantial impact of regulations which, in a simplified way, resemble the basic aspects of the funding regulations in place in Germany, Japan, the Netherlands, United Kingdom and the United States.

The analysis starts with a description of the liabilities of a final pay DB plan with indexation and contrasts them with those of plans without indexation and career average plans. Using demographic and economic data from OECD countries, the liabilities of a final salary plan with indexation are shown to be as much as double those of a career average plan without indexation, given a common accrual rate for both plans. Such cost savings can explain the reforms in plan design observed in occupational pension systems in recent years. In particular, the more explicit emphasis placed by Dutch pension funds in recent years on the conditional character of indexation clauses in pension contracts has reduced the average cost of pension provision and introduced a key element of flexibility that will allow the system to better weather storms in the future. The coetaneous move to career-average benefit formulas also has clear advantages from a risk management perspective, but it has not reduced average costs as accrual rates were raised. The flexibility introduced into the Dutch system also contrast with the situation in the United Kingdom, where statutory revaluation and indexation requirements have raised the cost of benefit provision substantially.

The regulatory impact assessment starts by prescribing the valuation methodology for pension liabilities. We find substantial differences among these systems and also compared to the results of the projected unit credit method used in the IFRS accounting framework. Different concepts of recognising accrued benefits (with or without projecting salaries at retirement) and different approaches to discounting future benefit payments lead to substantially different measures of liabilities. In particular, under the new international accounting standards (IFRS), pension liabilities increase considerably and become more volatile than under the methodologies prescribed by pension regulators. Additionally, we see different sensitivities regarding changes in interest rates and inflation. Under the regulatory system based on fixed discount rates (which resembles the German case), the liabilities have the lowest volatility and zero sensitivity to interest rate movements (duration). This contrasts with a duration of 22 years for the liabilities measured under IFRS.

The impact of regulations was assessed from the perspective of the sponsor of final salary and career average DB pension plans with guaranteed indexation by measuring their impact on the sponsor's funding costs, its liquidity demands for cash contributions, and the impact of the pension fund's funding status on the volatility of the balance sheet. The impact of regulations was then assessed from the regulator's (and beneficiaries') perspective of keeping the funding level to a prescribed minimum.

The funding costs are mainly determined by the investment performance of the asset portfolio. As in a liability driven investment concept the characteristics of the pension liabilities are the basis for the investment and contribution policy, the optimised asset portfolios differ between regulations, as do the surplus performances of the assets portfolios over the liabilities. An important finding is that, under all regulations, a liability-matching asset portfolio that fully replicates the (stochastic) liabilities cannot be derived, as common financial instruments are not able to rebuild the particular characteristics of the liabilities.

Regulations affect funding costs primarily through the choice of investment strategy. Asset regulations imposing quantitative limits on different asset classes reduce the set of otherwise admissible investment policies and can thereby affect funding costs. Funding rules can also have a strong influence on the investment and contribution strategies of pension funds, and hence on the net funding cost. Funding regulations that require full funding at all times and rely on fixed discount rates to calculate liabilities generally lead to higher investment in lower yield, lower risk instruments, raising the net funding cost. Market-based solvency rules in combination with short recovery periods can also have an impact on investment strategies (and hence on funding costs). As there is a risk of high liquidity demands (contributions) in scenarios with abruptly decreased funding levels, sponsors may choose a more conservative asset allocation. From the policymakers' perspective, these higher net funding costs must be traded-off against the lower likelihood of a sudden drop in funding levels and hence a higher level of benefit protection in case of plan termination or bankruptcy of the plan sponsor.

Finally, the paper shows that fair-value accounting standards (with immediate recognition of actuarial gains and losses) can contribute to a greater accumulation of assets than required by regulators. On the other hand, the mismatch in valuation methodologies under regulatory and accounting rules creates a dilemma, as the optimisation targets become ambiguous. Low volatility in cover ratios that satisfy sponsors may mean high volatility in funding levels that violate regulatory requirements, especially in countries where discount rates are fixed by regulators. Hence, greater coherence in valuation methodologies under accounting and regulatory standards would go a long way towards facilitating the implementation of optimal ALM strategies by pension funds. This is especially the case for some actuarial assumptions, such as mortality rates.

However, some aspects of the valuation methodology of IFRS accounting standards do not appear suitable for regulatory purposes. In particular, the IFRS measure of pension liabilities incorporates salary projections, which are normally excluded from the regulators' funding level calculations. This is because the regulators' focus is with ensuring the protection of benefits that have been accrued, excluding the revaluation of those benefits if the members were to continue working for the sponsoring company until retirement (as is done under IFRS). The regulator's valuation methods provide flexibility to pension funds to optimise the investment and contribution strategies for the additional funding needed to meet the cost of salary growth and benefit indexation.

The results concerning regulatory impact are specific to the plans modelled, final-pay and career average plans with indexation. Replacing the final-pay benefit formula by a career-average one leads to a lower level of uncertainty over the future evolution of liabilities, hence facilitating risk management. Similarly, a more explicit emphasis on the conditional character of indexation clauses (as is the case in the Netherlands) would reduce dramatically the value of the liability to be reported under IFRS on the sponsor's balance sheet. This would allow a more aggressive investment strategy for any buffers needed to finance the pension fund's indexation ambitions. Future research could model specifically how these alternative plan designs are affected by the different regulations reviewed in this study.

Notes

1. The model was developed by risklab Germany, which also prepared the main empirical results presented in this report. The study benefited from financial contributions from Allianz Global Investors.
2. The regulations considered were those in place up until July 2006. A summary of those regulations are contained in the Annex.
3. For an overview see e.g. Whittington (2006).
4. See, for example, Klumpes et al. (2003).
5. In the United Kingdom by April 2005, almost half of all UK DB plans active members were in a plan closed to new entrants. This statistic does not include "frozen" or "winding-up" DB plans, that is, plans where there are no longer any active participants (Government Actuary's Department (2006).
6. See Yermo (2007) for a review of the different perspectives taken by accountants and regulators when measuring pension liabilities.
7. There are also operational and governance risks, which are not the focus of this report.
8. See Stewart (2005).
9. For a detailed overview see e.g. Ziemba and Mulvey (1998).
10. Boender et al. (1998).
11. See Kortleve and Ponds (2006)
12. The UK Myner's Review of the investment industry in 2001 (review available at http://www.hm-treasury.gov.uk/media//843F0/31.pdf) claimed that "asset-liability modelling is a complex number-driven process, in which it is difficult to incorporate asset classes without reasonably long historic time series data. The outcome of such a process is unlikely to be investment in new or poorly researched asset classes, such as private equity. Yet according to investment theory, it is precisely among poorly researched asset classes that greater opportunities for enhanced return are likely to exist. More importantly, the outcome of the asset-liability modelling process depends crucially on a number of prior

decisions and qualitative judgments, such as assumptions about rates of return, and other economic indicators, and the division of assets into classes (an imprecise art, with elements of arbitrariness)."

13. See Exley et al. (2000).

14. This body of the financial economics literature originated in the United States in the 1970s. One of the first papers was Sharpe (1976). For an overview, see Orszag (2006).

15. See van Rooij et al. (2004) and Vlaar (2005).

16. In some of the countries studied, such as Germany and the United States, this assumption reflects very closely the reality, as the pension fund's governing board is often dominated by the sponsoring company (multi-employer plans in the United States are an important exception). In Japan and the Netherlands, the governing board is supposed to take into account the interest of all stakeholders (including sponsors) in its investment decisions, while in Japan the funding decision is taken jointly with the plan sponsor. In the United Kingdom, trustees were granted greater powers by the 2004 Pensions Act and, specifically, were assigned clear duties to set the funding and investment policy. The investment policy has to be consulted with the sponsoring employer, while the funding policy has to be agreed with the company.

17. A good example of a flexible system with risk sharing features can be found in the Dutch system, specifically with respect to the indexation of benefits.

18. See e.g. Vlaar, P. (2005), Boulier et al. (1996) and Van Binsbergen and Brandt (2007).

19. Current discussions among practitioners and academics point out that option valuation methods should be applied for a market consistent and fair valuation of pension liabilities seen as contingent claims. See, for example, Kortleve and Ponds (2006), and Kocken (2006).

20. For the same level of expected benefits, DB plans that pay benefits in the form of lump-sums are cheaper to run and less risky for plan sponsors as longevity risk is fully transferred to plan members.

21. A disability pension is paid in case of disablement before age 65. Members are entitled to a minimum disability pension: The total rate is at least as high as it would be if he/she reached age 55 as an active member.

22. Widows/widowers receive 60% of their spouse's current annuity or the disability pension he/she is entitled to respectively.

23. Note that inflation process is exactly the same as used in the capital market model. This holds also for the bond processes that are relevant for the discount rates.

24. Heubeck Richttafeln 2005 G; for more details, see Heubeck et al. (2006).

25. The German standard table within occupational pensions (Heubeck Richttafeln 2005 G) was used.

26. The simulations using the amortisation and corridor option are available from the authors.

27. See the Annex for a more detailed description of these regulations in the five countries considered.

28. If revaluation and indexation are not guaranteed (or are conditional on the funding level), the regulatory measure of liabilities does not take them into account.

29. Pension funds are required to reduce surpluses calculated on the basis of the projected unit credit method to max. 5% within 5 years.

30. The Pension Protection Act of 2006 increased the tax-relevant deductibility limit on contributions to 150% of the current liability.

31. Of the current liability, measured using the regulator's methodology.

32. See the Annex.

33. As result Reg-3, Reg-5 and Reg-6 funds have a smaller amount of assets at the beginning compared to Reg-1, while Reg-4 has slightly more.

34. The stochastic scenarios to simulate the financial market environment used for the analysis are produced with the economic scenario generator (ESG) of Risklab Germany. This structural cascade model provides a consistent set of all underlying driving risk factors.

35. DSP stands for „Dynamic Strategy Portfolio". In practice such dynamic risk controlling strategies prove to be a very effective instrument for an ongoing control of pension investment risk. The calibration of the risk profile of such a strategy requires some more information on the investor's preferences and circumstances. To avoid extra complexity within the case study the dynamic component is not incorporated into the LDI solutions.

36. For simplicity, we do not consider other risk management instruments such as derivatives and hedge funds.

37. In Reg-3 system, for example, a constant discount rate of 3.5% is always used, independently of movements of the term structure of interest rates. The underlying liabilities show no sensitivity to interest rate movements. The LDI portfolios for Reg-3 will therefore have practically no duration.

This is in contrast to the portfolios of the curve for Reg-1 or Reg-2. Here we have a high interest rate sensitivity.

38. See e.g. Dert (1998).

39. See e.g. Vlaar (2005) or Van Binsbergen and Brandt (2007).

40. For technical reasons in order to compare different approaches there will also be further contribution components such as target funding level contributions and comparison contributions. Since (especially in an open ongoing system) there is no final time point where one could compare the systems, we need to make sure that all systems start at the same level and end at the same level.

41. Additional contributions are valued at a lower discount rate. We use the five year corporate yield in order to account for the increased liquidity requirements. Restitutions are discounted with the particular portfolio return. Thus, a risky investment strategy will be valued less positively.

42. To ensure a realistic and tractable picture in such a multi-period and accounting based framework, this approach does not make use of generic utility functions but chooses key business figures that will be considered by the corporate sponsor when judging its financial situation.

43. For the application of state prices in a fair-value approach see Kortleve et al (2006) or Scherer (2006).

44. All simulations used here are performed on risklab Germany's proprietary simulation platform. To obtain a detailed picture of the consequences resulting from different investment strategies under different regulations in the simulation analysis some 245 evaluation figures are projected over 30 years into the future.

45. Additional contributions describe the amount of cash contributions, which exceed service costs for a given period.

46. Reg-1 and Reg-2 differ only with respect to payments to the protection fund, which are small relative to the size of the fund. Moreover, these payments do not affect the asset allocation of the fund or its contribution policy, only the net funding cost.

47. Value-at-Risk (VaR) measures the worst expected loss under normal market conditions over a specific time interval at a given confidence level (99% in this case). VaR answers the question: what's the most I can lose in x% of cases over a pre-set horizon.

Annex 4.A1

Pension fund design and regulations in five OECD countries

DB pension funds have been traditionally the main form of private pension provision in many OECD countries, but in some there is a growing trend towards plan closures and replacement by defined contribution (DC) ones, especially in Anglo-Saxon countries.[1] On the other hand, in some continental European countries, such as the Netherlands and Germany, as well as in Japan, DB plans have retained their importance and DC plans have only grown at the margins. These plans, however, have experienced major reforms, as epitomised by the Dutch reengineering of the pension deal (from final salary to career average and from unconditional indexation to conditional indexation).

The following section summarises the salient features of plan design and regulatory approaches. It will focus strongly on investment-relevant regulation, namely the regulation of plan assets, if existent, and funding rules.

Germany: 'Pensionskassen'[2]

'Pensionskassen' are special life insurance companies that serve one or several employers. Multi-employer 'Pensionskassen' (when not restricted to a group of companies under common control) are mostly operated by financial service providers or by the social partners. As the latter ones have been founded in the wake of the 2001 pension reform, their market share is still small. In terms of assets under management, company 'Pensionskassen'

---

1. This trend is most conspicuous in the United Kingdom, where as many as 60% of all DB plans are now closed to new entrants while over 10% have also stopped accruals for existing employees (NAPF estimates).
2. For Germany, this report will focus on 'Pensionskassen' only, as this is the most relevant and best documented funded pension vehicle in Germany. But the reader should keep in mind that it is only one in five available financing vehicles and accounts for roughly 20% of the German market for occupational pension plans.

dominates the market. The German pension fund market is growing strongly, mainly driven by employee-financed pension plans, to which all employees are legally entitled since the 2001 pension reform. Due to the hybrid nature of German pension plans, one might argue that this is more in line with the shift from DB to DC, than the exceptional phenomenon of a growing DB pension market.

German pension plans are overwhelmingly hybrid. Pure DC plans are legally not permitted; pure DB plans in the form of final salary plans are becoming increasingly rare. The dominating plan type is a 'contribution oriented' DB plan ('Beitragsorientierte Leistungszusage'), which is similar to the cash balance plans in the US. It is basically an average salary plan, where the employer guarantees a pension benefit based on pre-defined contributions. The pension benefit is calculated according to actuarial rules. As the calculation of this pension benefit is based on very conservative estimates, the promised pension benefit is actually a minimum benefit, which usually gets topped up by surplus benefits from investment returns. The 'Pensionskasse' determines the level of the guaranteed interest rate up to a maximum level, which is, in most cases, fixed by the Ministry of Finance (2.25% since December 2006). The guaranteed interest rate applies for the entire life of a contract. Retirement benefits are most often paid as lifelong pensions. By law, benefits must be indexed. There are different options available, but market practice today is the automatic 1% indexing of pension benefits for benefits from 1999 onwards. 'Pensionskassen' are mostly exempted from the indexation rule by using all pro rata surpluses to increase the benefits of the pensioners[3]. Today, many 'Pensionskassen' offer a variety of pension plans with different benefit structures employers and employees can choose from.

Germany is the only country of the analysed ones that still applies quantitative investment regulations for plan assets, although the rules have been considerably liberalised over the last years. The regulator defines the investment universe and imposes limits for the maximum investment per asset class or group of classes, which are basically diversification rules. The most important rule is the maximum of 35% for 'risk-taking assets', mainly equity, but also hedge funds and high-yield assets. German funding rules are strict. 'Pensionskassen' are required to be fully funded at all times with an additional solvency buffer of about 4.5%, which adds up to a required funding level of 104.5%. The 'Pensionskasse' is declared insolvent the moment the funding level falls below 100%. There is no upper funding limit. Germany is the only country covered in this report that does not apply fair value accounting for regulatory purposes. Assets are calculated in

---

3. According to the actuarial consultant firm BodeHewitt AG & Co. KG.

nominal terms on the basis of book values, which implies, that capital market volatility translates into hidden reserves (or losses). Liabilities are calculated on the basis of accrued benefits, discounted with the guaranteed interest rate per contract. The discount rate is therefore fixed per contract but does not necessarily apply to the whole balance sheet, which also reflects past discount rates.

EU-wide, the accounting world for the plan sponsor is today mostly governed by IFRS[4]. IFRS applies fair value accounting and calculates pension liabilities on the basis of projected benefits, discounted with a rate based on 'high quality' corporate bonds. Actuarial gains and losses have to be included in the disclosure of the balance sheet; the amount exceeding 10% of the pension obligation has to be amortised and included in the income statement ('corridor approach')[5]. IFRS accounting implies for the plan sponsor, that the pension liability changes significantly compared to the accounting world of the 'Pensionskasse', the liability increases and becomes much more volatile. Therefore, a sponsor might opt for an accounting according to DC rules. As the contributions are in most plans 'pre-defined' and most employers do not guarantee for shortfalls of the 'Pensionskasse' (beyond a general subsidiary liability), the plans are actually very close to a DC plan for the employer. It is further required that the sponsor does not profit from the surpluses of the 'Pensionskasse' in the future.

Due to the strict regulation, German 'Pensionskassen' are conservative and risk-averse investors. Pension fund managers are heavily disincentivised from risk taking because of the lay-offs consequent to insolvency. The maximum investment limit of 35% for 'risk-taking' assets was tapped with just 18% at the end of 2005[6]. The bulk of the assets are invested in bonds. Since September 2005, ALM is implicitly legally required.

Japan

Historically, there were two major types of pension plans in Japan, the Employer Pension Funds (EPFs) and the Tax-Qualified Pension Plan (TQPPs). A new type of DB pension plan, the Defined Benefit Corporate Pension Plan (DBCP) has proved popular since its introduction in 2001. This allowed the portion of the EPFs contracted out from the public pension system to be paid back to the government, whilst the remainder of these

---

4. Smaller, not capital-market relevant companies can still apply the commercial code HGB, which also covers the 'Pensionskasse'.
5. The second possible approach under IFRS is the 'SoRIE' approach: Gains and losses are recognised on the balance sheet in full immediately; but via a separate 'Statement of Recognised Income and Expense' (SoRIE), not in the profit and loss account.
6. Bundesanstalt fuer Finanzdienstleistungsaufsicht, Jahresbericht 2005.

funds are to be transferred into DBCP schemes (either contract or fund type). This section focuses on the EPFs and the DBCP (which are subject to the same regulation) as the government has required that all TQPPs are wound-up by 2012.

EPFs are mostly single employer or multi-employer pension funds and provide private pension benefits as well as part of the public pension (substitutional benefits). The stock-market weakness and low interest rate environment experienced by Japan since the early 1990s forced sponsoring employers to make additional contributions in order to meet investment returns related to the substitutional part of the benefits provided by EPFs. The ensuing financial difficulties led to EPFs switching to other types of plans without the substitutional component or to dissolution. The decline in the number of EPFs in recent years is striking. In 1996 there were 1,883 EPFs (12,096,000 participants) while in 2005 only 687 existed (5,250,000 participants).

DBCPs have been in existence since 2001 and attempt to offer increased protection to beneficiaries through strict funding requirements and fiduciary duties for the plan management. They have grown at a high pace since their introduction: the 1,432 plans cover 3,840,000 participants (2005).

Most EPFs and DBCPs are career-average salary plans (EPFs substitutional benefits had to mimic those of the public pension system), but recent years have also seen the introduction of hybrid plans such as cash balance plans, where members accumulate monthly pay credits at a specific interest rate per year (for example, 3%). Regarding EPFs, the indexation of substitutional benefits (see section on benefit adjustment) is financed by the government. Indexation for EPF's additional benefits and for DBCPs depend on plan rules and are not common. Cash balance plans do not normally provide indexation.

In 1997, a solvency test was introduced for EPFs, which was extended to the new DBCPs in April 2002. If the value of accumulated assets is less than 105% of the termination liabilities of the contracted-out portion or 90% of the termination liabilities of total plan benefits (no allowance for salary growth or early leavers, same discount rate for all funds based on risk-free rate, set by Pension Fund Association – 2.2% in 2005), the shortfall must be eliminated within a maximum period of 7 years. However, if the plan is severely underfunded and the employer is in financial distress, it is possible to reduce benefits. Conditions for reducing accrued benefits include approval by two-thirds of the plan participants and agreement of the labour union. Following further downturns in the stock market, the government introduced temporary relaxations of the minimum funding requirements, including a possible two-year suspension of deficit amortisations and an extension of the 7-year maximum amortisation period to 10 years.

Since 1989 there is also a Pension Guarantee Programme, managed by the Pension Fund Association (PFA) to provide termination insurance for EPF plans. The basic principle of invoking the guarantee is that the fund dissolution was caused by bankruptcy or similar financial difficulties of sponsoring companies. Premiums are determined by three components: per capita premiums according to the number of participants; premiums in proportion to the total benefit amount guaranteed; and premiums in proportion to the amount of unfunded liabilities. The maximum of the sum of first two components is set at Y8.82m. The maximum of the third component is set at Y0.861m. The ceiling placed on premiums means that larger companies pay lower guarantee premiums. Currently, premiums are further reduced by 35% from the sum of these components, as the Programme currently holds funds in excess of its targeted contingency reserve.

The Japanese accounting standard is called ASRB and was introduced in 1998 (operative for financial years starting April 1, 2000) among others in order to bring Japanese accounting standards in line with IAS 19. As in the case of IFRS, Japanese employers must recognise their pension liabilities on the balance sheet. The main difference with IAS 19 is that the Japanese standard does not use the corridor method for actuarial gains and losses. Also, the discount rate used to calculate the pension liabilities can be based on yield fluctuations during the previous five years of long-term government or high quality corporate bonds.

Investment regulations were relaxed in 1995, when a series of quantitative ceilings on broad asset classes were eliminated. Since then, pension funds can invest freely under the prudent person standard. In addition, the pension legislation stipulates that each pension fund should endeavour to avoid concentration of investment on a specific asset category and prohibits investment in securities with the purpose of pursuing interests of someone other than the pension fund.

ALM models remain relatively unsophisticated in Japan. Simple models are used, but given funds have been operating in a deflationary environment, these were not taken particularly seriously. Leading international companies such as Hitachi/ Toyota etc. do have regular, professional assessments of their liabilities, but they remain ahead of the curve and in the minority. The responsibility for pension plans has generally shifted from its traditional location within HR departments to finance departments, but the level of sophistication has not increased significantly. Some shift to equities has taken place since the deregulation of asset allocation structures, but bond weightings remain higher than in other countries, partly due to the existence of a liquid government (JGB) market. An important development since the mid-1990s has been the increasing use of hedge funds.

Netherlands

The Netherlands is still overwhelmingly a 'DB country', but most plans have been transformed from final salary to average salary ones. The Dutch pension funds worked successfully on restoring their financial position via a highly flexible system of burden sharing between the stakeholders.

Retirement benefits are paid as lifelong pensions. Indexation of pension benefits is an explicit goal of the pension policy of the Dutch pension funds, but indexing is neither stipulated by law nor an unconditional commitment of the funds. According to the new pension law, pension funds must explicitly declare their indexation policy and the conditions for indexing. With the shift from final salary plans to average salary plans, conditional indexing has become an especially powerful financial steering instrument for pension funds in the context of the pension deal. As only the nominal benefit is guaranteed, the indexation cutting instrument can be applied also to the benefit accruals of the active workers. The change to a conditional index-linked average-salary scheme during the last three years greatly enhanced the pension funds' control over their pension benefit levels.

Regulation is changing in the Netherlands. The new pension law was implemented in 2007. As the new law has been under discussion for quite some time, the effects in the market will probably be small. At the heart of the Dutch regulation lies a risk-based approach. Pension funds have to fully fund their nominal liabilities with a solvency buffer of 5%. The probability of undershooting 100% may not be larger than 2.5%, which has to be proven in a solvency test. According to model calculations by the regulator[7], this will require the average pension fund to be funded at approximately 130%. If the pension fund falls below 105%, they have a recovery period of 3 years. If a pension fund has a funding level between the targeted solvency balance (130% for the average fund) and the minimum funding level (105%), it is requested to prepare a recovery plan with a planned recovery period of up to 15 years, which must get approved by the regulator. Pension funds also have to pass a continuity test every three years, where they have to prove their long-term financial stability, including their indexation objectives, on the basis of an ALM study. The solvency test can be performed in three ways, which differ with regard to their complexity and

---

7. Pensioen en Verzekeringskamer, 2004, Financial Assessment Framework Consultation Document, Apeldoorn.

sophistication. The most sophisticated way in terms of risk management to perform the solvency test is the application of internal models, which were introduced to the banking industry with Basle II. Unfortunately, the parameters were chosen in a way that internal models will not be rewarded and therefore are unlikely to get implemented. In this respect, the Dutch regulation falls one step short of implementing a really sophisticated, risk-based regulation.

Investment regulations will not be affected by the new pension legislation. Current regulations are based on the prudent person standard. There are no investment ceilings other than a 5% ceiling on investment in the sponsoring employer (10% in the case of employer groups).

Under new legislation, Dutch regulation will be based on the fair value principle. Pension liabilities are calculated on basis of the accrued, nominal benefits, discounted with the term structure of Zero-Coupon interest rates. Indexation of benefits can be paid either by contributions or by investment returns or a combination. Conditionally indexed benefits are not included in the funding rule. The funding position of the Dutch pension funds was 125% at the end of 2005. A funding level of 150% is needed in order to achieve 100% funding in real terms (*i.e.* including revaluation and indexation objective).

The large industry-wide pension funds, which prevail in the Netherlands, have usually been classified as DC plans according to the Dutch standard RJ271, although the plans offer DB like features to the employees. The rationale is the low risk of additional contribution to the sponsor, due to *e.g.* the conditionality of indexation, the cost of which are also shared between employers and employees and pensioners. For all companies, which have to apply the IFRS accounting rules, this accounting practise would have become unsustainable, even if their pension fund is part of an industry-wide fund. This provision is still under debate in the Netherlands. Meanwhile, the IFRS regulations have triggered a move to Collective Defined Contribution (CDC) plans[8], in order to get the plan classified as DC. Pension funds fix the contributions for 5 to 10 years, withdraw the shortfall-guarantee but also give up the right to recover surpluses.

The Dutch pension funds are highly sophisticated investors. They are very liability orientated and deliberate risk-takers. ALM on a yearly basis is already market practice and has become mandatory with the new pension law. The SAA stayed virtually unchanged over the last years, with about

---

8. According to market experts, at least 15 pension funds have already changed to CDC, and about 1/3 of the company pension funds say they are considering the change.

40% in bond and equity each[9], but – according to market experts - about 1/3 of Dutch pension funds has implemented an overlay strategy based on derivatives to hedge out the downward risk. Trustees are rewarded for risk-taking as they can use the superior return for indexing. Therefore, liability-matching investment strategies are not popular in the Netherlands.

United Kingdom

The most significant current trend in UK private sector pension provision is the retreat by employers from providing defined benefit schemes. Some of these schemes are amended to be career average schemes, but often they are not amended but closed to new members. When this occurs existing members can usually stay in the schemes and continue accruing benefits. New members are frequently offered a DC plan instead – often with significantly lower employer contributions[10].

Retirement benefits are usually provided as lifelong pensions, often with an option to exchange up to 25% of the pension for a cash sum, paid free of tax. For pensions in payment, Limited Price Indexation must be applied to certain elements of the pension. Pensions in payment, which accrued after April 1997, must be indexed as a minimum in line with the lower of the retail price index (RPI) and a fixed rate of 5% p.a. From 2005 onwards this fixed rate was reduced to 2.5% p.a. Many funds also index pensions which accrued before 1997 at the same or similar rates. The indexation of deferred benefits is also a legal requirement in line with the indexation of pensions in payment.

UK pension regulation is changing significantly but incrementally. In general, regulation has become more risk-focused, looking closer at the funding level of pension funds and the covenant of the plan sponsor. Companies are encouraged to accelerate the funding of their pension funds' deficits. The Pensions Act 2004 established the 'Pension Protection Fund' (PPF), a protection scheme for pension benefits, as well as a new regulator: 'The Pensions Regulator'. The new regulation aims to protect the benefits of scheme members while avoiding the threat of 'moral hazard' inherent in the US system. Therefore, the PPF levy is partly risk-based, taking into account the covenant of the plan sponsor and the funding situation of the pension scheme. Also, a new funding regulation was introduced, but - unlike in other

---

9. See Kakes, J. (2006), 'Financial behaviour of Dutch pension funds', DNB Working Paper no. 108.
10. Theoretically, the change from DB to DC should be accompanied by higher contributions as a price for the risk, which is transferred from the employer to the employee.

countries - not clearly specified, as the UK regulation is scheme-specific and principle-based. Pension funds are required to adopt a 'Statutory Funding Objective', set out in a statement of funding principles. In general, funds should have 'sufficient and appropriate assets to cover their technical provisions (essentially their accrued liabilities)[11]. In case of a shortfall, the trustees have to prepare a recovery plan. As the new regulations are being phased in over 3 years with the forthcoming actuarial valuations, a new market practice has not yet evolved. To give the market some orientation, the Pension Regulator released its 'trigger points' for intervention, while stressing that these are not funding targets. In general, a funding target of either less than 100% in a PPF or IFRS valuation and/or a recovery period of more than 10 years may trigger some further investigation by the regulator.

Since pension schemes all use their own actuarial assumptions and valuation methods, for reasons of comparison, the valuation rules of the accounting standard FRS 17 are usually applied, although they apply for disclosure in the plan sponsor's accounts only and not for the funding of the pension scheme itself,. On a FRS 17 basis, UK pension funds are about 85% funded with a combined deficit of around GBP 40bn[12]. For accounting periods from 2005 onwards, UK listed companies are under EU law required to adopt IAS19. The two accounting standards are being harmonised, and both will require the recognition of the pension scheme asset or liability on the balance sheet, with pension fund deficits directly reducing shareholders' equity.

When a plan sponsor seeks to terminate the pension plan, he is liable to the buy-out liability with an insurance company. The buy-out liability will most often significantly exceed the pension liability in a regulatory or even accounting valuation[13]. Nevertheless, the interest of plan sponsors in disposing of their 'legacy cost' seems to be high, as is indicated by a number of new entrants into this potentially lucrative market.

As in the Netherlands, investment regulations are based on the prudent person standard. There are no investment ceilings other than a 5% ceiling on investment in the sponsoring employer.

In general, the discussion on the proper risk, a pension fund should take in its investment policy has become quite polarised in the UK. While most

---

11. http://www.thepensionsregulator.gov.uk/codesAndGuidance/codes/inForce/definedBenefit/index.aspx
12. 2005 NAPF Annual Survey, Pension Fund Investment.
13. Lane, Clark & Peacock estimates the total buy-out deficit of the FTSE 100 companies at over GDP 176bn in July 2006 compared to an IAS19 deficit of GBP 36bn (see: 'Accounting For Pensions: UK and Europe, Annual Survey 2006').

pension funds still adhere to the high risk-profile of the 'old 70:30 balanced mandate', where 70% of the assets are invested in equity and 30% in bonds, many have or are seeking to adopt 'Liability Immunisation Strategies', thereby significantly reducing investment risk, but also potentially decreasing investment returns and thus increasing the long-term costs for the sponsor. Although LDI strategies are still a much discussed niche product with 5% - 10% of overall pension fund assets estimated to be invested in LDI products, the change in the market SAA is already obvious, the equity exposure has been lowered from around 70% to around 60% with the balance being invested in lower-risk assets[14].

United States

In spite of the long-term, steady shift from DB to DC, DB pension plans still account for about 50% of pension assets under management in the US. Of those participants covered by DB plans, about 77% are covered by a traditional plan, of which over half have a final salary plan. However, despite some legal uncertainties that have slowed their adoption since the late 1990s, cash balance plans[15] have slowly gained in importance, and currently cover about 21% of DB plan participants[16]. Many large companies, particularly those in manufacturing and other older industries offer both DB and DC plans[17].

Although sponsors of DB plans are legally required to offer retirement benefits in the form of an annuity, about half of all participants have the option of receiving their benefit in the form of a full or partial lump sum. There is a huge variety of plan formulas among DB plans. Indexation is neither legally required nor market practice. Pension plans, especially those that are not collectively bargained, have to pass a series of coverage and eligibility test in order to maintain their tax-exempt status. To ensure compliance with these tests, most private sector employers established non-contributory plans (the contribution is paid by the employer only), where each member of the workforce is automatically enrolled upon meeting certain minimum requirements.

---

14. NAPF, Annual Survey 2005, September 2005.
15. Cash balance plans combine features of DB and DC plans. The employer specifies a contribution and guarantees an interest rate on that contribution. However, the accounts for individual participants are notional, and the plan is funded and invested by the plan sponsor. Benefits earned through participation in a cash balance plan are insured by the PBGC up to certain limits. In addition, although cash balance plans must offer participants the option of receiving their benefits in the form of an annuity, at retirement are usually paid as a lump sum.
16. See US Department of Labor (2006) Private Pension Plan Bulletin.
17. See: Mercer (2005). How Does Your Retirement Program Stack Up?

In August 2006, the Congress enacted comprehensive pension reform legislation. This new law, the Pension Protection Act of 2006, was aimed at improving the financial stability of the DB pension system and reducing the financial pressures on the 'Pension Benefit Guaranty Corporation' (PBGC), the government agency that insures benefits for private pension participants. In recent years, the PBGC has suffered a deterioration of its finances The PBGC's net position fell from a surplus of USD 7.7.bn in 2001 to a deficit of USD 18.4bn in November 2006 for its single-employer insurance program, due to the termination of a number of large underfunded pension funds by bankrupt sponsors, mainly in the steel and airlines industry. Given that at least several of these had been considered as adequately funded under the old regulatory regime, a consensus emerged that the existing plan funding rules were seriously deficient.[18] For example, under the old funding rules, sponsors were required to fund to between 90% to 100% of the plan's current liability[19], but were given considerable leeway in choosing the actuarial assumptions and methodology to reduce their contributions. At funding levels below 90%, sponsors were required to increase their contributions although other provisions had the actual effect of few sponsors ever making these additional contributions. In addition, sponsors had to be cognisant of not making too large a contribution in any single year to avoid exceeding the plan's maximum deductible contribution, which could threaten the plan's tax-exempt status. At least for some plans, this strict upper funding level prevented pension plans from accumulating reserves in times of good investment returns.

Under the Pension Protection Act 2006, US pension funds will ultimately be required to fully fund their pension liabilities. At first, the extension of relief measures to 2006 and 2007 – mainly the use of corporate bonds as discount factors for calculating the deficit reduction contribution as compared to the yield on 30-year Treasury Bonds – gives pension funds a 'funding break'. From 2008 onwards, pension funds are required to accelerate their contributions to amortise deficits over seven years. Pension liabilities will be discounted using a simplified yield curve based on a two-year average of high-grade corporate bonds. Actuarial assumptions and valuations methods will be prescribed by law. Furthermore, the funding level will affect not only employer's contribution, but also employees' benefits: If a pension fund is funded below 80%, the pension fund may not increase benefits, below 60% funding the accrual of promised benefits is

---

18. See e.g. United States Government Accountability Office: Report to Congressional Committees, May 2005, 'Private Pensions: Recent Experiences of Large Defined Benefit Plans Illustrate Weakness in Funding Rules'.
19. The current liability is the present value of accrued benefits calculated using partly mandated assumptions, e.g. mortality table, and a discount rate based on the yield of 30-year Treasury Bonds. It is calculated on a plan termination basis.

stopped; benefits are actually frozen. Some smoothing mechanisms for assets, liabilities and contributions will be still available, but restricted to 2 year-averages. The tax-relevant deductibility limit on contributions will be increased to 150% of the current liability already from 2006 onwards. While these measures are expected to increase the funding level of US pension funds, they are also likely to increase the volatility of contributions for the employer.

Besides the changes enacted in the Pension Protection Act, plan sponsors will also have to operate under a different set of accounting rules. According to the current rules, plan assets can be measured applying up to 5-year averages of market values. As under IAS 19 and FRS 17, liabilities have to be calculated as the projected benefit obligation. FASB's current rules regarding interest rate assumptions have been comparatively vague, requiring the discount rate to reflect the rate at which the pension benefit can be efficiently settled, but not prescribing a specific interest rate. Consequently, the use of the long-term expected rate of return on the plan's assets was widespread. For actuarial gains and losses the same smoothing mechanism are available as under IFRS rules. As the accounting rules were widely criticised for not reflecting the financial situation of pension funds[20], FASB set up a review project with two phases. FASB recently issued the results of phase one, which will apply from 2007 onwards. The first major change is that the funded status of the pension fund has to be explicitly recognised on the balance sheet and not simply acknowledged in the notes. In addition, plan assets and liabilities have to be recognised in the year in which they occur and measured as of the date of the financial statement. The second and more important change refers to the discount rate for valuing pensions, which must now be based on the yield of high-quality bonds instead of the expected rate of return on plan assets. Phase two comprises a new assessment of pension accounting and will take some years to complete and implement. Together, all of these changes imply that from 2007 onwards, also US companies will be exposed to considerable volatility due to pension funds in their accounting systems.

Investment regulations are based on the prudent expert principle, following modern portfolio theory. There are no quantitative investment ceilings other than a 10% ceiling on investment in the sponsoring employer, but extensive qualitative regulations, mainly via litigation.

The governance of US pension funds clearly provides incentives for risk taking by the pension fiduciaries. US pension funds are the only investor group analysed in this project that have actually increased the risk level of

---

20. See e.g. Ryan, R., and Fabozzi, F. 'Rethinking Pension Liabilities and Asset Allocation', in: The Journal of Portfolio Management, 2002, pp. 7-15.

their portfolio by moving out of bonds and into alternative assets. Although LDI has not yet reached the US market, this is widely expected to change under the new pension regulations, and the U.S. Labor Department has already accepted LDI strategies as conforming to the fiduciary requirements under ERISA[21].

---

21. see: http://www.dol.gov/ebsa/regs/aos/ao2006-08a.html

References

van Binsbergen, J. H. and Brandt, M. W. (2007), "Optimal Asset Allocation in Asset Liability Management", *NBER Working Paper #12970*, March 2007.

Boender, G. C. E., van Aalst, P. and Heemskerk, F. (1998), "Modelling and management of assets and liabilities of pension plans in the Netherlands." in *Worldwide Asset and Liability Modelling*, J. M. Mulvey and W. T. Ziemba (eds.). Cambridge, Cambridge University Press: pp. 561 - 580.

Boulier, J., Michel, S., and Wisnia, V. (1996) "Optimizing investment and contribution policies for a defined benefit pension fund", AFIR Colloquium.

Dert, C. (1998), 'A Dynamic Model for Asset Liability Managing for Defined Benefit Pension Funds', in *Worldwide Asset and Liability Modelling*, Mulvey, J. and W. Ziemba (eds.).

Exley, J., Mehta, S. and Smith, A. (2000) 'Asset and Liability Modelling for Pension Funds', paper presented to the Joint Institute and Faculty of Actuaries Investment Conference June 2000.

Government Actuary's Department (2006), "Occupational Pension Schemes 2005: The thirteenth survey by the Government Actuary", London: The Government Actuary's Department, June 2006.

Heubeck, K., Herrmann, R., D'Souza, G. (2006), 'Die Richttafeln 2005 G – Modell, Herleitung, Formeln', DGVFM-Blätter, April 2006.

Kocken, T. P. (2006), *Curious Contracts: Pension Fund Redesign for the Future*, 's-Hertogenbosch: Tutein Nolthenius.

Kortleve, N. and Ponds, E. (2006), "Pension deals and value-based ALM", in Niels Kortleve, Theo Nijman, and Eduard Ponds (eds.) *Fair Value and Pension Fund Management*, Oxford, Amsterdam, Elsevier: pp. 181-209.

Kortleve, N, Nyman, T. and E. Ponds, edited, (2006), *Fair Value and Pension Fund Management*, Oxford, Amsterdam, Elsevier.

Klumpes, P., Li, Y. and Whittington, M. (2003), "The Impact of UK Accounting Rule Changes on Pension Terminations," *Warwick Business School Working Paper*, August 2003.

Orszag, J. M. and Sand, N. (2006), "Corporate Finance and Capital Markets". in the *Oxford Handbook of Pensions and Retirement Income*. G. L. Clark, Alicia H. Munell and J. Michael Orszag (eds.), Oxford, Oxford University Press: pp. 399-414.

van Rooij, M., Siegmann, A., and Vlaar, P. (2004), "A Pension Asset and Liability Model for the Netherlands", *DNB Research Memorandum WO no 760*, April 2004.

Scherer, B. (2006) (ed), "Asset and Liability Management Tools: A Handbook for Best Practice", B. Scherer. London, Risk Books.

Sharpe, W. (1976), 'Corporate Pension Funding Policy', in the *Journal of Financial Economics* 3/2, pp. 183-93.

Stewart, F. (2005), "Developments in Pension Fund Risk Management in Selected OECD and Asian countries", www.oecd.org/dataoecd/38/52/34030924.pdf.

Vlaar, P. (2005) "Defined benefit pension plans and regulation", *DNB Working Paper No. 63*, De Nederlandsche Bank, December 2005.

Whittington, G. (2006), 'Accounting Standards for Pension Costs', in 'The Oxford Handbook of Pensions and Retirement Income' Gordon L. Clark, Alicia H. Munnell, and J. Michael Orszag (eds.), Oxford University Press, 2006; Oxford.

Yermo, J (2007), "Reforming the Valuation and Funding of Pension Promises: Are Occupational Pensions Safer?", this volume.

Ziemba, W. T., J. M. Mulvey, et al. (1998), *Worldwide asset and liability modeling*, Cambridge, Cambridge University Press.

ISBN-978-92-64-02810-4
Protecting Pensions: Policy Analysis
and Examples from OECD Countries
© OECD 2007

Chapter 5

Pension Fund Guarantee Schemes

by
Fiona Stewart

I. Introduction

The issue of pension benefit security is currently in the foreground of both economic and political debate in many OECD countries. After a 'golden age' for pension funds, which enjoyed high investment returns and funding surpluses throughout the 1990s, a more troubled period has emerged since the start of the millennium. With equity market corrections, (and the subsequent questioning of long-term equity return assumptions), a low interest rate environment, asset liability mismatches, severe underfunding (highlighted by accounting changes), ageing populations, financial scandals and loss of pension benefits, the whole defined benefit pension system in many countries is under assault. Once the rise in defined contribution schemes (and the uncertainty they inherently entail) as well as the scaling back of government pensions are also taken into consideration, people of all ages are rightly asking what retirement income they can rely on? Though the subject has been debated on many occasions, recent events have ensured that the topic of pension benefit security has once again become a focus for policy discussion.

Some countries have dealt with benefit protection via strong funding rules (the route taken for example by the Dutch authorities). This paper examines an alternative method of increasing benefit security in retirement – pension benefit guarantee schemes (the option current being introduced in the UK). The ultimate risk faced by beneficiaries of defined benefit occupational pension schemes, (or defined contribution type schemes where the pension fund itself is responsible for any return, benefit promise or guarantee), is the loss of their retirement income were their corporate plan sponsor to go bankrupt whilst the company pension plan is underfunded. Given rising bankruptcy levels and widespread underfunding, the likelihood of such an event seems to have increased in several countries. Benefit guarantee schemes, also known as insolvency guarantee schemes, cover lost pension income in such cases. This paper will examine the arguments for and against such schemes at both a theoretical and practical level. Detail studies of the countries where these schemes exist will then follow.

II. Arguments for Benefit Guarantee Schemes.

i. Market Failure

The main theoretical argument in favour of benefit guarantee schemes is derived from the concept of market failure. In theoretical terms, pensions can be seen as deferred wages, provided by companies in return for workers sacrificing some current income or other form of compensation. In estimating how much current wages they are prepared to give up in order to receive a pension income in retirement, employees calculate the perceived security of the sponsoring firm honouring these future promises. The lower the sponsoring firm's bankruptcy risk, the more wage concessions a company can extract for a given level of promised pension benefits. In a perfectly competitive market with full information workers in poorly funded plans with a near- bankrupt employer will grant few or no wage concessions as they do not believe that their pension will ever be paid. Consequently, compensation for bankruptcy and loss of pension should already have been considered through this trade off mechanism[1].

The problem with this theory (as pointed out by Mitchell (1987), Ippolito (1985/ 1987) and others) is that workers do not necessarily understand the bargains and calculations they are making, and do not always have all the information necessary to make such decisions – given the complicating issue of asymmetric information between workers and employers. They consequently remain more exposed to the bankruptcy of the sponsoring firm than their wage bargaining implies. The recent outcry over the loss of pension benefits by workers of several UK firms would certainly suggest that this is the case[2]. The justification for pension benefit guarantee schemes is that they provide an extra layer of security for beneficiaries against a sponsor's bankruptcy and therefore compensate for any asymmetric information situation and correct for any market failure.

Cooper and Ross (1994) describe this market failure in terms of 'market fragilities' and contracting problems. Markets are fragile when buyers may lose confidence that sellers will not stay in the market long enough to fulfill their contractual obligations. The problem arises in any buyer-seller setting where the current action of the buyer is taken in anticipation of a future action by the seller. Guarantee funds have been set up in many sectors (pension benefits, deposit insurance, travel packages etc.) in order to support trade in such potentially fragile markets, by acting as a substitute or backup in case a seller cannot commit to future market participation and cannot honour a contract. Pension benefit guarantee funds operate by providing confidence to workers who may otherwise be concerned about the future viability of their firm and its ability to honour its pension promises. If workers become concerned enough, they might leave the firm or demand higher wages today, either of which could hurt the company and make the very bankruptcy event they fear a self fulfilling prophesy. As in the case of deposit insurance, pension guarantees can avoid this type of behavioural run.

ii. Diversification

A further aspect of the market failure discussed above is the issue of diversification. Even if it is accepted that workers do have all the information required to make an efficient trade-off between current wages and future retirement income, a market failure may still occur due to the problem of diversification. Workers in occupation pension schemes receive their current and future income from the same source, and are therefore highly dependent on their employer, suffering a 'double blow' if the company enters bankruptcy. Portfolio theory argues that efficient risk bearing requires sufficient diversification across asset classes and individual issuers. Yet it may be difficult for employees to diversify the risk posed by their current and future income coming from a single source. Most employees are unlikely to have assets or portfolios of sufficient size or the investment expertise necessary to hedge the risk of their pension assets, as for many workers occupational pension benefits constitute a large proportion of total retirement savings. Only the most highly compensated managerial employees may have the financial wealth and knowledge required to diversify away the risks of their defined benefit pension claims, yet even they may face restrictions (*e.g.* on short-selling the firm's securities). Diversification is especially difficult if membership of the corporate pension scheme is mandatory, or for life time employees who work for a single firm during their careers. The problem with this situation is pointed out by Bodie (1996). Despite the fact that they are unable to diversify their pension risk, when it comes to their pension benefit workers often wish to have as low a risk exposure as possible to their retirement income. Bodie therefore argues that few employees would consciously agree to accept default risk on their pension benefits in order to increase their expected cash wages, even if they have all of the relevant information necessary to assess the default risk of the firm - which in most cases they do not which makes the welfare loss even greater.

The problem of diversification becomes even more key when pensions are funded via a book reserve system. In such cases, pension benefits are not secured by an external pool of diversified assets, as pension assets form part of the plan sponsor's balance sheet. As a consequence a book reserve system can be likened to a funded system in which all of the pension plan assets are invested in a single security – *i.e.* the debt of the sponsoring firm. If the plan sponsor were to go bankrupt the accrued pensions of both active and retired workers would clearly be at risk. In theory pension fund trustees could overcome this concentrated exposure, for example by shorting the sponsoring company's stock. However restrictions will usually be in place to prevent this and, where the pension fund is particularly large compared with the market capitalisation of the sponsoring firm, such action could have an extremely adverse effect on the share price. Hence benefit guarantee schemes are often compulsory for firms operating internal forms of funding (as is the case in Germany and Sweden).

III. Challenges for benefit guarantee schemes.

i. Moral Hazard

The main theoretical argument against pension benefit guarantee schemes is moral hazard. This is a classic problem with any type of insurance, where the buyer of the insurance product adopts riskier models of behaviour as an undesirable response to the financial protection provided by the insurance carrier. In the case of pension benefit guarantees, if a plan sponsor knows that upon bankruptcy their pension fund liabilities will be covered, even if sufficient assets are not available to back these promise, they may be incentivised to indulge in irresponsible behaviour, leaving others to cover the costs of the pension promises they have made. Such behaviour may include raising benefits to unsupportable levels, cutting their own contribution rates, or pursuing a risky investment strategy. Moral hazard can be avoided to some extent, for example by not covering increases in benefits awarded in a period leading up to bankruptcy (as is the case with in PSVaG in Germany). Other measures can be put in place to reduce incentives to abuse the insurance system, such as limiting the pension benefit covered (as is the case with the Ontario fund) or by imposing strict funding rules to limit the size of the potential claim taken on by the guarantee scheme. Moral hazard can also be limited by charging higher premiums as the pension becomes more underfunded, or if a risky investment strategy is followed. However, if premiums paid to the guarantee fund do not fully reflect the risk presented by the insured it is impossible to eliminate moral hazard completely.

ii. Adverse Selection

The problem of adverse selection also stems from the mispricing of premiums. If, when setting the premium rate, due consideration is not taken of the contributing firm's bankruptcy risk, pension funding level and investment policy, stronger member firms will inevitably end up subsidising weaker ones. If these cross subsidies are too high the problem of adverse selection kicks in, with financially secure firms finding ways of pulling out of the guarantee system (*e.g.* by replacing their defined benefit schemes with defined contribution ones). Guarantee scheme members therefore have the incentive to follow others out of the system in a 'bank run' type fashion to avoid being the last solvent member shouldering the burden of the underfunding of all bankrupt members.

The risk pricing of premiums does, however, seem to be very difficult to achieve in practice. Various studies have shown that premiums charged by existing pension guarantee schemes are not properly priced as they do not truly adjust premiums to take account of all sources of risk[3]. Most schemes do adjust for underfunding levels (*e.g.* PBGF of Ontario or the Japanese guarantee fund), but do not adjust for the solvency of the corporate plan sponsor, despite corporate debt markets making such judgments on companies daily. The UK authorities have indicated that their new guarantee scheme will take account of insolvency risk and the pension fund's investment policy, but the details have not yet been set. The problem seems to be that fully risk adjusted premiums would be too expensive for many firms to bear, with proper firm specific pricing of premiums pushing the weakest firms into bankruptcy, thereby hurting the very workers the insurance system was trying to help. Another problem may be that to fully reserve for possible future claims and therefore to keep the guarantee system adequately funded would also be prohibitively expensive, given that claims tend to be 'lumpy' and several standard deviation risks would have to be covered[4]. A further conundrum raised by properly risk adjusted premiums is that they could spell the final nail in the coffin for defined benefit schemes by making these too expensive for plan sponsors to operate and therefore finally persuading them to move to DC style plans (which once again places more risk in the hands of the beneficiaries the scheme was initially supposed to protect).[5]

iii.   Systemic Risk Issues

One reason given as to why pension guarantee premiums are not priced correctly (and indeed cannot be as they would be prohibitively expensive) is that there is systemic risk involved in guaranteeing pension benefits. This stems from the fact that the bankruptcy and underfunding risks of plan members are correlated, meaning that the insured risk cannot be spread sufficiently. The basic principle underlying any insurance system is the sharing of non-systemic risk. Insurance works when the incidence and severity of events covered by the insurance scheme are relatively independent across the insured population. Pension benefits can be insured for non-systemic events (such as poor corporate management, fraud etc.). They cannot, however, provide cover for systemic ones, such as macroeconomic weakness, which increases the bankruptcy risk of all companies, or sharp equity market and interest rate declines (which are systemic problems given the similar liability structure of occupational pension schemes and their tendency to follow the same asset allocation patterns). To make matters worse, bankruptcy risk is highly correlated with underfunding, as plan sponsors tend to stop making contributions to their pension funds when they get into financial difficulty. In addition, guarantee schemes which actually take over the assets of failed pension plans (such as the PBGC in the US and the future PPF in the UK) may face an extra layer of correlation if they invest the assets which they have taken over in the same manner as the pension funds which they are guaranteeing. If their investment returns turn negative at the same time as their clients, their own financial position worsens. Other schemes, such as the PSVaG in Germany are not exposed to this risk as they cover the pension liabilities which they take over by buying annuities. As pension funds become a larger part of the corporate capital structure it is possible that this systemic risk will increase even further (and in some cases insolvent pension funds may even cause the bankruptcy of the company).

Some argue that systemic risk may be the reason why *private sector* pension benefit guarantee insurance is impossible, but actually explains why *government sponsored* schemes are necessary. Pesando (1996) argues that due to systemic risk private markets may not be able to provide plan termination insurance even if demanded or that this insurance could exist only at premium rates that are commensurate with these risks. The subsequent argument is that governments must therefore step in to provide beneficiaries with the necessary coverage. However, given developments in financial markets, financial (risk hedging) products and the increasing sophistication of private sector investment banks, it is really possible to argue that the private sector is still not capable of providing coverage for pension benefits?[6]

However, the major difficulty with government backed schemes is persuading tax payers to accept the burden of pension insurance costs. In practice this means tax payers, (who are, it should be noted, in many countries seeing their state pensions being reduced), subsidising or indeed bailing out those lucky enough to still be in corporate defined benefit schemes, and who tend to be relatively well paid – a situation which may not be tenable. The fiscal burden of such guarantee schemes can be lessened to some extent, for example by imposing strict funding rules or asset matching requirements (which prevent pension schemes from becoming severe underfunded), or by placing a ceiling on benefits covered (as is the case with the scheme in Ontario, which provides protection only up to CAD$12,000). Yet governments are inevitably expected to be the final protectors of retirement income in times of systemic stress and, particularly if these schemes are mandatory or incentivised, surely it is difficult for the government *not* to act as a lender of last resorts should systemic problems arise?

IV. Practical Issues

i. Political vs. Economic

Following on from the observations on possible governmental involvement in these schemes, it should be noted that pension benefit guarantee schemes have generally been set up in reaction to political events. Maybe the justification for the existence of such schemes can really be found in the realm of politics rather than economic efficiency, as they often have implicit, if not explicit, cross-subsidy and transfer objectives? For example, it has been argued that the PBGC was set up during in the USA during the 1970's to support mature industrial sectors of the economy.[7] Meanwhile, it is interesting to note that the only Canadian province to offer pension insurance is Ontario, which is often seen as the industrial heartland of the country, and that this guarantee fund was set up in 1980 following a series of threatened plant shutdowns. The decision to introduce a guarantee scheme in the UK follows intense political pressure to cover pension losses for over 65,000 members of company schemes who have seen their plan sponsors become bankrupt in recent years. Yet it has been forcefully argued that whatever the merits of industry support subsidies, there are good reasons not to use cheap pension guarantees as the way to subsidise firms as these are not highly visible and can lead to serious market distortions in resource allocation.[8]

If these schemes were set up for political reasons in the past, could a similar argument be made to justify their continued existence today? Are the increased bankruptcy levels experienced in several countries in the last few years simply cyclical, a legacy of the 'dot com' bubble and the last vestiges of industrial decline? Or do they represent a structural change, as a more aggressive, competitive form of capitalism takes hold, particularly in countries such as Japan and Germany which previously ran 'corporatist capitalism' models where few firms failed? Has pension underfunding also become more of a structural rather than a cyclical issue, given the lower return but higher volatility environment of the capital markets, combined with pressure from increasingly demanding and public accounting requirements? If the latter is the case, could there be an argument that pension benefit guarantee schemes will be more necessary in future?

ii. *Alternatives*

Pension benefit guarantee schemes cannot be discussed entirely in isolation, given they should act as the last barrier in the protection of retirement income, in place in case all other measures fail. Indeed it could be argued that they are unnecessary if the rest of the system is properly structured. For example, if the academic theories discussed at the start of this paper hold true, market failures could be overcome by providing workers with proper information and education in order to make their wage/pension trade off effectively (though it should be stressed that in reality this is highly unlikely). Alternatively, asset allocation rules could be applied so that pension liabilities are fully immunised and matched with appropriate assets. Likewise, pension claims could be given high bankruptcy priority or secured creditor rights, so that liabilities would be covered by the firm's assets, ahead of other creditors, in the case of bankruptcy of the plan sponsor.

One alternative way of guaranteeing pension benefits is to impose strict funding rules, ensuring that pensions are never underfunded - the solution which has been adopted by the Dutch authorities[9]. Pensando (2000) and others have, however, stressed that it is impossible to ensure that pension funds are always 100% funded, for example when investment returns deteriorate sharply, when actuarial assumptions prove incorrect, or when instruments required for full 'immunisation' are not available. Full funding is additionally challenged by the fact that corporate plan sponsors tend to stop making pension contributions as their financial situation become more difficult. Funding rules may also conflict with other policy objectives (such as surplus funding being taxed). Pension benefit guarantee schemes may, therefore, have a role to play, even when stringent funding regulations are in place.

What can, however, be stressed is that a pension guarantee fund works more effectively when combined with adequate funding rules. Overly lax (and loosely applied) funding regulation has been cited as one of the main causes of the financial difficulties of the PBGC in the USA (see country discussion). Likewise in the UK, despite minimum funding rules proving inadequate in the past, concerns are being raised over whether new scheme specific funding rules will provide sufficient protection for the new PPF scheme. Without adequate funding rules claims on pension guarantee schemes have effectively no upside limit, potentially making premiums extremely (if not prohibitively) expensive. Strict funding and investment rules should be seen as compliments to any pension guarantee scheme. For example, if funding rules and guarantee schemes are designed to work together the problem of 'systematic underfunding' (where a company deliberately cuts back on pension contributions as it gets into financial difficulty) can be tackled.[10] Insolvency schemes can also be combined with other pension protection measures, such as asset allocation controls or priority bankruptcy rights, to ensure that there is some upside protection to the level of claims.[11] This prevents all the responsibility for pension benefit protection falling onto the guarantee scheme, a responsibility which may prove prohibitively expensive, making the scheme unworkable.

iii. Other guarantee schemes

Perhaps practical arguments in favour of pension guarantee schemes can be found through looking at equivalent schemes which have been successfully operated in other sectors – notably insurance?[12] Policyholder protection funds or guarantee schemes within the insurance sector are fairly common across OECD countries, usually for a specific class of insurance (compulsory motor insurance being the most common), but also in some countries for more general insurance contracts. The arguments put forward for these schemes are largely the same as those for pension protection funds, including overcoming an asymmetry of information and injecting confidence into the system to prevent bank deposit style runs. The drawbacks are also very similar, focusing on moral hazard, cross subsidy and structural correlation problems. As with pension guarantees, insurance guarantee systems were often introduced in reaction to political pressure following insurance company failures and their necessity is seen as differing according to the specific situation in countries (*e.g.* those countries placing insurance policy holders high in the bankruptcy creditor list are seen as having less need for an additional insurance system). Government guarantees stand explicitly or implicitly behind most schemes. Yet despite these insurance guarantee schemes received resounding support from the European Commission in a recent Working Paper,[13] the Commission is not recommending such guarantee funds be introduced for pension benefits (perhaps because most European countries either operate DC pension funds, or apply strict funding and asset allocation rules so that guarantee schemes would only be required in a few countries).

V. Conclusion

Pension benefit guarantee schemes do not come without their difficulties. One case where a definitive argument can, however, be made in their favour is when pensions are funded using a book reserve system. In this case, the lack of diversification seems to be an overriding issue and some form of benefit guarantee system is therefore required. Indeed, the OECD's 'Guidelines on funding and benefit security' highlight just such a situation:[14]

1.3 Occupational defined benefit plans should in general be funded through the establishment of a pension fund or through an insurance arrangement (or a combination of these mechanisms). Additional protection may be provided through the granting of priority creditor rights to plan members and beneficiaries and through insolvency guaranty schemes that protect pension benefits in the case of insolvency of the plan sponsor.

1.4 Private unfunded plans should generally be prohibited. The establishment of an insolvency guaranty scheme should in general be required for occupational defined benefit plans that are financed through the book reserve system.

1.5 Insolvency guaranty schemes should rely on appropriate pricing of the insurance provided in order to avoid unwarranted incentives for risk-taking (moral hazard).

For autonomous pension funds, the need for a pension benefit guarantee scheme is less clear cut. Their inherent difficulties (moral hazard, cross subsidies, systemic correlations) imply that other (less political) means for protecting pension benefits should be introduced first. Good funding rules can achieve almost all of what a guarantee scheme is striving for, are arguably easier to design and manage and, especially when combined with other measures, (such as asset liability matching or priority bankruptcy rights), offer a high level of protection. If a guarantee scheme is successfully combined with funding rules or other protection measures it can effectively perform its task as a 'last resort' benefit protection measure.

A further conclusion which can be drawn is that if guarantee schemes are to be introduced they must be carefully designed in order to avoid their inherent weaknesses. The failure of the pension guarantee fund in Finland in the early 1990's,[15] or indeed the Savings and Loan fiasco in the USA in the

1980s, (see US country section), show how important it is to design any insurance system carefully. Positive aspects can be identified in all of the guarantee schemes currently in operation. For example, the PBGC in the US phases in improvements made to benefits, limits the amount of benefit covered and can impose involuntary terminations on corporations in a difficult financial situation, in order to prevent the size of the potential claim against the guarantee fund escalating out of control. The scheme operating in Ontario corrects for some of the mistakes made on the introduction of the PBGC in the USA, including prohibiting the voluntary termination of underfunded plans (thereby limiting moral hazard and the exercise of the 'pension put' against the guarantee fund by employers that could continue supporting their pension fund) and holding a lien on the assets of the plan sponsor. Meanwhile, benefit improvements granted in the two years before bankruptcy are not covered by the German PSVaG. The great strength of the Swedish insurance system is its strong collateral backing, whilst the Swiss scheme (like those in Germany and Sweden) buys out annuities, rather than taking on the assets of pension plans. The Pension Guarantee fund in Japan can refuse a claim if funding levels are too low.

Drawing on these practical experiences, both good and bad, the following principles for the successful operation of a pension benefit guarantee system can be identified:[16]

- *Limited benefit coverage:* in order to limit moral hazard, certain benefits should be excluded from coverage (including improvements granted prior to insolvency). A ceiling on benefit coverage also seems reasonable, to make payments more acceptable if tax payer's money is involved and to keep the system affordable.

- *Risk based pricing:* the key to any insurance scheme's success (avoiding moral hazard and adverse selection) is the proper risk pricing of premiums, based on the expected claim levels for the insured. In the case of pensions, premiums should reflect the likelihood of the plan sponsor becoming insolvent (could be via proxy measures such as credit rating, swap levels etc.), the likely size of the claim, the extent of the pension plan's underfunding, and the risk inherent in any asset liability mismatch. Market based pricing is essential. Over the long term the aggregate level of premiums (+ investment returns) should reflect aggregate claim levels (and maybe a surplus should also be built), with flexibility needed to adjust premium levels as reality veers from estimates.

- *Accurate and consistent funding rules:* pension benefits should as far as possible be fully funded, and plan sponsors should be required to act swiftly in order to limit losses. Successfully combining a guarantee scheme with funding rules ensures some upside limit to potential claims and makes the guarantee scheme affordable. In order to ensure stable funding, consistent and adequate financial measurement and disclosure are required.

- *Prudent asset liability management:* pension funds should be encouraged to follow prudent asset allocation strategies, which avoid large swings in funding levels, again limiting potential claims and making the guarantee scheme more affordable. Likewise the guarantee fund itself, if it takes over the assets of insolvent pension schemes, should follow an appropriate investment strategy, and one which avoids correlations between its own financial position and the funding level of the pension funds it is insuring. In order to avoid such correlations, guarantee funds may use annuities to buy out pension liabilities taken over.

- *Adequate powers*: a pension guarantee scheme needs to have adequate powers to avoid moral hazard, and prevent plan sponsors using their guarantee as a 'put' for their pension liabilities. For example, extra premiums or collateral must be requested (and paid) as a scheme becomes more underfunded or the risk of insolvency at the plan sponsor rises. This again requires transparent and timely disclosure of information by the plan sponsor. Proper powers to claim assets via the bankruptcy process may also help the funding and functioning of the guarantee scheme. Any guarantee scheme needs to operate without undue political influence.

In summary, pension benefit guarantee schemes should be run in a truly economically efficient manner, with properly market priced premiums. If this proves prohibitively expensive, the cost of guaranteeing pension benefits can be reduced by combining with other benefit protection measures. However, for the guarantee scheme to work effectively, subsidies should not be provided, either implicitly or explicitly, by governments.

VI. Country Studies

The case studies discussed below consist only of countries which offer explicit insolvency insurance for defined benefit pension plans, triggered when the sponsoring firm becomes bankrupt and the assets do not meet the accrued benefits of the pension plan. Implicit guarantees also exist in some countries, but will not be discussed here (*e.g.* 20 year minimum benefit in Chile). Elsewhere compensation funds exist, providing cover in the case of fraud and illegal activities for pension income (and sometimes other benefits, *e.g.* mutual funds), but these are also not discussed.

United States

i. Description

History: A series of corporate failures (such as the Studebaker auto company in the 1960s) provoked the ERISA pension legislation which was eventually adopted in 1974. This included a guarantee programme, known as the Pension Benefit Guarantee Corporation (PBGC).

Coverage: The PBGC administers separate programmes for single and multiple employer defined benefit pension plans. As of 2006, the single employer insurance covers 34.2 m workers in 28,800 pension plans and the multi employer program 9.9m workers in 1600 plans. A total of 1.3 million people are currently receiving or owed benefits from the PBGC, whose annual benefit payments now total $3.686 billion.[17]

Operations: The PBGC is liable for the payment of guaranteed benefits with respect only to underfunded, terminated plans. Distress terminations occur when a company voluntarily terminates its pension plan (having filed for bankruptcy, or if the pension costs are proving unreasonably burdensome due to a decline in the number of employees covered). Involuntary terminations occur when the PBGC terminates a pension plan due to a lack of funding, or if the loss to the PBGC is expected to increase unreasonably if the plan is not wound up. In the event of the insolvency of a member corporation, the PBGC becomes the trustee of the plan assets and administers the payment of future plan benefits up to a specified maximum annual pension (c$47,659 per year for a 65 year old in 2006, with adjustments for other ages). Some other benefits (unvested, early retirement) are not protected. Guaranteed benefits that are created by plan amendments less than 5 years old are phased in at a rate of 20% a year. In the case of multi-employer schemes, the PBGC steps in when a covered plan no longer has assets available to make benefit payments (not when the sponsor is bankrupt). Assistance is usually provided in the form of loans, though companies often cannot fully repay them. The maximum guarantee under the multi-employer scheme is $12,870 per year. The PBGC has dealt with 3,595 terminated plans during its history, 120 new claims being made as of September 2005.

Premiums: The scheme has three main sources of income: premiums, trustee assets, and investment income. Premiums are charged on flat rate basis (raised from $19 to $30 per plan participant as of 2006) and there is also a variable component ($9 per $1000 of underfunded vested benefits). Premiums for the multi-employer plan are charged at $2.60 per head. Premium income from single employer plans in 2006 amounted to $1.44bn (flat rate premiums $883m, variable rate $550m). Although the PBGC is not funded from general tax revenues, it is a government agency, and as a consequence is a contingent liability of the U.S. government and tax payers. Changes to the premium structure require legislation from Congress and have historically been updated several times - including in 1991 when the cap on insurance premiums paid by underfunded plans was removed. The Pensions Act passed by the Bush Administration in 2006 involves changes designed to strengthen retirement security. As well as reforming funding rules (*e.g.* introducing funding targets related to the financial strength of the plan sponsor, restricting benefit improvements at underfunded plans), which indirectly help the guarantee scheme, the bill also reforms the PBGC's premium structure. The flat rate premium has been raised from $19 to $30 and will be index linked, whilst the risk-based premium will be based on the level of underfunding, adjusted regularly and will be payable by all underfunded plans[18].

Investment: Policy requires all premium income be invested in fixed income assets (in what are known as Revolving Funds), whilst assets taken over from terminated plans may be invested in equities (via Trust Funds) – which may seem contradictory, given that terminated liabilities are known, and therefore would seem to be better matched with bonds, whilst equity investment would appear to be more appropriate for premium income, which is designed to cover future claims. The PBGC uses external portfolio managers to invest these funds, with their oversight. The overall asset allocation of the organisation is set by the Board of Directors (which includes the Secretaries of Labour, the Treasury and Commerce) and in 2006 consisted of 77% bonds (the majority of liabilities are matched on a $ duration basis), and 23% equities. Revolving fund assets were $15.2bn whilst Trust Fund assets were $44bn. $2.2bn investment income was generated in 2006.

ii. Issues

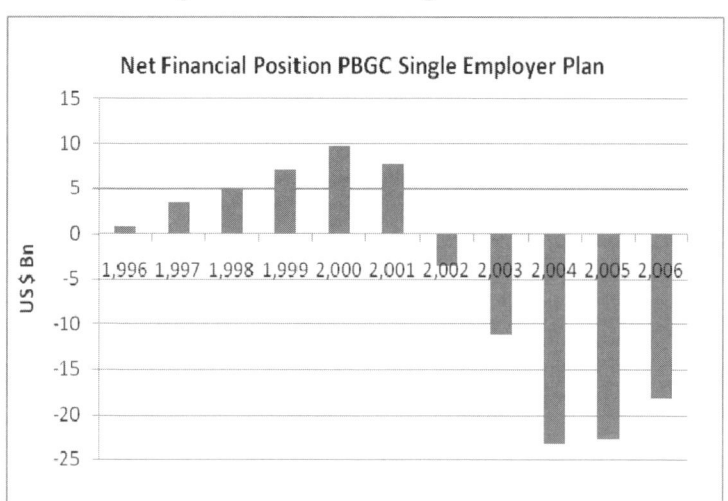

Figure 1: PBGC Funding Position

[Chart: Net Financial Position PBGC Single Employer Plan, US $ Bn, years 1996-2006. Values approximately: 1996: 1; 1997: 3; 1998: 5; 1999: 7; 2000: 9.7; 2001: 7.5; 2002: -3; 2003: -11; 2004: -23; 2005: -22.5; 2006: -18.]

(Source: Pensions Insurance Databook)

The PBGC has had a troubled financial history ever since its foundation. After enjoying several years of surplus during the late 1990's (hitting $9.7bn in 2000), the scheme is now facing a huge and extremely troublesome deficit (see figure 1). The 2006 annual report of the organisation, (for the fiscal year ending September 2006), declared assets worth $61.2bn, and liabilities at $80bn, creating an $18.8bn shortfall. The organisation was hit hard by the market and consequent economic correction from 2000 onward. Over and above the $18.8bn shortfall, the PBGC estimates that it has a further $73bn possible exposure to companies which are likely to become insolvent in the near term (*e.g.* having extremely low credit ratings). The multiemployer plan may also require further assistance. The latest estimates from the organisation for the total underfunding of US pension funds which it insures exceeds $450bn[19]. The PBGC's rapid swing from surplus to deficit is causing concern amongst plan sponsors, lawmakers and the tax-paying public, and its very survival is in question, raising the possibility of a required bail out through government funds[20]. Indeed the US General Accounting Office has characterised the scheme as 'high risk'.[21] There has been much debate over how such a huge deficit within the scheme came about. Some of the main causes are outlined below:

- *Concentrated exposure:* the PBGC's risk pool is concentrated in industries affected by global competition and the movement from an industrial to a knowledge based economy. In 2001 almost half the insured participants were in plans sponsored by firms in manufacturing industries (steel, autos etc.), many of which are heavily unionised and run flat rate schemes. These have always placed the PBGC particularly at risk as they promise to pay a nominal amount, with contracts being regularly renegotiated retroactively, and often substantially, to offset inflation and provide benefit improvements. As increases in pension promises cannot be funded in advance (due to tax limitations) automatic, and often large, underfunding situations are created at these schemes, which entail similarly large potential exposure for the PBGC. Although the PBGC's "problem" will eventually go away (as flat benefit plans are generally legacy costs of shrinking heavy industries, and many others shift to DC schemes) the funding situation of the organisation may get worse before it gets better. The PBGC remains highly exposed to the steel and particularly airline industries, from which it has recently suffered large claims (see Figure 2).[22]

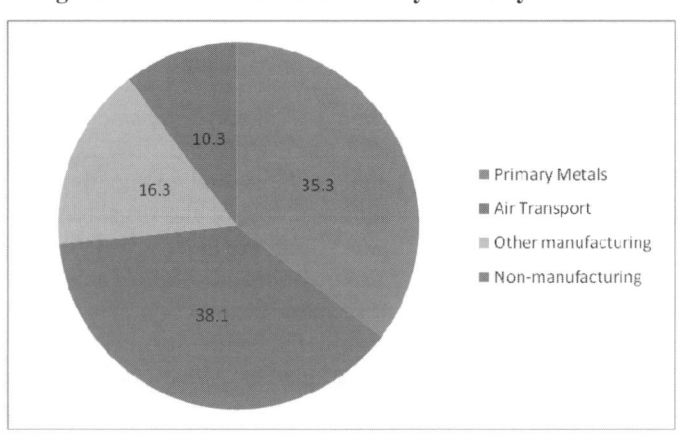

Figure 2: Historic PGBC Claims by Industry 1975-2005

Pie chart values: 35.3 (Primary Metals), 38.1 (Air Transport), 16.3 (Other manufacturing), 10.3 (Non-manufacturing)

Source: PBGC Pension Insurance Database 2005

Note : Primary Metals (i.e. steel) + air transport account for only around 5% of total employees covered by PBGC

- *Asset liability mismatch:* a further cause of the extreme deficits at the PBGC is the asset allocation mix widely adopted by pension funds in recent years, and indeed by the PBGC itself. It can be argued that a typical US pension plan has long duration bond-like liabilities, but asset allocation has typically been as high as 70% in equities, with the fixed income portion in bonds with far shorter durations. What has consequently been described as a severe asset liability mismatch left pension plans, and therefore the PBGC, particularly exposed to the low interest rate, poor equity return environment which occurred from 2000 onwards. The PBGC's own sensitivity to interest rates have been claimed to be a large part of its deficit (around one third of the move from c$10bn surplus to over $10bn deficit in 2001 was said to be due to interest rate sensitivity and duration mismatching). The PBGC could offset some of its exposure to poor equity market and macro conditions with a counter cyclical investment policy. Yet it still raised equity weightings itself during the 1990's (though the scheme announced a reversal to this approach during 2004)[23].

- *Weak funding rules*: weak funding rules, allowing pension plan underfunding to reach extreme levels, are a further cause of the PBGC's large deficit. US funding rules employ extensive smoothing and deferral mechanisms which can insulate companies from having to fund emerging deficits and past service liabilities in a timely fashion, meaning that when accelerated contributions are finally required companies are often not in a position to make them[24]. Steven Kandarian, former Executive Director PBGC, has identified poor funding rules as one of the main causes of his organisation's problems, and has pointed out several key weaknesses in these rules. These include the systematic understating of liabilities, partly as estimated current liabilities rarely bear any relation to the true amount of money a pension fund needs to meet its obligations (as these calculations do not consider lump sums, price annuities properly, factor in early retirement etc.), and partly as only highly probable, near term distress terminations (*i.e.* companies close to bankruptcy) are recognised as contingent liabilities. He also criticises contribution holidays and maximum funding rules (with tax disincentives to building up a surplus)[25]. The PBGC's own proposals for addressing its current problems focus on improving funding requirements, and government suggestions for stricter regulations are also currently being discussed.

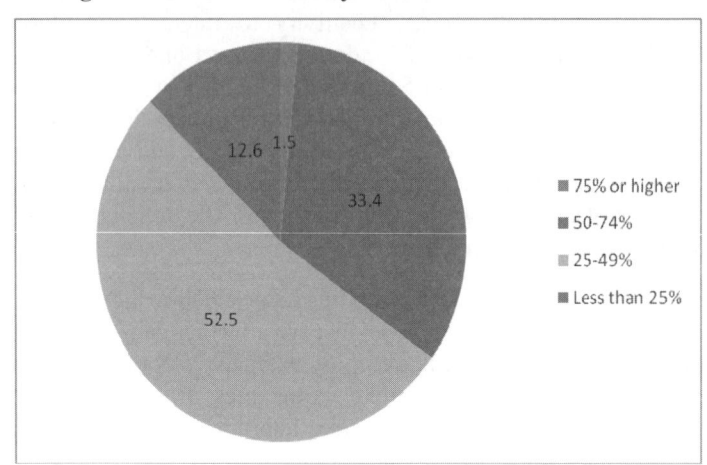

Figure 3: PBGC Claims by **Funded Ratio 1975-2005**

- 75% or higher: 1.5
- 50-74%: 12.6
- 25-49%: 33.4
- Less than 25%: 52.5

Source: PBGC Pension Insurance Database 2005

- *Political interference:* Interference from Congress has made, and continues to make, the underfunding situation even worse. Under intense lobbying pressure, politicians have intervened to assist companies in financial difficulty by providing temporary relief, which effectively make the already weak funding rules virtually meaningless. In April 2004 temporary legislation was passed which reduced the required contributions sponsors must pay to their defined benefit plans by an estimated $80bn by changing the discount rate used to calculate liabilities. Congress also provided an additional $1.6bn relief to the steel and airline industries - sectors with some of the most underfunded pension plans and which represent the greatest exposure for the PBGC, both historically and potentially. These moves by Congress directly counter the PBGC's own plans for strengthening the funding environment, and, though temporarily helping troubled industries, the measures will likely worsen the agency's financial condition[26]. Political interference also comes at the level of specific bankruptcy workouts, as priority rankings and compensation levels are subject to negotiations.[27] The PBGC's problem is not that is does not have sufficient powers to protect itself. Such powers range from demanding larger premiums as underfunding rises, to potential bankruptcy priority claims, to involuntary termination. The organisation also operates an 'early warning system', working with companies which it sees as entering into difficulties to try and ensure continued solvency. The issue is more that political interference stops the PBGC exercising the powers which it has. The fact that any changes to the PBGC premium or operational structure must receive Congressional approval also seems to hamper the PBGC's ability to react in a correct, long-term and timely fashion to its problems. Comments made by Dr. Alicia Mundell as far back as 1982 (quoted in Smalhout (1996)) sum up this position:

"The PBGC's vulnerability stems from its inability to control the action of the plan sponsors. Often it does not have access to detailed information about a pension plan until the company decides to terminate. Hence, the PBGC will always remain financially vulnerable and the federal government may well end up as the insurer of the nation's private pension system."

- *Mispriced premiums:* continuing on the theme of political interference, the PBGC's premiums are set by Congress, and have consequently been criticised as being set at politically judicious rather than economically viable levels. Premiums are not market priced, and do not take into consideration all the risks to which the PBGC is exposed (*e.g.* there is no adjustment for the potential insolvency of the plan sponsor). Over the long term, the premium income of a guarantee scheme should equal its benefit obligations and operating expenses. However, whilst the PBGC's benefit payments have increased through more plan terminations and its liabilities even more dramatically (partly due to interest rate and inflation exposure), its premiums have not, which has inevitably led to a deficit position. On top of the mispricing issue, which means that premiums are too low, Ippolito (2004) also points out that even these premiums are not fully collected, which makes the PBGC's position even more troublesome. The organisation is supposed to collect a variable rate premium equal to $9 for each $1000 of underfunding. Given the organisation's $400bn underfunding estimate in 2002, premiums of $3.6bn should have been collected. In reality, $787m were received, $586m coming from the fixed assessment of $19 per member. The PBGC therefore collected only $200m, or 50cents per $1000 of underfunding, around 5.5% of the prescribed $9 charge[28]. The changes introduced in the Pensions Act of 2006 do attempt to address these issues.

Canada

i. Description

History: of the 10 jurisdictions that regulate private pensions in Canada only the province of Ontario operates a scheme guaranteeing pension benefits, the Pension Benefit Guarantee Fund (PBGF). This was introduced in 1980, around the time when plant closures at heavy industrial companies were being discussed in this the centre of Canadian industry. As this guarantee system started six years after the PBGC was introduced, some of the perceived mistakes of this operation were ironed out (including that the event covered being the insolvency of the plan sponsor, that a lien on employer assets equal to the full amount of the insured shortfall of pension assets was set up, voluntary terminations by underfunded plans were not allowed and no provision for funding waivers for employers experiencing financial difficulties is available).

Coverage: the Ontario fund protects the basic pension benefits of over 1 million beneficiaries. As in the US, the scheme in Ontario covers many flat rate pension plans in heavily unionised, industrial sectors.

Operations: when a company with an underfunded pension plan covered by the PBGF fails a plan administrator is appointed and makes a 'PBGF declaration', valuing the guarantee promised by the organisation. The PBGF then makes an allocation to the pension fund, and this cash is used by the fund to cover its liabilities (*e.g.* by buying annuities). Benefits are guaranteed up to a maximum of CAD$12,000 per year, far lower than the US, PBGC scheme coverage. This amount is not inflation linked and has not been altered since the guarantee scheme was introduced. Neither liabilities of a plan less than three years old are not covered, nor any benefit improvements made within three years of termination. Multi-employer schemes are also excluded.

Premiums: initially premiums were set at 0.2% of any unfunded liability, but soon an annual charge of C$1 per member was added. Following a huge claim in the early 1990s from Massey-Combines (the farm equipment producer) which caused the fund to borrow from the provincial government, (the subsequent interest costs absorbing all premium income), a new premium structure was introduced with a sliding scale for the risk adjusted component. For plans unfunded on a termination basis the risk adjusted charge increased to 0.5% of those unfunded liabilities representing up to 10% of total liabilities. For additional unfunded liabilities representing up to 20% of total liabilities the annual charge rose to 1% and for unfunded liabilities above that the charge is 1.5%. The PBGF is currently in deficit again (largely due to a large claim made in 2001 on the reorganisation of the Algoma Steel company). The financial statements for the organisation[29] from the end of March 2005 show assets of CAD$291m and liabilities of CAD$529m, giving a deficit of CAD$238m. In addition, in 2004 accounts the PBGF notified of three companies in bankruptcy proceedings - *i.e.* operating under a stay under the Companies' Creditors Arrangement Act - whose pension plans could represent very significant claims on the fund (one estimated at CAD$50m, another at CAD$65.4m). The 2005 accounts note that the PBGF is still closely involved in the bankruptcy and insolvency proceedings of 2 funds. The financial statements also show that the Province of Ontario has made an interest free loan of CAD$330m to the organisation to assist with its current financial difficulties (payable at CAD$33m a year over 11 years), and it is expected that premium charges will also have to be increased.

Investment: As of March 2005, the PBGF's CAD$223m investments were held in short term deposits (35%), government and corporate bonds (65%).

ii. Issues

Currently, the only jurisdiction in Canada to implement a pension benefit guarantee fund has been Ontario. While the federal government has indicated that it is open to considering ways to strengthen existing protections in federal pension legislation, pension experts have indicated that a federal pension guarantee fund is not a practical option, particularly as federally registered DB plans account for only 5% of all pension plans in Canada (420 federal DB and combination plans as of March 2004, versus over 3000 plans registered in Ontario). In addition, a few of the federally registered pension plans are relatively quite large, with 10 accounting for roughly 70 per cent of the assets of all federally registered DB plans. Consequently, the ability of pension plans in a fund to distribute risk of loss is seen as difficult, particularly should a large plan terminate with a significant deficit.

UK

i. Description

History: under the UK's existing pension system, implicit insurance for pensions was offered for the contracted out portion of the earnings related portion of the state pension (SERPS). These commitments were absorbed back into the public system if a sponsoring company went bankrupt. A compensation scheme to cover pension beneficiaries who lost out due to fraud at the sponsoring company was also introduced during the 1980s (following the scandal at the Maxwell pension fund) [30]. The UK has introduced an explicit pension benefit compensation scheme, the Pension Protection Fund (PPF), which began operating from 6th April 2005. This Fund has been introduced on account of intense political pressure, following over 65,000 workers in various companies losing large amounts of their pension benefits in recent years on the bankruptcy of their sponsoring companies (including ASW the UK's second largest steel manufacturer).

This pressure came in the wake of other pensions scandals in the UK (such as Equitable Life, and misselling issues) and, as well as providing GBP 400m compensation for workers who had already lost out, the government felt it necessary to put a new compensation structure and new funding rules in place[31] in order to try and restore faith in the defined benefit pension system in general. Lawrence Churchill, formerly head of UK insurance at Zurich Financial Services, is the new organisation's first Chairperson.

Coverage: the PPF operates to provide compensation to members of eligible defined benefit occupational schemes with around 10 to 15 million pension fund members being covered.

Operations: the PPF will meet payments from a central fund. The scheme will pay 100% level of compensation to those above the normal pension age and to those of any age who are already in receipt of an ill health or survivors pension at the start of PPF involvement with a scheme (subject to the removal of any rule changes in the past 3 years the aggregate effect of which was to increase the scheme's overall liabilities). Furthermore, subsequent increases will be paid in accordance with PPF rules (as opposed to the scheme's which could result in increases which are less than the scheme may have provided). A 90% level of compensation will be paid to those below retirement age subject to inflation adjustments[32] and an annual cap set at £25,000 in 2005/06 for an individual retiring at 65. Again this is all subject to a review of the rules of the scheme and subsequent increases will be paid in accordance with PPF rules. Indexation will only be paid on rights accrued after 6th April 1997 in line with Retail Price Index (capped at 2.5%). The PPF will also pay survivors' benefits for eligible spouses, civil partners and unmarried partners at half the rate of members' periodic compensation. The costs of the PPF will depend on claims that it experiences in future. The Pensions Act 2004 also introduces a new, much more active Pensions Regulator with powers to investigate and impose action. New codes of practice requiring compliance, and threatening a range of punishments from the freezing of assets to the removal of trustees have been introduced.

Premiums: two types of PPF levy apply to eligible pension schemes during the first year of operation – 2005/2006[33]. The initial levy is a flat rate charged according to number and type of member (GBP 15 for active members and beneficiaries, GBP 5 for deferred members). Meanwhile, the administration levy is designed to cover start up and ongoing costs and is charged per member according to bands (2-11 members GBP £24 in total, 12-99 GBP 2.50 per member, adjusting gradually to a 0.74p charge for scheme with over 10,000 members. The formula is quite complex in order that the smallest schemes in a size don't pay less than the larger ones in the size below them. For example, for schemes of 10,000 or more, the rate is

0.74p per member, but with a minimum of £10,600). A fraud compensation levy is also paid by both defined benefit and defined contribution schemes if and when the (separate) fraud compensation fund needs to pay out substantial sums after a case of fraud occurs. From 2006/2007 the initial levy will be replaced by a Pension Protection levy which will be made up by a scheme-based element and a risk-based element. The scheme-based levy will relate to the level of a pension scheme's unfunded liabilities and may consider the number of members, and the amount of pensionable earnings in respect of active members. The risk-based levy will take account of the level of the scheme underfunding and the likelihood of sponsoring employer insolvency. It may also take account of a scheme's asset allocation and/or any other risk factors as set out in regulations. Ultimately, at least 80% of the estimated amount must be collected via the risk based levy of the pension protection levies. The risk based levy will be introduced over a transitional period to control costs – schemes will be required to provide a Pension Protection Fund valuation at the same time as their triennial valuation is undertaken. After the first year of the PPF's existence, when an initial levy will be set by the Secretary of State (to get the PPF up and running as quickly as possible), the Board of the PPF will have the power to alter the charge in order to regulate the total amount collected and therefore keep the PPF solvent, though within legislative limits (a 25% maximum annual increase and an overall levy ceiling). The PPF must consult with the government and appropriate stakeholders when it wishes to change the rate of the levies, and at least every 3 years if no changes are made. If the finances of the PPF are in trouble once the levy ceiling rate has been reached, the Act provides for the Board to borrow and to reduce indexation and revaluation to zero. Once it has reduced revaluation and indexation to zero it can recommend that the Secretary of State to vary the 90% and 100% levels (if Secretary of State agrees this will then require further regulation). The government is keen to stress that it is at arm's length to the fund. It is self-financing, and the Act gives the Board significant freedom to determine the levy structure, within set parameters as contained within legislation. The government hopes this will prevent the PPF from becoming run for political objectives and experiencing the financial difficulties currently troubling the PBGC.[34] The relationship between the PPF and the new Pensions Regulator will be important, as the latter will act almost as a watch dog for the PPF, with powers to stop schemes becoming severely underfunded. The regulator will also take on some outsourced tasks for the PPF, including the collection of the levies.

Investment: like the PBGC, the PPF will take on the assets and liabilities of insolvent schemes, rather than buying annuities. Two external fund managers have been appointed to invest the guarantee funds assets (Insight Investments and Pimco), currently with fixed income mandates designed to match liabilities, with Goldman Sachs given a deferred appointment. The strategic asset allocation of the funds will be reviewed at least annually, and will change according to adjustments in liabilities[35]. This approach may reflect an 'Anglo Saxon' approach to markets (contrasting with the approach of the PSVaG in Germany), and a belief in the ability to generate extra investment income, therefore reducing costs. In addition, the impact on cash-flow is lessened by paying benefits out over time as this allows the levy to gradually make up any deficit, (paying out benefits out at once would require the PPF to have much bigger cash reserves making the levy more erratic). The PSVaG's PAYG approach would also be difficult to operate in the UK or US where pension funds hold high equity weightings, causing their funding levels to swing from year to year. This in turn would make the PPF premium volatile, making it difficult for corporate CFO's to budget efficiently in advance for the charge. The Pensions Act also outlines new scheme specific funding requirements.

ii. Issues

The UK is an interesting real world example of the difficulties involved in introducing a pension benefit compensation scheme. Concerns were raised even before the new scheme began operating, which, aside from the generic ones discussed above, include the following:

- *Costs:* one of the major concerns over the new UK pension compensation scheme is that it will increase costs for defined benefit schemes, thereby encouraging even more of these to shift to a defined contribution basis[36]. The Association of British Insurers, the Association of Consulting Actuaries and the Pensions Management Institute have all expressed such concerns. The government, however, insists that companies will actually enjoy savings under the new pension regulations of around GBP130 million, rising to 210million when taxes are simplified, (*e.g.* from reduced administration costs, and from indexation requirements being relaxed). However a survey by the National Association of Pension Funds (NAPF) taken during 2003 found that 50% of pension fund respondents believed that the PPF would make it less attractive to run DB schemes. Meanwhile the Government is still claiming that the levy represents only a very small percentage of the flow of contributions into DB schemes, and that the scheme will greatly increases the value of DB pensions to firms, as they will be useful for recruiting and retaining the best staff. There is also the suggestion that, with the new European Pension Directive, defined benefit funds could locate in another European state which does not operate such a compensation scheme (such as Ireland) in order to avoid paying the levies – raising the possibility of 'adverse selection' with only the weaker funds which may need such insurance remaining[37].

- *Asset liability mismatch*: though firm details are not yet available, concerns have been raised that the new funding rules may actually encourage, rather than alleviate pension funds' asset liability mismatching. The Pensions Act 2004 specifies that risk premiums for the PPF will consider, amongst other risk factors, the "risks associated with the nature of the scheme's investments when compared with the nature of its liabilities."[38] However, this should not necessarily be taken to imply that funds will be directed to fixed income assets for immunisation purposes, given government comments that: "Our proposals (regarding scheme specific funding requirements) will allow schemes greater flexibility to match their investment strategy to the profile of their members – for example, schemes with younger members may be freed to invest more heavily in assets expected to give a higher return over the long term."[39] Even if fixed income holdings are to receive a lower premium, what mechanisms are in place to ensure that funds do not simply switch their asset allocation at the end of year to ensure lower charges and then to switch them into higher return assets for the rest of the period? There are also concerns over how the PPF will invest its money. Despite warnings from the actuarial profession, the plan seems to be intending to invest premiums in the same way as its pension fund client, holding both equities and bonds (though initial investments are to be made only in fixed income assets). The asset allocation will be determined by the Board of the PPF, who are aware of these potential problems, and stress that their own allocation will be set according to the liabilities they take over (*e.g.* equity investments may be used to cover the liabilities of younger schemes[40]).

- *Lack of funding:* though the PPF initially estimated it would raise around GBP 300m a year, though this was raised to GBP 575m at the end of 2005.[41]. Though a risk based levy will be introduced from 2006/2007, some observers remain concern regarding the organisation's funding over the long-term. Studies have shown that bankruptcies are 'lumpy' and therefore the Fund risks being overwhelmed at any one time, but particularly early on when built up premium reserves are low. Indeed if claims may be so skewed that it would be practically impossible to build up the multiyear reserves required, leaving the scheme almost inevitably exposed at some point in future (see McCarthy/ Neuberger model[42]). Some actuarial studies estimate that the fund needs closer to GBP 600m a year to remain fully solvent, and could therefore be facing a deficit of GBP 3bn in 10 years time[43]. The issue of a government guarantee should the fund get into financial difficulties has also been discussed. The government is ruling out the use of taxpayers' money, but retains reserve powers to reduce the level of compensation if there are large claims (though this can only be operated following a request from the Board). Some argue that aggrieved pensioners will not believe that the PPF is not an arm of the government if the system were to get into trouble, whilst others believe the government should take an even more explicit role, possibly committing tax payers' funds up front.[44]

- *Mispriced premiums:* despite the PPF attempting to take more risk factors into account than any other existing guarantee fund when pricing premiums, concerns still remain that these will still not be set at proper market rates (though practically a balance has to be struck between setting market rates and keeping premiums affordable to avoid the further closure of DB schemes). Concerns have also been raised over the new funding rules. In a study conducted for Watson Wyatt, Anthony Neuberger (of London Business School) and David McCarthy (from Imperial College, London) concluded that a minimum funding standard is an inevitable component of a successful pension protection system. Replacing MFR with scheme-specific regime seems attractive and flexible, but the problems of moral hazard and adverse selection remain[45]. It is not yet clear how the new scheme specific funding rules will operate in relation to the PPF (though some suspect that these will simply migrate towards the PPF's own required standards). There is also concern over how quickly the PPF will be able to adjust premiums in the face of a deteriorating position at a firm. The new Pensions Regulator should operate as an 'early warning' system, alerting the scheme to severely underfunded plans etc. Yet if premiums are only set once a year, severe damage could be done (via non contributions etc.) before actions are taken.

- *Anti- avoidance*: rather than being swamped with initial claims from insolvent companies on its inauguration, initial controversy around the PPF has instead focused around a restructuring deal made with a firm still in operation - insurance broker Heath Lambert. The Pension Regulator, utilising his clearance powers, approved a deal whereby the PPF guarantees the pensions of the firm in return for up to a 30% stake in the company. The Regulator insists that the company would have become insolvent without this deal, which therefore offers more upside to the PPF. However, concerns have been raised on several levels, including whether this will set a precedent, raising the moral hazard problem with other firms facing financial difficulties attempting to remove their pension liabilities to the PPF[46].

Germany

i. Description

History: the Pensions-Sicherungs-Verein Versicherungsverein auf Gegenseitigkeit (PSVaG[47]) is an independent body by law, operating as a mutual insurance association, and designated by parliament as the sole carrier of mandatory pension termination insurance since its foundation in 1974. It was founded by the Bundesvereinigung der Deutschen Arbeitgeberverbände e.V., the Bundesverband der Deutschen Industrie e.V., and the Verband der Lebensversicherungs-Unternehmen e.V. The PSVaG is subject to supervision from the Federal Financial Supervisory Authority (BaFin). If it were to withdraw the PSVaG's authorisation, or its functioning become impossible for other reasons, the organisation's liabilities would be transferred to the KfW-Mittelstandsbank. Prior to the introduction of the guarantee system, pensions in Germany were treated as wage claims in bankruptcy, with the book reserve system consequently forcing workers to take on significant risk. The insolvency insurance system was conceived as a way of retaining necessary public support for book reserve funding.

Coverage: book reserve, pension funds, support funds (Unterstützungskassen) and under certain circumstances direct insurance have statutory insolvency coverage from the PSVaG, which protects current and future beneficiaries in the event of employer insolvency. As of the end of 2005 59,636 companies were covered, comprising of around 8.7 million beneficiaries (3.8m retirees, 4.9m with vested entitlements), with a PV of insured benefits of €251bn, with around 440,000 individuals currently receiving €55.2m in monthly payments. The employers covered by the PSVaG hold around two-thirds of all German occupational pension plan liabilities. From 2002 some companies in Luxembourg have also been covered. The PSVaG does not insure retirement annuities purchased directly from life insurance companies and Pensionskassen[48].

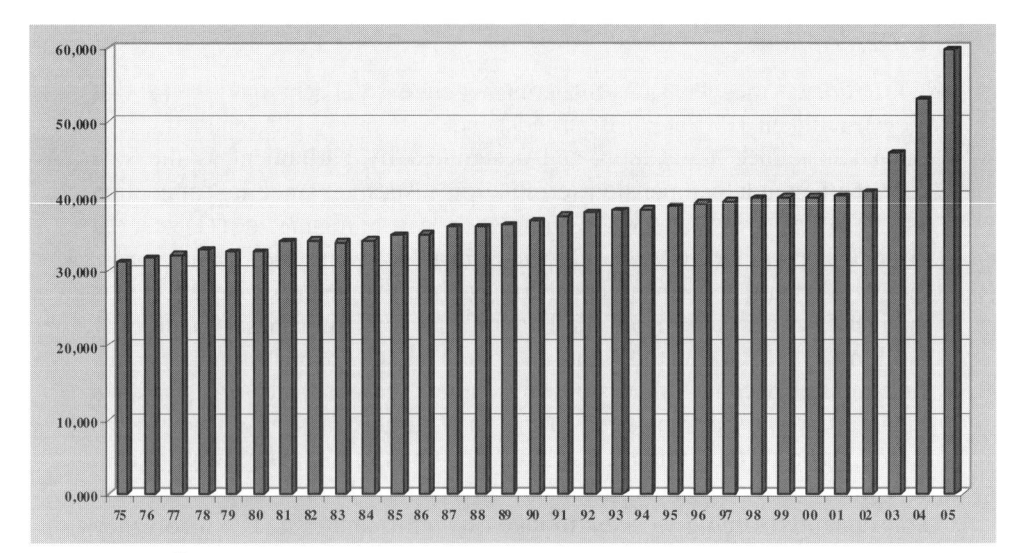

Figure 4: Number of Member Firms

Source: PSVaG[49]

Operations: a key difference between the PBGC in the USA and the PSVaG in Germany is that on the insolvency of a member the latter purchases annuities from a consortium of life insurance companies (this was made up of 58 companies in 2005 – Allianz being the largest). The PSVaG does not take over the assets of the pension fund, and consequently operates more like an intermediary, buying out benefits through private insurance companies. Benefits are secured up to a limit of 3x a reference monthly salary (€7,245 in 2004), with some being excluded, such as increases granted in the two years before insolvency and non-vested benefits. German law also apparently gives the PSVaG the authority to withdraw insurance cover if benefit commitments are changed by troubled firms to exceed levels prevailing elsewhere. Insured benefits are paid in full even if the bankruptcy involves criminal behaviour or if a firm's contribution payments are not up to date. With the exception of the some steel companies, most claims involve small firms. The system therefore involves extensive cross subsidy, but large companies seem to accept that this is a small price to pay for continued access to internal financing via the book reserve system.

Premiums: the PSVaG is financed via contributions in the form of an annual insurance premium, taking a PAYG approach to financing. Each year's premium is based on estimated losses during the previous 12 months, with this estimate divided by the contribution basis (the insured pension liabilities) to give a contribution rate. Premiums paid therefore reflect the experience of the year, with a little smoothing of premiums over time, and this has led to volatility in contribution rates (highest on AEG bankruptcy in 1982 at 0.69% of plan liabilities, 0.49% 2005, 31 year average 0.26%). Apart from the fact that the premium paid to the PSVaG in respect of pension funds is 80% lower than that for the book reserve or support funds (reflecting the fact that they are funded), no risk adjustment occurs to the premium charged. The number of insolvency claims in 2005 for the PSVaG amounted to 580, resulting in total claims of €574m.

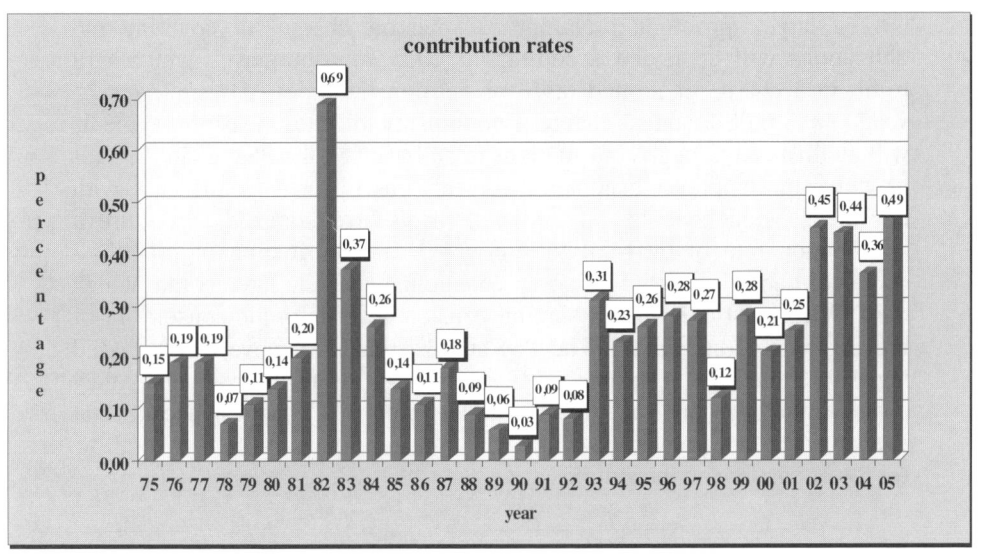

Figure 5: Total Contribution and Rates

Source: PSVaG

Investments: As of 2005, the PSVaG's investments amounted to €962.6m, with 16% held in shares, 42% in fixed income and 42% in deposits.

ii. Issues

A major reform of the PSVaG has been proposed, with a bill passing through the Germany parliament during 2006[50]. The government plans to change financing of the PSVaG from the current PAYG system to a fully funded status. Reform is being driven by two factors. First, changes in German pension law in recent years have caused a shift away from book reserves and other pension scheme financing arrangements that require little or no PSVaG coverage (*e.g.* due to the recently simplified option of transferring pension obligations to pension funds) – which results in a thinning of the contribution base. 'Old obligations' will therefore have to be spread across a smaller number of contributing firms, causing contribution rates to rise. The reform is also being driven by increasing bankruptcies in recent years, which has also put upward pressure on contributions (*e.g.* total contributions amounted to €1.2bn in 2005, an increase of 36% from the €882m collected in 2004). The proposal is for a new fund to be created, into which employers will pay for a period of 15 years (the period over which most of the outstanding obligations mature) covering the cash value of the current payable and vested benefits – amounting to €2.5bn of entitlements or 'old obligations'. The PSVaG estimate that building up this funding will not have a large impact on premiums. A one off charge for covering old obligations will be levied according to 2005 contributions – which will result in a charge of around 0.9% of pension liabilities, payable over 15 years, *i.e.* a 0.06% annual charge. Entitlements to future pension payments will be financed through contributions to be levied by the PSVaG in the year in which the employer becomes insolvent – as is currently the case with payable pension benefits. Future entitlements are estimated to require a contribution rate of 0.04-0.05% - giving total contribution of c0.10% - 0.11% of liabilities. Other proposed change includes the interest rate which the PSVaG must use when assigning pension benefits to the consortium of life assurance companies[51]. The PSVaG also plans to move to risk-based levies, provided they can obtain external ratings for all the companies they cover. Employers are said to support the proposed changes, hoping that investment returns generated on the accumulated funds in future will allow for lower employer contributions.

Sweden

i. Description

History: aside from schemes covering public sector workers, there are two main occupational pension schemes in Sweden. The first, known as the ITP, is for private-sector, white- collar workers. Funds which are run through the establishment of a pension foundation or book reserves (not those directly insured with insurance company Alecta) must insure the risk of insufficient assets in the case of insolvency with a guarantee fund managed by the Pension Guarantee Mutual Insurance Company (FPG). Founded in 1961, this is a mutual non-life insurance company which transacts insurance only for the safeguarding of pension rights. Its board of directors consists of representatives of policyholders (*i.e.* around 1560 sponsoring employers) and trade unions (one from each of Sif and Ledarna) and the organisation is non-governmental. A third entity, the PRI (Pension Registration Institute), records the pension promises made by each employer, calculates the value of these obligations on a standard basis and serves as an intermediary that receives the employer contributions and eventually makes the payments to retirees. The second main occupational scheme is for blue-collar workers. Previously known as the STP, insurance was provided by the AMFK when employers borrowed against their pension funds. From 1999 the STP was replaced by the SAF-LO. This is safeguarded through member directed life insurance and the AMFK is now in run-off.

Coverage: Swedish pensions are provided on a contractual basis, with the majority of employees (90% of the workforce) being covered by collective agreements between unions and employer confederations. It is Sweden's trade unions rather than the government which requires pension schemes to subscribe to the guarantee system. The FPG covers around 200,000 employees. In the case of both the FPG and the AMFK only creditworthy companies are allowed to participate in the guarantee scheme, or those who are able to provide adequate collateral.

Operations: in the case of a company insolvency, the FPG buys out benefits with the insurance company Alecta – meeting the full cost for securing the benefits in the case that liabilities were book reserved, and the shortfall in cases where liabilities were partially funded. Since inception the scheme has tried to assess the risk of a corporation to insolvency and to cover its exposure accordingly. It does so by effectively running an in house rating agency, analysing corporate accounts, historical performance, profitability, industry factors, leverage and where applicable external ratings. The insurers can respond in 4 ways to firms applying for coverage: 1. insurance is provided to financial strong companies; 2. insurance is offered to slightly riskier companies contingent on the assignment of capital; 3. insurance can be offered to subsidiaries with a security bond from the parent company; 4. insurance is offered only if the company provides a backup credit guarantee from a bank (which is tantamount to a rejection). Contracts can last up to 3 years and a key time for stepping in and demanding more collateral if the situation looks to be deteriorating is when the renewal is due. In the direst circumstances, the FPG can require the entire amount outstanding to be wound up over 5 years through the purchase of annuities from an insurance company. Demand for immediate termination arises in special situations such as when operations cease or a change in ownership takes place which could undermine the company. On average a far higher percentage of bankruptcy claims are recovered than by other guarantee programs, largely due to the surety bonds provided by parent companies. Uniquely amongst guarantee schemes the full benefits are covered with no restrictions. FPG and AMFK reinsure their liabilities to protect themselves against extraordinarily high claims in any single year.

Premiums: in the case of employers using the book reserve method, the yearly contribution (as of 2006) was 0.3% applied to total book reserved pension liabilities. Premiums for pension obligations funded via a foundation are reduced (to 0.1% in 2006) for the part which is covered by assets in the fund. The company pays the same premium to the FPG regardless of whether collateral has been pledged or not, or whatever its credit rating, except where the entire pension commitment is covered by a bank guarantee (when a lower premium applies), but this is unusual. Policyholders have an obligation to help the FPG to meet claims should reserves be totally exhausted. In this case additional charges may be made, capped at 2% of pension liability of a company. Members who have been policy holders for 10+ years qualify for a policy holder's bonus if board of FPG decides to grant one and this is based on the sum of premiums paid during the last ten years. In 2005 premiums of SEK248m ($34m) were collected and a bonus of SEK 147 m ($20m) was granted. Insurance exposure amounted to SEK120bn ($16.6bn), with 6 claims being made.

Investments: as of 2005, assets of SEK15.2bn ($2.1bn), were invested 67% in fixed income, 32% in equity.

ii. Issues

The Swedish model is probably the most successful currently in existence. The issue is therefore whether it could be transferred to other countries wishing to introduce a pension benefit guarantee scheme. One of the major obstacles would be implementing such a rigorous screening procedure on a large scale, mainly due to cost. Could an external credit rating of some form therefore be used? As the major rating agencies have become somewhat discredited in recent years (*e.g.* failing to pick up on the Asian crisis or scandals at US companies such as Enron), another proxy, such as credit default spreads (CDFs) or other credit swap derivatives could be used (though research suggests that these are also not always accurate predictors of insolvency). The system may also be difficult to introduce as bankruptcy laws may have to be changed, and the collateral demands made could push up the cost of debt. The system is therefore interesting in theory, but would need an independent rating agency with significant powers to make it work.

Others

i. Switzerland

History: the Sicherheitsfonds[52] was established in 1986 by the federal government as an independent, public foundation.[53] The supreme body is the Foundation Board, on which the top-level organisations of the social partners, the public administration and a neutral member have seats. The guarantee fund insures pension obligations up to a maximum specified in the country's Law of Old-age, Survivors and Disability Pension Plans (BVG / LPP 1985) and was designed to cover a considerable variety of plan designs (Swiss funds largely being DC in nature with guaranteed minimum returns). The guarantee fund supports all mandatory benefits promised by second tier, occupational plans, (including old age, survivor, disability benefits etc.). An interesting feature of the Swiss scheme is that protection is provided on the bankruptcy of the fund rather than the sponsoring firm (reflecting the strict legal separation of pension funds and their sponsoring corporations in Switzerland). In theory the guarantee fund could take on the responsibilities for a solvent company, but in practice this has not happened (as companies feel an unwritten moral obligation to make sure their funds are covered themselves).

Coverage: employer and employee organisations must establish and manage a safety fund (sicherheitsfond) at the federal level. The scheme is mandatory for defined benefit and DC occupational schemes, including both those schemes providing government specified minimum benefits and those providing above the minimum. Around c3,800[54] funds, or 3.2m insured persons are covered. Even though some public funds have an underlying guarantee from the state, canton or city and therefore do not require further insurance, they still are legally obliged to pay contributions to the foundation.

Operations: a pension fund is deemed insolvent in Switzerland if it cannot pay statutory or regulatory benefits which are due and if restructuring is no longer possible (*i.e.* if liquidation, bankruptcy or similar proceedings have been initiated against it). The guarantee scheme then attempts to secure pension benefits with suitable institutions (*e.g.* insurance companies), operating like the PSVaG in Germany by buying annuities, rather than taking on the assets of insolvent schemes. Benefits are maintained in their entirety, with an insured salary cap of 1.5x the Social Security Upper Earnings limit. Insurance is provided for fixed monetary amounts that are uniform across all plan types. As well as the usual main function (*i.e.* secure the payment of benefits if pension institutions are insolvent), the Swiss fund also has additional and unique roles, such as to pay subsidies to pension institutions with financial difficulties due to an unfavourable age structure, and payments to meet extraordinary costs of Auffangeinrichtung (collective scheme set up to administer vested benefits not transferred to a new employer and to provide a legal minimum benefits where an employer has not setup a plan). Furthermore the scheme may sue trustees or fund managers when insolvency occurs due to fraud.

Premiums: the fund is financed through levies which are determined by the scheme's board and approved by the Federal Social Insurance Office. In 2005 contributions for insolvency insurance were 0.03 %, applied to the sum of all vested rights and 10x the sum of pensions in payment. Extra contributions (covering the subsidy for funds disadvantaged by an older work force) of 0.07 % on the basis of the payroll totals coordinated on a pro rata basis pursuant to BVG are required for registered funds providing benefits. These contribution rates will remain the same for 2006. No direct link exists between the exposure of the guarantee fund and premiums charged. 2212 claims were made in 2005 (vs. a peak of 2821 in 2002), involving insolvency payments of CHF 46.7m. The situation for occupational benefit schemes has improved and stabilised in the past three years. Subsidies paid to funds with an older work force increased somewhat to CHF 72m. Although the scheme does not take over the assets of insolvent pension funds, but buys out their obligations with annuities, excess contribution income has allowed the guarantee scheme to build up a reserve fund of CHF 192.3m.

Investment: the scheme can invest assets with the same restrictions as apply to pension funds. As of 2005, 58.6 % of funds were invested in CHF bonds, 4.3 % in cash, 10.4 % in domestic equity, 16.8 % in foreign equity and 9.8 % in foreign bonds. This is one potential source of moral hazard which is not found in the Swiss system, as the investment policy of Swiss pension funds has been very conservative. This is partly due to culture, and also as fixed and legally required interest must be paid on mandatory pension credits combined with the contribution levels. There is also no doubt who owns the pension surplus in Switzerland – the workers – and consequently there is little incentive for plan sponsors to follow high risk, high return strategies (though this may change as returns are viewed and compared more in an international context).

ii. Japan

History: although defined contribution schemes are now allowed in Japan, many occupational schemes remain defined benefit in nature, including traditional lump sum severance pay plans funded by book reserves. Many Employee Pension Funds (EPFs) were established in the

1960s and 1980s. These are pension plans with over 500 members for single-employer schemes or over 3000 for multi-employer schemes (for EPFs newly introduced after April 2005, over 1000 members are required for single-employer schemes and over 5000 members for multi-employers schemes). As well as providing private pension benefits, EPFs also manage a portion of the public pension scheme - the Employee Pension Insurance or EPI, which is the employment related social security pension for private sector employees. This public pension portion of the EPF is known as the 'Substitution Component'. The Pension Guarantee Program was set up in 1989 by the Pension Fund Association (PFA) to provide termination insurance for EPF plans (other occupational pensions, know as Tax Qualified Pension Plans or TQPPs are not covered as they do not have any funding rules and are not covered by the PFA annuity programme). The Employees Pension Insurance Act (EPIA) states that the PFA is able to carry out the Pension Benefit Guarantee Program with the approval of the Ministry of Health Labour and Welfare. The EPIA does not describe the Program in detail – implying that it should be designed and operated appropriately based on the consensus of member EPFs. The essential characteristics of the Program are that it is a mutual aid system of EPFs, which aims at securing Minimum Preserved Benefits, within certain limits, in the case of 'inevitable' dissolution, due to bankruptcy or business deterioration of sponsoring companies. It is based on the understanding that every EPF makes its best efforts to secure rights of its own plan participants. Before setting up the fund in 1989, suggestions were sought by the PFA from the PBGC in the US. The following three suggestions were given: to make the program as simple as possible; not to extend the guarantee range beyond financial capabilities; to make efforts to prevent the dissolution of underfunded plans. These pieces of advice determined the basic structure of the Program which was then implemented.

Coverage: all EPF funds must make contributions to this scheme. The PFA Articles state that all member EPFs should participate in the Program (in 1989 the MHLW gave approval of the implementation of the Program on the condition that the PFA Article made participation obligatory, and in 2001 the PFA General Assembly unanimously adopted a resolution reconfirming the obligatory requirement). There has been discussion of the introduction of a Statutory Pension Benefit Guarantee Scheme to cover all DB plans (and possibly also DC schemes in cases of fraud). Indeed the Welfare Committee of both Houses of the Diet adopted resolutions requiring the government to give further consideration to the issue of the introduction of such scheme when the Defined Benefit Corporate Pension Bill was passed in June, 2001. However such a move is strongly resisted by employers (who are unwilling to give support to other companies for the sake of preserving severance allowances and who consider that defined benefit plans are derived from severance allowances). With such situation in mind, the next statutory revision of the pension system is expected in 2006 or 2007. Yet pressure for the introduction of such a fund may grow as the social security pension is scaled down and sooner or later corporate pensions have to assume a greater role in the retirement income.

Operations: if an EPF is wound up, the PFA takes over the Substitution Component in exchange for collecting the amount equal to the minimum funding required for this component (known as the 'Minimum Technical Provision of the Substitution Portion' or MTPSP). Any remaining assets are distributed to all plan participants, who can chose to take the portion of these residual assets due to them either as a lump sum or an annuity (which is paid by and known as the PFA Annuity). The guarantee scheme covers only those participants who choose the annuity option. The maximum guaranteed benefit is 0.3x the Substitution Component and half of the benefits exceeding this amount. The present value of the maximum guaranteed benefit is called as the Ceiling Amount[55]. In principle the benefits which the program pays out should be equal to the unfunded liability (*i.e.* the sum total of the Ceiling Amounts of all participants minus the amount of residual assets). However, a ceiling of Y7bn (cUS$70m) is imposed on the amount of the unfunded liability[56], which was introduced in 2000 to keep the Program solvent with affordable amounts of contribution.

Figure 6: Ceiling of the Applicable range of Guarantee for Individual Participants (*i.e.* Ceiling Amount)[57]

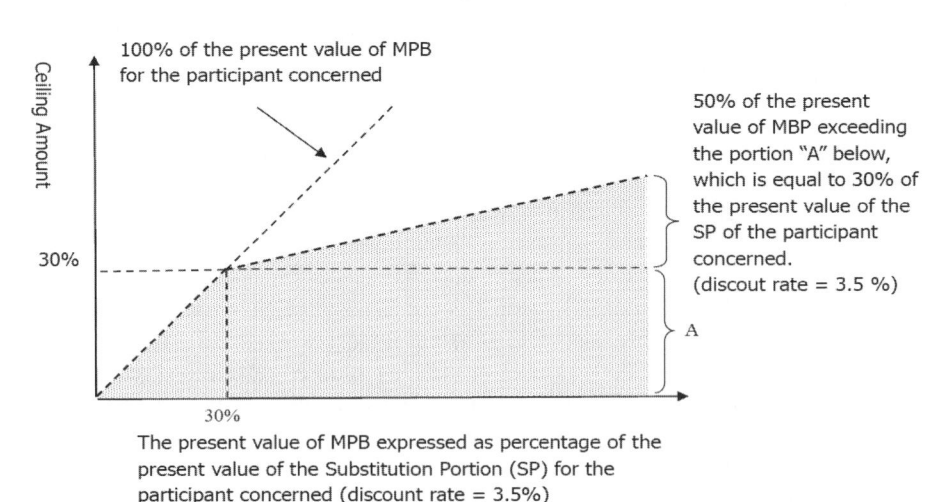

100% of the present value of MPB for the participant concerned

50% of the present value of MBP exceeding the portion "A" below, which is equal to 30% of the present value of the SP of the participant concerned.
(discout rate = 3.5 %)

The present value of MPB expressed as percentage of the present value of the Substitution Portion (SP) for the participant concerned (discount rate = 3.5%)

Insurable events cannot be described shortly in fine detail, because they include various fund dissolutions due to financial difficulties of sponsoring companies. However, with the accumulation of precedence, the criteria of invoking the guarantee have been clarified gradually. The basic principle of invoking the guarantee is that the fund dissolution was caused by bankruptcy or similar financial difficulties of sponsoring companies. Insurable events include 'inevitable' dissolutions due to: bankruptcy of sponsor companies; business deterioration of sponsoring companies or industries as a whole to which the sponsoring company belongs; or other circumstances under which the sponsoring companies are considered having been unable to sustain the EPF. There are criteria for applying the latter two conditions for the case of single-employer EPFs including: the sponsoring company having had a balance sheet in the red consecutively for several years before dissolution and the balance sheet having been in a situation where debts exceeded assets or cumulative deficits, excluding the retirement benefits provisions; also that the number of active participants at the EPF had been decreasing substantially, the plan is very mature and contribution rates were considerably high in comparison with those of other EPFs with similar levels of benefits, and further contribution hikes were considered to be unavoidable. In addition to these insurable events, benefits covered can be reduced based on the funded status of the EPF. If the funded ratio is below 50% a reduction formula is imposed. Program benefits may also be reduced due to inappropriate management of the EPF when: directors of the EPF are considered to have neglected their duties (reduction of the Program Benefits by up to 20% of the Unfunded Liability); when the administration or operation of the EPF are considered having been inappropriate (reduction of the Program Benefits by up to 20% of the Unfunded Liability); when appropriate measures have not been taken to secure assets after resolution to dissolve the EPF was adopted, and substantial amounts of assets were consequently lost (reduction of the Program Benefits by up to 30% of the Unfunded Liability). In terms of governance, the Program is operated under the control of the Steering Committee, which is composed of representatives of member EPFs. The PFA operates the Program in compliance with the recommendations of this committee, including whether to invoke the guarantee (the Program Benefits) to individual cases, whether to reduce the Program Benefits and to what extent. The committee also investigates key issues such as benefit structure, ceiling on guarantees, contributions of member EPFs to the Program etc. In other words the Program is self-governed by EPFs and is not directed by the government. The decisions of the Steering Committee are completely disclosed to all EPFs. There have been 36 claims as of March 31, 2005 and among these cases, the Steering Committee has recommended invoking the guarantee for 22 cases. As experience is gained, fewer claims with a scare chance of being approved by the Steering Committee are being received.

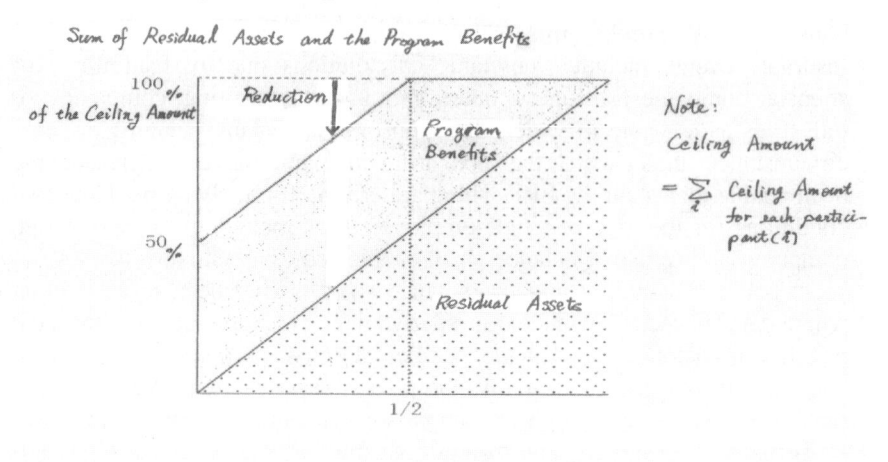

Figure 7: Program Benefit Reduction Formula

Sum of Residual Assets and the Program Benefits

[Graph showing: Y-axis labeled "100% of the Ceiling Amount" at top and "50%" midway; X-axis with "1/2" marked. The graph shows a "Reduction" region, "Program Benefits" area, and "Residual Assets" area.]

Note:
Ceiling Amount
$= \sum_i$ Ceiling Amount for each participant (i)

$$\text{Reduction Rate} = \left(1 - \frac{1}{2 \times (1 - \text{Residual Assets}/\text{Ceiling Amount})}\right) \times 100 \ (\%)$$

The government also allows another *de facto* type of protection for the Substitution Component via a system known as '*daiko henjo*'. Since April 2002, EPF schemes have been allowed to hand back this Substitution Portion to the government (the EPI)[58], a measure recognised as part of the de-regulation of the operation of corporate defined benefit pension plans. This move was partly due to the stagnation of Japanese financial markets and poor investment return for over a decade, but also due to changes in the Japanese accounting standard on retirement benefits introduced in 2000, which requires that companies evaluate the liability of the Substitution Portion in the same way as the rest of the occupation pension scheme (*i.e.* the purely private part of retirement benefits), irrelevant of the legal liability of the Substitution Portion - the MTPSP[59]. Any EPF scheme which carries out a daiko henjo operation will be converted to a 'New Defined Benefit Pension Plan' (as of September 2004 a total of 784 new DB funds had been set up, 546 via daikyo henjo operations).

Premiums: premiums are determined by three components: per capita premiums according to the number of participants; premiums in proportion to the total benefit amount guaranteed; and premiums in proportion to the amount of unfunded liabilities (the sum total of the Ceiling Amounts of all participants plus the MTPSP minus the amount of assets). The maximum of the sum of first two components is set at Y8.82m. The maximum of the third component is set at Y0.861m. The ceiling placed on premiums means that larger companies pay lower guarantee premiums. The premium ceiling was really imposed to persuade larger companies to accept the introduction of the guarantee fund. Currently, premiums are further reduced by 35% from the sum of these components, as the Program currently holds funds in excess of its targeted contingency reserve (*i.e.* by which the solvency of the Program is expected to be kept for 5 years without further contribution, with 90% probability). The excess amount is Y8.05 billion, and by assuming that the excess amount is withdrawn during 20 years, it is possible to reduce the total premiums by Y450 million, which corresponds to 35% of the total contribution.

Table 1: Contributions to the Program (applied from 2005)

Contribution proportionate to the number of participants		Contribution proportionate to sum total of ceiling amount		Contribution proportionate to the amount of unfunded liability
Average weight:45		Average weight: 45		Average weight:10
Y114 per participant	+	0.0083%	+	0.0123%
		Upper limit (1+2) Y8.82m per fund		Upper limit Y0.861m per fund

Investment: reserves at the Pension Guarantee Fund have been increasing since 1998, with the amount invested by the PFA now at Y30bn. The financing of the institution has remained on an even keel, partly as, despite the continued underfunding of occupational pension schemes in Japan[60], rising bankruptcy levels, and therefore rising claims against the Pension Guarantee Fund, the criteria for invoking the guarantee only include fund dissolution due to bankruptcy or similar financial difficulties of sponsoring companies, the criteria have been strictly applied, and the automatic benefit reduction formula based on the funded status of dissolved funds is also incorporated. Since the Program started its operation in 1989, there has been 36 claims (as of March 2005), with 14 cases being rejected. However, it should be noted that there have been far more funds wound-up during the same period, many underfunded in comparison to the MFSA, which means that the rights of participants have not been properly protected by the funding rules alone.

5. PENSION FUND GUARANTEE SCHEMES

Table 2: History of the Programme Implementation (From April 2002 to March 2005)

No.	Fund Name	Date of Dissolution	Claimed Amount (in mil. yen)	Applied Amount (in mil. yen)	Reduction Rate (%)
22	Fund V	Feb. 2001	955	346	63.7
23	Fund W	Apr. 2001	296	Not applicable	-
24	Fund X	Jan. 2002	73	21	70.7
25	Fund Y	Sep. 2001	247	158	36
26	Fund Z	Oct. 2001	65	58	10
27	Fund AA	Apr. 2002	1,049	608	42
28	Fund AB	May 2001	780	377	51.7
29	Fund AC	Jul. 2002	31	16	50
30	Fund AD	Jan. 2003	477	331	30.6
31	Fund AE	Mar. 2003	936	Not applicable	-
32	Fund AF	Jan. 2003	368	328	11
33	Fund AG	Dec. 2002	264	151	43
34	Fund AH	Sep. 2002	1,829	611	66.6
35	Fund AI	Feb. 2003	652	Not applicable	-
36	Fund AJ	Mar. 2002	254	229	10

Table 3: Major Pension Insurance Programs

Country (programme)	Who is covered	Coverage amount	Premium/ Cost Structure	Claim process	System status
US (Pension Benefit Guarantee Corporation)	Participants in private DB plans.	Vested benefits up to a $44,300 maximum.	Charge based on number of participants and underfunded amount.	Assets and liabilities taken over in case of corporate bankruptcy.	Surplus of $7.7bn in 2001 eroded to a deficit of $23.3bn 2004.
Canada – Ontario (Pension Benefit Guarantee Fund)	Participants in private DB plans.	Vested benefits up to CAD 12,000 (US $10,000) annual maximum.	Charge based on number of participants and underfunded amount.	Cash allocation made to plan administrator to cover guaranteed benefits.	CAD $100m deficit (US $84M), with several further large potential claims pending.
UK (Pension Protection Fund)	Participants in eligible DB plans (this will include some public sector schemes that do not have a	Pensioners, survivor and ill health pension at 100% (subject to a review of the rules of the scheme),	Administration and fraud compensation flat based levies. To fund compensation payments: an	Assets and liabilities taken over in case of corporate bankruptcy.	PPF proposed to be in place from April 2005. Government estimates GBP 300m (US $550m)

5. PENSION FUND GUARANTEE SCHEMES

Country (programme)	Who is covered	Coverage amount	Premium/ Cost Structure	Claim process	System status
	full crown guarantee).	with increases in accordance with PPF rules. Under pensionable age, 90% capped (estimated GBP 25,000 US $46,000) – again increases subject to PPF rules.	initial levy (in year 1) and then a scheme based and a risk based levy. Ultimately the risk based levy must collect at least 80% of the total.		annual funding to be raised.
Germany (Pensions-Sicherungs-Verein)	Participants in book reserve, support fund or pensions fonds financed plans.	Statutory vested benefits up to €86,700 (US $112,000) annual maximum.	Charge is a % of liabilities, and reflects experience in prior year.	Insolvency of a member company triggers annuity purchase.	Ex post premium ensures ongoing solvency of PSV.
Sweden (Forsakrings bolaget Pensionsgaranti)	Contractual coverage of white collar employees.	Full benefits.	Charge is % of liabilities; collateral required if insolvency risk deemed high.	Insolvency of a member company triggers annuity purchase.	End of 2003 reserves of $1.7bn and potential insurance exposure of $15bn.
Switzerland (sicherheitsfonds BVG)	Participants in DB and Swiss-style DC schemes.	100% of government-mandated minimum benefits; Additional benefits are subject to salary cap.	Charged based on liabilities.	When pension plan declared insolvent, annuities are purchased.	Reserves of CHF 300m ($217m) in early 1990's have eroded to CHF19m ($14m).
Japan (Pension Guarantee Programme)	Members of EPF.	0.3x substitutional component and half of any benefits in excess of this amount.	Premiums related to size of company, size of benefit and risk adjusted for level of underfunding.	Unclear what events trigger a claim.	Reserves of Y30bn (US $285m).

Notes

1. As expressed by Pesando (1996): "Compensating wage differentials will, in a competitive labour market, internalise risks associated with underfunded pension promises." See also Lindeman (2004).

2. See www.pensionstheft.org, the website of a pressure group claiming compensation for lost occupational pensions on the bankruptcy of their plan sponsors. Members claim they were never made aware of this risk to their pension, and that they were led to believe that their pension was 'guaranteed', quoting publications from the Financial Services Authority and the Department of Work and Pensions. They also argue that the government should bear responsibility as they were incentivised to join their corporate pension scheme.

3. Most of these studies focus on the PBGC of the United States. It is well known from financial literature that the guarantee provided by the PBGC is analogous to a put option. The value of this put, and therefore the correct level of premiums, can be derived from options pricing theory. Hsieh, Chen and Ferris (1994), for example, found that the PBGC approximately correctly charges over-funded pension plans but significantly under-charges underfunded ones. Summary of studies of the PBGC premium levels in McCarthy (2003).

4. See David McCarthy and Anthony Neuberger's claims model in: *"Will the PPF go the way of the US fund?", Pensions Management, April, 2004*, available on http://www.pensions-management.co.uk

5. It is interesting that one of the few defined benefit schemes to be set up in recent years in the US was by a charity (the United Methodist Church) and therefore outside the PBGC's jurisdiction. *See Financial Times 3 September 2004: 'Benefits or bailouts? Fund deficits may topple US pension policy into crisis.'*

6. Ippolito (2004) puts forward the radical suggestion that private insurance should be compulsory, with market pricing taking into account funding levels and investment policy restrictions, doing away with need for complex funding rules and encouraging asset matching and full funding. See also Lindeman (2004).

7. For example, Michael Gordon, one of the key architects of ERISA, has written that the actuarial soundness of the PBGC was deliberately sacrificed at its inception point in order to gain political support for the passage of ERISA- "The supposition that Congress was prepared to accept loss of jobs and further industrial decline in return for sound insurance principles is preposterous and is why, even today, there will be stiff resistance to redesigning pension insurance..." From dissenting comments on Ippolito's *'The Economics of Pension Insurance' (1989).* Quoted in Ippolito (2004).

8. Pension Academic Zvi Bodie for one has argued that if politicians wish to subsidise weak firms they should do so directly, not through changing accounting rules and through the pension back door, see *The Economist, 13th February 2003, ' Discount them at your peril.'*

9. Dutch funding rules require pensions to be fully funded at all times. On the liabilities side this includes the immediate coverage of all salary increases, pension indexing or retroactive plan improvements, and on the asset side the immediate correction of negative investment returns. Various reserves must be held by funds, including a general risk reserve of 5%, an investment reserve (sufficient to address such events as an immediate 25% in share values – 30% for emerging markets – a 15% decline in real estate values and including equivalent buffers for interest rate and inflation risk, foreign exchange risk etc.) a future pension adjustment reserve, and any additional reserves demanded by the regulator (PVK). As a result, required funding levels are generally around 120-135% of accrued liabilities. If the 105% funding requirement cannot be met the PVK must be informed immediately, a plan for returning to full funding developed within 3 months, and action taken within three years.

10. The problem of systematic underfunding arises from the issues of 'tax arbitrage' and the 'insurance effect'. The former states that financially secure firms have an incentive to make their pension contributions as large as possible in order to gain the maximum tax advantage. Meanwhile, companies in financial trouble, paying no tax, have the opposite incentive, to reduce pension contributions, underfund their pensions, and follow a risky asset allocation policy. These tendencies are made even worse by providing insurance for pension benefits – *i.e.* the insurance effect. Funding requirements should therefore be carefully coordinated with any guarantee scheme to ensure that companies maintain funding levels, even when in financial difficulty. See Smalhout (1996).

11. Though in the case of funding rules care needs to be taken not to make defined benefit pensions prohibitively expensive to run, and with priority

bankruptcy rights the implications for credit availability and the broader economy must be considered.

12. The following is based on arguments taken from OECD publication: *'Insurance and Private Pensions Compendium for Emerging Economies: Book 1 Part 1: 2) b Policyholder Protection Funds: Rationale and Structure'*, author Takahiro Yasui 2001.

13. European Commission Working Paper on Insurance Guarantee Schemes: MARKT/2525/03. Arguments in favour of insurance guarantee schemes, and ones refuting arguments against, which could also apply to pensions include:

- flexible and faster at providing compensation than wind up process and guarantee a minimum
- consumer confidence has been hit by the crisis within the insurance industry and will be even more destroyed if claims are not met in the case of a winding-up
- as social security shifts towards private products reliable protection and safety nets are needed
- political pressure to introduce schemes rise following corporate wind-ups without full compensation
- Member States which have already set up insurance guarantee schemes seem to have positive experience in this regard – same with banking and securities sector
- *Moral hazard:* no evidence has been presented that this exists, providing coverage is limited
- *Other safety measures:* (technical provisions/ special treatment in wind up hierarchy/ effective supervision etc.) might not be sufficient if the event of a winding-up due to a lack of assets
- *Costs:* no increase in premiums observed in those Member States which already have insurance guarantees.

14. See *OECD Guidelines on Funding and Benefit Security in Occupational Pension Plans* in the Annex.

15. The Central Pension Security Institute (CSPI) provided specialised credit insurance to Finnish employers who obtained loans from their pension funds. Losses began to accumulate in 1989 as the Russian communist economy collapsed, causing many Finnish firms (de facto part of the Russian state model) to lose their guaranteed order flow. The CSPI's eventual collapse in 1993 was due to operational and well as systematic factors, including political influence (e.g. the Finnish Parliament set the rate which companies could borrow against their pension funds), weak credit analysis and a lack of intervention powers. The Finnish experience

shows that pension insurance used to promote other goals (supporting industries etc.) can lead to a misallocation of resources, and that an inherently unstable system can survive for years before suddenly collapsing due to unanticipated losses. For details see Smalhout (1996): p214-223. It should be noted, however, that the collapse of the Finnish system did not cause any losses for members and beneficiaries, as the guarantee insurance was only a part of the guarantee scheme in statutory private pension scheme in Finland. The main guarantee scheme is the joint-liability of financing the pension benefits. This means in practice that if a pension institution became insolvent, the insurance portfolio would be transferred to another pension institution and the potential.deficit in funding would be covered by the contribution.

16. See also *'Insuring the Uninsurable?'* published in Morgan Stanley's March 2004 Global Pensions Quarterly, authors Nigel Cresswell and Aurelie Rabou. Extract available in Investment & Pensions Europe July/August edition, also available online at www.ipe.com

17. Current numbers and annual report available on www.pbgc.gov

18. http://www.dol.gov/opa/media/press/opa/retirementsecurityfactsheet.htm

19. The PBGC also uses a complex model to estimate future claims, incorporating stochastic movement in stocks, interest rates, employment levels, bankruptcies and other factors .The PBGC's 2003 Annual Report shows the possible projected outcomes in 2013. The expected net position (*i.e.* the average of all possible positions in 10 years time) is a deficit of $18.7bn – yet the position reported for 2004 is already worse than this projected average. The model estimates a 1 in 5 chance that the organisation will enjoy favourable enough conditions to return to surplus, but also 10% chance that the deficit will be $49bn, a 5% chance that it will be $60.3bn and a 1% chance that it will reach $82.5bn (see Ippolito 2004).

20. *Financial Times 18th November, 2004*: *'Pension safety net's $78bn hole'*: the amount required has been estimated at $78bn, $100bn if all potential claims from the airlines are included.

21. *Financial Times 31st August, 2004: 'Retirement worries move up US agenda'*: the article reports that the US Treasury is said to have created a task force to examine how to save the PBGC in the event of a default by United Airlines, with the White House is considering legislative solutions. Bradley Belt, then executive director of the PBGC is quoted as saying: "This is not an immediate liquidity crisis, but unless something is done now, that hole will get bigger and bigger and raise the inevitability of a taxpayer bailout of significant magnitude." Meanwhile Elaine Chao, Secretary of Labor, has been quoted as saying: "While the PBGC is not in

crisis…it is clear that the financial integrity of the federal pension insurance scheme is at risk."

22. In September 2005 Delta and Northwest airlines filed for bankruptcy protection, leaving the PBGC to face potential pension insurance claims of $8.4bn and $2.8bn respectively. This follows the settlement reached between the PBGC and United Airlines in April 2005 which saw the guarantee scheme taking on a $6.6bn claim from the airline's 4 pension plans, as well as a $2.3bn claim from US Airways in February of the same year. For background details on United's claim see: *Financial Times 28th July, 2004: 'Financial safety nets under threat', 20th December 2004: 'United stirs up a hornets' nest on pensions.'*

23. This ALM problem has led to comparisons between the PGBC and the FSLIC, the insurer of the Savings and Loan Institutes which collapsed, at huge expense to US tax payers, during the 1980s. These institutions got into trouble when interest rate levels and volatility rose in the 1970's, exposing their asset liability mismatch between short term, variable deposits and fixed, long-term mortgage liabilities. They received a fatal, double hit with the collapse of the real estate market in the 1980s. Due to fierce lobbying and delayed action by politicians, hundreds of weak S+Ls were allowed to stay open, capital requirements were reduced and they were encouraged to expand into new risky deals. The cost of $150-200bn which it took to eventually solve the problem would have been much smaller if it had dealt with sooner. Commentators have warned that the political climate surrounding the current PBGC's situation is alarmingly parallel to the S+L fiasco, though it should be noted that the obligations of the PBGC are due to be paid over a far longer time horison than the S+Ls, so that insolvency is not a pressing issue. See John Ralfe, writing in *'The Times Online'4/12/04 'Britain must learn from US pension pain'. Financial Times 13th September, 2004: 'A slow motion re-run of the S&L disaster: Stand by for a pension bail-out.'*

24. The $9 charge for every $1000 of underfunding is measured on a current liability, rather than a termination basis. This charge for underfunding can be avoided if a company shows it is generally 90%+ funded on this current liability basis. Hence US Airways made no risk adjusted contributions for underfunding in the 4 years prior to its pension plan being taken over by the PBGC. The funding level was estimated to be 104% in 2000 on the current liability basis but only 50% using termination calculations 2 years later. Similarly Bethlehem Steel, (which made no payment for the 3 years prior to termination), was 45% funded when taken as a claim in 2003, vs. the previous estimate used in the calculation for contributions of 84%.

25. Steven Kandarian's comments taken from his testimony before the Governmental Affairs Committee, Subcommittee on Financial Management, the budget, and international security of the United States Senate, September 15 2003 and from his evidence given before the Senate's Special Committee on Aging, October 14 2003.

26. Indeed the PBGC itself has warned that the rules to accelerate funding relief which Congress has waived will cause its shortfall to grow by $4bn over the next 4 years.

27. Smalhout (1996) discusses the example of TWA and the influence of the company's owner, Carl Icahn.

28. PBGC's strategic plan (available via www.pbgc.gov) states that average premium paid to the PBGC per participant is $23. This compares with average homeowner insurance of $487, auto insurance $786 or, Federal + State unemployment insurance $250. Though the PBGC claims this demonstrates their cost effectiveness, the premium level does seem too low given the organisation's current deficit position.

29. See www.fsco.gov.on.ca
http://www.fsco.gov.on.ca/english/pensions/pbgf-20050331.pdf

30. Some problems ironically arose out of the 1985 Pension Act which introduced additional protection for pensioners. Priority bankruptcy rights were given not only to existing pensions, but also to pension increases. Consequently, although retirees were largely protected when companies such as ASW went bankrupt in recent years an employee, due to retire in 1 week, lost up to 80-90% of his or her promised pension. This has been changed in the 2004 Pension Bill, with pensions promised to active members ranking above future pension increases for current retirees.

31. *Economist September 26th 2002 'How safe is your pension?'*: when steel company ASW went bankrupt in July 2002 its pension fund, though compliant with UK minimum funding regulations, was only sufficient to pay around two thirds of pensioners' accrued benefits.

32. *I.e.* 90% of the pension an individual had accrued at the start of PPF involvement with the scheme, revalued in line with the RPI (maximum 5%) between that date and the date the compensation comes into payment in line.

33. For details see: 'A guide to the Pension Protection Fund Levies 2005/06' available on http://www.ppf.gov.uk/guide_to_levies.pdf#search='pension%20protection%20fund%20a%20guide%20to%20the%20pension%20protection%20fund%20levies'

34. *See DAFFE/CMF(2004)12: "Developments related to corporate pension fund liabilities and funding gaps."* Comments taken from UK government response.

35. For details of the asset allocation strategic and governance of the PPF see: 'Statement of investment principles', available on http://www.pensionsprotectionfund.org.uk/sip.pdf#search='pension%20protection%20fund%20governance%20of%20the%20pension%20protection%20fund%20strategic%20management%20of%20the%20fund%27s%20assets'

36. *Investment & Pensions in Europe 1 August 2003, 'Piling on the agony'*, available on www.ipe.com

37. *Financial Times, June 13 2005, 'Great British Pensions Evacuation'*

38. Pensions Bill (Bill 57) Par 137 (3) (b)

39. See Department of Work and Pensions paper June 2003:*'Action on Occupational Pensions'*

40. *Investment & Pensions in Europe 3 March 2005, 'UK protection fund aims to set risk levy quickly'*, and 23 June 2005, 'UK's PPF names asset managers, custodian', available on www.ipe.com

41. It should be noted that after its first months of operation only 3 initial applications were made to the PPF, from MG Rover, Bristol Community Sport Ltd and Pearce Signs Group – See: *'PPF, in good shape', 1 June 2005*, available on www.ipe.com

42. Description of David McCarthy and Anthony Neuberger's claims model in: *"Will the PPF go the way of the US fund?"*, Pensions Management, April, 2004, available on http://www.pensions-management.co.uk

43. *Economist 15th April 2004 "Pensions: On the Cheap'. In addition*, John Ralfe, an independent pension consultant and formerly Head of Corporate Finance at the Boots company, has estimated that, taking into account credit risk, underfunding and asset allocation, the FTSE100 companies alone should be charged a PPF fee of £600m. See RBC Capital Market, Open Forum Notes Vol. 6, available on www.JohnRalfe.com Standard and Poor's simulations see the annual claim on the PPF at GBP 1.5bn, in their worst case scenario – see *Investment & Pensions in Europe 18 April 2005, 'S&P see up to €2bn annual claim on UK's PPF'*, available on www.ipe.com

44. *Financial Times 21/7/2004 'Companies UK: A bad idea'* Martin Dickson. Idea put forward in the FT by Sir Tim Chessels, chairman of trustees at BT's pension fund (which NB is in deficit and still has a high equity

weighting), that the government should put tax payers' money into the PPF.

45. *Accountancy Age 17 December 2003: 'Pension safety net worries financial directors'* available on www.accountancyage.com : article reports that a survey by the UK insurance group Prudential of financial directors found that 42% had reservations about new PPF, mostly on the basis that strong companies will end up bailing out weaker ones.

46. *Financial Times* coverage of the case includes, *'Pensions watchdog primed to protect benefits not jobs', 8 July 2005*

47. Numbers quoted from the English summary of PSVaG annual report 2005. 2004 summary available on line at http://www.psvag.de/pdf/gb04e.pdf#search='psvag%20summary%20of%20annual%20report%202005'http://www.psvag.de/pdf/gb01e.pdf#search='PSVaG%20summary%20of%20annual%20report%202003

48. The insurance industry recently launched a voluntary projected €500m insolvency protection fund which 'de-regulated' Pensionskassen (which serve a range of companies and account for around one-fifth of occupational pension assets) may join. *Investment & Pensions in Europe, 24 May 2006, 'Pensionskassen get insolvency protection'* – available of www.ipe.com

49. The sharp increase in the number of firms mainly comes from employers who have became subject to insolvency insurance as a result of wage and salary conversions

50. *Investment & Pensions in Europe 2 May 2006 'Germany plans huge pension insolvency fund'* – available on www.ipe.com

51. The current legal obligation of 2.75% being applied for payable pension benefits with a less conservative 3.67% applying to entitlements (including 'old obligations').

52. Also known as the LOB (Law on Ocuupational Benefits) Guarantee Fund. See: www.sfbvg.ch/en/bvg/bvg_home.htm

53. It is unclear if there is implicit government support behind the scheme and if public funds would be used to support the organisation if it were in difficulty. Certainly increased premiums, reserves and even bank loans may be used to cover heavy losses before this were the case.

54. This number includes the 2600 registered pension funds and 1200 non-registered pension funds. Registered pension funds are authorised to provide the mandatory part of the second pillar. Note that pension funds often also insure (voluntarily) additional parts of workers salaries.

55. The discount rate for calculating the present value is fixed at 3.5% at present, therefore is greater than the discount rate for calculating the 'Minimum Funding Standard Amount' or MFSA of the pure private benefits.

56. This corresponds to the ceiling on the contribution to the Program (annually 65% of Y9.681m per fund).

57. Following charts taken from Nobuhiro Shimizu's presentation on 'Protection of Participants and the Pension Benefit Guarantee Program of Japan', made at the OECD/ IOPS Conference on Private Pensions in Asia, Bangkok, Thailand, 27-28 April 2005 http://www.oecd.org/dataoecd/56/39/34723067.pdf

58. Goldman Sachs 'Portfolio Strategy', October 2002, author Japan strategist Kathy Matsui

59. The MTPSP is evaluated, in actuarial terminology, by the retrospective method - *i.e.* the MTPSP is the termination value of cash inflows and outflows (premiums corresponding to the Substitution Portion and benefits paid out) with actual interest rates performed by the investment of social security fund (EPI). In other words, EPFs do not have any responsibility of paying additional contributions as long as the investment return is not less than that of the EPI.

60. In the fiscal year ending March 2004, assets at 283 of Japan's biggest corporate pension funds covered 77 per cent of their payment obligations, up from 62 per cent the previous year, according to Greenwich Associates, the US consultancy. See *Financial Times*, 26 July 2004, "Mood of crisis lifts in Japanese pension funds". A survey of all listed companies (3,414) by Nomura Securities found a lower funding ratio of 56% as of March 2004,'*Corporate Pension Obligations*' *Nomura Daily Report, 7th September, 2004.*

References

BODIE, Z., (1996), 'What the pension benefit guarantee corporation can learn from the Federal Savings and Loan Insurance Corporation', *Journal of Financial Services Research, Volume 10, 83-100, March 1996*

BODIE, Z., MITCHELL, O.S., TURNER, J.A., (1996), 'Securing employer-based pensions: an international perspective', Pension Research Council, Wharton School of the University of Pennsylvania

BOYCE, S., IPPOLITO, R.A. (2002), 'The cost of pension insurance' *Journal of risk insurance, 69:2 pp 121-70*

COOPER, R., ROSS, T.W., (1994), 'Public and private guarantee funds with market fragility', *The Journal of Risk and Insurance, Vol. 66, No.2, June 1999, pp 163-184*

GALE, W.G., (1999), 'Public Policies and private pension contributions', *Journal of money, credit and banking, Vol.26, No.3, Part 2: Federal Credit Allocation: Theory, Evidence and History, August 1994, pp710-732*

HSIEH, S-J, CHEN, A.H., FERRIS, K.R., (1994), 'The valuation of PBGC insurance premiums using an option pricing model', *The Journal of Financial and Quantitative Analysis', Vol.29, No.1, March 1994, pp 89-99*

IPPOLITO, R.A. (1985), 'The labour contract and true economic pension liabilities', *The American Economic Review, Vol. 75, No.5, December 1985, pp 1031-1043*

IPPOLITO, R.A., (1987), 'The implicit pension contract: developments and new directions', *The Journal of Human Resources, Vol.22, No.3, Summer 1987, pp441-467*

IPPOLITO, R.A., (2004), 'How to reduce the cost of federal pension insurance', Cato Institute's *Policy Analysis no. 253, August 24th 2004*

LINDEMAN, D., (2004), 'A note on Benefit Security', *OECD Financial Market Trends, No.86, March 2004*

MCCARTHY, D. (2003), 'How much does a central guarantee fund cost?' Watson Wyatt research briefing 2003-04, July 2003

MITCHELL, O.S., (1987), 'Worker Knowledge of Pension Provisions', Working Paper NO. 2414, National Bureau of Economic Research, Cambridge, MA

PESANDO, J.E. (1996), 'The government's role in insuring pensions', in BODIE, Z., MITCHELL, O.S., TURNER, J.A., 'Securing Employer-Based Pensions', The Pension Research Council, University of Pennsylvania Press, Philadelphia, 1996

PESANDO, J.E., (2000), 'The containment of bankruptcy risk in private pension plans', in Private Pension Systems and Policy Issues: OECD Private Pension Series No.1, 2000

SHIMIZU, N. (2005), 'Protection of Participants and the Pension Benefit Guarantee Program of Japan', OECD/ IOPS Conference on Private Pensions in Asia, Bangkok, Thailand, 27-28 April 2005 http://www.oecd.org/dataoecd/56/39/34723067.pdf

SMALHOUT, J.H., (1996), 'The uncertain retirement', Irwin Publishing, Chicago, 1996

ISBN-978-92-64-02810-4
Protecting Pensions: Policy Analysis
and Examples from OECD Countries
© OECD 2007

Chapter 6

Benefit Security: Priority Creditor Rights for Pension Funds

by
Fiona Stewart

I. Introduction

A topic which leads naturally on from the discussion of pension benefit guarantee schemes[1] is the issue of the position of pension fund claims within bankruptcy proceedings. The rights of pension fund beneficiaries within the corporate bankruptcy process has returned as a topic for debate in several countries, due to a series of high profile corporate failures which caused defined benefit occupational pension fund members to lose part of their expected retirement income.

The ultimate risk for pension beneficiaries is the loss of their retirement income. One way in which this can happen is if the corporate sponsor of their pension plan – which is responsible for the funding of the plan – becomes insolvent whilst at the same time the plan does not have sufficient assets to cover its pension liabilities. This is more likely if pension assets are not held separately from the sponsoring company's assets, but is also a risk even when pension assets are ring fenced as achieving full funding at all times is not always feasible. The following questions then arises - once it has been ascertained that the pension beneficiaries have such a claim on the sponsoring company's assets, where does this claim rank vs. other creditors? Do the accumulated pension rights of the plan beneficiaries have a higher ranking claim upon the sponsoring company's assets than other creditors, rank equally, or indeed do they come lower down the creditor rankings, only receiving any remaining company assets after other creditors have been paid? Where a pension benefit guarantee scheme exists, the scheme takes on the credit claims of the pension beneficiaries, and consequently faces the same issues of where its claim stands in the credit rankings - which inevitably has an impact on its financial stability and the cost of its premiums.

II. Arguments for Priority Rights

One form of benefit protection for pension fund beneficiaries would be to give their claims against company assets priority standing, ahead of other creditors – either through a 'preferred' creditor ranking, with priority over other unsecured creditors, or via a 'super preference' over even secured creditors. The arguments for giving such priority claims are similar to those used to justify the introduction of pension benefit guarantee schemes, namely:

- Employees, though they effectively act as creditors of their sponsoring firm, (trading current wages for the promise of future pension income), do not necessarily understand the trade off they are making, are exposed to issues of asymmetric information and do not necessarily undertake a rigorous credit analysis of their employer. They consequently remain more exposed to the bankruptcy of the sponsoring firm than their wage bargaining implies. Whilst an investor such as a bank or a credit provider can consider the risk of a default in pricing their rates, employees are not usually in a position to detect and price or bargain over the respective risks.

- Even if workers are aware of the credit risk to which they are exposed, they are unable to manage this risk effectively as it cannot be successfully diversified. Workers with an occupational pension receive their current and future income from one source, and their pension may be the only substantial financial asset they own. They therefore receive a double blow if their employer becomes bankrupt, and the pension scheme on which they are relying is under-funded, having no other source of income or savings. Other financial creditors, meanwhile, will have a portfolio of lendings, whilst trade creditors are likely to have a range of clients. Pension creditors therefore are especially exposed to credit risk, particularly if their pension scheme is mandatory, they have life-time employment with one firm or if the pension is financed by book reserves (though, as mentioned, extra protection may still be required even with a separating of assets as 100% may not always be achieved).

III. Actual situation

It would therefore seem natural to assume that, to the extent that pensions are an obligation of the plan sponsor and considering the fact that they are the promised benefit of a vulnerable group, pension credits would receive priority ranking over other creditors. Yet this is rarely the case, despite pensions frequently being recognised as deferred wages, and wage and other employment claims often having a priority ranking. For example though pensions may be legally recognised as deferred pay, bankruptcy courts may not recognise this status and offer no priority ranking. An added complication in some countries is that bankruptcy and pension law may actually clash, therefore in practice denying pension claims the priority rights they may have in theory. For example, the bankruptcy law in the USA does not recognise the priority creditor rights given to pensions by the ERISA pension legislation of the 1970s. The position of pension credit rankings remains contested, with current court cases attempting to secure these priority rights (*see USA country section for further details*).

International law also offers pension beneficiaries limited protection. The legislation of the European Union and the conventions of the International Labour Organization (ILO) do address protection for employees in the case of the bankruptcy of their employer, covering areas such as wages, outstanding holiday, sick leave and maternity leave (which receive priority rankings) - but surprisingly pensions are not covered (though the interpretation of international treaties does differ between countries).[2] One exception involves systems of severance pay, which have traditionally received greater protection - given, unlike funded pension plans, they are not funded by independent entities separate from the plan sponsor and are therefore exposed to the plan sponsor's insolvency risk at all times (not only in the case of the pension scheme being underfunded as with other funding arrangements). For example, the ILO sets out rules on the base level of entitlements in the advent of an employer's insolvency which employees should be able to expect. These include a severance allowance or separation benefits based on length of service[3]. Yet these systems are gradually being phased out (for example in Italy, Japan and Korea) and replaced with more conventional pension arrangements which generally receive lower creditor ranking in the case of the bankruptcy of the plan sponsor.

In reality, in some countries not only do pension beneficiaries not receive priority status, but may be disadvantaged vs. other creditors, particularly during the bankruptcy negotiation process, or when a corporate restructuring rather than a full bankruptcy takes place[4]. Though legally all unsecured creditors should be treated equally, this can happen in several ways:

- *Strategic Bankruptcies*: bankruptcies are normally considered to be the result of financial distress, but in some cases bankruptcy filings are made by companies as part of a corporate strategy. Such 'strategic bankruptcies' may be used as a way of employers to renegotiate wages or pension rights[5]. It has been suggested that such tactics have been used by companies within the airline industry[6], whilst a major steel company was accused of similar tactics by the PBGC[7] - indeed, the risk can be argued to exist where companies have the opportunity to pass on their pension obligations to a guarantee scheme.

- *Legal Incentives*: bankruptcy laws themselves may sometimes make the position of the pension beneficiaries more difficult. For example, courts or parliaments may have the power to grant plan sponsors facing financial difficulty pension contribution suspensions, which may increase any underfunding which already exists at the sponsor's pension plan. Indeed pension regulation may also have unforeseen effects, such as loopholes allowing solvent firms to terminate pension plans, thereby improving cashflow and the position of other creditors. For example, the initial ERISA pension legislation in the USA, by determining the event insurable by the pension benefit guarantee scheme as the termination of the fund rather than the insolvency of the plan sponsor, allowed many solvent companies to hand their underfunded pension plans over to the guarantee scheme the PBGC, until legislative amendments were made in the 1980s (see McGill, Brown etc. (1999)).

- *Avoidance tactics:* various 'tactics' can be used by sponsoring firms in financial trouble to avoid paying pension contributions. For example, where obligations are the liability of the controlled group as whole, companies may try to break ownership links or rearrange the corporate structure in order to avoid payment. Likewise, some creditors, sensing that a firm is heading for financial difficulties, may try to improve their position in the creditors rankings – for example by extending or increase the size of a short-term loan when it comes due in return for becoming collateralised against specific assets such as those held in inventory. Indeed in many bankruptcy cases substantive deviations from priority rules do occur. Legal safeguards exist to protect against such evasive behaviour[8], but it is often hard to prove that the main purpose of the action was to evade liability for pension underfunding.

- *Work-out negotiations*: the insolvency process in some countries allows companies experiencing financial difficulties a period of time in which to negotiate new terms and settlements with its creditors in an attempt to keep the firm as a going concern and avoid full liquidation. Different creditors have different incentives for either keeping a firm as a going concern or to liquidate, these incentives also being affected by the size and seniority of the different creditors. Deviation in the priority of creditors is more likely (and indeed less of an issue) in work-outs, as creditors negotiate with each other as they try to find a satisfactory deal and avoid full bankruptcy procedures (see Franks, Nyborg (1996)). An issue often up for negotiation is the payment of pension contributions, particularly where underfunding is considerable. An interesting counter to such practices exists under Australian bankruptcy law by which employees' entitlements, including superannuation contributions, cannot be avoided through agreements and transactions, even if approved by the courts.

Pension creditors may well be adversely affected by such work-outs and negotiations as current and retired workers are often not able to defend their position, and have been described as the 'lost voice' in bankruptcy proceedings. Where they exist, unsecured creditors committees tend to be dominated by larger financial institutions, which do not necessarily share the interests of the former employees, with the 'natural' representatives of pension claims potentially not having such a strong voice (*e.g.* unions may be weak, pension fund trustees inexperienced or guarantee funds, where they exist to take on pension creditor claims, may be politically constrained). Former and current workers may also have lost a great deal of their wealth and therefore may not be able to afford representation and consequently may not be able to make their position fully heard in the reorganisation process. In some countries the restructuring courts can require the debtor to cover third party legal or financial expert costs to ensure proper representation[9]. German bankruptcy proceedings prove a notable exception, where the major pension creditor, the PSVaG, has a strong voice on the creditor committees of the major cases affecting the organisation, and all creditors are able to vote on restructuring agreements (*see German country section for further details*). The pension regulator in the UK is also encouraging pension fund trustees to be more assertive when making deals with corporate plan sponsors[10], with the pension fund representatives of the UK auto parts company Turner and Newell being an interesting current example of trustees playing a more active role in bankruptcy negotiations[11].

IV. Arguments against priority status

One argument against awarding pension creditors priority status is that if this were allowed a range of social issues could come forward claiming priority rights, such as health benefits or environmental claims. The vulnerability of pension vs. other creditors can also be challenged. For example, should small, unsecured creditors, highly exposed to one corporate client, rank behind what could be high financially secure pension beneficiaries (given that higher paid workers are more likely to be members of occupational pension plans than the lower paid in many countries)?

However, a strong case can be made against changing the position of pension claims within the creditor rankings, centering upon the fact that - aside from the complications of changing bankruptcy legislation - doing so may be harmful to capital markets and therefore the investment climate of a country. If pension funds rights increase in status other creditors (who may themselves be small trade and personal creditors) naturally have to drop in the rankings, increasing their credit risk, which might be passed onto corporations in the form of more expensive capital or a general impact on the markets with increased bad debts and potential failures. The impact of 'super priority' rights over secured creditors would of course have an even bigger potential impact, particularly on small trade and personal creditors.

The argument countering priority status for pension credits is outlined in the World Bank's 'Guidelines for Effective Insolvency and Creditor Rights Systems'[12]. This argues that as a general principle creditor rights through commercial laws should both preserve the legitimate expectations of creditors and, most importantly, encourage greater predictability in commercial relations by upholding to the maximum extent possible the relative priorities of creditors established prior to insolvency. The easiest way to ensure this is to have a flat hierarchy of priorities, which consists of only two levels: secured and unsecured creditors, with few deviations from this general rule. The more predictable and transparent the insolvency process the greater the chance of retrieving collateral in the advent of bankruptcy and the more willing lenders should be to lend at rates that reflect lower risk premiums[13]. Similar arguments were made in Germany, where the abolition of rights of preference was one of the main aims of the insolvency reforms in 1999. This implies that employment contracts, which cover pension rights, should be treated in the same way as other trade and service contracts. This is not to say that the repayment of employee entitlements is of less importance than payment of collateral, but rather that there may be more efficient ways of ensuring workers entitlements while still preserving a strong and predictable financing market (for example in the case of pensions through strict funding rules).

It could also be argued that any change in the ranking of pension obligations would now have an even greater impact on credit cost and availability than in the past. New accounting standards increasingly treat such pension obligations the same as other forms of debt and demand that they are shown on companies' balance sheets. Though noting that there are differences between pension obligations and other forms of debt– notably the size of the debt is uncertain and indeed volatile – the major creditor rating agencies are increasingly acknowledging the impact of pension deficits on their corporate credit ratings. They also acknowledge the importance of the priority of creditor's rankings[14]:

"Standard & Poor's treats unfunded pension liabilities, health care obligations and all other forms of deferred compensation as debt-like....For companies with significant unfunded post retirement benefit obligations, the standing of such obligations in bankruptcy can be an important consideration for creditors. It may affect their willingness to lend, as it obviously has a bearing on ultimate recovery in a reorganization or liquidation. Analysis of this matter is highly specific to the legal system and type of benefit in question, as well as to the legal structure of the corporation."

"In its credit analysis of pension obligations, Moody's places greatest emphasis on assessing the future cash flow requirements to fund a company's defined benefit pension plan....Moody's views underfunded pension liabilities as debt-like and incorporates them into certain adjusted leverage measurements as debt equivalent... It is crucial to understand how pensions can affect a company's overall credit quality, including... potential issues affecting priority of claims."

Large underfunded pension schemes are already impacting the credit ratings of companies in the USA (notably the auto companies GM and Ford) and Europe[15]. Different methods for dealing with pension underfunding can also have different impacts[16]. Even the premiums due to the new Pension Protection Fund in the UK could potentially have an impact on other creditors (these being paid from cashflow which is therefore being used to protect one class of creditors – *i.e.* pension fund beneficiaries, including other unconnected employers with relevant pension schemes). Pension debt has also been impacting M&A deals[17]. 'Pension debt' is therefore already increasingly impacting other creditors as both funding and accounting standards move towards fair or market valuations. The potential disruption to capital markets from ranking pension creditors preferentially ahead of other unsecured creditors, or even 'super preferentially' ahead of secured creditors as well, could be huge. Yet some may argue this would be a good thing as it would mean pension obligations being priced properly by markets – being reflected through the increased cost of the rest of the plan sponsor's debt (see Lindeman 1993). The impact could also be lessened by 'grandfathering' in the change in rankings so that it only applied to new debt issuance. It is also interesting to consider the example of Sweden, a country with well functioning capital markets, where the major pension creditor has a strong position within the insolvency process (through the ability of the guarantee scheme - the FPG - to take collateral lines against company assets – see OECD Working Paper on Pension Fund Guarantee Schemes for further details).

V. Conclusion

The issue of the rights of pension creditors within bankruptcy proceedings is clearly a complex one – not least as it may be difficult to establish what contractual, debt-like obligations a plan sponsor is actually liable for. Are plan sponsor pension contributions a contractual (legal) obligation or conditional one? Does the plan sponsor decide the contribution rate or is this done by the pension trustees[18]? Is the plan sponsor liable for pension underfunding due to poor investment performance, incorrect assumptions etc. – or can extra contributions also be required from plan members? The first conclusion which can be drawn is that the obligations of the plan sponsor toward the pension fund should be clearly laid out in the plan documents.

Once established, where these pension obligations should stand in creditor rankings needs to be assessed. Though arguably more vulnerable than other creditors, in many countries pension beneficiaries do not receive priority treatment within the bankruptcy process. Should this be the case? What can be said is that pension creditors should be treated *at least as well* as other unsecured creditors. They should receive proper representation within insolvency and bankruptcy proceedings (*e.g.* on legally required creditors' committees), ensuring their position is articulated as clearly as other, often more heavy weight, financial and trade creditors – the German bankruptcy system being a possible example of good practice. What should also be ensured is that loopholes and other incentives do not exist within the bankruptcy system allowing plan sponsors to avoid pension contributions in order to improve cashflow and pay other unsecured creditors ahead of pension beneficiaries – the UK, for example having recently moved to close down such possibilities.

Whether pension creditors should receive *priority rights* is more controversial. It may be possible to 'grandfather' in preferential rights ahead of other unsecured creditors in order to minimise the impact on financial markets and credit availability. However assigning 'super priority' rights ahead of even secured creditors would likely have a major impact on capital costs, particularly given increasingly market based pension accounting and funding standards. Whether these rights should be extended beyond due and unpaid contributions to underfunding is also controversial, and possible priority for such underfunded claims only being given in cases where the fund is to be terminated.

The OECD *'Guidelines for the protection of the rights of members and beneficiaries'*[19] recommend that, in the event of the insolvency of a plan sponsor with an underfunded pension scheme, there should be rules to allocate available assets to members in accordance with accrued rights and with general principles of equity, as well as rules concerning the responsibility of plan sponsors for any unfunded liabilities. Where insolvency guaranty schemes do not exist, there should be a priority position for due and unpaid contributions, equal to at least the position of due and unpaid taxes[20] (NB in some countries this would imply a 'super preference'). Where such guarantee schemes do exist they would normally become a preferential creditor. The guidelines recommend that priority rights may also be appropriate for underfunded pension commitments that are the responsibility of the plan sponsor –depending on whether a guarantee scheme exists and the likely impact on credit availability. As in the discussions on other benefit protection measures, it should be stressed that priority creditor rights should not be seen in isolation – rather protection measures should be looked at in combination. Given that bankruptcy laws are difficult to change (due to their economic, social, political impact), it may be simpler to focus on introducing efficient funding rules as a 'first line of defense' with additional measure such as benefit guarantee schemes and priority creditor rights being introduced as back up measures, protecting pension beneficiaries in the 'worst case scenario' of their plan sponsor becoming bankruptcy whilst the pension scheme (for which they are responsible) is underfunded. The combination of protection measures used should reflect the nature of the pension system in individual countries.

4.2 The legal provisions recognise the creditor rights of pension plan members and beneficiaries in the case of bankruptcy of the plan sponsor, unless benefits are assured by insolvency guaranty schemes. Where such schemes do not exist, priority rights relative to other creditors should be required for due and unpaid contributions. Priority status may also be recommended for underfunded pension commitments (with reference to the terminal liability) that are the responsibility of the plan sponsor.

VI. Country Profiles

Australia

Outstanding contributions due to superannuation funds from a corporate employer are preferred creditors within the Australian bankruptcy system. Under section 556(1)(e) of the Corporations Act 2001, employment entitlements are given priority over other unsecured debts, except liquidation expenses. Where money is available to pay employees entitlements it is allocated in the following order: wages, superannuation contributions, injury compensation, leave entitlements, and retrenchment payments. A further provision (section 596AA) protects employees entitlements, including superannuation contributions, from agreements and transactions entered into with the intention of defeating the recovery of those entitlements (even if the company is not a party to the agreement or transaction or the agreement is approved by a court).

Canada

Canada's insolvency system is primarily based on two statutes, the *Bankruptcy and Insolvency Act* (BIA) and the *Companies' Creditors Arrangement Act* (CCAA). The BIA provides the framework for bankruptcy as well as for commercial and consumer proposals to restructure debts. The CCAA is a corporate restructuring statute, which provides the basic framework for a court-driven process of reorganisation. Any entity may choose the proposal process under the BIA, while only companies with debts in excess of C$5 million may choose to reorganise under the CCAA. With respect to private pension plans, the federal and provincial governments share jurisdiction depending on the industry. The statute governing pension plans established for employees in areas under federal jurisdiction, such as banking, inter-provincial transportation, and telecommunications, is the federal *Pension Benefits Standards Act, 1985* (PBSA). While some 1,300 pension plans fall under the purview of this act, this represents only 10 per cent of the assets of all registered plans in Canada. All of the provinces except Prince Edward Island have legislation governing pension plans under their jurisdiction.

Currently, pension obligations are not specifically addressed in the priority-ranking scheme in bankruptcy proceedings. As such, outstanding pension funding obligations are treated as unsecured debts. That said, pension funds are held in trust separately and apart from the assets and as such do not form part of the bankrupt's estate. Where the outstanding contributions are subject to a trust, pension legislation states that the contributions will also not form part of the estate (see below for description of the "deemed trust").In CCAA cases or proposals under the BIA, pension obligations may be altered by negotiation between the parties- provided consent is obtained from the appropriate regulatory body- along with all other claims.

At present, the creditor priority rankings in bankruptcy proceedings are as follows:

- Unpaid suppliers, who have a right to repossess goods delivered within 30 days of a bankruptcy under certain circumstances, and farmers and fishers, who have a right to a priority charge on the inventory of the bankrupt.
- Canada Revenue Agency with respect to source deductions (*i.e.*, amounts deducted by the employer from employees' pay cheques in respect of income tax, employment insurance and Canada pension plan and not remitted).
- Secured Creditors.
- Preferred Creditors
    1) Reasonable funeral and testamentary expenses of the debtor
    2) Costs of administration of estate
        - Expenses and fees of receivers
        - Expenses and fees of trustees
        - Legal costs
    3) Levy due to Superintendent of Bankruptcy
    4) Wages to a maximum of 6 months or $2000 and disbursements to a maximum of 6 months or $1000
    5) Family support claims accrued in the year prior to bankruptcy
    6) Municipal taxes accrued within 2 years immediately preceding bankruptcy
    7) Rent owed to a landlord accrued within 3 months of bankruptcy and for up to 3 months following a bankruptcy, if applicable
    8) Legal fees related to first garnishment order made against the bankrupts property
    9) Claims resulting from injury to workers where government program for workers' compensation does not apply
- Unsecured Creditors

Currently, unless the outstanding contributions are subject to a trust, pension obligations are treated within the insolvency system as unsecured debts. Therefore, in insolvency law, pension obligations do not have a priority status. Both federal and provincial pension legislation, however, provide protection for pension plan members by creating a "deemed trust" in favour of the pension plan for specific employer and employee contributions owed to the pension fund. While the wording of the "deemed trust" provisions varies by jurisdiction, they also usually require that these monies do not form part of the employer's estate in the event of bankruptcy or insolvency. Conflicts may arise between provincial pension legislation and federal bankruptcy and insolvency laws. For example, there may be questions about the application of provincial "deemed trust" provisions under provincial pension legislation with respect to bankruptcy, which is governed by federal legislation.

In a restructuring, whether under the CCAA or a BIA proposal, creditors are entitled to vote on the plan. The creditors are divided into classes based on commonality of interest and each class may vote on the proposal. To be binding on the class, creditors who are the majority in number and holding two-thirds of the claims of that class must approve the plan. This ensures that, while larger creditors generally participate more extensively in the bargaining, the smaller creditors have rights during the restructuring approval process.

Pension beneficiaries may generally be divided into two groups – retirees and active employees. The first group currently receives pension benefits and the second are potential recipients. Because their interests are not necessarily the same, they may be represented separately in either a bankruptcy or restructuring event. In a bankruptcy, there is no obligation to create an official creditors' committee. Rather, at the creditors' meeting the claimants may make their views known. In addition, the claimants may choose to create a creditors' committee for dealing with the trustee or receiver. In a restructuring, a union may represent both retirees and active employees. In that situation, the union negotiates amendments to the collective agreement, which dictates employer pension obligations post-restructuring. However, because of differing interests, retirees may have their own representation. Any reduction in pension benefits or accrued pension benefits must be authorised by the regulator.

Proposed Legislation

On June 3, 2005, the Canadian government introduced Bill C-55, An Act to establish the Wage Earner Protection Program Act, to amend the Bankruptcy and Insolvency Act and the Companies' Creditors Arrangement Act and to make consequential amendments to other Acts, in the House of Commons. The Bill proposes to provide greater protection for pension contributions during corporate restructuring and bankruptcy. The Bill would provide regular employer and employee pension plan contributions, which are unremitted at the time of bankruptcy or receivership, with a priority claim over the claims of secured creditors. In a restructuring under both the BIA and CCAA, the payment of unremitted contributions has to be addressed in the plan of arrangement unless otherwise agreed to by the company, the pension beneficiaries, and the pension regulator. At this point in time, there is no guarantee that the Bill will come into force or that it will remain in its present form. However, if Bill C-55 comes into force in its present form, the following changes would occur.

In CCAA cases and BIA proposals, the court could not approve a plan unless it requires the payment of unremitted regular employer and employee pension plan contributions. However, the parties can reach an agreement to allow for payment of a lesser amount with the approval of the relevant pension regulator.

In bankruptcy, the following priority ranking would apply:

- Unpaid suppliers, who have a right to repossess goods delivered within 30 days of the bankruptcy under certain circumstances, and farmers and fishers, who have a right to a priority charge on the inventory of the bankrupt.

- Canada Revenue Agency with respect to source deductions (*i.e.*, amounts deducted by the employer from employees' pay cheques in respect of income tax, employment insurance and Canada pension plan and not remitted).

- Wage earners, who have a claim for unpaid wages, including disbursements and commissions, are granted a priority charge over current assets.

- Regular employer and employee pension plan contributions, which are unremitted at the time of bankruptcy, are granted a priority charge over all assets

- Secured Creditors

- Preferred Creditors

    a) Reasonable funeral and testamentary expenses of the debtor
    b) Costs of administration of estate
        i) Expenses and fees of receivers
        ii) Expenses and fees of trustees
        iii) Legal costs
    c) Levy due to Superintendent of Bankruptcy
    d) Wages to a maximum of 6 months or $2000 and disbursements to a maximum of 6 months or $1000

e) Secured creditors whose security was compromised by the priority charge described in (2) to the amount that the security was compromised
f) Secured creditors whose security was compromised by the priority charge described in (3) to the amount that the security was compromised
g) Family support claims accrued in the year prior to bankruptcy
h) Municipal taxes accrued within 2 years immediately preceding bankruptcy
i) Rent owed to a landlord accrued within 3 months of bankruptcy and for up to 3 months following a bankruptcy, if applicable
j) Legal fees related to first garnishment order made against the bankrupt's property
k) Claims resulting from injury to workers where government program for workers' compensation does not apply.

- Unsecured creditors.

- Creditors whose claim relates to damages arising from the purchase or sale of shares, units or other ownership interest in the bankrupt entity.

Germany

Prior to the introduction of the pension guarantee insurance corporation, pensions in Germany were treated as wage claims in bankruptcy, with the book reserve system consequently forcing workers to take on significant risk. Since the introduction of the PSVaG in the 1970s, pension beneficiaries have received virtually full protection of their pension promises in the case of bankruptcy of their plan sponsor. Direct pension pledges by employers (*i.e.* book reserves), support funds (Unterstützungskassen) and pension funds (pensionsfonds) are covered by the PSVaG. Upon insolvency the obligations of the corporate plan sponsor (both pensions and vested entitlements up to a ceiling level) are taken on by the PSVaG, which covers these with an annuity (see German country section in OECD Working Paper on Pension Fund Guarantee Schemes for further details). Pensionskassen and direct insurance schemes fall outside the PSVaG's protection[21], but the risk to plan members is limited (these being supervised as insurance funds, protected via solvency margins etc. – indeed no defaults at Pensionskassen have taken place).

From 1999 onwards Germany bankruptcy law was changed so that all unsecured creditors are treated the same and priority rankings were basically disbanded. The PSVaG therefore stands in the same position as all other creditors, and indeed it should be noted is a *private* creditor like all others, being a private company and not an agency of the State. What is perhaps different in Germany to other bankruptcy systems is that the 'onminium creditorum' position is genuinely applied, with all unsecured creditors treated equally, including employees. All creditors also have the right to representation through the 'creditors committee' (which may be established by law), and the ability to object to either the appointed bankruptcy administrator or the reorganisation plan. The PSVaG, having only around 140 staff members, but facing 500-700 claims in recent years[22], is not able to sit on all these committees but will be a major voice where large claims of economic significance are involved. What is also different in Germany is the structured nature of the bankruptcy process (with the administrator usually achieving a quick insolvency work-out solution). Less negotiation is possible on the part of individual creditors than, for example, within the US bankruptcy system)[23]. Priority rights may not exist in Germany, but at least the PSVaG has a strong place at the negotiating table when bankruptcies do occur. The asset recovery rate for the organisation is still low (informally estimated around 5%). What the German system does seem to show is that pension creditors do not necessarily need priority ranking within the bankruptcy process to receive fair representation. Rather what are needed are clear, objectively fair and rigorously applied bankruptcy proceedings, operating for the benefit of all creditors equally.

Italy

Severance pay has been the traditional form of retirement income in Italy (though a transition is taking place to DC style pension plans). This is known as Trattamento di Fine Rapporto (TFR), and is calculated as a career average lump sum (indexed annually for 75% of inflation + 1.5% fixed rate), and is accrued as an unfunded liability in the company's book reserve.

Bankruptcy proceedings in Italy are governed by the Royal Decree 16th March 1942 n.267, and the priority rights of creditors are also affected by the rules of the Civil Code. According to these, all credits relating, in general, to the salary due by the employer, included the TFR (severance pay) are priority credits on the movable properties of the debtor. The same status is awarded for credits related to the non-payment of the contributions to the first pillar (compulsory State pension system) and the non-payment of the contributions to others forms of social protection. A wide interpretation of the code could take this to include contributions to pension funds, but there have not been any court decision to clarify this point. The ranking within priority creditors themselves is as follows:

- credits for judicial expenses;

- credits regarding, in general, the salary due by the employer, included the TFR;
- credits regarding the non-payment of the contributions to the 1st pillar (compulsory state pension system)
- credits for the payment of the taxes
- credits regarding the non-payment of the contributions to others forms of social protection

The Decree on bankruptcy discipline also prescribes the institution of a creditor committee formed of 3 or 5 members, generally chosen from all creditors (*i.e.* there are no special rights for workers and retirees).

From 1992 a further Decree (n. 80/1992) instituted a Protection Fund against the risk of the non-payment of employer pension contributions in the event of the employer's bankruptcy.

Ireland

Section 285 of the Irish Companies Act 1963, (as amended by s.10 of the Companies Act 1982), gives certain debts a priority status over other claims made against a company during the insolvency process, namely:

- All sums due to any employee pursuant to any scheme or arrangement for the provision of payments to the employee while he is absent from employment due to ill health
- any payments due by the company pursuant to any scheme or arrangement for the provision of superannuation benefits to or in respect of the employees of the company whether such payments are due in respect of the company's contribution to that scheme or under that arrangement or in respect of such contributions payable by the employees to the company under any such scheme or arrangement which have been deducted from the wages or salaries of employees.

As the definition of superannuation benefits includes pensions, unpaid pension contributions are therefore given preferential treatment in the winding up of companies. However, any claim in respect of enhancement of the value of the pension fund, if admitted, will rank only as unsecured debt. Section 285(7)(a) of the Act says that where there is an insufficiency of assets to meet these preferential debts then the assets will be divided on a pro rata basis (all preferential creditors will rank pari passu). It also states that this preferential treatment will occur only if the liquidator is notified of or becomes aware of the creditor's debt within 6 months of his advertisement for claims. Preferential creditors rank as follows within the hierarchy of debts:

- fixed charges
- liquidators' fees and expenses, examiners fees and certified creditors in an examinership
- preferential debt (including unpaid pension benefits)
- floating charges
- unsecured debts
- members of the company

The Government also protects employees of companies in liquidation by providing that the Minister for Enterprise, Trade and Employment can make payments to employees from the Social Insurance Fund in accordance with the Protection of Employees (Employers' Insolvency) Acts, 1984 to 2003[24]. The Acts provide for the payment into the assets of an occupational pension scheme of certain outstanding pension contributions. The outstanding contributions covered are those which both the employer and the employee were liable to pay in respect of the employee's occupational pension scheme during the year prior to the date of insolvency of the employer. In the case of contributions payable on behalf of an employee, payment can be made only where the amount of the contributions was deducted from the pay of the employee but was not paid over to the trustees/administrators of the occupational pension scheme. In the case of contributions payable on an employer's own account, the lesser of the following is payable under the Acts:

1. the balance of the employer's contributions remaining unpaid in respect of the period of twelve months immediately preceding the date of the employer's insolvency, or

2. the amount certified by an Actuary to be necessary for the purpose of meeting the liability of the occupational pension scheme on dissolution to pay the benefits provided by the scheme to or in respect of the employees concerned.

Where a payment is made out of the Social Insurance Fund in respect of unpaid pension contributions, the Minister is subrogated to the rights of the members as a preferential creditor in the liquidation or receivership (s.10(3) of 1984 Employee protection Act.)

Japan

Severance pay: this was the traditional form of retirement benefit in Japan, though it is now largely supplemented by or converted to more conventional externally funded pension or lump-sum arrangements. Under the new Corporate Reorganisation Law, one-third of the claim of a dismissed employee for his/her severance allowance up to 6 times of his/her monthly salary is given priority over other debts owed by the employer (*i.e.* is treated as one of the 'Claims of Common Interests' and should be paid back prior to any other debts, including collateralised debts and tax payments). Under the new Bankruptcy Law, the claim of a dismissed employee for his/her severance allowance up to 3 times his/her monthly salary is given priority over general preferential claims, although inferior to collateralised debts.

Employee Pension Funds: Many Employee Pension Funds (EPFs) were established in the 1960s and 1980s. These are pension plans with over 500 members for single-employer schemes or over 3000 for multi-employer schemes. For EPFs newly introduced after April 2005, over 1000 members are required for single-employer schemes and over 5000 members for multi-employers schemes. As well as providing private pension benefits, EPFs also manage a portion of the public pension scheme (the Employee Pension Insurance or EPI, which is the employment related social security pension for private sector employees). This public pension portion of the EPF is known as the 'Substitution Component'. The following priority rights exist in relation to EPF pension claims:

1. EPFs have a priority claim over employer contributions

2. the Pension Fund Association has a priority claim over the Substitutional Component

3. EPFs have a claim for the uncollected contribution due from the public nature of the EPF

If an EPF converts to the new pension system and decides to become one of the new Defined Benefit Pension Plans, the position of claims for contributions moves down in the rankings as the plan loses its public nature (as it 'hands back' the Substitutional Component to the government by the system known as 'daiko-henjo').

What is more complex in Japan is the nature and amount of contributions which are due from the plan sponsor, and what benefits they have an obligation for. This stems from the fact that historically retirement benefits were paid in the form of severance pay and that ways existed for companies to reduce the amount of severance allowance which they had an obligation to pay. When pension funds were subsequently introduced it was therefore difficult to include clear vesting rights. The new Defined Benefit Corporate Pension Law of 2002 set up common rules for the vesting issue but with some changes still needed, and clarified the termination liability which the plan is obliged to pay immediately to the plan participants when the plan is wound up. The termination liability is based on the concept of the 'Minimum Preserved Benefit' (MPB) – *i.e.* a scheme participant's vested or regarded-to-be-vested benefit corresponding to his/ her past service period and the benefit provision of the plan. The sum total of the present value of the MPBs minus the amount of plan assets is treated as uncollected contribution (*i.e.* this is the liability of sponsoring company when the plan terminates). The discount rate for calculating the present value is self-determined, with the range between 80% and 120% of the five year average of subscriber interest rates of 30-year Japanese Government Bonds. The sum total of the present value of the MPB is called as the 'Minimum Funding Standard Amount' (MFSA). EPFs and DB plans are required to keep the funded ratio above 100% (90% until 2007) of the MFSA. When the funded ratio goes below 100% (90% until 2007)–the EPFs or DB plans should in principle draw up and implement a recovery plan to shore up the funded ratio to over 100% within 7 years(90% within 10 years until 2007).

Pre 2005	*From 1st Jan 2005*
Taxes	Taxes / Labour Creditors
Pension Creditors (EPF)	Pension Creditors (EPF)*
Labour Creditors	
Private Creditors	Private Creditors

* Part of Pension creditors can be regarded as Labour Creditors

However, these funding rules are relaxed in the case of insolvency. As a temporary measure, EPFs are allowed to reduce the amount of contribution which the sponsoring company is obliged to pay into the fund for making good the shortfall to the minimum funding requirement for the Substitution Portion alone – know as the 'Minimum Technical Provision of the Substitution Portion' or MTPSP[25]. Therefore in reality it is only the Substitutional Portion which is protected, not the purely private part of the occupational pension. The normal procedure after the dissolution of an EPF is that the Pension Fund Association (PFA) collects amounts equal to the MFPSP – in exchange for which it provides an annuity corresponding to the Substitutional Portion. Dissolved EPFs then distribute residual assets to plan participants, either in the form of a lump sum or an annuity (also provided by the PFA and known as the PFA Annuity) – however as funding has been reduced to cover only the Substitional Portion, few residual assets are likely to remain. Since 1989 the Pension Fund Association has also operated a Pension Benefit Guarantee Program (PBGP) to provide a minimum guarantee to participants of dissolved EPFs, which supplements the PFA Annuity (*i.e.* it only covers participants who chose the annuity rather than the lump sum option regarding residual assets).

Other pension funds: Non EPF type defined benefit pension plans do not receive any priority status in bankruptcy proceedings, and rank in the same position as private creditors. However, if the pension benefits provided are legally regarded a severance (and the promise of paying the benefits are explicitly stated in the office regulations or in the severance allowance regulations of the sponsoring companies), they may then be treated as labour credits, ranking as a preferential claim (receiving the lowest priority order amongst these). However this status still exists only in theory and there is as yet no established precedence as the Defined Benefit Corporate Pension Law was introduced only in 2002.

Korea

Corporate retirement income in Korea has traditionally operated as severance pay. This is treated as deferred wages and receives priority standing ahead of other creditors in case of the sponsor's bankruptcy. When the new occupational pension system goes into operation in Korea from the end of 2005, (by which companies can voluntarily convert their severance pay systems into DB or DC pension plans), retirement benefit rights of the new DB schemes will receive priority standing ahead of other creditors in case of the sponsor's bankruptcy, in the same way as severance pay.

The Labor Standards Act Article 37 (Preferential Claims for Wages) outlines the following details:

- Wages, retirement allowance, accident compensation, and other claims arising from employment shall be paid in preference to taxes, public charges, or other claims except for claims secured by pledges or mortgages on the whole property of an employer; provided, that this shall not apply to those taxes and public charges which take precedence over said pledges or mortgages.

- Notwithstanding the provisions of the preceding paragraph, the claim falling under any of the following subparagraphs shall be paid in preference to any claims secured by the right of pledge or mortgage on the whole property of the employer, taxes, public charges and other claims:

1. The wages of the last 3 months;
2. The retirement allowance of the last 3 years; and
3. Accident compensation allowance.

- The retirement allowance under paragraph (2) shall be the amount equivalent to a 30 days' portion of the average wage for each one year of continuous employment.

Netherlands

In the Netherlands laws governing bankruptcy, unemployment and pensions and savings funds provide a substantial safety net for pension fund beneficiaries. In the case of the bankruptcy of the plan sponsor, there is a special fund that will pay pension premiums with a backlog of maximum one year. Legislation requires that the Articles of Association and regulations of a pension fund contain provisions in respect of winding-up, including that if the plan sponsor ceases to exist, (or the relationship between the pension plan and the sponsor is terminated in another manner), all accrued benefits must be transferred to another pension fund or purchased through an insurance contract, or if pension fund assets are sufficient to pay accrued rights, become a closed pension fund. Pensions funded through the purchase of insurance contracts may be protected, in the event that the insurer encounters financial difficulty, through the early intervention arrangement for life insurers. In such a case, the insurance portfolio would be transferred to a special purpose vehicle company set up by the insurance industry.

It should be noted that Dutch pension funds are independent from the plan sponsor(s), so that the only creditor rights which a pension fund can have towards a plan sponsor are overdue premiums. The pension fund is treated equally to all other creditors in the bankruptcy process, though unpaid taxes and social contributions have legal priority over unpaid pension fund contributions. However, the Department of Justice has put forward a bill to change the Civil Act so that pension providers will get a preferential position in case of bankruptcy of the plan sponsor.

The bankruptcy of a pension fund itself is not technically possible as legislation requires that a pension fund have assets sufficient to meet its liabilities – *i.e.* it must be fully funded at all times[26]. In the event that a pension fund has to be re-insured and the assets of the fund are insufficient to pay the full insurance premium, the benefits of all members (active, inactive, retired) would be reduced. The allocation of pension fund assets on winding-up (whether these assets are larger or smaller than the pension fund's obligations) are not addressed in legislation (as is usually in the case in other countries – see Portugal, UK, USA), but are dealt with in the Articles of Association of the fund. Funding rules are the main protection measure for pension beneficiaries in the Netherlands – for example there is no Pension Benefit Guarantee Scheme operating. Overall, the legal structure and governance practices employed by pension funds in the Netherlands facilitate the adjustment of the benefits and contributions of a pension fund in response to changing circumstances. This contributes to the ability of pension funds to continue their operations, even in the face of financial difficulties, and lessens the need for a guarantee scheme.

Portugal

In Portugal occupational pensions schemes can be financed though the establishment of a pension fund or through an insurance contract, through no financing obligation exists in legislation. Occupational defined benefit (or hybrid) plans financed by pension funds, which are underfunded due to unpaid contributions due from the plan sponsor must be wound-up according to the legislation. In such cases the pension fund assets will be used to cover guaranteed pension benefits (*i.e.* pensions in payment, vested rights and accrued benefits). However, beneficiaries and active workers do not have any right to claim pension fund contributions due from the insolvent mass of the company, much less any priority credit status. Nor does a national pension benefit guarantee scheme exist.

When the assets of pension fund are liquidated under the terms laid out in the winding-up contract they should be distributed preferentially in the following order (on a pro-rata basis if necessary)[27]:

- Chargeable expenses (under Article 26 of the law)

- In the case of pension funds that finance contributory pension schemes, each member's individual account, that should be applied in accordance with the rules laid down in the incorporation contract or management regulations;

- Single annuity premiums that guarantee pensions in payment in accordance with the amount of the pension at the time of the winding-up;

- Single annuity premiums that guarantee payment of pensions relating to members of an age equal to or greater than the normal retirement age laid down in the pension scheme;

- A sum that guarantees the vested rights of the members existing at the time of winding-up that should be applied in accordance with the rules laid down in the incorporation contract or management regulations;

- A guarantee for accrued benefits as regards members who are not covered by the previous sub-paragraph;

- Sums that guarantee the up-dating of pensions in payment, provided that this is set forth in the contract.

Sweden

Occupational pensions for white-collar workers (ITP schemes) in Sweden are protected by a guarantee fund - the Pension Guarantee Mutual Insurance Company or FPG (see Swedish country section in OECD Working Paper on Pension Fund Guarantee Schemes for further details). The FPG is not a preferential creditor in a bankruptcy proceeding, except - occasionally - for a very small part (max 5 %) of the total claim, *i.e.* for pension rights earned three months before the bankruptcy. However, the FPG is in a strong position as it is able to demand collateral against the insured company's assets. Indeed the scheme only allows creditworthy companies to participate, or those who provide adequate collateral (the amount demanded of the company depending on the FPG's regular internal assessment of insolvency risk), or a surety bond issued by the parent company. During the last ten years FPG has had very few claims and the net losses, after recoveries, have been insignificant. What is interesting in the Swedish case is that the pension claims (through the FPG) are effectively even higher than preferential claims, and indeed rank as secured creditors. Yet the healthy capital markets in the country imply that this has not affected company's ability to raise capital or the cost of capital.

Other pension funds in Sweden, not covered by the FPG insurance system, receive general preferential rights. Pensions can also be safeguarded through life insurance provided by life insurance companies or friendly societies (a kind of mutual economic association). In the case of life insurance companies, the company is obligated to keep a special register containing assets held to cover technical provisions. In case of bankruptcy, the insured will have a priority right as concerns these assets. This system does, however, not apply to friendly societies (where the legislation is more complex), though funds are of course earmarked for pensions, as these societies are closed.

Preferential rights in respect of specific property
Particular liens
Mortgages on real property
Mortgages on site-leasehold right
Seizures
General preferential rights
Costs for petitions by creditors and company reorganisation
Costs for accounting and yearly mandatory audit
Business mortgage with a right to 55% in all remaining assets after creditors with superior rights have received dividend
Salary and pension claims

Switzerland

Regarding pension funds, when an employer is bankrupt or insolvent and is unable to make pension contributions, a special fund, known as the guarantee fund, intervenes to pay pension beneficiaries up to a ceiling level. The guarantee fund is subrogated to the rights of the members as a creditor within the bankruptcy proceedings but receives no priority ranking. Any benefits above the ceiling level remain with the beneficiaries, who do receive a preferential claim status (first class).

UK

Under a final salary scheme where the scheme's liabilities exceed its assets, the shortfall becomes a debt owed by the employer to the trustees of the scheme. If the company becomes insolvent the trustee's claims (other than those for some unpaid contributions) have to rank equally with all other non-preferential and unsecured creditors, so any recovery of the debt cannot be relied upon. There are some measures which the trustees can take to reduce the debt, other than relying on the company. A claim may be made for contributions due but unpaid by an employer to the state operated

National Insurance Fund through the Redundancy Payments Directorate of the Insolvency Service[28]. Where an insolvent employer has failed to pay contributions into a pension scheme, the scheme may be able to recover some of the missing contributions from the National Insurance Fund, via the Redundancy Payments Directorate. The contributions which may be recoverable are the employer's own contributions as well as any employee contributions which the employer has deducted from wages but not paid over to the scheme. Unpaid employees' contributions are payable up to the actual amount deducted from wages during the twelve months prior to the date of insolvency. Unpaid employers' contributions for the twelve-month period prior to the insolvency date are also payable but are subject to monetary limits depending on the type of pension scheme. The Secretary of State then takes on this claim against the company, taking on the benefits of scheme trustees and enjoying any preferential status within the creditor hierarchy which is as follows:

- Secured creditors – fixed (over company assets / property etc.);

- Preferential creditors – including employee claims (the government gave up claims to certain tax preferences in recent years). Employees rank as preferential for certain debts, and to the extent that the Secretary of State pays the employees, takes over that preferential status. The Secretary of State ranks as a preferred creditor for payments made as part of employment protection legislation (wages, holidays and the pension contributions mentioned above);

- Secured creditors - floating (no lien on a particular asset);

- Unsecured creditors – the rest of due pension payments ranking here, ranking pari passu with all of the other unsecured creditors.

This overall order of priority was debated as part of the Green Paper of the Pensions Bill (2004), but it was decided not to change the priority of pension claims within bankruptcy proceedings (due to concerns over capital market disruption and the effect on the other creditors generally).

The new Pension Protection Fund offers an additional layer of protection for pension obligations to defined benefit scheme members from April 2005. Its position as a creditor within the bankruptcy system is also as an unsecured creditor. The PPF also covers shortfalls in any pension schemes caused by fraud or theft.

The priority of rights amongst pension claims themselves has also been revised in the UK (where there is a statutory priority order established by law which overrides the priority order in pension scheme rules, unlike in the Netherlands where the hierarchy established in the Articles of the individual pension fund applies). The 1985 Maxwell scandal (hurting actual pensioners) resulted in the Pensions Act 1995. Regulations made under powers in the Act placed not only pensions in payment but also future increases in pension benefits ahead of the accrued pension rights of active, working members of the pension scheme. The recent round of companies becoming insolvent with underfunded pension schemes saw pensioners at some firms having their pension secured, whilst active members (even if one week away from retirement) lost a large percentage of promised benefits. The Regulations were amended for schemes which began winding up on or after 10 May 2004. The priority order was changed to put the rights of active pension scheme members ahead of the rights of existing pensioners to future pension increases.

A new statutory priority order was introduced under the Pensions Act 2004 for schemes which commenced winding up on or after 6 April 2005 when the Pension Protection Fund (PPF) commenced operations. The new Statutory Priority Order is broadly as follows:

1. any liability for pensions or other benefits to the extent that this does not exceed the corresponding PPF liability;
2. remaining voluntary contributions not covered in (1);
3. any other scheme benefits not covered in (1) or (2) above.

It will ensure that broadly speaking individual scheme members will be no worse off if their scheme winds up than they would be if the PPF were instead to assume responsibility for the scheme and pay compensation to members. The PPF will pay two levels of compensation:

- One level, commonly referred to as the "100% level of compensation" – this is for people who, at the start of the PPF's involvement with a scheme (the assessment date), have reached the scheme's pension age or are in receipt of survivors' benefit or a pension on the grounds of ill-health. In broad terms, this means a starting level of compensation that could equate to 100% of the pension in payment immediately before the assessment date (subject to a review of the rules of the scheme by the PPF). However, only the part of this compensation that is derived from employment on or after 6th April 1997 will be increased each year (up to a maximum of 2.5%) – this could, potentially, result in a lower rate of increase than the scheme would provide.

- The second level is referred to as the "90% level of compensation" – this is for the majority of people below the scheme's normal pension age. The 90% level is based on the pension an individual had accrued immediately before the assessment date (again subject to a review of the scheme by the PPF). This amount is then re-valued in line with the increase of the Retail Prices Index between the assessment date and the commencement of compensation payments (subject to an overall maximum calculated by assuming RPI increased by 5% each year) – this helps to ensure the pension holds its value. Once revaluation is calculated a cap is then imposed – in 2005 / 06 this has been set at £27,777.78 per year at age 65. The cap will be reduced if members receive compensation before reaching 65 or if they have opted to commute part of their pension for a lump sum (as otherwise their overall compensation 'package' would be of a higher value and this would be unfair to other members). The final compensation is then 90% of the capped amount. Once in payment this is subject to the same increases as the 100% level of compensation.

The new Pensions Act also introduced various measures to close some of the loopholes which saw pension beneficiaries losing out to other creditors, particularly during pre-bankruptcy negotiations. Previously when a sponsoring company was unable to cover the cost of buying out the required benefits, the trustees were allowed to come to a deal with the employer on how much of a contribution to accept[29]. Before entering into a compromise deal with the company, trustees had to take appropriate independent expert advice (likely to include legal, actuarial and accounting advice). Whilst compromising on the debt paid is still possible, it has been actively discouraged. If scheme trustees decide to do this they are likely to make their scheme ineligible for the Pension Protection Fund. If most of the trustees are senior members of the company, and are therefore not deemed to be sufficiently independent, the Pensions Regulator can appoint an independent trustee to oversee any negotiations involved.

The Pensions Act 2004 also contains a number of measures to address the risks of so-called 'moral hazard'. Moral hazard is the risk that, because the Pension Protection Fund will compensate scheme members if their employer has become insolvent and the scheme is underfunded, employers will deliberately manipulate their affairs so as to shift their deficits to the Pension Protection Fund, thus increasing the Pension Protection Fund levy costs for responsible employers. Three key elements of the Pensions Regulator's moral hazard powers are its ability to impose either a contribution notice, financial support direction or restoration order. Contribution notices are a regulatory tool intended to allow the Regulator to require a person (which can include a company) who has been involved in a deliberate act to avoid pension liabilities, to put money into a pension scheme up to a specified amount. However, before issuing a contribution notice to anyone, the Regulator must be satisfied that it is reasonable to do so and there are a number of factors which must be considered set out in the legislation. Financial Support Directions are intended to allow the Regulator to direct that associated and connected persons put in place arrangements to guarantee the pensions liabilities of an employer who is insufficiently resourced to do so itself, or which a "service company" is as defined in the legislation. When an employer has been subject to a "relevant event", if the assets of the scheme have been reduced by virtue of a transaction at an undervalue involving assets of the scheme, the Regulator may make a restoration order to put the position back to what it would have been had the transaction not occurred. This applies to occupational pension schemes but not money purchase schemes, a prescribed scheme or a scheme of a prescribed description. The Regulator may only make an order in certain circumstances where a "relevant event" has occurred and where the transaction was entered into on or after 27 April 2004 and not more than two years before the occurrence of the "relevant event."

USA

Occupational defined benefit pension funds in the US are secured (up to a ceiling level) via compulsory insurance with the Pension Benefit Guarantee Corporation which takes over the position of pension creditor in case of the bankruptcy of the plan sponsor (see USA country section in OECD Working Paper on Pension Fund Guarantee Schemes for further details). There is, however, contention over the priority bankruptcy rights of the PBGC. The PBGC argues that the ERISA pension legislation of the 1970s affords the organisation priority treatment for certain of its claims against bankrupt employers with underfunded pension plans. In cases where plan termination occurs *before* a bankruptcy petition has been filed, the organisation argues these priority claims cover a shortfall of up to 30% of the net worth of the sponsoring firm and affiliates. In the bankruptcy courts this is known as the PBGC's employer liability claim. Plan underfunding is typically large relative to the net worth of the firm terminating its plan, so the 30% rule normally applies. When the laws were introduced, Congress stipulated that this claim of employer liability would be treated as a tax due to the US, therefore being granted priority over general unsecured creditors. However, in the opinion of the PBGC, Congress *also* intended that the 30% net worth claim would have value *after bankruptcy had been filed*. The PBGC goes on to assert priority treatment for missed minimum funding contributions in excess of $1m^{30}. However, these priority claims have been challenged by many bankruptcy lawyers, who dispute the PBGC's interpretation of ERISA, the tax code and the bankruptcy code. They also argue that after a firm has filed for bankruptcy, it is not longer responsible for its minimum contributions to an ongoing pension plan as these are payments for 'pre-petition debt'. The PBGC counters the argument by saying that pension promises are non-cash wages for workers' ongoing labour and that pension contributions should be paid in full just like wages and other current compensation during bankruptcy.

The PBGC is again asserting its rights in the courts, trying to avoid companies exercising what is known as the 'pensions put', passing its pension obligations onto the guarantee fund before starting up again with lower costs. Bradley Belt, Chief Executive of the PBGC, wishes to strengthen the agency's status in bankruptcies. He has proposed a modest change to the law that would allow the PBGC to force the collection of due and unpaid contributions from companies in bankruptcy. In October 2004 he called on Congress (via the Senate Commerce Committee) to strengthen the agency's hand in seeking to attach assets of bankrupt companies to protect those companies' pension plan participants (explaining that the PBGC has the power to place a lien on non-bankrupt company assets if the company misses pension contributions, but is not able to do so for bankrupt companies)[31]. In order to enhance the PBGC's ability to recover its claims, the organisation is also arguing that pension contributions should be treated as administrative expenses, thereby receiving priority status within bankruptcy proceedings - ongoing cases involving United Airlines being important test cases for this argument.[32]

The following statutory ranking for the allocation of pension benefits supersedes any procedures laid out in plan documents. A PBGC regulation also permits for limited subclasses within each category (*e.g.* based on age, disability etc.).

- Benefits attributable to voluntary employee contributions (active workers, assets in individual accounts)
- Benefits attributable to mandatory employee contributions
- Benefits of a participant or beneficiary that had been in a pay status for at least 3 years on the date of the insured event, and the benefits that would have been in pay status for 3 or more years if the participants had retired with normal benefits 3 years prior to the insured event. Priority only for the lowest benefit level under the plan during 5 years prior to retirement (three years' lowest benefit level to those already retired).
- All other benefits up to the applicable limits that would be insured except for the aggregate limit
- All other vested benefits
- All other benefits under the plan

Country	Pension Credit Priority	Ranking	Other Protection	Comments
Australia	Unpaid employer contributions	Behind insolvency charges and secured creditors Ahead tax and other unsecured	Clause overriding agreements to reduce superannuation contributions	
Germany	No – all unsecured creditors rank equally		Guarantee scheme, PSVaG, covers most pension obligations	PSVaG strong representation in work-out process
Italy	Severance pay Unpaid employer contributions to state pension Theoretically unpaid to occupational pensions	Behind judicial costs, ahead of tax State contributions as above Occupational behind tax	Protection fund for unpaid contributions	
Ireland	Unpaid contributions only	Behind fixed secured creditors Ahead floating secured creditors	Social Insurance Fund covers unpaid contributions	
Japan	Severance pay (capped) EPF substitutional component (public pension) + employer contributions	Behind secured creditors, ahead preferential Behind wages/taxes, ahead private creditors	Guarantee scheme for EPF funds	Funding rules and contribution requirements mean that in reality only the substitutional component is protected
Korea	Severance pay and new DB schemes	Ahead tax and secured creditors		Pension benefit guarantee scheme under consideration

Country	Pension Credit Priority	Ranking	Other Protection	Comments
Netherlands	No		Social fund covers one year backlog	Legislation currently under review.
			Strict funding rules	Plan sponsor not responsible for underfunding – full funding required.
Portugal	No			
Sweden	No - ITP plans		ITP plans covered by guarantee scheme - FPG	FPG takes collateral lien on company assets
	Yes - others	Behind secured creditors + bankruptcy costs, ahead unsecured creditors		
Switzerland	No – guarantee fund subrogation		Guarantee fund exists	
	Yes – excess claims remaining with beneficiaries			
UK	Limited unpaid contributions only	Behind fixed secured creditors, ahead floating secured creditors	Unpaid contributions covered by National Insurance fund	Closing loopholes to avoid pension contributions in new Pensions Act
			New guarantee scheme – PPF	
USA	No		Guarantee scheme – Pension Benefit Guarantee Scheme	Priority status claimed by PBGC not recognised by bankruptcy courts
				Claim secured status for underfunding up to 30% of firm's net worth, + priority status unpaid contributions over $1m (ranking with tax and administrative charges)

Notes

1. See OECD Working Paper on Pension Guarantee Funds

2. There is EU legislation on pension transfer rights in the event of M&A (under the 1998 European directive amendment), and the 'Barber Judgement' of the European Court has recognised some pensions as deferred pay. See: http://www.law-lib.utoronto.ca/Diana/fulltext/flyn.htm.

3. See ILO convention C173: 'Protection of Workers Claims (Employer's Insolvency) Convention' (1992): http://www.ilo.org/ilolex/cgi-lex/convde.pl?C173.

4. It should be noted that such renegotiations may be for valid business reasons. For example, where a company faces financial difficulties due to a large increase in pension contributions required due to an 'actuarial deficit' (e.g. caused by changes in assumptions), it may well make sense to renegotiate contribution terms with pension beneficiaries. Equally, if a restructuring results in an on-going company, the pension deficit is in effect 'actuarial' and can be made up over a period of time.

5. See paper from Pace University: http://webpage.pace.edu/jteall/Corp7.pdf#search='chapter%2023%20corporate%20bankruptcy,%20restructuring%20and%20divestiture

6. *See the Economist, 'Nest Eggs without the yoke', 8 May 2003.*

7. The PBGC's claims centred around the use of 'follow on' plans, For case details see: http://www.usdoj.gov/osg/briefs/1989/sg890430.txt.

8. See article on 'avoidance powers' and exceptions in US Bankruptcy code: http://www.weil.com/wgm/cwgmpubs.nsf/475bf0f96efe96638525679b0053248d/076afb0ea7d645d7852567990078692a?OpenDocument.

9. The employees of the US firm Enron organised an official committee to represent their interests in the bankruptcy process (regarding deferred compensation, health and welfare benefits etc. – the PBGC handling pension claims directly). Their motivation was the fact that: "The existing unsecured creditors' committee is dominated by the largest financial institutions in the United States. It does not share the interests of

former employees and retirees and cannot adequately represent their interests" – according to David P. McClain (of McClain & Siegel the Houston bankruptcy firm acting on behalf of former employees). Richard D. Rathvon, co-chair of the Employee Committee pointed out that: "The Committee has ensured that the interests of employees were not eclipsed by more powerful creditors as the cumbersome bankruptcy process rolled forward." For details see www.employeecommittee.com.

10. See: *'Opra warns of 'inappropriate' trustee deals'*, 20 December 2004, available on www.ipe.com.

11. For coverage of the case see *Financial Times, 'T&N trustees can vote against US plan'*, November 3 2004, *'T&N fund members stand to loose 70% of benefits'*, December 7, 2004

12. http://www.worldbank.org/ifa/icrosc_template.pdf#search='World%20Bank%20Principles%20and%20Guidelines%20for%20Effective%20Insolvency%20and%20Creditor%20Rights%20Systems%20April%20%202001'.

13. It should be noted that, though transparency is important, it does not necessarily mean that priority rankings in a liquidation situation need to be the same as the pre-bankruptcy order. Lenders need to be able to obtain information necessary to make lending decisions taking account of the priority situation in event of bankruptcy.

14. Standard & Poor's, *'Ratings Direct: Corporate Ratings Criteria – Post Retirement Obligations'*, 28 October 2004. Moody's Investor Service Global Credit Research, *'Rating Methodology – Analytical Observations related to U.S. Pension Obligations'*, January 2003.

15. www.ipe.com *'Pension deficits to hit German group's ratings'*, 12 September 2002.

16. e.g. ICI 'ring-fenced' cashflows and assets, giving pension contributions priority over other payments – see *Financial Times 'ICI assets to insure pensions', 16 October, 2003*. US auto firm GM and UK retailer M&S, meanwhile raised debt – *see Financial Times 'Standards that encourage delusion', 19 December 2003*, and *'M&S issues bond to bridge gap'*, 1 June 2004, available on www.ipe.com. For an assessment of the impact of these different strategies see Moody's Investor Service Global Credit Research, "*Special Comment – Analytical Observations Related to 'Underfunded' Pension Obligations when using UK and IAS GAAP"*, May 2003 and *Financial Times 'ICI pension move hit by Moody's review'*, 23October 2003.

17. See Lane, Cark & Peacock's "*11th Accounting for Pensions Survey -- 2004*", August 2004, available at www.lcp-actuaries.co.uk. For details on

WH Smith and Marks & Spenser cases in the UK see: *"Fund remains steadfast in its duty"*, Financial Times Fund Management, 16 August 2004, and the *Financial Times: 'Pension deficits hit harder'*, January 9th 2005.

18. e.g. as is the case with the pension fund of retailer Marks and Spencer in the UK, which caused problems in a recent M&A deal. See *'Pensions key in 13.5bn bid for M&S'*, 3 June 2004 available on www.ipe.com.

19. See 'OECD Guidelines on Funding and Benefit Security in Occupational Pension Plans' in the Annex.

20. In some cases income tax taken from employees' pay but not yet remitted to the authorities would be considered, whilst corporate taxes due to the state could be considered.

21. In some limited cases direct insurance is covered by the PSVaG.

22. Details available from PSVaG Summary Annual Report –the 2003 report available in available in English on line at http://www.psvag.de/pdf/gb03e.pdf#search='PSVaG%20Summary%20of%20Annual%20Report%202004'.

23. Following the drawing up of insolvency papers a 3 month period exists when the company is run by an administrator – who is a person not a company - appointed by the court. Many of these are well known to the PSVaG, and the resulting close cooperation with insolvency executors ultimately serves to promote the fulfilment of the functions and responsibilities of the PSVaG. Employees are paid by the government in this period, during which much of the insolvency process will be worked out by the administrator (the bidding process, decisions on which divisions are to be sold etc.). Official bankruptcy proceedings then open, and the administrator's plan is taken to the creditor committee and all creditors can vote on it.

24. After the case *Re Cavan Rubber Ltd. (in liquidation)* [1992] ELR 79, the Employment Appeals Tribunal (EAT) decided that a scheme which would not constitute an occupational pension scheme for the purposes of the pensions acts as it was not revenue approved, needed a lesser standard to be considered as an occupational pension scheme for the purposes of being eligible to recover funds from the Social Insurance Fund.

25. The MTPSP is calculated in a retrospective manner, using actual rates of return achieved by the Social Security Fund (including the performance of the GPIF).

26. Dutch funding rules require pensions to be fully funded at all times. On the liabilities side this includes the immediate coverage of all salary increases, pension indexing or retroactive plan improvements, and on the

asset side the immediate correction of negative investment returns. If the fund assets are less than accrued liabilities plus a required buffer to protect against adverse investment experience (such as an immediate drop in equity values), then the shortfall must be rectified within 15 years. Furthermore, if the fund assets are even less than 105% of the accrued liabilities, the shortfall must be addressed in principle within three years (up to one year if certain conditions are not met).

27. According to Article 24 of Decree-law no. 475/99, of the 9th of November, available in English on www.isp.pt.

28. See Faculty and Institute of Actuaries (www.actuaries.org.uk) GN4: Insolvency of Employers: Safeguard of Pension Scheme Contributions. Opas – Office of the Pensions Advisory Service www.opas.org.uk/PensionRights/WindingUp/index.htm

29. This principle was agreed by the Courts in the Bradstock case, where the trustees wanted to accept a lower contribution from the company than was required to secure the minimum benefits, rather than making the company insolvent by requesting the full amount. Opas – Office of the Pensions Advisory Service www.opas.org.uk/PensionRights/WindingUp/index.htm

30. Since enactment of the Pension Protection Act of 1987, a statutory lien on the assets of the controlled group arises 60 days after a contribution has been missed and the total amount of missed contribution exceeds $1million. The amount of the lien is the amount of missed contributions in excess of $1million. In general, the remaining portions of the PBGC's bankruptcy claims are not entitled to priority status and are treated as general unsecured claims.

31.. See Washington Post, 8 October 2004, 'Pension Guarantor Calls for Changes – PBGC Asks Congress for New Powers', available on: http://www.globalaging.org/pension/us/private/2004/guarantor.htm.

32. For details of the cases see press releases from the PBGC available on their website: www.pbgc.gov.

References

BODIE, Z., MITCHELL, O.S., TURNER, J.A., (1996), 'Securing employer-based pensions: an international perspective', Pension Research Council, Wharton School of the University of Pennsylvania.

CARROLL, T.J, NIEHAUS, G., 'Pension Plan Funding and Corporate Debt Ratings', *Journal of risk and insurance, 1998, Vol.65, No.3, p427-441.*

COHEN, N., *Financial Times, September 26th, 2004: 'Time to rethink a bankruptcy system'.*

The Council of the European Communities, *Council Directive 80/987/EEC on the approximation of the laws of Member States relating to the protection of employees in the event of the insolvency of their employer (1980).*

FEBER, M.M., (2003), 'Employee Entitlements in Insolvency: Comparison between Australian and German Concepts', 10th October, 2003 - www.CIMEJES.com.

FRANKS, R. J., NYBORG, K. G., 'Control rights, debt structure and the loss of private benefits: The case of UK Insolvency Code', *The Review of Financial Studies, vol. 9, no. 5, 1996.*

ILO (International Labor Organization) *C95 Protection of Wages Convention, C158 Termination of Employment Convention.*

IPPOLITO, R.A. (1985), 'The labour contract and true economic pension liabilities', *The American Economic Review, Vol. 75, No.5, December 1985, pp 1031-1043.*

IPPOLITO, R.A., (1987), 'The implicit pension contract: developments and new directions', *The Journal of Human Resources, Vol.22, No.3, Summer 1987, pp441-467.*

LINDEMAN, D.C. *'Underfunding and bankruptcy: Pension's plagues and the PBGC." The American Enterprise March/ April 1993, Vol. 4, No. 2, pp72-80.*

LINDEMAN, D., (2004), 'A note on Benefit Security', *OECD Financial Market Trends, No.86, March 2004.*

McGILL, D.M., BROWN, K.N., HALEY, J.J., SCHIEBER, S.J., 'Fundamentals of Private Pensions', Pension Research Council, the Wharton School of the University of Pennsylvania, 7th Edition, 1996.

MITCHELL, O.S., (1987), 'Worker Knowledge of Pension Provisions', Working Paper NO. 2414, National Bureau of Economic Research, Cambridge, MA.

OECD, 'Benefit Security: Pension Guarantee Funds': Working Paper No. 5 http://www.oecd.org/dataoecd/6/8/38328502.pdf

PESANDO, J.E. (1996), 'The government's role in insuring pensions', in BODIE, Z., MITCHELL, O.S., TURNER, J.A., 'Securing Employer-Based Pensions', The Pension Research Council, University of Pennsylvania Press, Philadelphia, 1996.

REITH, P., 'Protection of Employee Entitlements in the event of employer insolvency', Ministerial Paper, Australian Ministry Employment, Workplace Relations, and Small Business, August 1999.

SMALHOUT, J.H., (1996), 'The uncertain retirement', Irwin Publishing, Chicago, 1996.

World Bank, 'Principles and Guidelines for Effective Insolvency and Creditor Rights Systems' April 2001.

ISBN-978-92-64-02810-4
Protecting Pensions: Policy Analysis
and Examples from OECD Countries
© OECD 2007

Annex 1

OECD Council Recommendation on Guidelines on Funding and Benefit Security in Occupational Pension Plans

THE COUNCIL,

Having regard to Articles 1, 3 and 5(b) of the Convention on the Organisation for Economic Cooperation and Development of 14 December 1960;

Having regard to the Recommendation of the Council on Core Principles of Occupational Pension Regulation [C(2004)41], to which this Recommendation is complementary;

Considering that the funding of private pension plans is central for benefit security;

Considering that regulations should encourage prudent levels of funding so as to meet the retirement income objectives of the pension plan;

Considering that the Guidelines presented in this Recommendation are based on previous work carried out in this area by the Insurance and Private Pensions Committee and its Working Party on Private Pensions and are complemented by the Annotations, which may be reviewed as necessary from time to time by the Insurance and Private Pensions Committee;

Considering that the Guidelines address regulatory concerns that arise in the funding of occupational, private pension plans;

Noting that these Guidelines are intended to apply to occupational, private pension plans;

Noting that these Guidelines may also apply to funded, non-occupational plans and funds;

Noting that the Guidelines identify good practices for the regulation of pension funds, where "regulation" is understood to include a broad variety of instruments, *e.g.* laws; tax requirements; standards set by supervisory authorities; codes of conduct developed by professional associations; collectively bargained agreements and plan documents;

Recognising that evolutions of the structure and operation of private pension plans may call for further updating and adaptation of these Guidelines;

On the proposal of the Insurance and Private Pensions Committee and its Working Party on Private Pensions;

I. RECOMMENDS that Member Countries invite public authorities to ensure an adequate regulation of funding and benefit security in occupational pension plans, having regard to the contents of the Guidelines, which form an integral part of this Recommendation.

II. INVITES Member Countries to disseminate these Guidelines among pension funds.

III. INVITES non-Members to take account of the terms of this Recommendation and, if appropriate, to adhere to it under conditions to be determined by the Insurance and Private Pensions Committee.

IV. INSTRUCTS the Insurance and Private Pensions Committee and its Working Party on Private Pensions to exchange information on progress and experiences with respect to the implementation of this Recommendation, to review that information and to report to the Council not later than three years following its adoption and, as appropriate, thereafter.

Guidelines on Funding and Benefit Security in Occupational Pension Plans

I. Funding of occupational pension plans

1.1   *Occupational pension plans should be funded.*

1.2   *Occupational defined contribution plans should be funded through the establishment of pension funds, pension insurance contracts or the purchase of other authorised retirement savings products from financial institutions.*

1.3   *Occupational defined benefit plans should in general be funded through the establishment of a pension fund or through an insurance arrangement (or a combination of these mechanisms). Additional protection may be provided through the recognition of creditor rights to the pension fund or the plan members and beneficiaries and, in some cases, through insolvency guaranty schemes that protect pension benefits in the case of insolvency of the plan sponsor or the pension fund.*

1.4   *Private unfunded plans should generally be prohibited. The establishment of an insolvency guaranty scheme should in general be required for occupational defined benefit plans that are financed through the book reserve system.*

1.5   *Insolvency guaranty schemes should rely on appropriate pricing of the insurance provided in order to avoid unwarranted incentives for risk-taking (moral hazard). The level of benefits guaranteed should also be limited.*

II. Measurement of occupational pension plan liabilities

2.1   *Legal provisions[1] should be in place requiring the determination of occupational pension plan liabilities corresponding to the financial*

---

1. Throughout this document, legal provisions are defined in a broad sense. They may include the main body of the pension law, related laws (e.g. trust law, tax requirements, standards set by pension and financial sector supervisory authorities, codes of conduct developed by professional associations (e.g. a pension fund association), collectively bargained agreements, or plan documents (e.g. trust documents).

commitments or obligations which arise out of the pension arrangement. The ongoing liability is normally defined as the accrued benefit rights of pension plan members and beneficiaries excluding future service but taking into account the projected benefits to be received under estimated retirement, mortality, and early leaver (also known as membership termination or job separation) patterns. The termination liability takes into account the pension benefits accrued if the plan were to be terminated at the time of the valuation.

2.2 Any definitions of ongoing and termination liability should reflect any benefit indexation factors prescribed by law or plan terms (unconditional indexation) that apply from membership or plan termination to the annuity starting date and, if relevant, after the annuity starting date, provided that these factors are predictable. These definitions should also reflect benefits that become vested upon plan termination.

2.3 These legal provisions should require the use of appropriate calculation methods, including actuarial techniques and amortisation rules that are consistent with generally recognised actuarial standards and methods.

2.4 The legal provisions (referencing generally recognised actuarial standards and methods) should require the use of prudent actuarial assumptions which are considered appropriate for the calculation of the pension plan's liabilities. These assumptions would include, among others, the mortality table (representing the assumed level of mortality of plan members and beneficiaries as at the date at which the plan's liabilities are calculated), future trend in mortality (representing permanent changes in mortality that are assumed to occur after the date at which the liabilities are calculated) and retirement and early leaver patterns at different ages (taking into account the actual retirement and early leaver behaviour of those covered by the plan).

2.5 The legal provisions (referencing generally recognised actuarial standards and methods) should require the use of prudent discount rates for determining liabilities that are consistent with the methodologies used in the valuation of assets and other economic assumptions. These legal provisions (or the actuarial profession) should provide guidance as to the factors that may be considered in determining the discount rate for ongoing and termination liabilities.

2.6 The calculation of pension liabilities should take place at least once every three years, while a certification or report of the adjusted development of the liabilities and changes in risks covered should be required for the intervening years. All actuarial valuations should be carried out by an actuary, or by another equivalent specialist, who has had appropriate training and experience in the field of pensions.

2.7 As part of the process of defining its funding policy, the governing body of the pension fund should seek the advice of the actuary or other relevant specialist regarding the assumptions and methods to be used in calculating pension liabilities and funding levels. This advice should be provided in a clear and timely fashion.

III. Funding rules for occupational pension plans/funds

3.1 The legal provisions require the identification and maintenance of a level of assets that would be at least sufficient to meet accrued benefit payments. The targeted funding level may be based on the termination or the ongoing liability. It should also take account of the plan sponsor's ability and commitment to increase contributions to the pension plan in situations of underfunding, the possibility of benefit adjustments or changes in retirement ages, as well as the link between the pension fund's assets and its liabilities.

3.2 Approved funding methods (also known as actuarial cost methods) for the ongoing liability should attempt to prevent sharply rising cost curves over time by spreading the actuarial (or accrued) liability over the expected career path of plan members. In order to ensure adequate funding levels over time, ongoing funding methods should take into account factors such as future salary growth, mortality, disability, early leaver (separation) and other relevant events.

3.3 In addition to normal costs (the present value of benefits that have accrued on behalf of the members during the valuation period), contributions should reflect other factors, including, to the extent appropriate to the accrual of benefits under the plan, work before a plan's inception, plan amendments that increase liability attributable to past service, deviations of actual results from assumptions (experience gains and losses), and the effects of changes in assumptions (actuarial gains and losses). These supplemental costs should be amortised as even currency units or at a minimum as even percentages of payroll. Amortisation periods should in general not be longer than the expected future period of service of active plan participants.

3.4 The legal provisions should not prevent funding methods that seek to dampen the short term volatility in firms' funding contributions. Prudent amortisation of supplemental costs over time might help achieve a smoother contribution schedule and more stable funding levels.

3.5 These legal provisions set out the different mechanisms and the recovery period for correcting a situation of underfunding, taking into account the sources of underfunding and the type of underfunding (ongoing or termination basis). Funding rules may grant some reprieve on contribution obligations only under restricted circumstances and to defined limits. Temporary reductions of contribution obligations may be considered with a clear waiver procedure managed by the pension regulator.

3.6   Funding rules should aim to be countercyclical, providing incentives to build reserves against market downturns. They should also take market volatility into account when limiting contributions (or their tax deductibility) as a certain funding level is reached. Tax regulations should not discourage the build-up of sufficient reserves to withstand adverse market conditions and should avoid restricting the full funding of the ongoing or termination liability. Temporary suspension of contribution obligations may be appropriate in circumstances of significant overfunding (calculated on an on-going basis).

3.7   Funding rules should take into account the extent to which the autonomous pension fund itself as opposed to the plan sponsor or the plan members is directly responsible partly or wholly for the commitments represented by the pension liabilities. Where the pension fund itself underwrites the pension liability without any guarantee from the plan sponsor or members, it should be required to hold additional assets over and above those necessary to fully fund the pension liabilities on a plan termination basis. This capital requirement or solvency margin should be determined taking into account the nature and size of assets held and liabilities due that are the responsibility of the pension fund and the extent to which benefits may be reduced.

IV.   Winding-up

4.1   The allocation of plan assets and the responsibility for underfunding in the event of plan termination should be clearly established. In the event that assets exceed promised benefits on a termination basis, there should be rules in place as to the allocation of the funding excess or surplus. In the event that assets are insufficient to cover promised benefits, there should be rules concerning the benefit payment allocation.

4.2   Whenever plan benefits are guaranteed by sponsoring employers, the creditor rights of pension plan members and beneficiaries (either directly, via the pension fund, or, where relevant, via insolvency guarantee schemes) should be recognised in the case of bankruptcy of the plan sponsor. Priority rights relative to other creditors should be required for at least due and unpaid contributions.

Annotations to Guidelines on Funding and Benefit Security in Occupational Pension Plans

I. Funding of occupational pension plans

Benefit security in both defined benefit and defined contribution occupational plans calls for the funding of pension benefits, that is, the identification and accumulation of assets to be used exclusively to meet pension commitments and related expenses (for example, the cost of pension plan administration).

Different methods of funding exist in occupational plans. For defined contribution plans, where sponsoring employers do not make any benefit or performance commitments, the legal separation of pension plan assets from those of the employer should be mandatory. The assets may be held in a pension fund or they may be managed directly by financial institutions through pension insurance contracts or other authorised products.

For occupational defined benefit plans, plan assets should normally be legally segregated from the plan sponsor through a pension fund or an insurance arrangement (a pension insurance contract) in order to ensure a minimum level of protection against the possible insolvency of the sponsor. Countries sometimes buttress these funding requirements with priority creditor rights in the case of insolvency of the sponsor and, more occasionally, with insolvency guaranty schemes that protect benefits against the insolvency of the sponsor. In most countries, insolvency guarantee schemes only insure benefits promised in a pension plan up to a specific ceiling.

In occupational defined benefit pension plans financed through the book reserve system benefits should be protected against the risk of default of the plan sponsor through an insolvency guaranty scheme. In practice, only certain defined benefit plans offered by some companies to specific workers (*e.g.* senior executives, so-called "top hat" schemes) are sometimes managed on an unfunded basis without such schemes. Such plans may be permitted but should not benefit from tax advantages. Plans that benefit from tax deductibility (and which are normally expected to cover most of the sponsoring company's workers) should not be run on an unfunded basis without insolvency insurance.

Insolvency guaranty schemes may be privately or publicly managed. In general, it is important that such schemes rely on appropriate pricing of the insurance provided in order to avoid unwarranted incentives for risk-taking (moral hazard). These arrangements also function most effectively when the underwriting entity has priority rights for missed or unpaid contributions in the case of insolvency of the plan sponsor.

Insolvency guaranty schemes (and in some cases, bankruptcy priority) may also be required for defined benefit plans financed via pension funds, in order to provide an additional layer of protection against bankruptcy of the plan sponsor. The need for such schemes should be evaluated taking into consideration the effectiveness of funding and investment rules in mitigating the consequences of sponsor bankruptcy on benefit security and the potential impact of such schemes on the plan sponsor's ability to raise capital and, consequently, on its ability and willingness to continue to support the pension plan. It is important also that insolvency guaranty schemes rely on appropriate pricing of the insurance provided, taking into account, inter alia, the extent of under/overfunding and the default risk of the sponsoring entity.

Plan sponsors may also contract directly with insurance companies to purchase policies to cover their pension commitments. In defined benefit plans, such policies may include savings products providing rate of return guarantees, annuities, and survivors' insurance. In general, however, for those countries in which final salary benefits accrue with respect to future salary increases, insurance companies do not provide instruments to fully insure final salary benefit promises for plan members that are still accruing benefits (annuities are the relevant policies for those who have retired)[1]. Such plan formulas, therefore, would normally call for the establishment of a pension fund to meet commitments that are not covered by the insurance policy.

II. Measurement of occupational pension plan liabilities

The legal provisions usually define one or more measures of ongoing liability to be used in determining annual contribution requirements to occupational pension plans. Ongoing liabilities are normally valued by presuming that the plan remains in place and by treating current members and beneficiaries of the pension plan at the time of valuation as a closed

---

1. German Pensionskassen, although treated as insurance undertakings under the Insurance Supervision Law, do provide such instruments.

group. An actuarial cost method is then consistently applied to allocate an appropriate part of the total projected cost of the pension plans to the period ending on the valuation date (the "accrued liability") and subsequent years (the "normal costs"). One such method is the projected unit credit method, which includes any assumed future salary increases and excludes future service. Alternative measures of ongoing liabilities may include also prospective benefits that are accrued from future service. The reporting of the total projected cost of the pension plan, net of projected future contributions, should be required if measurement of the accrued liability and normal cost alone, may fail to disclose future deficits to be funded by plan members and beneficiaries. In calculating ongoing liability plan sponsors and pension entities should take into account the particulars of all plan benefit formulas and rights using appropriate assumptions and discount rates (see below).

A clear measure of termination liability (also called winding-up liability) that reflects the country's laws about the rights of participants if the plan were to be terminated on or about the time of valuation (accrued rights) may also be required. These rights often correspond to the rights of workers (early leavers) who leave plan coverage (separation) before retirement with a vested benefit payable at the plan's annuity starting date. The termination liability is calculated with reference to current salaries (and indexation if required). The concept of termination liability can be important for minimum funding rules (see below).

The legal provisions (referencing generally recognised actuarial standards and methods) also need to provide guidance concerning the appropriate range of actuarial assumptions for the measurement of ongoing liabilities. There will normally be distinct assumptions with respect to early leaver (separation) and disability during active service, mortality, salary or wage growth (including any indexing requirement), expected income from assets, and, if relevant, future increases in benefits (*e.g.* unconditional indexation). Guidance is required in order to promote the adoption of prudent assumptions that encourage adequate funding levels. Separate guidance should be provided for the determination of assumptions for calculating the termination liability where required.

The legal provisions (also referencing generally recognised actuarial standards and methods) should also provide guidance on longevity after benefits become payable (retirement age or annuity starting date). Specific guidance is needed with respect to the use of mortality tables that are up to date and relevant to the population covered. The pension regulator may require that any standard tables used (*e.g.* those from census/statistical offices or tables based on annuity transactions of life insurance companies) are appropriately adjusted to take account of any systematic differences in longevity characteristics between pension plan retirees and beneficiaries and the population covered by those standard tables. The legal provisions should require that retirement assumptions take into account the actual retirement and early leaver (also known as membership termination or job separation) behaviour of those covered by the plan.

The legal provisions (also referencing generally recognised actuarial standards and methods) should also require that the discount rates used to calculate pension liabilities are prudently chosen taking into account the plan liabilities' risk and maturity structure. Those used for the calculation of ongoing liabilities usually differ from those used in calculating termination liabilities, but both normally take into account the market yield of high-quality corporate or government bonds. Discount rates used for calculating the termination liability may alternatively be based on the yields implicit in annuities sold by market providers for benefits equivalent to those offered by the pension plan. When choosing discount rates, due attention should be paid to the maturity and risk profile of the pension plan's liabilities.

Regular monitoring of the plan's pension liabilities is important to ensure that any imbalances in funding levels are identified at an early stage and hence corrective measures can be implemented on a gradual manner. Valuations should take place at least every three years, but the regulator may deem it necessary to require more frequent valuations on plans that may be more prone to funding imbalances. Such intervening valuations may be limited to a certification or report reflecting the adjusted development of the liabilities and changes in risks covered. The calculation of pension liabilities should be carried out by an actuary or by another equivalent specialist in this field. Actuaries have specific reporting and whistleblowing responsibilities that are outlined in the pension fund governance guidelines [DAFFE/AS/PEN/WD(2001)2/REV5]. In particular, they should be required to disclose to the governing body in a clear and timely manner the actuarial assumptions and methods used for calculating pension liabilities and funding levels.

III. Funding rules for occupational pension plans/funds

The legal provisions (referencing generally recognised actuarial standards and methods) should provide guidance concerning appropriate actuarial funding methods to allocate a pension plan's actuarial (or accrued) liability over time, balancing the security of members' benefits and the plan sponsor's ability to pay. These provisions should require a regular contribution obligation (normal cost) derived from such allocations either based on the ongoing or the termination liability.

The target funding level should take into account the plan sponsor's ability and its commitment to raise contributions if the plan were to become underfunded, as well as the extent to which benefits can be adjusted or the retirement age changed. The relationship between the fund's assets and its liabilities, and in particular, the extent of matching between their respective future cashflows, should also be taken into consideration when choosing a target funding level.

The periods chosen for the amortisation of funding costs arising from work before a plan's inception, plan amendments that increase liability attributable to past service, and experience and actuarial gains and losses should be chosen so as to keep plan contributions on a path consistent with the plan's normal cost. By spreading these funding costs over time (as even currency units or at a minimum as even percentages of payroll), the short term volatility of funding contributions can be reduced. In general, however, amortisation periods should not be longer than the expected future period of service of active plan participants. Long amortisation periods should be discouraged as they can lead to low funding levels, below the plan termination liability, even when ongoing funding methods are based on projected benefits. Short amortisation periods may be envisaged for experience and actuarial gains and losses in order to rapidly correct underfunding.

The amortisation periods for liabilities related to work for plan sponsors prior to plans being adopted should balance prudential interests and allowing sponsoring employers to provide retirement benefits to workers who were employed by the firm sponsoring the plan before the plan's inception. Similarly, with respect to changes in the law that require sponsors to recognise or accelerate the recognition of liabilities, legally established amortisation periods should balance prudential interests, the effects on sponsors' reported earnings and cash flows, and the willingness of sponsors to establish and maintain occupational pension plans.

Corrective measures in the case of underfunding should take into account the source of the underfunding and the type of underfunding (ongoing or termination basis). In particular, it should firstly be established whether the underfunding is due to changes in the valuation of the assets or liabilities or to a failure to collect the required contributions from the sponsoring employer or/and plan members. The latter should be addressed through appropriate channels, including judicial procedures where relevant.

Funding rules should also set out the different mechanisms permitted for correcting underfunding, such as the payment of a lump-sum by the plan sponsor, an increase in future contributions by the sponsor or/and plan members, and adjustments in future benefit accruals and other benefit parameters such as the retirement age. Funding rules should also provide for recovery periods for correcting underfunding, taking into account the source and type of underfunding. The chosen recovery period needs to balance the goal of benefit security of accrued benefits and that of plan continuity.

Exemptions to funding requirements may also be granted on a discretionary basis by the pension regulator, but only under defined circumstances with a clear waiver procedure managed by the regulator. The procedure should have the option to require any sponsor granted a waiver to collaterise the waived contributions with secured liens on company assets or otherwise provide security on behalf of the pension plan and, if relevant, any public or private insolvency insurer or guaranty fund.

Funding rules should aim to be countercyclical, providing incentives for the build-up of reserves against market downturns. They should also avoid putting in danger the employer's continuation of the sponsoring of the plan. The building of reserves is all the more important when the spreading of experience and actuarial gains and losses are restricted. Asset price and discount rate volatility can then cause wide swings in funding ratios and funding requirements. Tax regulations, which set ceilings on contributions or their tax deductibility when a certain funding level is reached, should not discourage the build-up of sufficient reserves to withstand adverse market conditions and should avoid restricting the full funding of the ongoing liability. When setting such ceilings it is of paramount importance to consider the potential volatility of discount rates and asset values.

Optimally, sponsoring employers should be permitted to more rapidly recognise and amortise unfunded liabilities and make deductible contributions that exceed annual contribution obligations. Such provisions may include more rapid amortisation of unfunded liabilities attributable to past service or acceleration recognition of the future liabilities over a worker's remaining expected service with the sponsoring employer.

In some countries, the pension fund itself may be directly responsible for ensuring that assets are sufficient to meet liabilities without any guarantee from the sponsoring employer or members. This is the case for accrued liabilities in some countries. Where autonomous pension funds underwrite directly some of the pension liabilities without an employer or member guarantee, they should be subject to a capital requirement over and above the level of assets necessary to fully fund the pension liabilities on a plan termination basis. Such pension funds act to a certain extent in a similar way to life insurance companies. Solvency rules regarding pension funds should therefore also take into account the specific role and functions of other institutions providing occupational retirement benefits.

IV. Winding-up

In the event that a plan is terminated and promised benefits exceed assets, there should be rules to allocate available assets to members and other beneficiaries in accord with accrued rights. There should also be rules concerning the responsibility of plan sponsors for any unfunded liabilities. In the event that assets exceed promised benefits on a termination basis, there should be rules in place as to the allocation of the funding excess or surplus between plan sponsors, plan members and other beneficiaries. In some jurisdictions, however, excess assets may only be returned to the plan sponsor while in others they may be shared only among members and other beneficiaries. There is also a need for clarity in allocating plan assets to cover benefits due to current pensioners and active workers when assets are insufficient to cover promised benefits.

Bankruptcy and company insolvency laws should provide priority position for due and unpaid contributions at the time of plan termination. The position should equal at least the position of due and unpaid taxes at the time of plan termination. Where insolvency guaranty schemes are present, the underwriting entity normally becomes a preferential creditor of the insolvent sponsor.

Priority rights may also be appropriate for underfunded pension commitments (with reference to the termination liability) that are the responsibility of the plan sponsor. The need for granting such rights will depend on various factors, such as the extent to which there are in place insolvency guaranty arrangements that may help recoup any funding gap in the case of plan terminations as a result of bankruptcy of the plan sponsor. Due consideration should also be given to the likely impact of such rights on a plan sponsor's ability to raise capital and, consequently, on its ability or willingness to continue to support the pension plan.

OECD PUBLICATIONS, 2, rue André-Pascal, 75775 PARIS CEDEX 16
PRINTED IN FRANCE
(21 2007 06 1 P) ISBN 978-92-64-02810-4 – No. 55893 2007